# KING ARTHUR'S

## BATTLE FOR BRITAIN

# KING ARTHUR'S

## BATTLE FOR BRITAIN

### ERIC WALMSLEY

Matador
9 Priory Business Park,
Wistow Road, Kibworth Beauchamp,
Leicestershire. LE8 0RX
Tel: (+44) 116 279 2299
Fax: (+44) 116 279 2277
Email: books@troubador.co.uk
Web: www.troubador.co.uk/matador


ISBN 978 1780884 004

British Library Cataloguing in Publication Data.
A catalogue record for this book is available from the British Library.

Typeset in 11pt Adobe Garamond Pro by Troubador Publishing Ltd, Leicester, UK

**Matador** is an imprint of Troubador Publishing Ltd

*To my friend and mentor*
*Frank Hopton*

*"How lucky you are, Britain*
*More blessed than any other land,*
*Endowed by Nature with every benefit of soil and climate*
*Your winters are not too cold,*
*Your summers are not too hot,*
*Your cornfields so productive,*
*Your herds innumerable,*
*The dairy herds overflowing with milk."*

The Emperor Constantine, 310 AD.

# CONTENTS

# LIST OF MAPS & ILLUSTRATIONS

# INTRODUCTION

The inspiration for this book came to me following a visit to South Cadbury Castle, Somerset, in the late summer of 1969 when Leslie Alcock and his team of young archaeologists from the University of Wales were in the final stages of exploring the site.

Their excavation revealed that this formidable fortress had been re-occupied during the late fifth and early sixth centuries AD, when the ramparts and walled defences of the fort had been extensively rebuilt.

The dramatic discovery of the remains of a fortified gate-tower that had once guarded the south-western entrance to the fort, and the locating of an Arthurian feasting-hall on the summit plateau of the castle caused so much national interest and excitement that many came to believe the long-held local rumour that South Cadbury Castle was indeed Arthur's Camelot.

Soon after the completion of the Cadbury-Camelot project in 1970, Leslie Alcock summarised the archaeological findings in his book *Arthur's Britain*, a comprehensive study in which he reviewed a number of Arthurian documents, highlighting key texts that supported the argument for the existence of Arthur, not as a legendary king whose court was at Camelot, but as a powerful Dark Age military leader who rallied his warriors to defend Britons against the savage attacks of Angles, Saxons, Scots and Irish marauders who were hell-bent on the destruction of Britain.

One particular text caught my attention: it was a list of Arthur's twelve battles, copied in immaculate hand-written Latin from an earlier Welsh war-poem or battle-list rescued from a collection of early historic documents by an intelligent cleric called Nennius in the early ninth century. Known as the *Historia Brittonum* or *History of the Britons*, Nennius' compilation is an invaluable treasure of early British history that includes a *Northern British History* as well as a record of *Easter Annals*, perhaps better known as the *Annales Cambriae*.

It appears something of a miracle that these historic documents relating directly to Arthur's lifetime, albeit copies of copies of the original texts, have survived to the present day, preserved intact for almost twelve-hundred years; and if we can accept that the major events recorded in these texts are authentic and part of a genuine attempt to preserve the early history of Britain, then it is our good fortune to have access to material that not only reveals details of Arthur's battle for Britain, but also provides, within the *Annales*, a timeframe for the events described.

Armed with an authentic list of Arthur's battles, I considered the idea of bringing the battles to life in an imaginary form but in the style of a drama-documentary that would be based as far as possible on known historical facts relating to the Arthurian period. But before I could put pen to paper two major problems arose: first, it appeared that of the twelve battles listed by Nennius, only two or three of the battle-sites mentioned could be located with any certainty; secondly, I soon discovered that authentic factual references to Arthur and the events of his era were extremely limited.

Consequently my search for Arthur's battle-sites was both arduous and time-consuming; but after more than a decade searching windswept moors, rivers, mountains and lakes in England, Wales and Scotland, whilst poring over maps of Ancient and Roman Britain, I believe that I have at last solved the enigmatic problem associated with the obscure names of Nennius' Latin list by finding convincng locations for all Arthur's battles, including Camlan.

For the dramatic action of the battle scenes I have relied very much on my own imagination, coupled with some strategic and tactical guesswork on behalf of the opposing army commanders that inevitably relates to the geographical features of each battle-site; and this has been achieved by close reference to the Ordnance Survey Landranger maps of the areas in question.

With ideas, stories and references gleaned from the earliest sources, I have attempted to flesh-out the bare skeleton of Nennius' battle-list in the style of a war-correspondent's report from the battle-front, covering the action of friend and foe alike. My sources include works by Gildas and Nennius, early Nordic and Welsh poetry, including the *Welsh Triads*, as well as the poetry of Aneirin and Taliesin, and the entertaining tales from *The Mabinogion*. Whilst researching the later medieval Arthurian works, particularly the notorious *History of the Kings of Britain* by Geoffrey of Monmouth, and the legendary tales of Sir Thomas Malory's *Le Mort d'Arthur*, I came across a few rare strands of fable that could possibly relate to the true story of Arthur, but which were so deeply interwoven with legendary embellishment that they had become barely recognisable.

Nevertheless, by developing a scenario for each of the twelve battles in the chronological order of the original list, a storyline has emerged with a natural progression that depicts Arthur's lifetime struggle to defend his country from the late fifth, to the early sixth century.

The story reveals that Arthur's battles were not just skirmishes that took place over an unknown decade of the Dark Ages; they were in fact a serious response to full-scale attacks by nine different enemies who threatened the security of the whole island of Britain. From his first battle with Angles at the mouth of the river Glen to his final victory over the Saxons at Mount Badon, Arthur's Battle for Britain endured for more than thirty years.

There can be no doubt that the spirit of courage and sacrifice shown by our own "Knights of the Air", the brave pilots who flew Hurricanes and Spitfires in the Battle of Britain that raged over our skies from July to October 1940, was the same spirit shown by Arthur and his young warriors who took up arms to fight for their country in the first battle for Britain, so many years ago.

My personal quest to find the real locations of Arthur's battles has proved a great challenge that has forced me to piece together a jig-saw puzzle of events in Dark Age Britain. By searching out clues from all the available sources, I have found plausible answers to some of the perennial questions that have puzzled Britons for centuries:

*"Who was King Arthur?"*

*"Where was Camelot?"*

*"Where did Arthur's battles take place?"*

*"Where exactly is Mount Badon?"*

*"Who was Arthur's real enemy at the Battle of Camlan?"*

*"Where is the legendary Isle of Avalon?"*

and finally:

*"Where is King Arthur's grave?"*

But first and foremost it is necessary to review the written evidence about Arthur, for only then can we discover more about the real person behind the legendary king.

ERIC WALMSLEY
Seer Green, April 2012

Craig Phadraig

Duneidion
*Burghead Fortress*

**CALEDONIA**

Dundern
Loch Voil · Balquhidder
Dunadd
Dunblane
Stirling
Alcluith
EDINBURGH ■

Arthur's Seat

Newstead
*Trimontium*
Broomholm Fort ·

HADRIAN'S WALL

Corbridge
*Coria*
Carlisle
*Lugvvalium*

Catterick
*Cataractonium*

York
*Eboracum* ■

Dragonby

**B R I T A N N I A**

Lincoln
*Lindum*

**H I B E R N I A**

Dublin
*Dun Laoghaire*

Kildare ·

Din Rig ·

Moyarney Abbey ·
King's Bay Quay · · Wexford
Our Lady's Island
THE ISLE OF AVALON

Holyhead
Caer Gybi
Deganwy Fort

Chester
*Deva* ■
Dinas Emrys
Dinas Bran

Cregiau
Gwineu

Barmouth
Forden Gaer
Aberdyfi
Caersws

Wroxeter
*Viroconium Cornoviorum*
Caer Caradoc

Brancaster
*Branodunum*

Longthorpe ·

Burgh Castle
*Gariannonum*

Castell Dinas

Warwick
*Guerensis* ■

Colchester
*Camulodunum* ■

Carmarthen
*Moridunum*
Neath

Brecon y Gaer
Isca
*Caerleon* ■

Gloucester
*Glevum* ■

Cirencester
*Corinium* ■
Silchester
*Calleva Atrebatum*

St Albans
*Verulamium* ■

LONDON
*Londinium*

Isle of Thanet

Canterbury ·

Dunster ·

Glastonbury ·

South Cadbury
*Caer Cadarn* ■

Winchester
*Venta* ■
Portchester Castle

Castle Dore ■

Map 1 Arthur's Britain c 500 AD
© C.M.Walmsley

# CHAPTER 1

# THE EVIDENCE FOR ARTHUR
## Clerics and Kings

*"What place is there within the bounds of the Empire of Christendom to which the winged praise of Arthur the Briton has not extended?*

*Who is there, I ask, who does not speak of Arthur, since he is but little less known to the peoples of Asia than to the Britons, as we are informed by our palmers who return from the countries of the East?"*
Layamon, *The Brut*

Almost a century after the Imperial Army had sailed for Rome, leaving Britain defenceless in the face of invading Angles and Saxons, a young British warrior-chieftain took up the challenge, leading his armoured cavalry against the foe in a brave attempt to fight for the freedom of his country and his fellow Britons.

Stories of the exploits of Arthur and his band of Dark Age warriors, his battle campaigns and his momentous victories, were passed on from father to son in the vernacular tradition of court poets who spoke the Brythonic language of the fifth century; as raconteurs of epic battles, praise poems and eulogies for princes and valiant warriors lost in battle, they held the history of the age in their hearts and minds for many years before their memories were captured in the earliest poetry and prose to be written down in Welsh and Latin.

By the time of the Norman conquest of Britain, threads of the true story of Arthur's life had been deeply woven into a rich tapestry of medieval literature. Embellished with Celtic myths and magic fables for over six hundred years, the real story of Arthur the Warrior gradually evolved into the popular legend of 'King Arthur and his Knights of the Round Table' whose lifelong quest, when his valiant battle for Britain had been long forgotten, became the honourable attainment of the mystical Holy Grail.

The most extraordinary feature of Arthur's success as a British battle-leader is that his achievements came to be so fearsomely admired by his Anglo-Saxon enemies that their English descendants acclaimed him as their own king. Even William the Conqueror tried to prove his lineage from King Arthur, and his royal patronage stirred medieval troubadours and court bards to embellish the story of Arthur and his Knights with mystical prowess and magical powers; but in the early twelfth century Willliam of Malmesbury, a monk of Malmesbury Abbey in Wiltshire who took a serious approach to historical research, made an indignant protest in his book *Gesta Regum Anglorum, the Acts of the Kings of the English*:

*"It is of this Arthur that the Britons fondly tell so many fables, even to the present day: a man worthy to be celebrated, not by idle fictions, but by authentic history. He long upheld the sinking state, and roused the broken spirit of his countrymen to war."*

William made this bold assertion and told us that Arthur fought alongside the British war-leader Ambrosius Aurelianus in battles against the Angles, although he did not reveal the source of this statement. William also confirmed that Arthur was victorious at the siege of Mount Badon, and we know this information comes from a reliable source, the *Historia Brittonum,* a compilation of early historical documents transcribed into Latin in the early ninth century by a monk called Nennius who lived in Bangor, North Wales.

Nennius explained: *"I have heaped together all that I found, from the Annales of the Romans, the Chronicles of the Holy Fathers, the writings of the Irish and the Saxons and the traditions of our own wise men."*

In his introduction Nennius makes a humble plea: *"I ask every reader who reads this book to pardon me for daring to write so much here after so many, like a chattering bird or incompetent judge. I yield to whoever may be better acquainted with this skill than I am."*

We should certainly congratulate him for having the good sense to transcribe a wealth of material relating to the history of the fifth century, including a Kentish Chronicle recording events between 425 and 460 together with the evidence of a chronographer who recorded exact dates for events in early fifth century Britain. Many of the original documents that Nennius copied are now lost, so we owe him a debt of gratitude for his foresight in giving us this window into the distant past; it is perhaps a minor miracle that his book the *Historia Brittonum* has itself survived, protected by the Church during turbulent periods of war and strife for over a thousand years.

Thankfully, Nennius recorded one literary treasure that has great historical significance for Arthurian scholars: it is a list of Arthur's twelve battles, each set in an enigmatic location with place-names that are, for the most part, unrecognisable; it appears to have been copied from an early battle poem that extolled the great achievements of Arthur:

in rub o igneo. secundo modo in monte q̄
draginta dieb; & q̄draginta noctib; ieiuna
uit. tercio modo similes fuer̄ etate centu̅ ui
ginti annis. quarto modo sepulchru̅ illi̅ ne
mo scit: S; mocculto humat̄ nemine sci
ente. quindeci̅ annis incaptiuitate. in ui cesi
mo quinto anno ab amatheo sc̄o episcopo o
subrogat: occingentoru̅ & quinq; annoru̅
inhibernia p̄dicauit. & es aut exigebat
ampli̅ loqui de sc̄o patricio. sed tamen p̄
copendio sermonis uolui breuiare.

n illo tempore saxones inualescebant in
multitudine & crescebant inbrittannia.
(M)ortuo aut hengisto occha fili̅ ei̅ transi
uit de sinisthali parte brittanni̅e ad reg
nu̅ cantoru̅. & de ipso ori̅s reges cantoz.
une arthur pugnabat contra illos.
millis dieb; cu̅ regib; brittonu̅. s. ipse dux erat
belloru̅. Primu̅ bellu̅ fuit inostiu̅ flumi
nis quod dicit̄ glein. secu̅ & tciu̅ & q̄r
tu̅ & quintu̅. sup aliud flumen quod
dicit̄ dubglas: q̄s in regione limnuis.
Sextu̅ bellum sup flumen quod uocat
ē bassas. Septimu̅    fuit bellu̅
in silua celidonis. idē cat coit celidon.
(O)ctauum fuit bellu̅ incastello guinin
oir. Inquo arthur portauit imagine̅
sc̄e marie ppetue uirginis sup hume
ros suos. & pagani uersi s̄ infuga in
illo die. & cedes magna fuit sup illos
p̄ uirtute̅ d̄ni n̄ri ih̄u xp̄i & p̄ uirtute̅
sc̄e marie uirginis genitricis ei̅. Nonu̅
bellu̅ gestu̅: inurbe legionis. Decimu̅
gessit bellu̅ inlitore     fluminis quod
uocat̄ tribruit. Vndecimu̅ factu̅:
bellu̅ inmonte qui dicit̄ agned. Duo
decimu̅ fuit bellu̅ inmonte badonis.
inquo corruer̄ inuno die n̄ genti sexa
ginta uiri de uno impetu arthur.

The Arthurian battle-list, transcribed by Nennius from an early British text and
included in the *Historia Brittonum;* known as Harleian MS 3859, this is the earliest
surviving manuscript to mention Arthur, and is held by the British Library in London.

*"At that time the Saxon invaders strengthened and increased their numbers in Britain. When Hengist died, his son Octha came from the north of Britain to the kingdom of the Cantii where he founded the royal line of Kent. Then Arthur fought against them in those days with the kings of the Britons, but he himself was their Dux Bellorum (or battle-leader). The first battle was at the mouth of the river Glein. The second, third, fourth and fifth were fought upon another river called Dubglas, in the district of linnuis. The sixth battle took place on the river called Bassas. The seventh battle was fought in the forest of Caledonia, that is Cat Coit Celidon (in the British language). The eighth battle was in Castell Guinnion in which Arthur carried the image of Saint Mary, ever virgin, on his shield and that day the pagans were turned to flight and great was the slaughter brought upon them through the virtue of our Lord Jesus Christ and the virtue of Saint Mary the Virgin, his mother. The ninth battle was waged in the City of the Legion. The tenth battle he fought on the shore of the river called Tribruit. The eleventh battle was waged on the mountain called Agned. The twelfth battle was on Mount Badon where nine hundred and sixty men fell in one day from one charge by Arthur, and no-one overthrew them except himself alone. And in all these battles he was the victor."*

Although most of the battle sites have been obscured through transmission from the original Brythonic language to the formal Latin of Nennius' text, we are still able to recognise some of the locations: for example, the first battle placed at the mouth of the river Glein, is most likely to be the river Glen that runs into the Wash by Surfleet in Lincolnshire. Furthermore, as Caledonia was the Roman name for Scotland, it would not be beyond the bounds of possibility to imagine Arthur following in the footsteps of Agricola by pursuing the Picts in a forest somewhere between Stirling and the Grampian Mountains; and the ninth battle was most probably fought at Chester, the legionary headquarters of Hadrian's Legio XX that came to be known as 'Cair Legionis.'

Significantly, Nennius' list reveals that battles were fought over the length and breadth of Britain; it also contains vital clues that enable us to piece together the jigsaw puzzle of Arthur's military campaign in his battle for Britain. But in order to reveal the true story of Arthur's life we must seek-out the factual evidence relating to his allies as well as his enemies, and play out the drama on the stage-map of post Roman Britain.

Nennius' text depicts Arthur charging into battle with an image of the Virgin Mary on his shield: he appears as the champion of post-Roman Britain fighting the pagan invader, yet surprisingly, Nennius does not refer to Arthur as a king but as a warrior who was the Commander of Battles.

Another source of evidence is the British monk Gildas, who as a contemporary of Arthur ranks as an important witness to events in sixth century Britain. In his book *De Exidio Conquestu Britanniae, On the Ruin and Conquest of Britain,* written around the year 540, he mounts a tirade against the miscreant kings of Britain and he also reprimands the people for their waywardness and lack of faith. At the same time he gives us an extraordinary insight into the state of the country and the attitude of its people:

*"Their leader was Ambrosius Aurelianus, a modest man who alone among his Roman family had survived the shock of this tempestuous storm* (the Saxon invasion) *in which his parents, who had worn the purple, were both killed. Now in our time his descendants have not lived up to their grandfather's excellence. Under his leadership our people regained their strength and challenged the conquerors to battle: and with the Lord's help they were victorious."*

*"From then onwards, victory went now to our countrymen, then to their enemies, so that in His own way the Lord could test the people, these New Israelites, to see if they loved Him or not: this continued until the year of the siege of Mount Badon, which was virtually the last slaughter of the bandits, and certainly not the least. And as I know, that was the year of my birth, for one month of the forty-fourth year since then has already passed."*

*"Even now the cities of our country are not inhabited as they were before, but to this day they are in ruins, deserted and squalid: our wars with foreign enemies have ended, but not our civil wars. For both the terrible destruction of our island and its unexpected recovery was long remembered by those who witnessed both momentous events. And because of this, kings, public officials and private citizens, as well as priests and churchmen all kept to their stations: but when they all died they were succeeded by a generation who have not experienced the storm of war and who only know the present calm. Indeed, amongst the kind of people I have mentioned, all vestiges of truth and justice have been discarded, except for a very few who, because so many rush daily on all fours into hell, are such a small minority that even the holy mother Church does not even recognise her own true sons who reside with her."*

Gildas is fired with emotion as he tells the story of the conquest and destruction of Britain but when his Latin text is translated into English the complicated sentences and erratic style lead to ambiguous meanings. He presents us with a conundrum over his suggested date for the Battle of Mount Badon, for there are two ways of interpreting his statement: either that he is actually writing 44 years and one month after the battle, or that he is referring to the period of 44 years and one month that has elapsed from the time that Ambrosius first challenged the Saxons until the overwhelming British victory at Badon.

Fortunately the English historian Bede answers this problem in his *Historia Ecclesiastica:* writing only two hundred years after Arthur's great victory at Badon,

Bede closely follows Gildas' text, sometimes copying word for word, at other times editing his original text to clarify the meaning. In this passage he makes some omissions as well a significant change to the original:

*"And from this time now our citizens and now the enemy were victorious, until the year of the siege of Mount Badonicus when they inflicted not the smallest slaughter upon their enemies, in about the forty-fourth year from their coming into Britain."*

Bede also confirms that the Anglo-Saxons were the invaders.

Now that we have clarified Gildas' enigmatic clue to the battle, we must look for further historical evidence in order to confirm the exact date. The *Annales Cambriae*, or *Welsh Annals*, is an eleventh century copy of a tenth century historical summary that has a brief entry for each year recorded, and when the early entries are compared with independent sources they are shown to be accurate; for example, the battle of Cair Legion is recorded in the year 613, and this same battle of Chester is ascribed to the same year in the *Annals of Tigernach*, an independent chronicle.

The Battle of Badon is entered under the year 518: *"The Battle of Badon in which Arthur carried the cross of Our Lord Jesus Christ for three days and nights on his shoulders, and the Britons were the victors."*

Gildas names Ambrosius as the British leader who challenged Hengist when the Saxons began their campaign to conquer Britain, starting a war that lasted forty-four years and ended with the renowned British victory at Badon. Curiously however, in his chronicle Gildas makes a glaring omission: he fails to mention Arthur as the victor of Badon and gives no credit to the leader who performed what he himself described as a miraculous event.

But we know from Nennius that it was Arthur who led the cavalry charge at Badon, and the *Annales Cambriae* confirms the siege as Arthur's victory. So why did Gildas remain mysteriously silent by not mentioning Arthur? One good reason may have been that following Arthur's death in the civil strife at Camlan, the most powerful king Maelgwn of Gwynedd had forbidden Britons to mention Arthur's name, whose death was to be kept secret. The very fact that Arthur had been killed in a civil war, possibly even murdered by his own countrymen, was devastating news for the British people and if word of this event were to reach the ears of the Saxons, they would very soon be spurred into resuming their attacks on the heartland of Britain.

Another possible reason for Gildas' silence is that he held a bitter prejudice against Arthur as a result of a strong political or personal disagreement. When Gildas relates the story of the Saxon's first coming into Britain he describes them as: *"ferocious Saxons, a name not to be spoken, hated by man and God."* They are despised and unmentionable in Gildas' own words, but how could he really put Arthur in the same category?

In his book *The Life of Gildas* written in the twelfth century, the Welsh monk Caradoc of Llancarfan confirms that Gildas was the contemporary of Arthur *"the king of the whole of Britain,"* whom he diligently loved and whom he always desired to obey. Caradoc reveals that Gildas was one of the twenty-four sons of Caw, a king of the north who lived near the Clyde; but his warrior brothers refused to pay allegiance to Arthur constantly rising against him, routing him, and driving him out from the forest and battlefield. Heuil, the elder brother was an active and distinguished warrior who *"submitted to no king, not even Arthur."* He provoked Arthur's anger by swooping down from Scotia with a raiding party, then carrying off the spoils with victory and renown.

Arthur responded with a hostile pursuit and following a council of war in Mynau, he killed the young plunderer. Here Caradoc has mistakenly taken Mynau to mean the Isle of Man, but as Heuil's refuge was north-west of Stirling, Mynau must refer to the Manau Guotodin, a district around the head of the Firth of Forth close to the kingdom of the Gododdin, or Votadini, who were allies of Arthur.

*"After that murder the victorious Arthur returned, rejoicing greatly that he had overcome his bravest enemy."* Gildas wept when he heard that his dear brother had been slain by Arthur, and he prayed daily for Heuil's spirit, praying as well for Arthur, his brother's persecutor and murderer, thus fulfilling the commandment that says: *"Love those who persecute you, and do good to those that hate you."*

The shock of this bereavement would explain Gildas' ambivalence towards Arthur and may well be the reason why he would not mention his name or give him the direct credit for the victory of Badon; but on the other hand, Gildas may well have made some obscure references to Arthur using code-words that would have been easily recognised by his contemporary audience. Caradoc explains that Gildas and Arthur were later reconciled when Gildas was courteous to his enemy and kissed Arthur as he prayed for forgiveness, accepting the penance imposed upon him by the bishops who were present. However, a tradition recorded by Giraldus Cambrensis reveals that Gildas had written a book about Arthur, but in his despair over the death of Heuil, had cast his book into the sea.

For the most part Gildas, as a reclusive monk, was not concerned with military matters but at the very least he acknowledged that under Ambrosius the Britons regained their strength, challenged the invaders to battle, and with God's help were victorious. However, separate testimonies from Nennius and the *Annales Cambriae* reveal that it was Arthur who carried the image of the Virgin Mary and the Cross of Christ on his shield, or over his shoulders, in different battles. Evidently Arthur became the great champion of the Christian cause against the pagan invaders and he was indeed the victor at the battle of Badon in the year 518.

Gildas made an oblique reference to Arthur in his diatribe against the evil-doing kings of Britain: he asks king Cuneglas:

*"Why have you fallen back into the sewage of your past wickedness, ever since your youth, you bear, the rider over many men and the driver of the chariot which carried the bear; you are a despiser of God, and the oppressor of his lot, Cuneglassus, whose name in Latin means 'red butcher'. Why do you wage such a war against men and God? Against men, that is our countrymen, with arms special to yourself; against God, with infinite sins?"*

Knowing that "artus" is the Celtic word for bear, here we find Gildas cleverly playing word-games by referring to Arthur as "the bear" and at the same time revealing to us that Cuneglas was a cold-blooded murderer: for the name Cuneglas does not really mean "red butcher" in Latin. But why does Gildas also address Cuneglas as "you bear"? This is unexpected, because we know that this epithet is reserved for Arthur alone. Is this Gildas telling us in one word that Cuneglas is closely related to Arthur and has inherited his position, together with his land, wealth and the people he protected? Is Gildas trying to tell us something else when he calls Cuneglas the oppressor of God's lot? Is he in fact accusing Cuneglas of cruelly tearing apart Arthur's established peace by waging a civil war against his own people, and subjugating them with special weapons?

Arthur features in another medieval Welsh story, the *Life of Saint Cadoc* composed by Lifris about 1100, who relates a lively tale about the saint's parents. Gwynllyw, king of Glamorgan, eloped with princess Gwladys from Brecknock (Brecon) and rode off with her to his own country with her father in pursuit. Fleeing over a hill, they came across Arthur playing a game of dice with Cei and Bedivere; at first Arthur is filled with desire for Gwladys but his companions remind him of their custom to help those in distress. Arthur challenges the angry father, and then escorts the lovers to the safety of Gwynllyw's palace where they marry without delay, and in due course their first-born child is named Cadoc.

Many years later when Saint Cadoc was abbot of Llancarfan, he gave sanctuary for seven years to a man who had killed three of Arthur's warriors. When Arthur eventually found the hiding-place he brought his army to the bank of the river Usk to argue with Cadoc across the river over the legitimacy of the period of sanctuary. When Cadoc refused to release the guilty man, an arbitrator awarded Arthur a herd of cattle in compensation, but he demanded that the cattle be part red and part white. The monks overcame this impossible request with divine aid and drove the cattle across a ford, but when Arthur's soldiers took over, the cows changed into bundles of fern. Arthur realised that he could not argue further and recognised Cadoc's right to give sanctuary for seven years, seven months and seven days.

Here we find Arthur challenging the authority of the Church, being awarded a herd of cattle for the loss of three warriors, then losing his compensation either by divine intervention or with a clever trick by Cadoc's monks; then finally accepting the Church's right to give sanctuary to an enemy. The story echoes the feeling that Welsh monastic tradition was not friendly towards Arthur as a military leader; he may well have paid homage to Christian duty, but he was first and foremost a hard-bargaining warrior out to get whatever he could from the Church to support his military campaigns.

The idea that the monks disliked Arthur because he harassed them and tried to extort goods from them is confirmed in a story from the life of Saint Carantoc, who floated an altar on the sea and vowed to preach wherever it landed: eventually he tracked it down to the coast of Dindrathov (Dunster in Somerset) where Arthur ruled as a junior aid to prince Cadwy. By the time Carantoc arrived the altar had disappeared, but Arthur was there looking for a huge serpent that was frightening the people of Carrum. When Carantoc asked where the altar was, Arthur promised to tell him if he would help him to chase off the serpent; he agreed, banished the serpent and Arthur confessed to commandeering the altar himself to use as a table, but everything he put on it fell off. Arthur thanked Caradoc by granting him estates and allowing him to settle at Carrum. (Carhampton)

The *Life of Saint Padarn* written in the twelfth century, makes a contemptuous reference to *"a certain tyrant by the name of Arthur"* using the word tyrant to mean: 'one who seizes power without the authority of Rome.' Here we discover Arthur bursting into St Padarn's cell and demanding the tunic presented to him by the Patriarch of Jerusalem. Padarn refuses but Arthur enforces his demand: as he does so the earth opens and he sinks in up to his neck. Once again Arthur is forced to apologise before making his escape.

We must be aware that most of the Lives of the Saints were written over five hundred years after the period they describe. With the aim of enhancing the reputation of their subjects, authors embroidered their biographies with miraculous and metaphorical events as well as linking their saints' lives to the great hero Arthur, who had lived in an earlier age; but when the mystery and magic is stripped away there remains an element of reality in the names and places mentioned in the texts. Arthur is featured challenging the monastic establishment and riding rough-shod over holy ground, although not always getting what he wants and eventually having to back-down in humiliation; but more importantly, each mention of Arthur appears to give a cameo of his life, what he was doing and where he was at the time.

When king Gwynllyw eloped with princess Gwladys it must have been more than co-incidence that he bumped into Arthur on a nearby hilltop; the story not only suggests that he had a romantic eye for the young ladies but also gives a position report for Arthur, on a hill somewhere between Brecon and Glamorgan. We might be tempted to ask what he was doing there together with his trusted aides Cei and Bedivere? Could he have been on a reconnaissance mission to plan for a future battle?

Similarly, Arthur's meeting with Cadoc has an extraordinary element in the story, for why would Arthur bring his army to the bank of the river Usk just to have a discussion with the Abbot of Llancarfan? However we must consider that Cadoc was no ordinary abbot: he inherited his father's secular kingdom and became "*abbot and ruler over Gwynnliauc after his father.*" He possessed many tenanted estates and unlike any other British saint, maintained a garrison of one hundred men-at-arms in the hill-fort near his monastery.

Arthur may have needed to bring his army to the Usk in order to challenge the power of the dissident kings of Dyfed and Brecon; his compensation of a herd of cattle from the wealthy monastery would have been accepted as a traditional method of payment for military services. But Arthur's request for them to be part red and part white may have a deeper meaning because the colours relate to the national opponents involved in the war. Red signifies the Red Dragon of the Britons, and white relates to the White Dragon of the Anglo-Saxons (who later became the English of the eastern part of Britain). Perhaps Arthur was asking the Church for funds to pay for his army, half to pay for a civil action against the dissident states of South Wales, the other half to be spent on military action against the invading Saxons.

Cadoc's monastery at Llancarfan was over twenty miles west of the river Usk and the nearest strategic position for Arthur's army base would have been the old Roman fortress of Caerleon on Usk. Indeed, the fact that legend supports the idea that Arthur used Caerleon with its Roman amphitheatre for meetings of the 'round table' is not without foundation, for Arthur would have called a council of war with the local kings, including Cadoc's father, who were his allies and who could provide aid in the form of levies of men-at-arms together with cattle for the army's sustenance prior to battle. Thus, in the saint's life-story we find Cadoc not just inheriting his father's estate, but by poetic licence, having his father's encounters with Arthur superimposed upon his own story.

In the tale of Saint Carantoc, we find the young Arthur acting as a junior aid to Prince Cadwy at Dunster Castle. Perhaps Ambrosius had asked Arthur to help with the urgent task of strengthening the northern coastal defences of Dumnonia in order to repel frequent raids by Irish pirates. In fact, Arthur's request for help in fighting off the 'serpent' may not be as fanciful as it sounds if the serpent he is alluding to is seen as the prow of a sea-raider's warship appearing out of the mist and striking fear into the local people. Recent archaeology confirms that British hill-forts were re-occupied and their defences strengthened in the fifth century: in this area we find one strategic line of defence along the coast from Gloucester to Dunster, and another line of defence running across the country in a south-easterly direction from Brent Knoll in Somerset, through Glastonbury, Cadbury Castle, Hod Hill and down to Badbury Rings in south Dorset.

According to a chronicler, Brent Knoll, a hill-fort close to Dunster, once belonged to Arthur, but he graciously gave it to the monks of Glastonbury. Further south the hill-fort of South Cadbury held a key strategic position as the guardian of central Dumnonia; exactly half-way between the north and south coast it barred the path of any Saxon army that attempted to invade the south-western peninsula of Britain. Its strategic importance was paramount in the defence of Dumnonia, and it is highly probable that Cadwy and the young Arthur worked together to reinforce the defences of Cadbury to make it the strongest and most formidable fortress in the south-west.

Not surprisingly, local folklore strongly upholds the tradition that Cadbury Castle is Arthur's "Camelot" of legendary fame, a belief recorded as far back as 1542 when Henry VIII sent John Leland, the great antiquarian and traveller, to investigate the Arthurian claims; he reported: *"At South Cadbyri standith Camallate, sumtyme a famose toun or castelle. The people can tell nothing thar but they have hard say that Arture much resorted to Camalat."* Leland found the hill-fort *"wonderfully enstrengthened of nature"* and admired the still extant foundations of the great hall and other buildings. From these early times the summit plateau, which towers some five hundred feet above sea-level, was renowned as the site of "King Arthur's Palace"; even today, rumours still abound that the hill is hollow and that it conceals a cave where King Arthur can be found sleeping.

The name 'Cadbury' is derived from both Celtic and Saxon sources: the 'bury' is an English word taken from the earlier Saxon 'burh' or 'burgh' meaning a fortified dwelling place or town. Coins found with the name 'CADANBYRIG' revealed that a mint had been established there by Ethelred the Unready early in the eleventh century, and as an inhabited centre within a secure boundary wall the mint qualified as a 'burh'. The 'Cad' may be based on the Celtic word 'cad' meaning 'battle' a word that may also relate to the personal name of the heroic ruler Prince Cadwy or Cado, mentioned in the *Life of Saint Caradoc*. If the translation of 'Cadbury' is literally 'battle-fortress,' then how did the association of Cadbury with the legendary 'Camelot' arise?

A few miles to the west of South Cadbury lies the village of Queen Camel, originally known as Camel; the village and the fort are linked by the river Cam which flows through the meadows just to the north of the fortress. The Brythonic 'cadarn-leoedd' also means 'fortress' and it is possible that an association between the village and the fort resulted in the combination of 'Camel-leoedd', slipping off the tongue as "Camelot", thus linking Cadbury with the medieval legend of Arthur. In fact, Cadbury was listed as 'Cameletum' in 1544, but on later Elizabethan maps was shown as 'Camelleck.'

It was the French storyteller Chrétien de Troyes who first introduced Camelot in his Arthurian romances composed between 1160 and 1180, proclaiming it to be the many towered city where King Arthur held his court, and the only clue he gave to its location was, *"where Roman gladiators fought to the death."* As far as we know from archaeological evidence there were only three cities in Roman Britain where gladiatorial contests were held: Caerleon, Chester, and Colchester, otherwise known as 'Camulodunum' the first city of Roman Britain.

The original British name was derived from 'Camulos' the Celtic God of War, but when the Romans adapted this to 'Camulodunum' the local Britons would have shortened it to 'Camulod.' Here then is the direct link to Chrétien's 'Camelot.' Camulodunum was the first Roman capital of Britain and would have been inherited first by Ambrosius in the fifth century and later by Arthur as an important fortress in the defence of eastern Britain and a vital port with established trading links to Gaul. In the medieval stories, *"Arthur's knights rode out from Camelot"* to engage in chivalrous quests through the 'wasteland' of Britain; but the imaginary quests were invented by storytellers long after the real battles had faded from memory.

As Britain's *Commander of Battles,* Arthur would have been planning campaigns and fighting over the length and breadth of the island, so that his visits to Camulodunum would have been rare occasions concerned with strengthening the garrison and ensuring the safety of vital supplies from across the Channel. However, his rare visits to Camulodunum appear to be in direct contrast to Cadbury Castle where the local story that Arthur was reputed to have made frequent visits to the fortress was confirmed by Leland.

If Colchester is in fact the true 'Camelot' of Arthur's time, then Cadbury Castle's claim to fame must be seen as a separate development linked by local legend that has always projected a strong association with Arthur; thus the many towered west-country fortress has evolved over the centuries into the legendary Camelot.

The "Quest for Camelot" became a reality in 1965 when the Camelot Research Committee raised funds and commissioned a team headed by Leslie Alcock of University College Cardiff, to carry out a detailed survey and excavation of the site in a serious attempt to prove Arthur's link with Cadbury Castle. Over the next two years exploratory ditches were dug through the defensive earthworks and pits were excavated across the plateau of the site, revealing evidence of human settlement dating back to the Neolithic period over five thousand years ago, and confirming that a

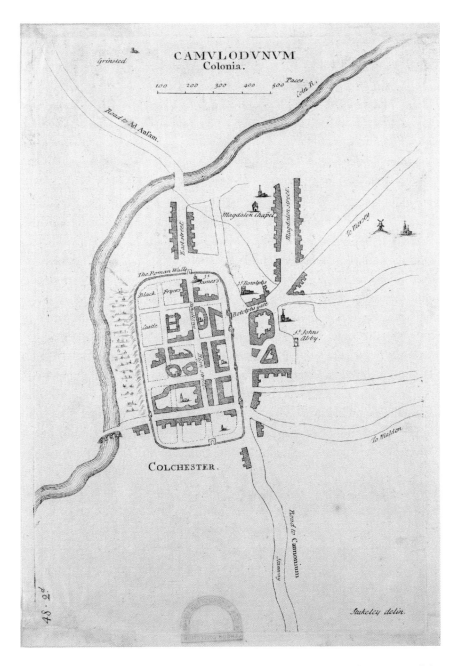

Camulodunum Colonia. A map of Roman Colchester showing the extent of the city walls that protected the Legionary Fortress, Temple, Amphitheatre and Baths within. The French poet Crétien de Troyes located King Arthur's Court at 'Camelot', a name that is closer to Camulod (unum) than any other Romano-British city. Courtesy of Essex Records Office.

13

Celtic village had flourished within the stronghold for hundreds of years before the Romans stormed the castle; but the most exciting discovery was that the fortress had been re-occupied and re-fortified in the late fifth or early sixth century, in fact, within Arthur's lifetime.

On the highest plateau, Leslie Alcock and his team discovered the foundations of a large timber hall measuring some 63 feet long by 34 feet wide; with its walls defined by post-holes cut deep into the bedrock, it was similar in construction to early medieval timber-framed barns that had been traditionally used as feasting halls by great British chieftains. Here on the renowned site of Arthur's Palace was firm evidence that a wealthy warlord had secured a military base for a band of warriors, servants and horses. Remains of wine-jars imported from the Mediterranean in the sixth century showed that the occupants had enjoyed the luxuries of wine and olive oil, to complement spit-roast pork and venison.

Another important discovery was made at the south-west entrance to the fort, where the team found that the top-most rampart had been strengthened and raised: this massive compaction of stones and rubble was named 'the stony bank' by the excavators, and it formed the core of an imposing rampart over 16 feet thick; this had originally been faced with an inner and outer stone wall. Gaps in the stone about six feet apart showed where timber posts had been secured to support a wooden breastwork, with timber towers constructed at key points along the 1200 yards of battlements that enclosed the fortress. At the entrance the remains of a gatehouse were found, consisting of a square wooden tower, approached by a cobbled roadway ten feet wide, that passed through two sets of timber doors on each side of the gatehouse.

The extent of Cadbury's massive re-fortification, after its almost total destruction by the Romans three hundred years before, is unparalleled elsewhere in Britain except for the rebuilding at Wroxeter, Roman Viroconium. It was almost certainly rebuilt in the late fifth or early sixth century, the Age of Arthur, and its purpose was to defend the regional headquarters of an important British chieftain.

Amongst the finds unearthed during the excavation were Roman military bronzes: one cuirass hinge and part of a shield binding as well as a gilt-bronze letter 'A'. The hope that this find might prove the link with Arthur, as the first letter of his name, was dashed when it was dated to the third or fourth century AD; it was suggested that there could have been a Romano-Celtic temple at Cadbury, and the 'A' may have been part of a votive inscription to the deity Apollo.

Another extraordinary find was the discovery of a foundation trench that revealed the cruciform plan for a church. The design was based on a uniform Greek cross, with a central tower in the style of the prototype church of the Holy Apostles in

Constantinople, built in the year 337, a style that was most frequently adopted in the fifth and sixth centuries. The plan could therefore be attributed to the Arthurian period, but although it represented an ambitious architectural project that reflected the hopes of a Christian community, the foundations were only partly completed and the church was never built.

If Arthur had been the driving force behind the re-fortification of Cadbury Castle, it is not surprising to find that local tradition also records his association with Glastonbury. The holy 'Island of Glastonbury' lies only twelve miles to the north-west of South Cadbury and it is claimed that these historic sites are linked by an Iron Age track known locally as 'Arthur's Causeway.'

Glastonbury Tor is a natural mount of Jurassic blue limestone capped by a mass of hard sandstone that rises dramatically to a peak five hundred feet above the Somerset Levels. On a clear day you may scan the horizon in all directions for over twenty miles, and to the west, follow the river Brue as it winds through marshland towards Bridgewater Bay in the Bristol Channel; but in post-Roman Britain this view would have appeared alarmingly different, for a significant rise in sea-level flooded the plain to a depth of about eighteen feet, effectively making the Tor an island. A landing-stage for visiting ships would most probably have been constructed at the foot of Wearyall Hill on the south-western slopes of the island, close to the Old Church and Chalice Well; to the east the remains of a causeway exists that linked the Tor to the higher ground of the 'mainland' towards Shepton Mallet.

Recent excavations (1964-1966) have shown that the Tor was occupied as a defensive site in the sixth century with evidence of timber buildings whose occupants enjoyed eating beef, lamb and pork, together with wine and olive oil imported from the Mediterranean. Hearths with crucibles found nearby were used to make iron and bronze artifacts, such as a remarkable miniature bronze head that was possibly part of a bucket escutcheon or the head of a staff: the bronze was cast around an iron core and the face shows Celtic characteristics that feature a domed helmet with ear-protectors.

Glastonbury Tor's natural function as a small but effective stronghold meant that its garrison could perform the role of protector and guardian of the early Christian settlement that had become firmly established on its western terraces. It is worth noting that Glastonbury holds the honour of being the earliest known Christian site in Britain, for the church was founded within a few decades of the crucifixion, possibly even during the lifetime of those who had known Christ and his disciples.

Our respected historian William of Malmesbury, in his *De Antiquitate Glastoniensis Ecclesiae* of 1130, revealed the existence of accredited documents that acclaimed: '*No other hands than those of the disciples of Christ erected the church of*

*Glastonbury.'* William mentions no names but legend has it that Joseph of Arimathea built the small wattle church dedicated to the Virgin Mary. Seeking refuge from the wrath of the Romans after the crucifixion, it was reported that Joseph had sailed to Britain bringing with him precious relics: a sprig from the crown of thorns grew into the famous thorn tree of Glastonbury; and the cup that Christ used at the Last Supper became the focal point of the Legend of the Holy Grail.

True or not, much of this story may well be credited to the inventive ideas of the monks who added their own embellishments to the original legend over several centuries; but this factor apart, Glastonbury has, for some very special reason, become a landmark as one of the earliest holy sites in Britain. Excavations have revealed evidence of Roman occupation from the first century continuing through to Romano-British settlement in the later third and fourth centuries. Without doubt the earliest Roman presence here would have included a small temple for the worship of one or more of the Roman pantheon of pagan deities. The most imposing site for this temple would have been the summit of the Tor and the Roman tiles discovered there may well have come from the roof of an original temple. Today, only the ruined tower of the medieval church dedicated to St. Michael stands at the summit as an imposing edifice to the shrines of earlier times.

In the late fifth and early sixth century Glastonbury enjoyed a period of revival as the monastic movement gained a stronger hold over the teaching and practice of Christianity in western Britain and Ireland, and the holy site became a magnet to the religious leaders of the age. Legend claims that St Patrick, the great Apostle of Ireland, became abbot of Glastonbury in his later years, and contributed greatly towards the development of the original monastery; it is said that when he died in 460, Patrick was given a ceremonial burial in the cemetery of the Old Church of St Mary. However, this version of events is hotly disputed by the Irish, who claim that St Patrick is buried at Down Cathedral in County Down, alongside St Brigid and St Columba.

Gildas was drawn to the Abbey because it gave him the seclusion to complete his book *On the Ruin and Conquest of Britain* and offered him protection from the claws of the five evil kings whose acts of atrocity he angrily exposed in his diatribe against them. Glastonbury was also a long way from the threat of the dreaded and unmentionable Saxons. Gildas expressed the wish to be buried in the Abbey he so dearly loved, and when he died in the year 570, the abbot observed his request, and *"with very loud wailing and with the most befitting of funeral rites"* he was buried in the middle of the pavement of St Mary's church, a position of significance close to the sacred pyramid shrines of St Indracht and St Patrick.

The first record of Arthur's connection with Glastonbury is found in *The Life of*

*Gildas* by Caradoc of Llancarfan about 1150. He mentions that King Melwas, who reigned over the summer country, now Somerset, had abducted Arthur's wife Guinevere and held her prisoner at Glastonbury's fortress because it was considered invulnerable, being surrounded by thickets of reed, river and marshland. After a year searching for his wife, *"the rebellious tyrant Arthur"* raised both armies of the Cornovii and the Dumnonii: he then besieged the city and prepared for battle; but the abbot, together with Gildas the wise and the clergy, intervened between the two armies advising King Melwas to restore Guinevere to Arthur in peace and goodwill. When this was done, the two kings bestowed a gift of many lands upon the abbey and they came to pray at the church of St Mary. So the kings were reconciled and promised the venerable abbot never to violate the most sacred place of Glastonbury.

Whether or not Caradoc's story is true is very much open to conjecture, for only twenty years earlier William of Malmesbury's research on the history of Glastonbury made no mention of Arthur, Guinevere or Avalon; but he did reveal the existence of a charter granted by a king of Dumnonia dated to the year 601. Caradoc clearly included Arthur in his story for good measure, for his purported gift of land to the abbey would have carried the authenticity of *"the king of the whole of Britain."* Thus we find by the twelfth century, when Caradoc is writing, that Arthur's status has evolved from a fifth century battle commander to the 'King of Britain;' yet in the same breath, Caradoc reflects the sixth century monastic view of Arthur by calling him a rebellious tyrant.

The echo of this disregard for Arthur some six hundred years after his lifetime has a ring of truth to it, for it shows that Caradoc is quoting his story from an earlier source; in fact, the statement that Arthur raised his army from the Cornovii, centred on Powys in the lowlands of mid-Wales, and Dumnonia, which included Somerset and Devon, is perfectly plausible because they were key areas in the defence of central and southern Britain in Arthur's time.

In contrast to this disdain for Arthur, the Celtic church paid much greater respect to its saints, honouring them with elaborate funeral rites and erecting magnificently carved shrines to their memory. William of Malmesbury relates how devoted Irish pilgrims came to Glastonbury to worship their saints, quoting a ninth century document that proclaimed *"the scots used to resort to a sanctuary of their own."* The 'Scots' referred to in this early document were the Scotii tribe from Ireland, and their most venerated saint was St Patrick.

Another Irish saint said to have visited Glastonbury is St Brigid, a contemporary of both Gildas and Arthur; St Brigid established a monastery at Kildare and is said to have written to Gildas as an admirer of his preaching and his wise instructions to the monastic priesthood. A small chapel at Beckery, close to the Abbey on the western plateau of the Tor, became the focus of Irish Christians on their pilgrimage to honour St Brigid, and according to tradition, her wallet and distaff were preserved there as relics sacred to her memory.

Local legend relates how Arthur was first converted to Christianity when he saw a vision of the Virgin Mary here at Beckery, the centre of a Marian cult that was also predominant in Ireland; but the 'vision' may have been a painted image of St Mary that encouraged Arthur to have the portrait emblazoned on his shield, for this would not only give him Divine protection in battle but also demonstrate that he was fighting for the Christian cause.

A further testament to the importance of Glastonbury as a centre for Christian worship in Arthur's time is found in one of the Welsh Triads where *"at Glastonbury, Amesbury and Llantwit Major, choirs sing the praise of God by day and by night."* The original wattle church was still standing in the year 600 when Paulinus, Bishop of Rochester under Augustine, protected the church with a new roof of timber planks. This providential gift from a Saxon bishop prolonged the life of the crumbling building for another eighty years; it was a gesture that again confirmed the special nature of the Old Church. William of Malmesbury added that the church had one remarkable feature: it was held to be so sacred that any oath taken there was eternally binding.

As the Saxon warbands forged westward in their conquest of Britain, Amesbury was destroyed, but fortunately Glastonbury was spared by Cenwalh, the Saxon king who conquered central Somerset in 658. As a convert to Christianity he made Glastonbury a place of reconciliation between the Saxon invaders and the Britons of the south-west. But by the close of the seventh century the Old Church of St Mary had crumbled beyond repair, and it was Ine, the Saxon king of Wessex who took up the challenge of building a new church in the continental style introduced by St Augustine. The hallowed ground of the original church was preserved and the new larger church sited just to the east. King Ine became a great benefactor of the church at Glastonbury, confirming its possessions and bestowing new grants to support the monastic establishment.

Just over two hundred and fifty years later in 943, King Edmund appointed St Dunstan Abbot of Glastonbury. Dunstan extended Ine's church with imaginative plans and new buildings, transforming the abbey into a centre of culture. Under his care both art and industry flourished and the monastery became the wealthiest in the land. St Dunstan enclosed the ancient cemetery with a stone wall and raised the area of the old tombs and an ancient mausoleum. *"The area within was raised to form a pleasant meadow, removed from the noise of the passers by, so that it might be said that bodies of the saints lying within, that they repose in peace."*

But in 1184 a disastrous fire destroyed the monastery and consumed the sacred shrine of Glastonbury. The ancient religious texts, relics and treasures were lost in the fire; a single chapel and a bell tower were all that remained of St Dunstan's magnificent church.

As the rebuilding of St Mary's Church began, the monks turned their attention to the bodies of the saints reposing in the cemetery. It is said that the bodies of St Patrick, St Gildas and even St Dunstan, who was in actual fact resting in peace at Canterbury, were exhumed to be enshrined in the new church. Their holy shrines attracted hundreds of pilgrims whose offerings helped to restore the seriously depleted coffers of the monastery.

Then, just six years after the fire had devastated the monastery, the monks made another miraculous discovery: it was nothing less than the tomb of the renowned King Arthur and his wife Guinevere, found in the ancient cemetery between two great standing stones near the Lady Chapel. The discovery of Arthur's grave in 1190 was as fortuitous for the monastery as it was for the monarchy because it coincided with the success of Geoffrey of Monmouth's *History of the Kings of Britain,* a book that had revived everyone's interest in the story of Arthur and as a result had become a 'best-seller'. A curious blend of historical fact and fiction based on early Celtic legends, Geoffrey's story was the first to introduce Merlin as Arthur's wisest adviser and court magician; and first to claim that after the battle of Camlan the mortally wounded Arthur was borne away to be healed of his wounds on the mystical Isle of Avalon.

Geoffrey's work found favour with the Norman kings who were pleased to associate themselves with the ancient heritage of the kingdom their ancestors had conquered; but the legend of Arthur's mysterious disappearance, the traditional belief that his grave was unknown and the rumour that one day he would return to lead the Britons against them, became a lasting concern for the Plantagenets. Giraldus Cambrensis, who visited Glastonbury in 1192, revealed that it was King Henry II who had suggested the exhumation. Henry feared the threat of a revolt by Celtic Britons led by his own grandson Arthur, son of Geoffrey of Anjou and Constance of Brittany, whom people believed to be the reincarnation of the great 'King Arthur'. Henry realised that he could give the lie to the Celtic tale of Arthur's imminent return by actually finding his body: this would be the de facto evidence that would lay Arthur's ghost to rest for all time; and with its earlier Arthurian associations and recently disinterred saints, what better place than Glastonbury for such a momentous discovery?

But Henry died in the year 1189, leaving his successor Richard I to accomplish his plan. Richard appointed Henry de Sully as the new Abbot and with his approval the monks excavated the suggested site between the two ancient 'pyramids' or standing stones; at a depth of seven feet they found a leaden cross bearing an inscription in Latin:

HIC IACET SEPULTUS INCLITUS REX ARTURIUS IN INSULA AVALONIA

HERE LIES BURIED THE FAMOUS KING ARTHUR IN THE ISLE OF AVALON

Digging down a further nine feet they revealed a large coffin that, according to Giraldus was made from a hollowed oak and contained the skeleton of a large man; a lock of golden hair found in the coffin is said to have crumbled to dust when a monk tried to snatch it away. Adam of Domerham, a Glastonbury monk writing a century after the event records:

*"The Abbot and convent, having raised up the remains, joyfully translated them into the great church, placing them in a double tomb, magnificently carved. The King's body was set by itself at the head of the tomb, that of the Queen at the foot or the eastern part, and there they remain to the present day."*

Endless controversy surrounds the discovery of Arthur's tomb but the fortunate beneficiaries were clearly King Richard, his Abbot, and the Abbey's coffers. That the whole event was a masterful forgery there is little doubt, and the evidence for this is revealed by the design and inscription of the leaden memorial cross, as illustrated in the 17th century engraving by William Camden.

First, the shape of the cross is a kind of cartoon version of what a medieval monk thought would pass for a sixth century memorial: it is remarkably similar to the tenth century leaden crosses found nearby at Wells cathedral, whereas a sixth century memorial would have had a text engraved below a simple circular Celtic cross. Secondly, the script is a giveaway to the forger's art, taken from the style of late Saxon silver pennies: perhaps the forger found similar coins readily available in the Abbey's treasury. Furthermore, the words of the inscription describe Arthur as 'Inclitus Rex' the famous King; but in his own time Arthur was known as the 'Dux Bellorum' or Leader of Battles. However, Arthur's status had been elevated by the authors of the Lives of the Saints, so that by the year 1150 he had become renowned as 'King of all Britain'.

This fact, together with the reference to the 'Isle of Avalon' confirms that the script was a twelfth century forgery. Geoffrey of Monmouth first wrote of Avalon in 1138, but after the 'discovery' of Arthur's tomb Giraldus Cambrensis, who had witnessed the exhumation, put his historical seal of approval on the event in his *De Principis Instructione* by declaring Glastonbury to be 'The Isle of Avalon', Arthur's last resting place.

Thus by devious means King Arthur's shrine became the wonder of pilgrims at Glastonbury; but it is ironic that in his lifetime Arthur's attempts to raise money from the church earned him the reputation of a rebellious tyrant, yet some six hundred years later the fame of his shrine ensured a constant flow of pilgrims and wealth to the Church in return. But the enshrined 'Arthur' was not allowed to rest in peace. In 1287, some eighty years after his entombment in the abbey, King Edward I ordered the shrine to be opened and the bones secured in the abbey treasury. Adam of Domerham recorded the event:

*"The lord Edward with his consort the lady Eleanor came to Glastonbury to celebrate Easter. The following Tuesday at dusk, the lord King had the tomb of the famous King Arthur opened; wherein, in two caskets painted with their pictures and arms, were found separately the bones of the said King, which were of great size, and those of Queen Guinevere which were of marvellous beauty. On the following day the lord King replaced the bones of the King, and the Queen those of the Queen, each in their own casket, having wrapped them in costly silks. When they had been sealed they ordered the tomb to be placed forthwith in front of the high altar, after the removal of the skulls, for the veneration of the people."*

This extraordinary event was no more than a clever publicity stunt by King Edward whose aim was to revive the public awareness of Arthur as the greatest ruler of Britain. The ceremonial exhibition of Arthur and his Queen not only once more revived the Abbey's income, but was politically expedient for Edward, whose current claim to the overlordship of Wales and Scotland was based on the rights of King Arthur to the whole realm of Britain. As king of England, Edward's aim was to conquer the Welsh and Scots with his powerful army, and proclaim himself as 'King over the whole of Britain.'

Without doubt, Arthur's fame brought great prestige and wealth to the Abbey for many years, but the final chapter in the history of St Mary's Church came as a sudden shock. It was also the greatest irony that, having survived the destruction of the Saxon invasion, it was a Tudor king of Welsh descent who delivered the final crushing blow: Henry VIII ordered the demolition of the Abbey. In 1538 at the Dissolution of the Monasteries, Henry sent auditors to assess the enormous wealth of Glastonbury Abbey, whose estates in the 16th century were second only to Westminster's. It was found that, in the previous year, fifty four resident monks had feasted on more than six hundred lambs and two hundred and fifty suckling pigs; and the auditors reported that of an amazing annual revenue of around £3000, (current value over £500,000) the Abbey had given only £140 to charity.

Richard Whyting the abbot, stubbornly refused to surrender the Abbey's estates, further angering the king. Henry arrested him and ordered a search of the Abbey:

his soldiers found as much embezzled treasure *"as would have sufficed for a new abbey."* After a short trial, the abbot and his two treasurers were condemned to death. They were hanged on the summit of the Tor, their bodies dismembered, and the abbot's head spiked above the Abbey's main gateway. It was a horrific warning to every abbot in the land to "defy King Henry VIII at your peril!" Although Henry had desecrated St Mary's Church and harvested its wealth for his own treasury, he could not wish away the hallowed ground that marked the Old Church of Glastonbury.

Arthur's tomb was destroyed and the bones dispersed. Today the site is marked by a simple plaque in the meadow by the crumbling ruins of the Abbey Church. Nevertheless, the mystery of Arthur's grave remains, and we are reminded of the words of an early Welsh poem *The Stanzas of the Graves*. It lists the last resting places of Celtic heroes:

> *"A grave for March, a grave for Gwythur,*
> *A grave for Gwgawn Red-Sword,*
> *The world's mystery, a grave for Arthur."*

# CHAPTER 2

# THE EVIDENCE FOR ARTHUR

## *Texts and Poetry*

*"Arthur of far flung fame,*
*Bear of the host, giver of shelter,*
*Arthur of the terrible sword*
*Your enemies shall fall before you."*

This early anonymous poem entitled *The Prophecy of the Eagle* celebrates Arthur's fame as a victorious battle-leader, and in the first two lines the author links the name of Arthur with the 'bear of the host' confirming that the names 'Arthur' and 'Bear' are synonymous. Evidently, the name 'Arthur' was originally taken from "artus" the Celtic word for 'bear' and combined with "ursus" meaning 'bear' in Latin; the name would thus have been easily recognisable by both Brythonic and Latin speaking people of Britain.

In Arthur's day, wild bears freely roamed the highland forests and they were undoubtedly the strongest and most feared of all the wild animals in Britain. The suggestion that Arthur, as a young warrior, gained great prowess by killing a wild bear single-handed, is open to conjecture; however, there is no doubt that as the strongest and most fearsome leader, Arthur truly earned his reputation as ' the bear of the host.'

The opening lines of the poem are an example of the early use of the epithet 'Bear' for Arthur, who is the first renowned fearsome killer, the crusher of the enemy Saxon host, and they verify the reference that Gildas made to Arthur as 'the bear' in his written reprimand of Cuneglas of Powys. The poem also has an important religious message for Arthur: following a discussion over good and evil, the eagle explains to Arthur that his sins will be absolved if he prays to Christ.

In *The Gododdin*, a sixth century battle poem by Aneirin, the renowned bard of the royal court of Din Eidyn (Edinburgh Castle), we find strikingly similar lines in praise of Merin ap Madain, the foremost lord of the war-band:

> *"Steadfast boulder before the host*
> *Terrible bear, killer, crusher,*
> *He trod on spears when battle came*
> *In an alder trench..."*

Aneirin's work is one of the earliest British battle poems to have survived from the last years of the sixth century and it relates the epic story of the Battle of Catraeth, Catterick, in the year 598. Looking at the map of Roman Britain, Catterick appears to be in the middle of nowhere, but in the sixth century it held a significant strategic position between the Saxon coastal settlements of Deira, north of the river Humber, and Bernicia to the north of the Tyne.

Some thirty six miles north of the British stronghold of York, the tribal city of Cataractonium guarded the main route to the north with a Roman *vexillation fort positioned just south of the Dere Street Bridge over the river Swale. The fort commanded the approach to Scotch Corner, where the road branches north-west through Stainmore forest to Carlisle, with Dere Street continuing north via Corbridge to Hadrian's Wall, then onward to Edinburgh. * (A vexillation fort was an outpost of the main garrison, manned on a temporary basis to give advance warning of enemy raids).

When the Saxon king Aelle of Deira conquered York in the year 580, the sudden loss of this great kingdom alarmed its northern neighbour: king Urien of Rheged, who ruled the north-east from his headquarters at Carlisle, immediately called upon the kings of the north to strengthen the British alliance. Urien's first move was to take Catterick and establish a British garrison there, both to defend Rheged against invasion by Deira, and to prevent Aelle from joining forces with Bernicia. In response, the Saxon king Aethelric rallied his Bernician warlords and challenged Urien to battle. Aethelric, known to the British as 'Flamddwyn' the Firebrand, first demanded hostages as a prelude to a peace treaty; but when they were not forthcoming, he attacked at the head of four war-bands. Urien stood firm:

> *"If a meeting for concord's to come*
> *Let our banners rise on the mountain*
> *And let our faces appear over the edge*
> *And let our spears rise over men's heads*
> *And let us charge Flamddwyn amid his men*
> *And let us kill both him and his comrades.*
> *Before Argoed Llwyfain*
> *There was many a dead man*

*Crows were crimsoned from warriors,*
*And the tribe charged with its chieftain!"*

The site of the battle of Argoed Llwyfain, the Forest of Leven, is unknown, but by tracing Aethelric's route from Bernicia towards Urien's base we may find the most likely place of conflict. The Saxons of Bernicia claimed that Hengist's son Ochta had established their kingdom, and they were determined to carry out his plan to conquer northern Britain. Having pushed the British Votadini out of their territory to the south of the river Tweed, the Saxons took over the Royal Palace of Yeavering Bell and the surrounding hill-forts of Peniel Heugh and Woden's Law. From these strongholds the Saxon warlords and their warriors could strike suddenly against British positions at Edinburgh, the Clyde and Carlisle.

Yeavering Bell, just to the west of Wooler in Northumberland, is seventy miles from Carlisle. If Aethelric had mustered his four war-bands here, he would have faced a route-march of two days or more, first following Kale Water into Teviot Dale; then moving south-west through Harwick and Langholm, he would have rested his men prior to the final assault on Urien's fortified city of Carlisle. But British scouts spotted the Saxon advance and raised the alarm: "*Goddau and Rheged were marshalled in Dyfwy, from Argoed to Arfynydd, they were given not one day's delay.*" Both Votadini and Cumbrian forces were called to prepare for battle at very short notice.

If Urien had marched his assembled army twenty-five miles eastward to meet Aethelric's war-band he would have reached the high ground to the east of Langholm, just a few miles from Kershope Forest. Tinnis Hill and Black Edge are relatively high mountains that would have offered a tactical advantage with the element of surprise over an enemy trudging through the valley below. Significantly, about one mile east of Black Edge we find 'Lookout Hill' exactly where scouts would have been positioned to spot an enemy advancing along the Ewes Water valley. This is the most likely area for the battle of Argoed Llwyfain where Urien's army clashed with Flamddwyn and his warriors, halting the Saxon advance into British territory.

Did Aethelric live to fight another day? He did indeed survive the battle and retreated with the remnants of his army to his own territory. Urien however, did not rest on the laurels of his victory but strengthened his forces by negotiating an alliance with his former enemies: Riderch of the Clyde, Gaullac of the Upper Forth and Morcant of Lindisfarne; he also invited Aedan of the Dal Riada Scots and king Fiachna of Ulster to join the war against the Saxons. Nennius confirms the story:

*"Four kings fought against them, Urien, and Ridderch Hen, and Gwallawg and Morcant. Theodoric (Aethelric's brother) fought vigorously against Urien and his sons.*

*During that time, sometimes the enemy, sometimes the Cymry were victorious, and Urien blockaded them for three days and three nights in the island of Lindisfarne."*

Urien and his allies had all but annihilated the Bernician forces who were only saved from extinction by a twist of fate, when Morcant quarrelled with Urien for allowing king Fiachna to take Bamburgh as a prize of war in return for his aid, thereby giving away Morcant's rightful territory without his consent.

*"But during this campaign, Urien was assassinated on the instigation of Morcant, from jealousy, because his military skill and generalship surpassed that of all the other kings."*

Urien was acclaimed as 'The Pillar of Britain' on his victory over Bernicia, but when this great warrior fell the British lost their greatest war-leader since Arthur; following Arthur's shocking demise, Urien's life was also cut short by one of his own countrymen. Urien of Rheged was the most powerful king; chief of all the kings of the north he held power in the west from Galloway to Shropshire, and strove more than any other leader to fulfil Arthur's policy of uniting the Celtic kingdoms of Britain against their common enemies.

Soon after Urien's murder his son Owain rallied his men for a final battle with Aethelric. Ironically, in his poem *Lament for Owain ab Urien* Taliesin celebrates the last British victory in the north whilst mourning the death of Owain in the strife that followed:

> *"When Owain slew Flamddwyn,*
> *It was no more than sleeping.*
> *Asleep is England's broad host,*
> *With light on their open eyes;*
> *And those who fled not far*
> *Were bolder than was needed:*
> *Owain scourged them savagely*
> *Like a wolf-pack after sheep...*
> *Soul of Owain ab Urien, may the Lord care for its needs."*

Owain's death was the prelude to the total demise of Rheged: its leaderless army disintegrated and its erstwhile allies now turned enemies and closed in for the kill. With the destruction of Rheged, the British kings had unwittingly accomplished the strategic plan of their enemies and handed the balance of power in the north as a gift to the Saxons.

With the fear of imminent invasion foremost in their minds, the British leaders devised a battle-plan as a last-ditch attempt to halt the Saxon advance. More than three hundred of the best warriors were picked from each of the three British regions: Gwynedd and Powys in the west; Cumbria, Dumfries and Ayrshire in the northeast, and Edinburgh and Lothian in the north. Mynyddawg, king of Gododdin and his battle leader Cynon of Gwynedd, would host the allied war-band in the great hall at Din Eidyn. The warriors would be trained for one year having pledged their loyalty to their lord in return for sustenance; meat, wine and bragget, a malt drink made from beer and honey, were plentiful and the men celebrated every feast day and made merry late into the night. They slept where they dined, in the great hall, on soft feather pillows.

Aneirin, the court poet, also drank wine and mead in the great hall; he enjoyed his lord's hospitality and was thereby committed to take part in the forthcoming battle:

> *"I drank deeply of mead in my turn,*
> *Wine fed in one gulp!"*

His experience of this bloody battle, and his fortunate survival, has given us an invaluable insight into the warfare of the sixth century. Not one chronicle of Arthur's battles has survived, but Aneirin's report of the Battle of Catraeth gives us a first-hand picture of a bloody clash between mounted Britons and Saxon invaders fighting on foot, just sixty years after Arthur's time. His epic poem *The Gododdin* is therefore the closest reference we will ever have to an Arthurian battle.

Aneirin, unarmed and wearing his bard's distinctive purple cloak, was captured during the battle, clamped in chains, and thrown into a pit; he was rescued by a warrior of true valour, kind hearted and magnanimous:

> *"From a war-band his bright blade saved me,*
> *From a fell cell of earth he bore me,*
> *From a place of death, from a harsh land,*
> *Cenan ab Llywarch, bold, undaunted."*

Woven between verses that describe courageous warriors charging headlong into the thick of the fray, Aneirin reveals a stark fact about the men's fitness for battle:

> *"Men went to Catraeth at dawn:*
> *Their high spirits lessened their life-spans.*
> *They drank mead, gold and sweet, ensnaring;*
> *For a year the minstrels were merry…*

*Red their swords, let the blades remain*
*Uncleansed, white shields and four-sided spearheads,*
*Before Mynyddawg Mwynfawr's men.*
*… by candles' light we drank bright mead,*
*Though good was its taste, afterwards long detested."*

*"Where can heaven's lord of Britain be found?"*

asks Aneirin; (perhaps in despair he is referring here to Urien or Arthur?)

*"Resplendent the lord in Eidyn's great hall,*
*His mead made men drunk;*
*He drank vintage wine.*
*A reaper in war, he drank the sweet wine."*

and when the battle began:

*"Men launched the assault, moving as one:*
*Short were their lives, made drunk by pure mead,*
*Mynyddawg's band, renowned in battle.*
*For a feast of mead they gave their lives…"*

In fact we find over three-hundred well trained but well-imbibed mounted warriors charging into battle fully armed with swords, spears and shields, wreaking havoc in the fray and reportedly killing over two thousand of the enemy in the first hour of battle; but despite their bravery, being slaughtered by the overwhelming opposition. Cypno the battle leader *'will not declare'* or more to the point, *could not declare* the battle won or lost because he and his comrades had perished; only three warriors survived the carnage of the battle, as well as Aneirin himself. He named them for posterity:

*"Men went to Catraeth, they were renowned*
*Wine and mead from gold cups was their drink,*
*A year in noble ceremonial*
*Three hundred and sixty-three gold torqued men.*
*Of all those who charged, after too much drink,*
*But three won free through courage in strife,*
*Aeron's two war-hounds and tough Cynon,*

*And myself, soaked in blood, for my song's sake."*

Earlier in the poem Aneirin describes the survivors Cynri, Cynon and Cynrein of Aeron as "three monarchs of men from Britain" and towards the close of the poem he pays a special tribute to another warrior from Wales:

> *"More than three hundred of the finest were slain.*
> *He cut down the enemy's centre and far wing,*
> *This most generous lord was resplendent before the host;*
> *In wintertime he freely gave horses from his herd.*
> *Guaurdur brought black ravens to a fort's wall*
> *Though he was not Arthur –*
> *He counted amongst men mighty in feats*
> *Before the front line's sharp alderwood barrier, Guaurdur."*

Aneirin witnessed the events he described and thus paid Guaurdur the highest compliment by comparing his brave exploits in battle with Britain's greatest warrior, Arthur. Guaurdur's name is similar to, and in Welsh actually rhymes with 'Arthur,' and as a warrior from Gwynedd he would have aspired to achieve the prowess of his renowned predecessor.

The association of these rhyming names was a natural gift to the poet, but Aneirin saw this as a challenge to his word-craft and he cleverly conveyed his meaning in a few concise lines of Brythonic verse, ending each by rhyming with 'ur'

> *"gochore brein du ar uur*
> *caer ceni bei ef arthur*
> *rug ciuin nerthi ig disur*
> *ig kynnor guernor guaurdur"*

Guaurdur, like Arthur, led his noble warriors into battle. He cut through the enemy's front line and then attacked their far wing. He charged to the top of the ramparts and dispatched his foes along the wall of the fort, leaving their dead bodies as a feast for black ravens, just as Arthur had done when he had clashed with the Saxons, many years before.

The naming of Arthur in this passage of *The Gododdin* is of great significance because, not only is it the earliest known reference to Arthur in literature, but also it shows that Arthur was esteemed within the living memory of Britons who revered him as the greatest hero of their age.

The battle of Catraeth was a catastrophe for the fragile alliance of British kings. It was the final decisive event of the sixth century that marked the transfer of military power in the north from the established alliance of British kingdoms to the burgeoning alliance of the English kingdoms of Deira and Bernicia, present day North Yorkshire and Northumberland; it was from these regions that the Saxon kings mounted an offensive onslaught that would eventually secure their command over the whole island of Britain.

But Aneirin was not the only poet bewailing the bitter consequences of these belligerent times: Nennius mentions him along with Talhaearn Tad Awen, Taliesin, Bluchbard and Cian who were '*all famed in British verse at the time when Outigern fought bravely against the English.*' Outigern, the 'overlord' with the strongest army of spearmen had assumed Arthur's role as the defender of Britain a decade or more after his death: the overlord in question was 'Eleutherius of the Great Army' king of York, who opposed Ida the new Saxon king. In the year 547 Ida fortified Bamburgh and united Deira and Bernicia under his control, presenting a formidable threat to the British.

But of all the famous bards, only the work of Aneirin and Taliesin has survived to enhance our understanding of life amongst the Britons of the late sixth century. Whilst Aneirin is famed for his depiction of the stark reality of pitched battle in his poem *The Gododdin*, his great work shows a distinct contrast to the more imaginative, often esoteric verse of Taliesin, who was renowned as the 'Chief poet of the West.'

The legendary * *Story of Taliesin* first translated from a sixteenth century text by Lady Charlotte Guest as part of her collection of early Welsh tales called the *Mabinogion*, relates how the poet was abandoned as a babe, like Moses in Egypt, and found in a coracle caught in a salmon weir by the bank of the river Conwy. The child was rescued by Elffin, the son of one of Maelgwyn's noblemen, who, on seeing such a bright forehead remarked: "Behold, a radiant brow!" "Taliesin it is" replied the child, who thereupon composed his first poem *The Consolation of Elffin,* in which he re-assured his new patron that his unexpected catch would be of far greater value than a hundred salmon!

Elffin and his wife fostered the young poet until he was thirteen years of age, when Elffin took him to the Christmas Court at Caer Deganwy. There they listened to songs praising Maelgwyn, extolling him as the most powerful, handsome and generous prince, his wife as the fairest lady, and his bards as the wisest in the land; but when Maelgwyn overheard Elffin declare that his own wife was fairer and more chaste than the queen, and that his bard was more skilful than the king's, Maelgwyn threw him into prison until Elffin's words were proven to be true or false.

When Taliesin heard that Maelgwyn had asked his son Rhun to test the faithfulness of Elffin's wife, he persuaded his foster mother to exchange clothes with her maidservant and to give the girl her own ring. When he arrived at the house, Rhun was invited to join the lady of the house for supper; he duly plied the maid with wine, seduced her with softly spoken words, and when she had fallen asleep, cut-off her little finger with the ring to prove his conquest.

Maelgwyn presented Elffin with the macabre evidence and challenged him with the disgrace of his wife's infidelity; Elffin agreed that the ring was his, but denied that the finger belonged to his wife, and was promptly thrown back into prison until he could prove the wisdom of his bard. Angry with Maelgwyn for imprisoning Elffin for a second time, Taliesin entranced the court bards as they took their places for the Christmas feast, so that instead of praising the king, all they were able to do was to pout their lips and mouth "blerm blerm" before Maelgwyn.

Furious at this nonsense, Maelgwyn ordered his steward to strike the chief bard for his insolence; the blow broke the trance and Heinin the bard pointed the finger of blame at Taliesin. The king demanded an explanation, prompting Taliesin to reply with a poem full of wonder, eloquence and wisdom: *"Primary Chief Bard am I,"* he began. Humbled by the young poet's extraordinary intellect, Maelgwyn invited Taliesin to sing for him of the order of the world, of its creation and its ending.

Thus by proving his ability as a poet, and proving the innocence of Elffin's wife by revealing that she still had five fingers on each hand, Taliesin secured Elffin's release from prison.

Closer in time and place to the world of Arthur, and with first-hand knowledge of Deganwy, Taliesin mentioned more of Arthur than his younger contemporary Aneirin. Truly angered by the imprisonment of his lord and patron Elffin, Taliesin likened Maelgwyn's accomplices who tortured the innocent with *cunning tricks and crafty devices*, to the fools who opposed Arthur at Badon: fools who were now silent, because in their folly they had been struck down:

> \* *"Silent as fools as at the battle of Badon*
> *with Arthur, chief giver of feasts,*
> *with his tall blades red from the battle*
> *that all men remember.*
> *The king's battle against his enemies,*
> *woe to those fools ! "*

Nor was there any love lost between Taliesin and Maelgwyn:

> *"No word of grace or blessing upon Maelgwyn Gwynedd,*

*Because of this fearful wrong and ingenious cruelty.*
*Vengeance shall be the ending upon Rhun his heir:*
*May his life be short, may his lands be wasted,*
*May his exile be long:*
*This upon Maelgwyn of Gwynedd ! "*

from * *The Journey to Deganwy* by Taliesin.

The *Story of Taliesin* gives a glimpse of Maelgwyn's court at Deganwy Castle in Gwynedd, where this powerful king, trumped-up with pride by his flattering bards and doting courtiers, held sway over his fearful subjects. The intriguing tale brings the young poet into a head-on confrontation with the king over his unjust imprisonment of Elffin; yet with his intelligent command of the situation Taliesin overcomes Maelgwyn's trickery and secures Elffin's release from his 'golden chains.' Taliesin has the final say, cursing Maelgwyn for his wrong-doing and ingenious cruelty.

Talieisin's condemnation of Maelgwyn is reinforced by another contemporary witness: Gildas the monk, who gives a more detailed account of events at Deganwy: he openly condemns Maelgwyn, describing the path to corruption and depravity that earned him the reputation of the most evil king in Britain. Gildas tells us that, having *"cruelly murdered his uncle and nearly all his brave soldiers by sword, spear and fire,"* Maelgwyn showed some remorse for his evil deeds and vowed to become a monk; but his penance was short-lived and he soon broke his vows.

He left the service of God to become an '*instrument of the devil.*' Even as a monk, his presumptive first marriage was against the law of the Church, yet after a while he spurned his wife for the wife of another, a man who was none other than his brother's son. Then, with the collusion and encouragement of his nephew's wife, Maelgwyn crowned his sacrilege with two more murders, killing his own wife and his nephew. He then married his nephew's widow in a public wedding ceremony that was acclaimed legitimate by his parasitic followers. Gildas thought it a most scandalous act and condemned Maelgwyn's tyranny as one of the evils of the age: his depiction of Maelgwyn as the devil of Deganwy makes Taliesin's curse all the more poignant.

Gildas lived to witness his promise of Divine retribution delivered to the unrepentant king in the form of the yellow plague, an epidemic from Persia that spread through Mediterranean trade routes to Gaul. When the plague eventually reached Britain, tradition holds that Maelgwyn took refuge in the small chapel of Llanrhos, a mile or so north-east of Deganwy; but for him there was no escape. His death in 'the great mortality' of 547 is recorded in the *Annales Cambriae.*

From Deganwy, Taliesin moved to Rheged as chief bard to the court of king Urien, where he became renowned for his extensive repertoire of poetry. *"Three hundred and more are the songs of my singing"* he boasted; later in the fullness of life's experience he claimed to know *"four hundred songs which bards both older and younger cannot sing; nine hundred more, unkown to any other, I will sing concerning the sword stained red with blood."*

Yet from the small collection of Taliesin's work that has survived to the present day, we find poems that include many esoteric references to the Celtic Otherworld along with poetry that celebrates the wonder of nature, praises the warlord's hospitality and prowess in battle, and laments the death of heroic warriors.

In his poem *The Chair of the Sovereign* Taliesin writes of Arthur:

"Sing a brilliant song of boundless inspiration
Concerning the man who is come to destroy nations.
His staff and his entrenchment,
And his swift devastations,
And his ruling leadership
And his written number,
And his red-purple robes,
And his assault against the rampart,
And his appropriate seat
Amid the great assembly…

…The third deeply wise one
Is the blessed Arthur
Arthur the blessed,
Renowned in song,
In the fore-front of the battle
He was full of action."

In another poem attributed to *Taliesin, Arthur's enemies were not forgotten:

"The third profound song of the sage
Is to praise Arthur, Arthur the blessed,
With harmonious art: Arthur the defender in battle,
the trampler of nine enemies."

Confirmation of Arthur's nine enemies from this contemporary source gives credence to Nennius' list of Arthur's twelve battles: when we consider that four of the battles were fought against Ochta's Saxons on the river Blackwater, this would account for Arthur fighting twelve battles against nine enemies. In a further reference to Arthur's enemies, Taliesin reveals the only existing proof of a link between Arthur and Uther Pendragon, the 'Chief Dragon' who ruled over Gwynedd and Powys from his royal seat at Castell Dinas Bran by Llangollen. In the *Death Song of Uther Pendragon* two concise lines reveal a significant fact:

> \* *"Do I not share my protection,*
> *A ninth part with the battling Arthur?"*

asked Uther, a question that demonstrated his support for Arthur in the Battle for Britain: the question presupposes that Uther has either provided the funding for Arthur to fight one of his nine enemies, or alternatively, has provided one ninth of the total cost of the war, with the remainder funded by the other British kingdoms.

In another poem, certain lines allude to the hero of the age; without naming Arthur, Taliesin takes it for granted that his audience will understand whom he is describing:

> \* *"He was in conflict constantly while he lived,*
> *Worshipping the Creator,*
> *Defending the realm,*
> *Civilizing, chiding,*
> *Conquering with sharp steel."*

\* *Taliesin: The Last Celtic Shaman* by John Matthews with Caitlin Matthews published by Inner Traditions, a division of Inner Traditions International, 1991. All rights reserved. http://www.Innertraditions.com Reprinted with permission of the publisher.

In the *Book of Taliesin*, a fourteenth century manuscript that contains some of the earliest verse in the Welsh language, we find a reference to Arthur in a most enigmatic poem called *Preiddeu Annwn, The Spoils of Annwn*. Taliesin accompanies Arthur and the crew of his ship *Prydwen* across the sea to the Celtic Otherworld of Annwn; their quest is to steal the magical cauldron that gives life, sustenance and wealth in plentiful measure to all who possess it. The Cauldron was guarded by the Lord of Annwn and kindled by the breath of nine maidens; to reach it required great courage and Arthur and his men journeyed through the seven Cairs that represented seven levels of the otherworld that must be attained before they could reach the coveted prize of the Cauldron, the fount of creation.

A similar but more down to earth version of the quest for the Cauldron appears in the Mabinogion story of *Culhwch and Olwen*. Culhwch wishes to marry Olwen, daughter of the fearsome giant Ysbadadden, who demands that a number of seemingly impossible tasks are accomplished before he will agree to give his daughter's hand in marriage. Culhwch calls on his first cousin Arthur and his men to help him achieve the tasks, one of which is to seize the Cauldron of Diwrnach, who is steward to Odgar son of Aed, the king of Ireland. With a small force, Arthur sets sail for Ireland in his ship *Prydwen*. On reaching Diwrnach's house they are invited to eat and drink their fill, and when they have finished their meal, Arthur asks for the cauldron; but when Diwrnach refuses to part with it, Bedivere snatches the cauldron as Llenlleug seizes Arthur's sword, swinging it round in a circle and killing Diwrnach the Irishman together with his entire retinue. When Irish soldiers arrive to challenge Arthur he puts them to flight before boarding his ship and returning to Dyfed, with the cauldron stuffed full of the treasures of Ireland.

In a sequel to this tale, Arthur returns to Ireland with an army to subdue Leinster, provoking the king of Leinster to attack South Wales in a reprisal raid. In a metaphorical twist to the story, Arthur's enemy becomes 'Twrch Trwyth' an indefatigable boar that ravages through Dyfed and Brecon, killing Arthur's men, including his own son Gwydre. (This mention of Gwydre is unusual, for there is no other record of Arthur having a son named Gwydre).

In Culhwch and Olwen the storyteller has clearly drawn on real events that fit the category of seemingly impossible tasks fulfilled by Arthur in the distant past; he then weaves them into the story as the giant's challenges to Culhwch. In complete contrast, Taliesin the poet transforms a real event ~ Arthur's voyage to Ireland in *Prydwen* to secure the cauldron ~ into a transcendental voyage to the Otherworld where departed souls journey through seven stages before reaching their heavenly goal.

For Taliesin, the expedition becomes a '*sorrowful journey*' with a '*lamentable meeting*' that prompts the repetition of a forlorn statement that "*except seven, none returned.*" In his poem *Preiddeu Annwn* there is an echo of a real event: in all probability Taliesin had in mind Arthur's voyage to Avalon, the last journey of the wounded warrior to the lamentable meeting that preceded the secret obsequies of the king.

In complete contrast to Taliesin's dark-age lament, the author of Culhwch's adventure introduced some witty, light-hearted relief in a parody of Arthur's Court that was, in essence, the satirical equivalent of an early medieval version of *Monty Python's Flying Circus* that would have had his audience in fits of laughter.

When Culhwch invokes Olwen in the name of Arthur's warriors, he expounds an extensive list of two hundred and fifty warriors and camp-followers: beside the well-known celebrities of Arthur's Court, Cei, Bedivere and Gawain, the list features Gildas the priest and Bishop Bidwini, but is then extended to include Britons who lived long after Arthur's time, interspersed with nonsensical names such as Rheu Easy Difficult, Keudawg Half Wit, and Hwyrddyddwg, Drwgddyddwg, and Llwyrddyddwg (Late Bringer, Evil Bringer and Complete Bringer) and their three wives Groan, Shout and Outcry together with their daughters Bad, Worse and Worst of All. (note: the 'dd' in Welsh is pronounced 'th' in English, turning each name into an amusing tongue-twister.)

Between the comic asides, the gentle gold-torqued women of Britain are authentically recorded in Culhwch's list, including the first lady of the island, Gwenhwyvar, (Guinevere), her sister Gwenhwyfach, Kelemon daughter of Cei, and Gwenwldyr daughter of Gwawrddur the Hunchback. (As a valiant warrior Gwawrddur is compared to Arthur in the battle poem *The Gododdin* by Aneirin.) Indeg, daughter of Garwy the Tall is also named as one of the women of Arthur's court, and her name appears again in one of the Welsh Triads that lists the three mistresses of Arthur as Indeg, Garwen and Gwyl.

Earlier the story reveals the customs of Arthur's Court with particular emphasis on the role of the Gatekeeper, whose prime task is to prevent enemies from entering the fortress. When Culhwch approached the castle to seek Arthur's help, Glewlwyd Mighty Grasp the Gatekeeper denied him entry, for he arrived too late:

*"Knife has gone into meat, and drink into horn, and there is a throng in Arthur's hall: excepting the king of a lawful dominion or a craftsman who brings his craft, no-one may enter!"*

Culhwch is told that he will have to wait until tomorrow morning, when food for fifty men will be served in the guest-house where strangers and foreigners with no craft are billeted, with the promise of songs to entertain him and a woman to sleep with. But Culhwch will have none of this and threatens to bring dishonour upon the Court unless he is allowed to see Arthur without delay.

*Culhwch and Olwen* gives Arthur his first appearance in Welsh prose, but despite his nominal role, the story encapsulates a wealth of traditional lore, untainted by the influence of Geoffrey of Monmouth, and gives us a fuller understanding of life in Arthur's time.

Glewlwyd the Gatekeeper features in another early Welsh poem *Pa Gur?* or *What man is the Porter?* that was part of an anthology of early Welsh verse compiled at the

Augustinian Priory of St John's around 1250 entitled *The Black Book of Carmarthen*. As one of the oldest manuscript written in the Welsh language it is an important source of folklore and tradition that reaches back to the sixth century. Amongst the religious texts and the prophecies of Myrddin (the bard Merlin of legend whose name derived from the Roman fortress of Moridunum) are four poems that mention Arthur, including *Pa Gur?*

This is one of the most significant early poems, for it takes us into the dark-age world of epic poetry born of heroic action in fierce and bloody battles frequently interwoven with mystical encounters from the Celtic Otherworld:

> *"What man is the gatekeeper?"*
> *"Glewlwyd Mighty-Grasp,*
> *What man asks it?"*
> *"Arthur and Cei the fair"*
> *"What company is with you?"*
> *"The best men in the world"*
> *"They shall not enter here unless you vouch for them"*
> *"I shall vouch for them, you shall see them,*
> *The Vultures of Elei;*
> *The three great magicians:*
> *Mabon son of Modron,*
> *Uther Pendragon's servant;*
> *Cystaint son of Banon,*
> *Gwyn Goddyfrion,*
> *Strong servants all, defending the laws:*
> *Manawydan son of Llyr, great in council:*
> *(Manawyd returned with a shattered shield from Tryfrwyd)*
> *and Mabon son of Mellt, who stained the grass with blood,*
> *and Anwas the Winged and Llwch Llawynnawc*
> *who were both determined to defend dun Eidyn.*
> *A lord would give them refuge, would avenge them.*
> *Cei would plead for them, even as he struck three at a time!*
> *(When Celli was lost fury ranged free)*
>
> *Cei would entreat them even as he cut them down.*
> *Though Arthur was laughing he made blood to flow*
> *in Afarnach's hall, fighting the hag.*
> *He slew Pen-Palach in the house of Disethach.*

*On Eidyn's Mount he fought the dog-heads,*
*felled them by the hundred: by the hundred they fell*
*to Bedwyr the hewer.*
*On the shores of Tryfrwyd in battle with the dog-man,*
*furious his mean with sword and shield.*

*Vain was a host compared with Cei in battle:*
*he was a sword in battle, a giver of pledges,*
*a constant chief to the host, defending the land.*
*Bedwyr son of Rhyddlaw,*
*with nine hundred poised for battle,*
*and six hundred scattering*
*after his attack.*
*I used to have servants;*
*It was better when they were alive.*
*Before the Lord of Emrys I saw Cei in a hurry*
*Leading the host, long in wrath, heavy in vengeance,*
*Terrible was his fury in battle.*
*When he drank from his horn it was enough for four men;*
*When he came into battle he slew enough for a hundred.*
*Unless God achieved it Cei could never be slain,*
*Cei the Fair and Llachau, brave in battle,*
*Llachau before the pain of blue spears finished the fight.*
*On top of Ystawingun Cei slew nine hags;*
*He went to Mon to fight wild cats.*
*He set his shield against Cath Palwc."*
*When people ask: "Who slew Cath Palwc?"*
*The answer shall be: "that where nine-score warriors*
*and nine-score chieftains perished,*
*\*It was Cei the fair who vanquished Palug's panther."*
*\*(the last line of the original text is missing).*

*Pa Gur?* and *Culhwch and Olwen* are fine examples of the storyteller's art reflected in poetry and prose where strands of Celtic folklore originating from ancient Celtic myths have been woven into a tapestry that assembles fearsome giants ~ Awarnach, Wrnach and Ysbaddaden ~ and the hags of evil cults alongside pagan deities such as Mabon ap Modron, (whose name relates to the Romano-British god Apollo), and Manawydan son of Llyr, the Celtic god of the sea. These imaginary immortal beings are brought to life in fables where they take the stage alongside the real heroes of the past, Arthur, Cei, and Bedivere, and real warriors whose names echo the Celtic pantheon.

A medieval audience familiar with the story of *Culhwch and Olwen* may well have appreciated the touch of irony in the opening lines of *Pa Gur?* The gatekeeper is Glewlwyd Mighty Grasp, one and the same who challenged Culhwch at the gate of Arthur's fortress, now challenges Arthur, his own lord and master, who must obey the rule by naming and vouching for his men before being allowed to enter within. So the gatekeeper's challenge is used as a literary device that allows the poet to introduce famed characters and to extol their achievements. Words of praise from Arthur celebrate the prowess of his greatest warriors Cei and Bedivere; but lesser warriors are also included in the acclamation together with the battles in which they fought:

"*Anwas the Winged and Llwch Llawynnawc were each determined to defend Din Eidyn*" when Arthur fought the dog-heads at Edinburgh Castle. These lines are of great significance for they reveal that Arthur fought another battle that was not included in Nennius' original list of twelve battles. Equally significant in *Pa Gur?* the inclusion of 'Tryfrwyd,' Arthur's tenth battle as recorded by Nennius, is mentioned twice.

"*Manawydan returned with a shattered shield from Tryfrwyd*"
"*On the shores of Tryfrwyd in battle with the dog-man*"

Although the spelling differs from Nennius' 'Tribruit' it is clearly the same battle; the recording of this battle by two different sources strengthens the possibility that both *Pa Gur?* and the Nennius' battle list hold authentic information that dates from Arthur's lifetime. The author of *Pa Gur?* links the battles at Dun Eidyn and Tryfrwyd with the same enemy who are described as 'dog-heads', none other than Pictish warbands from the highlands who were fighting the British Votadini who ruled Edinburgh and the territory of Manau Gododdin as far north as Stirling.

Though they are listed together in the poem, it does not necessarily follow that both battles took place in the north. Dun Eidyn, the headquarters of the Votadini king, would be the most plausible location for a northern battle; but *the devastating raids from the north*" described by Gildas, confirm that the Picts were renowned for making reprisal raids much further south, suggesting that the battle on the shores of the river Tryfrwyd may well have been fought closer to Lincoln or York than to Edinburgh.

Another early poem found in the *Black book of Carmarthen* is *The Elegy for*

*Geraint Son of Erbin* a lament for Gerontius the young prince of Dumnonia who was killed in action at the Battle of Llongborth fighting alongside Arthur. The name 'Llongborth' is derived from the original Latin 'longa navis' or warship, and in this context means 'ship-port.' In the early years of the sixth century, Arthur's Saxon enemies continued to reinforce their settlements along the south-coast, strengthening the foothold territory secured by Aelle and Cerdic. In the year 501, the *Anglo Saxon Chronicle* records the arrival of new forces in the south, when invaders spear-headed landings in the Isle of Wight, Southampton, and Portsmouth Harbour, where Beida and Maegla *"slew a young Welshman, a very noble man."*

Three miles north of the harbour entrance, Portchester Castle holds sway over the wide expanse of sheltered water famed as Britain's major warship port on the south-coast. Built by the Romans as a defensive bastion, 'Portus Ardaoni' as it was then known, was the western-most of the Saxon Shore Forts listed in the Notitia Dignitatum a decade or so after the Romans had left Britain, and it presented the invading Saxons with an essential strategic target. As the defensive bastion to Britain's 'front door' in the south it was a prize worth fighting for, and it would reward them with command over Portsmouth Harbour together with its extensive seaboard.

The poet's eyewitness account records Llongborth as a bloody battle:

*"At Llongborth I saw slaughter, men quaking and heads bloodied."*
Their great battle-horses were red-shinned and blood-spattered in the fray.
*"At Llongborth I saw Arthur… the emperor, strife's commander."*

This is without doubt the most significant line in the whole poem, for it confirms Arthur's military leadership as Britain's supreme battle commander. At Llongborth, Geraint is the leader of loyal Dumnonian forces fighting under Arthur's command in the defence of southern Britain; and it was the young nobleman Geraint who gave his life that day for his country.

The *Elegy for Geraint* is written in Taliesin's style and follows the earliest tradition of a poet's presence at a major battle; the vivid description of the battle and the lament for the loss of a hero closely compares with Aneirin's first-hand account of the battle of Catraeth in *The Gododddin*, where one line *"though they were being slain, they slew"* is repeated in the Llongborth poem. Repetition is a feature of Taliesin's work, and in this poem no fewer than eight stanzas repeat the theme:

*"There were swift stallions under Geraint's thigh,*
*Long-shanked, raised on wheat-grain*
*Roans, spotted eagles assault."*

It is evident that the British cavalry were there in force, but they were not able to win the battle; the poet concludes with a tribute to a Christian prince:

*"When Geraint was born, heaven's gates were open,*
*Christ granted all our prayers.*
*A wonder to behold, the glory of Britain."*

The Saxons took control of Portchester Castle and recorded their victory; even the loss of a very noble Welshman was recorded in the *Anglo-Saxon Chronicle*. Llongborth was a strategic defeat for Arthur, whose attention was soon after diverted from Cerdic's claims in the south to the more serious threat of Ochta's Saxon army breaking out of Kent into central Britain. For the time being, the battle of Portchester Castle was best forgotten; yet even in the long-term, as Nennius' list shows, this was another battle of Arthur's that was officially unrecorded.

❧❧❧❧

The earliest and most important collection of *Englynion y Beddau* or the *Stanzas of the Graves* is also found in the *Black Book of Carmarthen* where Arthur is given an enigmatic entry in the list of the great Warriors of Britain:

*"There is a grave for March, a grave for Gwythur,*
*a grave for Gwgawn Red-sword;*
*the world's wonder a grave for Arthur."*

This single line confirmed that the Britons acknowledged Arthur's death; but it also proved that the custodians of Avalon had kept the secret of Arthur's last resting place, according to his wish.

A further source of Arthurian material lies within *Trioedd Ynys Prydein* the *Triads of the Island of Britain,* found in various manuscripts that date from the early thirteenth century with later additions in the fifteenth and sixteenth centuries. Formed by linking subjects into groups of three, the triads were used as an aide-memoire by bards recounting by heart their repertoire of traditional stories. Even though the earliest triads were written more than six and a half centuries after Arthur's lifetime, the key texts that mention Arthur show him as a rough diamond and an intrepid warrior: as well as being listed as one of the frivolous bards of the Island of Britain, Arthur is also called one of the three 'red ravagers of Britain,' ranking with Rhun son of Beli and Morgant the Wealthy. Of the three 'generous men of Britain,'

Nudd, Mordaf and Rhydderch, Arthur himself was counted more generous.

One of the earliest triads to name Arthur's warriors has an air of authenticity, for the names also appear in *The Dream of Rhonabwy* and in the long roll of Arthur's followers listed in *Culhwch and Olwen*:

> *"Three chieftains of Arthur's Court:*
> *Gobwry son of Echel Mighty Thigh,*
> *Cadrieth son of Portawr Gadw,*
> *and Fleudur Fflam (the Firebrand)."*

In another triad *The Three Powerful Swineherds*, Arthur is accused of attempting to steal a pig:

> *"Drystan son of Tallwch, who guarded the swine*
> *of March son of Meirchiawn, while the swineherd*
> *went to ask Essyllt (Isolde) to come to a meeting with him;*
> *and Arthur was seeking to get one pig from among them*
> *either by deceit or by force, but he did not get it."*

Yet another triad outlines three catastrophic events that proved disastrous for Britain:

> *"Three Unfortunate Counsels of the Island of Britain:*
> *To give place for their horses fore-feet on the land*
> *to Julius Caesar and the men of Rome*
> *in requital for \*Meinlas;*
> *and the second: to allow Horsa and Hengist*
> *and Rhonwen into this island;*
> *and the third: the three-fold dividing by*
> *Arthur of his men with Medrawd at Camlann!"*

\*(note: the British leader Cassivellaunus presented his horse 'Meinlas' to Julius Caesar as a peace offering when the Romans first landed in Britain).

This startling admission of an apparent tactical error by Arthur is, apart from the brief listing in the *Annales Cambriae*, the only other historical reference to the event of Arthur's overwhelming defeat at the battle of Camlan. If he actually divided his force into three *with* Medrawd, then Medrawd must have been fighting on Arthur's side against three opposing enemy forces that were poised to attack from three different directions. In the clash of battle the enemy combined to overwhelm Arthur's disintegrating army, and after the massacre of almost all his men, the name of his real enemy was suppressed, and the word spread that the faithful Medrawd had turned traitor. Who then was Arthur's real enemy?

The true cause of the battle of Camlan has vexed the minds of Britons for centuries. In the early medieval story of *Culhwch and Olwen*, a young warrior named Gwyn Hyfar is named "*as one of the nine who plotted the battle of Camlan;*" but over time his name has been misinterpreted as Gwenhwyfar (Guinevere) Arthur's wife, who is subsequently blamed for being the chief causer of the conflict. A triad was then composed to encompass this idea:

> "*Among the three harmful blows given in the Island of Britain,*
> *The second is the one Gwenhwyfach struck upon (her sister) Gwenhwyfar,*
> *And for that cause there took place afterwards the action of the Battle of Camlan.*"

The triad about *Three Unrestrained Ravagings of Ynys Prydein* highlights another violent attack upon Gwenhwyfar:

> "*The first, when Medrawd came to Arthur's court at Celliwig in Kernow; he left neither food nor drink in the court that he did not consume, and he dragged Gwenhwyfar from her royal chair; and then he struck a blow upon her. The second Unrestrained Ravaging was when Arthur came to Medrawd's court. He left neither food nor drink in the court.*"

The opportunity to eat one's host out of food and drink may well have been an accepted tradition in Arthur's day; but the violence inflicted upon Guinevere was certainly an exceptional event documented to show the growing bitterness that would eventually lead to civil strife. If Medrawd was not Arthur's real enemy, and his role in this triad is one of mistaken identity, then the dramatic events of the *Unrestrained Ravaging* may be an example of bards clutching at straws of hearsay in a vain attempt to resolve the cause of the battle of Camlan.

Geoffrey of Monmouth's embellishment of Arthurian legend in his *History of the Kings of Britain* disguised the true story of Arthur's reign for hundreds of years. Written in 1136, his book was accepted as the definitive version of the history of Britain; widely read, his story was believed by the majority of his contemporaries without question. In turn, Geoffrey's fantasies were further embellished by the French poets who introduced romantic tales of knights undertaking perilous quests for their ladies' favour. With Arthur's court at the 'many towered castle of Camelot' surrounded by an enchanted forest, the stage was set for unlimited romantic fantasy. It was the French poet Chrétien de Troyes who introduced the name of Camelot in the late twelfth century, and who developed the love story of Lancelot and Guinevere that ended in a tragic twist of unrequited love and death.

As late as the fifteenth century, three hundred years after Chrétien's romantic revelation, triads of the period persisted in linking Arthur's demise to Guinevere's adultery: of *The Three Faithless Wives,* Guinevere is more faithless than all three; but whatever the cause of the civil strife at Camlan where Britons engaged to kill fellow Britons, the triads ranked the infamous battle as the third and the worst of the *Futile Battles of Ynys Prydein.*

As essential mnemonic keys that unlock the detail of the storytellers' repertoire, the earliest triads allow brief glimpses into the real world of Arthur; yet through the centuries of the middle-ages, triads evolved to encompass all the elements of mythical and romantic fable that characterise the 'Legend of King Arthur' in its final form.

୬୬୬୬୬

The great esteem in which Arthur was held during his lifetime was reflected, following his death after the battle of Camlan, in poems that came to represent the collective memory of Welsh poets over a period of eight centuries. Early Welsh poetry is represented by two collections of work: first the *Cynfeirdd* covers the period of early poets from 600 to 1100; secondly, the *Gogynfeirdd* covers the later period from 1100 to 1400.

We must assume that the majority of the poetry and prose from the early years has been lost to the ravages of war and centuries of decay; but within the priceless body of material that has survived, the name of Arthur, or a reference to his battles, occurs on at least seven occasions, three of which are found in the *Cynfeirdd* and the remaining four in the *Gogynfeirdd.*

The first, and earliest known mention of Arthur, as previously discussed in detail, is in Aneirin's epic battle poem *The Gododdin* composed in the closing years of the sixth century, where the warrior Guaurdur is compared to Arthur: with his bold leadership in battle he is the front line's bulwark bringing black ravens to the fort's wall *"though he was not Arthur."*

The last days of Powys as a British kingdom are recorded in a collection of early poems known as the *Canu Llywarch Hen,* the *Song of Llywarch the Old.* Llywarch was a sixth century war-lord who survived the death of this first cousin king Urien of Rheged, who was praised in his lifetime and lamented on his death by Taliesin. When Rheged fell, Llywarch moved south with his sons to defend Powys against the invading

English. Llywarch's successors divided the country between them: Constantine took southern Powys as far as the river Wye near Hereford, and Cyndrwyn ruled northern Powys from Wroxeter. Cyndrwyn's son Cynddylan inherited Pengwern, the region around Shrewsbury, and continued the struggle against the Anglo-Saxons from his powerbase at Wroxeter, just as Arthur had done before him:

> *"White town by the woods twixt Tren and Trodwydd,"*

(the town appeared white because the houses were painted with a protective coating of lime-wash)

and close by, its great protecting fortress the Wrekin, that became the last refuge of the kings of Powys. Poems from the Heledd Saga show Cynddylan as a fearless young warrior king:

> *"Cynddylan, a Culhwch, wars' lion,*
> *His heart was as merry*
> *for fighting as for feasting…*
> *Cynddylan, a wild boars heart,*
> *when he charged in battle's onslaught,*
> *corps lay upon corps."*

The poets celebrated his victories at Maes Cogwy and Caer Lwytgoed (Roman Letocetum, now known as Wall just south of Lichfield) and when Oswy with his army of Northumbrian English overwhelmed Powys in the year 605, the bards mourned Cynddylan's loss. Now, in the land of Cynddylan, *"Pengwern's Court was a blazing fire;"* and around the stronghold of Wroxeter:

> *"More common were shattered shields from combat*
> *than ploughing of oxen at mid-day; …*
> *More common was blood on the field*
> *than ploughing of fallow."*

In *The Lament for Cynddylan* the poet writes in the same formal style as Taliesin:

> *"In the glory of battle, great the fortune*
> *that Cynddylan won, lord of warfare!*
> *Seven hundred heroes following*

*their bold commander rushing into danger.*
*But no bride was his; he died unwed."*

Then in a following stanza, the poet describes Cynddylan and his brothers as "*the heirs of Arthur*":

*"Brothers sustained me, it was better when they lived;*
*Heirs of great Arthur, our strong fortress.*
*At Caer Lwytgoed they were triumphant.*
*There were bloodstained ravens after fierce attack;*
*they shattered shields, Cynddrwyn's sons.*
*I shall mourn till I enter earth's bed*
*Cynddylan slain, lord of high renown."*

Since the descendants of Cunedda are known to have ruled Powys from the early sixth century to the mid-seventh century, from Cuneglas to Cynddrwyn and Cynddylan ~ all names that feature the Cunedda family prefix 'Cun' or 'Cyn,'~ the poets revelation that Cynddylan and his brothers are the heirs of Arthur is most significant , for it suggests that Arthur himself was related to Cunedda.

In another lament from the *Heledd Saga*, Cynddylan of Powys, the young prince is described as being clothed in purple, the traditional vestment of Roman Emperors. These statements appear to confirm that Cynddylan was a direct descendant of Arthur, and that he had also inherited Arthur's role as the king of Powys, the Commander of Wroxeter, and the bold battle leader who defended the last frontier of Britain.

The third mention of Arthur in the *Cynfeirdd* occurs in the poem *Geraint ab Erbin* where the poet gives a vivid description of the battle of Llongborth. Arthur *'the emperor'* is clearly present on the battlefield.

A poem by Gwalchmai ap Meilyr in praise of his lord Owain Gwynedd, ruler of Gwynedd from 1100 to 1170 marks the first reference in the Gogynfeirdd to one of Arthur's battles, when the poet compares Owain's battle at Aberteifi (Cardigan) with events at the battle of Mount Badon:

*"they cut through falling spears as at Badon Fawr (major)*
*Valiant war-cry!"*

This shows that the impact of Badon was deeply embedded in the collective memory of Britons for over six-hundred years.

Moving on to the poetry of the late twelfth century, a court bard praises Llywelyn ab Iorworth, known as Llywelyn the Great for his successful attempts to win back most of South Wales from the Anglo-Norman lords:

> *"Grieved a great lord, although England is his:*
> *A Welsh lion has won*
> *concord in the land he rules,*
> *equal in might, bold in battle."*

In the greatest compliment he compares Llywelyn with Arthur:

> *"Bold was Arthur once, and his men,*
> *spreading anguish on every side.*
> *Soldiers' dearly loved soldier,*
> *as you are today, bold man ..."*

In the *Lament for Gruffudd's three Sons* the poet Bleddyn Fardd laments the loss of Llywelyn, Owain and Dafydd, the three princes of Gwynedd who had won suzerainty over the whole of Wales in the late thirteenth century. After Llywelyn's death in 1282 at the hands of a Saxon, the poet compares his earlier victory at Caerphilly with one of Arthur's battles:

> *"Blood-spilling spear of Beli's lineage,*
> *Steel-speared, like Arthur, at Caer Fenlli,*
> *Dread lord's splendid assault, reddened gold sword,*
> *When Gwynedd's troops went to Teifi's lands."*

Beli is the legendary ancient British king mentioned by Taliesin in his poem *Protector of the Honey Isle*. Named after one of the earliest gods of Britain, Beli embodies the Dragon of Wales and represents the guardian spirit of Britain that upheld both Llywelyn and Arthur. The comparison is significant because it highlights a battle of Arthur's that is not included in Nennius' list. Caer Fennli is an Iron-Age fort near Ruthin in North-Wales that lies just a few miles south of Moel Arthur, a hilltop peak in the Clwydian Range: this was certainly an area under Arthur's territorial control so that an assault on Caer Fennli would have most likely involved a punitive attack against a rebellious local war-lord rather than a major battle against invaders.

Bleddyn Fardd was not the only poet to grieve for Llywelyn ap Gruffudd. Llywelyn's court bard Gruffudd ap Ynad Coch lamented the loss of his lord with loud wailing, the 'wretched keening' together with the rage he expressed at the Saxon who felled Llywelyn with a single sword-stroke: it was a bitter blow that ended Llywelyn's struggle to unify Wales and it dashed every Welshman's hope of gaining independence from the suzerainty of king Edward I of England. The poet captured the despair of the people of Wales:

*"See you not that the world is ending?*
*Ah God, that the sea would cover the land!*
*Many a side made red with slashes,*
*Many a foot in a pool of blood,*
*Many a widow wailing for him,*
*Many a heavy heart in pieces,*
*Many a son reft of his father,*
*Many a house blackened by fire-brand,*
*Many a place wasted from pillage,*
*Many a wretched cry, as at Camlan…"*

How truly these poignant words must echo the feelings of Britons who were engaged in the eight-hundred year struggle to fight the Anglo-Saxons for the freedom of their country. Yet Llywelyn's loss at the battle of Builth was as tragic for his countrymen as Arthur's demise was for the people of Britain after the battle of Camlan. After his last skirmish with the English, Llywelyn's head was severed by the stroke of a sword and delivered to King Edward: the conquest of Wales was complete.

☙☙☙☙

It is clear that most of the evidence for Arthur of Britain preserved in poetry and prose is linked by vernacular tradition to the momentous events of Arthur's lifetime. Drawn together, the snippets of information from different sources over a period of six-hundred years or more, paint a picture of a heroic battle leader who equipped his soldiers with fine horses and armour, tempered-steel swords and four-pointed steel-tipped spears, chain-mail vestments and hard lime-coated shields for their protection. Kind and generous to his own people, and famed for his hospitality when hunting and feasting, he was courageous and bold in battle; most certainly he was held in high esteem by his men, for he was regarded as *the soldiers' dearly loved soldier,"* a fitting tribute so valiant a warrior.

# CHAPTER 3

# VORTIGERN, AMBROSIUS AND ARTHUR

*"But later our people will arise, and will valiantly throw the English people across the sea."*
Ambrosius Aurelianus

The location of the Britons' military headquarters was a closely guarded secret: to mention it by word of mouth, or to pen its name in poetry or prose, was strictly forbidden. Although the Saxons were only too aware that both Ambrosius and Arthur struck like lighting from the west, and returned thence when battle was done, they had never set eyes on the fortress that guarded western Britain.

Ambrosius, as a member of a Roman family, would have remembered stories of the Roman conquest, and would have been aware that the military had established three powerful legionary fortresses as strategic support bases for their campaign to conquer Wales in the first century AD: Isca (Caerleon) on the bank of the river Usk in the south, Viroconium (Wroxeter) by the river Severn in the central border region, and Deva (Chester) on the banks of the river Dee in the north.

Wroxeter was known by the Romans as Viroconium Cornoviorum, (the settlement of Viroco of the Cornovii tribe) and was first established as a base for the XIV Legion under the command of Aulus Plautus in 44 AD: it was an ideal strategic position because, on a clear day, the commanders could see for miles across the flat plain towards the Welsh Marches, giving them control over a wide area of local territory as well as the nearby ford across the river Severn.

Towards the end of the first century the Roman Consul Julius Agricola chose Wroxeter as his base and planned a vicious attack on the Ordovices to avenge the infamous slaughter of a cavalry squadron that had been patrolling their territory. Commanding the XX Legion he moved rapidly into north-west Wales ruthlessly executing the opposing tribesmen, before crossing the Menai Strait to mount a

The Roman City of Viroconium. A reconstruction by Alan Sorrell of the south-western part of the city, showing the enclosure behind the temple that was used for equestrian training. © Shropshire Council.

fearsome assault on the Druids in their holy island refuge of Mon. (Anglesey)

In contrast to the severe treatment of the Ordovices for their stubborn resistance, both the Silures of south-west Wales, and the Cornovii of the upper Severn region were rewarded for their co-operation with the Romans by the gift of new cities, or *civitas,* that gave these Britons their first taste of the civilized life enjoyed by all citizens of the Roman Empire. Caerwent became the civitas of the Silures; set in an idyllic position five miles west of the Wye estuary and just a mile south of their original fortress at Llanmelin, it was endowed with all the features of a Roman city including a forum, basilica with bath-houses, and temples for the benefit of all three-thousand citizens. Town-houses were designed and built for wealthy magistrates, councillors and tribal magnates.

However, the measure of Wroxeter's importance as the new civitas of the Cornovii was confirmed in AD 130 by the arrival of the Emperor Hadrian himself, who combined an architectural eye and forceful hand to build a new forum on the site of the abandoned fort, and to extend the city with a magnificent basilica and heated baths; all for the enjoyment of its citizens and for the benefit of soldiers on recreational leave from the neighbouring forts of Caersws, Forden Gaer and

Bravonium. Before Hadrian moved north, via Chester, to build the great wall that would define the northern border of the Empire, the people of Wroxeter dedicated their new forum to the Emperor with a very fine marble inscription placed prominently above the colonnade's main entrance.

When Hadrian, with his Legio XX Valeria Victrix numbering over five-thousand soldiers moved to Chester, it must have been a severe economic blow for the people of Wroxeter. But their loss was Chester's gain; it was perhaps, some compensation for the fact that Chester had not been granted the official status of a civitas. Yet over the years the *vicus,* or settlement, that served the needs of the Roman army in its walled fortress, grew from a village to a city in its own right; with easy access to Irish Sea ports such as Meols, situated on the north-west coast of the Wirral, the merchants of Chester increased their trade with Ireland, and capitalised on the mineral wealth from nearby salt-mines to make their city a wealthy trading centre. From the strategic point of view, the Chester garrison guarded the northern edge of lowland Britain in the mid-west, securing this rich agricultural territory from raids by Irish pirates and other belligerent immigrants, as well as commanding numerous vexillation forts where troop detachments played an active role in subjecting the dissident tribesmen of North-Wales to the discipline of Roman rule.

The three centres of Roman power, Chester, Wroxeter and Caerleon, together with its satellite city of Caerwent, became established as the most important military bases of western Britain, each supporting a large population that thrived on the benefits of the new civilized way of life introduced by the Romans. The cost of this enhanced life-style and the price of peace guaranteed by the presence of the Roman army would be paid for by the people, who suffered the imposition of a strict tax regime, as well as the sequestration of their mineral wealth. Gold, silver, lead and tin mined in Britain was now shipped to Rome to swell the coffers of the emperor.

The fact that at some time in the last century of Roman rule, the *Notitia Dignitatum* listed the Cohors I Cornoviorum defending the fort of Newcastle on Hadrian's Wall, was of great historical significance, for it revealed that the civitas of the Cornovii was the only province in Britain that had the manpower and resources to support the formation of a cohort of a Roman legion. It was this region, encompassing most of present day Shropshire, Staffordshire and Cheshire, that later became known as Powys and with its capital city Wroxeter, became the strongest military power base in Britain.

But the power vacuum created when the Roman army withdrew from Britain in the early years of the fifth century put the Britons at the mercy of their enemies; over four hundred years of Roman modernisation and development was threatened with imminent destruction by marauding barbarians. Fearing invasion from Picts in the north, Saxons in the south and east, and the Scotii or Irish from the west, Britons fell back to the safety of the old Roman forts: Chester, Wroxeter and Caerleon now became the bastions of British defence in the west, safe havens in adversity, where the military leaders could recruit and train young men to form a new force for the protection of Britain.

On the exodus of the Romans, a descendant of the kings of Gloucester named Vortigern, who was described by Gildas as *"the proud tyrant"* because he ruled without the authority of Rome, seized the overlordship of Britain and made his powerbase at Gwytheyrnion in central Wales. His policy of appeasing the Saxons by allowing them to settle in the Isle of Thanet while engaging them as mercenaries to fight the Picts in the north, became a disastrous failure when the Saxons turned against their paymaster and set about the destruction of Britain.

Gildas, from his cloistered world of Biblical scholarship, viewed the Saxon scourge of Britain as God's inevitable punishment of a people who had refused to turn from their evil ways. He reported that the people, fearing for their lives, flocked to Ambrosius for protection, praying that they should not be completely destroyed. Gildas is remarkably sparing in naming individual characters in his *De Exidio Conquestu Britanniae*; although he freely names and shames six reprobate kings of western Britain, the fact that he singles out Ambrosius for praise is a measure of his great respect for him as a leader. Gildas describes Ambrosius as a nobleman of Roman descent, a true Christian whose ideals and attributes put him in direct conflict with Vortigern, the tyrant king who had betrayed his people.

But where was Ambrosius at this time of great distress for the Britons? Nennius records the legendary parable of *Dynas Emrys*, the Fortress of Ambrosius, a tale that reveals several important clues about the life of Ambrosius. First, the story relates that he was a child without a father, confirming Gildas' statement that his parents were Romans of Consular status who lost their lives in the Saxon storming of Britain. Vortigern's men were said to have found Ambrosius playing ball with other children in Maes Ellidi, a valley in Glywysing, possibly the Rhonda Valley in Glamorgan, South Wales, not far from the once thriving Romanised city of Caerwent.

Secondly, on the advice of his wizards, Vortigern retreated to a region called 'Gwynessi,' ceding power to Ambrosius, who then became ruler over the western provinces of Britain with the right to occupy the impregnable fortress of Dynas Emrys on the south-eastern escarpment of Mount Snowdon. Finally, the tale relates the prophecy that was eventually interpreted by the young Ambrosius, where the red dragon of the Britons engaged in battle with the white dragon of the English. At first the white dragon made three attempts to drive the red dragon out of the eastern half of the country, and the red dragon was seen to be the weaker of the combatants;

however, the red dragon eventually gained strength and rallied to push the white dragon right out of the country: *"but later our people will arise, and will valiantly throw the English people across the sea."*

Ambrosius made this prophesy with a promise to rally his people to the defence of Britain, and as a strong and effective leader he became the champion of the British cause in the war against the Angles and Saxons. The reference to the partition of the country and the expression of hope that the English would eventually be expelled from Britain, suggests a period in the first half of the fifth century for the origin of this story, just prior to Ambrosius taking command, when the invaders were gaining the upper hand in their conflict with Vortigern.

The tale of Dynas Emrys must encapsulate a period of thirty years or more; Ambrosius, as a child, was feared by Vortigern because he was the protégé of a Roman consul who had been endowed with the authority of Rome. Fear that the Romans would return to Britain and sanction Ambrosius' right to inherit this same authority, became a lasting threat to Vortigern. Moreover, the young Ambrosius of the story must have grown to manhood before being able to mount a challenge for the leadership of Britain.

Early in the fifth century Vortigern founded the royal house of Gwertheyrnion, a small province in mid-Wales with its power centre near Builth Wells at Caer Beris, a fortress where the kings of Builth and Gwertheyrnion held court. From this small central powerbase Vortigern cleverly expanded his realm by conquering the prized territory of the Cornovii, an area of rich agricultural lowland in the central area of the Severn Valley with its capital city Wroxeter. This was the 'land of the people' that became the new province of Powys.

Testimony to Vortigern's sequestration of Powys is the inscription cut into the weathered stone of a ninth century memorial cross near Valle Crucis Abbey in the Vale of Llangollen, north-east Wales. The Pillar of Eliseg, erected by Cyngen to honour his great grandfather Eliseg, is one of the most significant pieces of evidence that has survived from Dark Age Britain. This rugged edifice, carved from the same blue granite as the monoliths of Stonehenge, now points to the sky without its original circular Celtic cross; but the time-worn inscription names Vortigern as the founder of the royal line of Powys. Furthermore, the cross stands in the shadow of the mountain-peak fortress of Dinas Bran, the renowned Grail Castle of Arthurian legend, which in reality was the seat of power of the kings of Powys.

The inscription on the pillar of Eliseg names 'Britu' as Vortigern's son from his marriage to Severa, daughter of Magnus Maximus, but Nennius refers to this son as 'Vortimer' when describing his victories over the Saxons earlier in the fifth century; but just as 'Vortigern' is a description derived from the Latin word *vertifernus* meaning 'overlord,' so the name 'Vortimer' may have been given to the eldest son of the overlord.

The cup of friendship given to Vortigern by the Saxon leader Hengist and sealed by his marriage to Hengist's daughter Rowena, turned into a poison chalice. Britons felt betrayed by his allegiance with the Saxons and their loyalty turned to hatred. To make matters worse, Vortigern committed a major heresy against the Church of Rome by encouraging Pelagianism, a humanist doctrine expounded by a priest called Pelagius who emphasised personal responsibility for the salvation of the soul. Despite the logical simplicity of this idea, it came into direct conflict with the fundamental Catholic doctrine of original sin and its evident popularity became a serious threat to the established teaching of the Church.

Nevertheless Vortigern's approval of Pelagianism was not his only sin, for he stood accused of an incestuous relationship with his daughter who had given birth to a son named Faustus. The king's pathway to hell engendered the Papal wrath, and a course of correction was devised in the shape of Germanus, the wealthy and powerful bishop of Auxerre, who, as Pope Celestine's representative was sent to guide Vortigern and his wayward Britons back to the Catholic faith. When Germanus arrived in Britain in the year 429, he succeeded in reconverting the bishop and clergy of St Alban's; he then travelled widely across the country preaching and converting people to the true faith.

But being independently minded, the British soon reverted back to Pelagianism so that Germanus was forced to make a second visit in the year 447, when he finally took Vortigern to task. Nennius' source *The Life of St Germanus* relates how the shamed king locked himself into his castle at Caer Beris in Gwertheyrnion for forty days and nights while Germanus persuaded him to return to the Lord. Then, after making his escape from Caer Beris, Vortigern was pursued by Germanus and besieged by his cavalry while taking refuge in a remote castle in south-west Wales. At midnight on the fourth night of the siege, Vortigern was struck down by an act of God in the form of fire from heaven that destroyed his castle on the river Teifi in Demetia. It was said that Vortigern, together with his retinue and all his wives, perished in the flames.

This legendary tale echoes an earlier story from Germanus' visit to Britain when he besieged a 'great tyrant,' the evil heathen king Benlli in Moel Fenli his fortress near Ruthin, northern Powys. Significantly, Germanus instructs his companions to *"be watchful, and if anything happens in the fortress, do not look but continue praying and calling upon God without pause."* Very soon after this, night fire fell from heaven and the fortress burned to the ground, consuming the tyrant king and all his men. As an experienced soldier, Germanus had commanded Roman armies before his episcopal appointment; he was skilled in military arts and would have been familiar with the effective use of 'Greek Fire' in the form of arrows tipped with burning pitch. Now in his new role as a bishop this weapon became an instrument of Divine retribution: fire from heaven fell upon the evil tyrants who refused to listen to the word of God.

This earlier story of the downfall of one great tyrant named Benlli, may well have been superimposed onto the later life-story of another great tyrant, Vortigern. At least the storytellers concluded that both tyrants received their just desserts, but other sources suggest that Vortigern survived Germanus' last visit because it is recorded that his life was spared ten years later by Hengist following the massacre of the 'Night of the Long Knives.' Nennius also appears to have had doubts about the veracity of this story as he offers an alternative ending to the tale of Vortigern:

*"Because he was hated for the sin of inviting the Saxons into Britain, by all men of his own nation, mighty and humble, slave and free, monk and layman, poor and great, he wandered from place to place until at last his heart broke, and he died without honour."*

The final demise of Vortigern around the year 458, gave the Council of Britain the eagerly awaited opportunity to promote Ambrosius to leadership. Vortigern's sons Vortimer and Cateyrn predeceased their father, losing their lives in the war against Hengist, thereby leaving the youngest son Pascent to inherit his kingdom. Nennius confirms the change of leadership:

*"The third son Pascent, who ruled in the two countries called Builth and Gwertheyrnion after his father's death, by permission of Ambrosius, who was the great king among all the kings of the British nation." (Rex inter omnes reges)*

Gildas refers to Ambrosius by his Roman title of 'Dux' or the 'Duke of Britain' that gave him the most powerful position as the chief military commander and director of battles. This was in line with the command structure of Roman Britain shown in the *Notitia Dignitatum,* the central register of Roman Officers, and although the Romans had departed half a century before, it is clear that the title 'Imperator' or 'Emperor' was discreetly avoided, enabling Ambrosius to govern the states of Britain without being branded as a tyrant or appearing as a potential threat to the emperor himself.

Pascent, the youngest of Vortigern's legitimate sons, whose Roman name was derived from the Latin *'pax'* or *'pacis'* meaning 'peace,' evidently made a peaceful alliance with Ambrosius who, in a gesture of goodwill, now trusted Pascent to reign as king in his own right in part of his father's original kingdom; in return Pascent would send young recruits to be trained as warriors to fight in the new British army.

But it was Ambrosius who took the reigns of power over Vortigern's most prized possession, the land of Powys; not just for its wealthy farmland, but for its great attribute, the capital city of Viroconium. This thriving Roman city, now known as Wroxeter, would be his chosen command headquarters for the future establishment and training of a military force that would defend the realm of Britain.

For centuries the Romans had recognised the strategic importance of Wroxeter as the gateway to central Wales. In the first century, the Roman military machine carved vital trunk routes through the landscape of southern Britain, making a huge diagonal cross: the Fosse Way ran for 210 miles in a north-easterly direction from Axminster in Devon, via Cirencester and Leicester to Lincoln. Conversely, Watling Street (now the A5) ran for 150 miles in a north-westerly direction from London, via St Alban's, to Wroxeter. These major arterial roads crossed at Venonae or High Cross, a central point twelve miles south of Leicester, and from here Watling Street curved away to the west eventually cutting right through the heart of Wroxeter to reach the ford on the river Severn.

This important river linked Wroxeter with the port of Gloucester some eighty miles to the south at the head of the Severn estuary, where cargoes of wine and oil were imported from the Mediterranean, and where the western naval command was based. The recent discovery of a small Roman harbour cut into the bank of the river Severn at Wroxeter confirms that the city was supplied by boats plying the navigable reaches of the river over ninety miles from the estuary. Control of this vital supply route would have been of paramount importance to the rulers of Powys and it would therefore have been to their great advantage to control the source of this life-giving river.

Centuries before, the Romans had clearly reached the same conclusion, and the continuation of Watling Street that ran from Wroxeter in a south-westerly direction via the fort at Forden Gaer towards Caersws, reached into the heart of the Cambrian Mountains. It is here that the great peak of Plynlimon gives birth to both the Wye and the Severn, their springs significantly guarded by the Roman forts of Cae Gaer to the south, and Pen y Crocben by Dylife, to the north. The pure mountain streams that tumbled down to Lyn Clywedog gave the Romans an endless supply of fresh drinking water: this was the vital resource inherited by the rulers of Powys and the citizens of Wroxeter.

Control of the river sources guaranteed the supply of pure drinking water both for the army as well as the people, although the people of Wroxeter were also fortunate enough to have access to spring-water channelled to their homes by ducting from Bell Brook, a stream that ran along a small valley to the north of the city. Hence the great advantage of the city's upstream position, for the function of the river as an open sewer would have transformed the Severn from a fresh stream at Wroxeter, into a flow of putrid polluted water by the time it reached Gloucester.

It may well have been the urgent quest for pure water that prompted the overlords of Gloucester to secure the water sources at Builth Wells in mid-Wales, where more than six rivers converge, and to make this region of the Wye Valley their centre of power. Indeed, it is significant that Vortigern's grandfather was called 'Vitalinus,' a name derived from the Latin *vital* meaning 'life' or 'life-giver;' moreover in relating the genealogy of Vortigern, Nennius mentions the name 'Vitalis' as the son of Vitalinus the son of Glou, king of Gloucester. This leads to the suggestion that perhaps 'Vitalis' is actually the real name of Vortigern 'the Overlord.' Furthermore, control of the water sources gave the kings of Builth and Gwertheyrnion, Vitalinus and his son Vitalis, the supreme power of life-givers, for they were the royal providers of water to their people.

Ambrosius would also have been keenly aware of the importance of securing the local water sources as well as controlling the facilities centred on Caersws that provided a guaranteed water supply. These vital assets, together with the existing network of roads and navigable waterways, were the most important features of the Roman infrastructure inherited by Ambrosius. Other examples of excellent design and engineering were clearly evident in the many defensive fortresses and castles built by the Romans through the length and breadth of Britain: Portchester Castle near Portsmouth is one of the best surviving examples, its massive stone walls reaching a height of some thirty feet, built as straight as a die, and defended with projecting bastions that were designed as platforms for artillery weapons.

In contrast to the magnificent stone-built fortresses of Caerleon and Chester, the defences of Wroxeter's legionary fortress were of the more expedient, and much less expensive, ditch and bank construction, surrounded by a timber palisade with watch-towers at intervals and a wide main gate, the *porta praetoria,* in the centre of the western wall. The defences of the original fort enclosed an area of about 40 acres, but as the city grew in importance, new defences were built to protect a settlement that covered 180 acres, over four times the size of Caerwent and ten times the size of Cadbury Castle. Thoughtfully, the engineers who designed the city's new defences decided to include the valley of Bell Brook within the city walls, making their construction task much more difficult but ensuring the security of the water supply in the event of an enemy attack. Aqueducts channelled almost two million gallons of water a day from the stream to a central distribution tank that supplied the public baths and shops, as well as town houses and private villas.

Recent archaeological surveys have revealed the full extent of the development of Wroxeter, although for many centuries the only visible remains of the city was known as 'The Old Work', a large free-standing fragment of the south-wall of the basilica to the baths, so strongly constructed that it has survived the ravaging of weather and the plundering of its stones for over 1800 years. This landmark of Roman architecture was recorded in the reign of Queen Elizabeth I by William Camden, who concluded that the remains must have been part of a castle standing in the centre of the city; but the site then lay dormant until 1701 when a Mr Clayton, while digging for building stones, discovered the remains of a building with its hypocaust structurally intact. Then in 1788 Thomas Telford made further discoveries while constructing a new turnpike from Shrewsbury to Ironbridge that cut a diagonal scar right across the city from north-west to south-east (now the B4380), narrowly missing the site of the Roman baths by about one hundred yards.

However, it was not until the 1860's that the site of the baths was more fully excavated by Thomas Wright, who started by digging a large hole fourteen feet deep to reach the foundation of the Old Work, eventually leading to the discovery of the full extent of the basilica. But the intrusion of the archaeologist and his diggers infuriated the local tenant farmer who just wanted to get on with planting his turnips, so he threw the workmen off the field. Wright had to appeal to the landowner, the Duke of Cleveland, who intervened in the dispute and allowed the excavation work to continue on the south side of the site.

This ruction had unforeseen benefits: first Charles Dickens travelled down from London to see what all the fuss was about, and subsequently published an article entitled *Rome and Turnips* in his magazine *All the Year Round* giving great publicity to the dig at Wroxeter. Moreover, the enforced move to the south side of the site led Wright and his team to the exciting discovery of most of the important rooms of the baths, as well as the shops, the latrines and some rooms of the market-hall.

From Mr Clayton's first random but fortuitous spadework in 1701, the sporadic and haphazard sequences of excavation and piecemeal discovery have extended over three centuries, with the ancient Roman city of Viroconium finally yielding most of its secrets to a combination of modern aerial photography and geophysical techniques: the introduction of the latest ground-penetrating radar now gives archaeologists the opportunity to 'see' up to six feet beneath the surface without having to excavate.

The latest surveys confirm that the city was extensively built up, supporting a population of at least five thousand in its hey-day, and that the citizens of Wroxeter enjoyed a sophisticated lifestyle through most of the four centuries of Imperial rule. The public baths featured a complex of cold, warm, and heated rooms, all impressively decorated with mosaic floors, painted plaster walls and vaulted ceilings, complemented on the north side by an adjacent basilica that was as large as the nave of a medieval cathedral. This was used as a meeting place where bathers could converse and exercise together before entering the baths. Adjoining the basilica were taverns and a market hall that fronted the main street with public latrines conveniently situated at the rear of the premises.

Directly opposite the baths was the town forum, the main administrative centre that also housed a busy marketplace where trading stalls were set up in the large open courtyard; this was colonnaded on three sides with a row of shops fronting onto Watling Street. Just further south in the centre of the town, a *mansion* or inn provided accommodation and a change of horses for the couriers of the Imperial postal service. Grazing for horses and cattle was available in the pasture-land surrounding the outer defences: this area was a designated 'no man's land' known as the *prata legionis,* the legion's meadows; in contrast, the *forum boarium* or cattle market was a stockaded enclosure secured well within the city walls, purposely sited down-wind of the baths and residential part of the town, but close enough to Bell Brook to guarantee a constant supply of water for the livestock.

No fewer than three temples provided sanctuary for the worship of different deities: the largest, a classical style temple built on a stone pediment with a four-column facade was possibly devoted to Venus, or Epona the Celtic horse goddess. The two smaller temples were of Romano-Celtic design, whose worshippers would have served one or more of the Roman pantheon: Mercury, Apollo, Mars or Jupiter. However, the discovery of the distinctive plan of a simple church of Romanesque design suggests that the Christians of Wroxeter were also allowed to worship here openly. In AD 325, following his conversion, the emperor Constantine proclaimed Christianity the true religion of the Empire, and decreed that every city should have its own bishop. Previously persecuted for their belief by successive emperors, Christians now triumphed in their new freedom, and the importance of pagan gods began to decline. By the time Theodosius finally banned all forms of pagan worship in 391, Christianity had taken a strong hold among the Celtic peoples of Britain and the temples once dedicated to the old gods were despoiled and fell into decay.

Several impressive Roman courtyard houses found at Wroxeter have proved to be fine examples of the largest and wealthiest villas that feature an enclosed rectangular court with a front entrance gateway. Situated to the south of the baths, one excavated house shows evidence of rebuilding and extension by its prosperous owners in the fourth century; but by far the largest and most remarkable villa, revealed by distinctive crop-marks captured by an aerial photograph, is found at the western end of the road that runs adjacent to the baths and the forum. On the city's prime location overlooking the river Severn, this palatial villa occupied an elevated site set back from the high embankment; its wealthy owners would have enjoyed spectacular views to the west across open countryside towards the distant hills of Wales. With a western frontage of some 240 feet, the villa had as many as twenty-four rooms linked by corridors, and compared with other known contemporary houses of this status, would most probably have been equipped with its own hypocaust and private bath suites. Extensions at each end of the main house provided large living and dining areas with verandas overlooking the river, and the prevailing south-westerly breeze would have blown the wood-smoke and the unpleasant odours of the city away from the villa; that is, until the wind veered to the east.

Considering the scale of the villa and its most favourable location, this must have been the residence of a Very Important Person; only a king or a military commander would have been able to enjoy the right to the very best site in the city.

Whether or not royalty or military leaders were present, Wroxeter, like every other Roman city or *civitas,* had a governing council that met in the administrative rooms of the forum and it was this building that became the focus of daily life; by combining the place of governance and the administration of the law-court with the market-place, it became the city's centre of commerce. On market days the forum became a hive of activity with some stalls selling farm produce, others displaying a multitude of craft wares made by weavers and tanners, potters, carpenters and metal-smiths who worked in the city. Imported goods such as wine, oil, ceramics and glass were available to wealthier citizens in exchange for silver coins.

The latest techniques of modern archaeology have brought alive this glimpse of Wroxeter in its hey-day. Built not only as a show city by the Romans as a reward for Cornovian loyalty, but also as a base and recreational centre for the legion, Wroxeter thrived for over three centuries; but eventually as the Roman army posted more forces to the border garrisons on the Wall, the prosperity of the city began to wane. A major misfortune occurred around the end of the third century when the forum basilica burnt down in a disastrous fire that also destroyed houses in the north-east of the city. Some of the residential property was abandoned, confirming the severity of the fire, but surprisingly the forum basilica was not re-built, suggesting that the council was unable to raise funds for a major building project during a time of economic uncertainty.

To make matters worse, by the early fourth century the baths and basilica were showing signs of serious wear and tear; roof-tiles, the fabric of the walls and vaulted ceilings as well as the floor tiles all required refurbishment. So the funds saved by abandoning the rebuilding of the forum basilica were wisely used to give the baths another lease of life. At the same time, to save costs, the heated areas of the baths were reduced, and the baths basilica took on the main functions of the abandoned forum.

If the Roman commanders had received an advance warning of their recall to Rome in the year 410, then their parting gift to the Cornovii was to strengthen

Wroxeter's city defences. A detachment of troops was given the specific task of updating the original double-ditch system in front of the main embankment by cutting a single, deeper ditch around the whole perimeter of the city. The earth thrown up from the new ditch was compacted behind to reinforce the rampart, and in front to create a raised embankment that would effectively increase the depth of the ditch. This would have given the defenders standing at the top of the palisade a height advantage of 40 feet over an enemy trapped in the ditch below. Finally, the older, more heavily weathered timbers of the palisade and watch-towers that crowned the city gates were renewed to make a strong and effective fortification around the two mile perimeter of the city.

The refurbishing of the baths must have been popular with the people, and the later reconstruction of the city defences may have gone some way towards alleviating their fear of an enemy attack; but the real shock came when the Roman generals announced their final exodus from Britain, leaving Britons to their own devices: without the Roman Army as a peace-keeping buffer force against its enemies, Britain was left virtually defenceless. When the Council of Britain appealed to Rome for help in 410 following Saxon raids, the Emperor Honorius sent words instead of troops, advising the citizens to take up arms and look to their own defences.

By the time Ambrosius took over the reins of leadership in AD 460 the country was in chaos. Vortigern's policy of employing Saxon mercenaries in the north to keep the Picts at bay, had been expedient at the time because an effective British force was non-existant; this traditional Roman method of military reinforcement may have been an acceptable policy in a crisis, but it was despised after the event when the Saxon's treachery was unleashed on the Britons themselves. Vortigern stood aside from the conflict, leaving his son Vortimer to rally a force that successfully reversed the Saxon advance into Kent, pushing them back into the Isle of Thanet. Vortimer's demise, whether from mortal injury in battle or from poison administered by Hengist's daughter, was a bitter blow to the British. This was soon followed by a ruthless revenge attack by Hengist and his men on the 'Night of the Long-knives' when they massacred most of the British leaders and nobility. Now the Saxons had gained the upper hand, they took the offensive and set about the destruction of the cities of southern Britain; the fire from their rampage "*spread from sea to sea.*" Gildas gives us a glimpse of the horror:

"*All the major towns were laid low by the repeated battering of enemy rams; laid low, too, all the inhabitants ~ church leaders, priests and people alike, as the swords glinted all around and the flames crackled. It was a sad sight. In the middle of the squares the foundation-stones of high walls and towers that had been torn from their lofty bases, holy altars, fragments of corpses, covered, as it were with a purple crust of congealed blood, looked as though they had been mixed up in some dreadful wine-press."*

This picture illustrates the total devastation wreaked by Hengist's ruthless storm-troopers in the year 459: not only was it a lightning strike that struck fear into the heart of every surviving Briton, it was also the wake-up call for Ambrosius to muster every able-bodied man over 15 years of age to fight for the freedom, if not the very existence of their country: for now the Red Dragon was in real danger of extinction. Ambrosius took up the challenge to turn the tide of British misfortune, and from the lowest ebb, he achieved a gradual but planned and purposeful recovery. Gildas summarises this critical period in a few lines of prose: *"Under him our people regained their strength, and challenged the victors to battle. The Lord assented and the battle went their way."* However for Ambrosius, the reality of the challenge was not just one battle, but a war that lasted thirty years and more, leaving Arthur to eventually inherit his position as Dux Britanniarum and to champion the British cause for another fifty years.

From the secure headquarters of Dynas Emrys in North-Wales, Ambrosius planned his military campaign. His first priority was to recruit a new army of young warriors who would form the core of a mobile cavalry force that could strike back at the enemy. Wroxeter, with its strengthened defences and working Roman infrastructure would make the ideal base for this new army. The city was in a remote location, far from the threat of Irish raiders on the west-coast and even further away from the Anglo-Saxon settlements in Kent and the eastern coastlands of Britain. Yet its central position gave Ambrosius the strategic advantage of being able to deploy his forces rapidly to intercept enemy incursions from all points of the compass. Likely battle-fronts within a one hundred and twenty mile range of Wroxeter included the stronghold of York and the estuaries of the Trent and Humber to the north-east; the estuaries of the Wash to the east; Cambridge and St Albans to the south-east; Winchester, Cadbury Castle and Ilminster in the south, and Pembroke and St David's to the south-west.

But the formation of a new army presented Ambrosius with the complex problem of dealing simultaneously with the recruitment of men and a number of experienced or even retired military commanders to train them; the preparation of military headquarters with billeting for between five-hundred and a thousand troops; the supply of horses, stabling and saddlery; while at the same time re-establishing the supply of livestock and local farm produce to feed the soldiers as well as the citizens who supported them.

By this time the basilica of the baths at Wroxeter had become dilapidated from over three-hundred years of use as a public recreation centre; its tiled floor had become worn and rutted, and the heavy tiled roof was in need of constant repair:

but its sheer size was a gift to Ambrosius, for in this great hall he could quarter his troops. This ample space would have been used not only for meetings and exercise, but also as a refectory; then, at the day's end converted into dormitory accommodation, for the men followed the tradition of sleeping 'in hall' stacking their oak benches on the tables, then spreading straw palliasses on the wooden floorboards for the night, with their weapons lying close to hand.

Recent excavations have revealed that the worn floor-tiles of the basilica were overlaid at this time with timber boards, an expedient and relatively low-cost refurbishment of a large floor area that would have provided a practical solution for day-to-day use as a military headquarters. The absence of any new building during this period is significant because it confirms that Ambrosius' priorities lay elsewhere: by commandeering Vortigern's magnificent Wroxeter villa for himself and his officers, and by billeting his men in the great hall of the basilica, Ambrosius was able to concentrate his limited resources on the procurement of vital equipment and supplies for his new army.

The supply of iron, copper, lead and tin for use in the manufacture of arms and armour would have been of prior importance to Ambrosius, together with the need to commission metalworkers and armourers who could make keen swords and strong shields for his warriors; of equal importance was the supply of hides to the tannery for the making of saddlery and leather battle clothing that were the mainstay of his new cavalry force. Without doubt, the supporting craftsmen, blacksmiths, potters and tilers would have been kept busy repairing the fabric of the city's buildings and defences, as well as maintaining the vital services of water supply and drainage.

The unopposed sacking of southern Britain by the Saxons brought a wave of slaughter, destruction and desecration that plunged the survivors into a wartime economy and hastened them towards poverty and starvation. In the fifty years of independence from Rome, coinage had gradually fallen out of use; by this time the breakdown of the economy had given way, out of necessity, to the old system of trade by barter, and the highly organised method of state taxation introduced by the Romans had regressed to the arbitrary control of greedy local rulers who levied unfair taxes in kind on rich and poor alike.

For his part, Ambrosius urgently needed funds to prepare for war, and these were most likely provided by contributions from the Council of the Kings of Britain; but over the long term Ambrosius may have been forced to re-introduce the Roman *Annona Militaris,* a tax in kind specifically to maintain the army: to provide food for the men and their horses, clothing, and weapons of war.

Ambrosius' battle-list has not survived to give proof of his victories and military prowess, but the limited evidence points to the eventual success of his campaign against the Angles and Saxons. Gildas' few words *"from then on victory went now to our countrymen, now to their enemies..."* reveal that the war was a constant struggle of battles won and battles lost, with neither side able to gain true ascendancy or declare a long-term victory; but the fact that the Anglo-Saxon Chronicle is silent for eight years from 477 when Aelle came from Saxony with an invasion force of three ships to attack the coast of Sussex, suggests the presence of a strong British force that largely succeeded in holding back the English advance.

Knowing that the major threat of an Anglo-Saxon invasion was on the east coast of Britain from the Humber estuary in Lincolnshire to the Blackwater estuary in Essex, we can be reasonably certain that the majority of Ambrosius' battles took place in the quadrant of central Britain defined by an area that extends north-east from Wroxeter to the Humber, and south-east from Wroxeter to Basingstoke. Furthermore, one vital aim of Ambrosius' defensive strategy was to prevent the Saxons of Kent joining forces with the Angles holding new ground on the east-coast, and to achieve this he drove a wedge of British forces between their settlements. Forming a strategic spear-head with its base between London and St Albans and its point reaching sixty miles east to Camulodunum, modern Colchester, he secured this vital port for the British, and kept open the traditional Roman trading link with Gaul.

A few place-names exist that may bear silent witness to the evidence of fifth century battle zones; Ambroseden for example, a small village three miles south-east of Bicester, may have taken its name from a nearby 'fort of Ambrosius.' The most likely position of this hill-fort is a distinctive raised mound seven miles to the east, now the site of a great 19th century house, Waddesden Manor, built by Baron Ferdinand de Rothschild to display his art treasures and to entertain fashionable society in the Victorian era. However, as a hill-fort, this site not only commanded an elevated position over the Vale of Aylesbury and the Icknield Way, but also controlled Akeman Street, the Roman road that ran eastward to St Albans. If Akeman Street had formed the shaft of Ambrosius' strategic spearhead, then this hill-fort would have made the ideal marshalling base for his campaign in south-eastern Britain.

Ambrosius knew that his fledgling cavalry force would face the difficult challenge of patrolling almost two hundred miles of eastern seaboard against hostile raiders, but he was determined to close the window of opportunity opened by Vortigern, who had allowed the Saxons to commandeer Kent, and the Angles to gain a foothold in the coastal areas of East Anglia. Whilst the earliest English settlements at Abindon, Luton and Cambridge may have been first populated by retired Saxon foederati who had been engaged by the Roman army to strengthen the garrisons of Hadrian's Wall and the Forts of the Saxon Shore, Vortigern's open invitation to Saxon mercenaries encouraged new settlements along the coastlands from Norfolk to Lincoln. North of the Humber, the English who had built homesteads at Market Weighton and Driffield deferred to the British of York, but further north lay Hengist's original colony of Bernician Saxons, a mercenary buffer force stationed along the Northumbrian coast to intercept Pictish raids south of Edinburgh; but because these settlers were so remote, they were not deemed to be a significant threat to the balance of British power in the south, and they were left to grow in number and strength, unhindered by Ambrosius.

Although Ambrosius and his Council may have reluctantly accepted these Germanic settlements that had been allowed by Vortigern in return for military service, with the ever increasing threat of invasion, the British were caught on the horns of a dilemma: how could they stem the relentless tide of hostile immigrants breaching the coastal defences and settling alongside fellow countrymen who had already established their homes and smallholdings in Britain?

Ambrosius drew a bold red line on his map of Roman Britain: from the south bank of the Humber, through Lincoln, he followed the route of Ermine Street down to Peterborough and on to the Roman fort of Godmanchester twenty miles further south; then moving to the south-east he scored through Cambridge and onward to finish at Colchester. *"There is our eastern-front: one hundred and sixty miles from north to south, from Lindum to Camulodunum,"* he said with a flourish as he addressed his commanders. *"And there is your challenge: to stop the enemy, whether they are Angles or Saxons, from crossing that line."*

Ambrosius deployed his front-line cavalry force to garrison the three great Legionary fortresses of Lindum (Lincoln) in the north, Longthorpe in the central position, and Camulodunum on the south-east coast. Although the Romans had abandoned these forts over half-a-century before, the new British force erected their tents, repaired the defences and made makeshift stables for their horses. With each commander controlling a sector that extended to a thirty mile radius of the garrison, Lincoln controlled the seaboard from the Humber to the Wash, Longthorpe, the Roman fort just west of Peterborough, covered the area from Boston to the river Ouse and round to Cambridge in the south; and Colchester controlled an area that encompassed Thetford, Diss and Saxmundham on the east coast. Mounted scouts patrolling each sector would thus be able to report an enemy incursion and raise the alarm within two hours of the first sighting, allowing the garrison commander to call his cavalry force to battle readiness.

The speed and flexibility of mounted cavalry gave Ambrosius' British force the great advantage of surprise as they could engage the enemy within three or four hours of a sea-borne landing and smash into them with a powerful and fearsome cavalry charge. The garrisons of Lincoln and Longthorpe would have been reinforced from Wroxeter, the British training base just one hundred miles to the west; and for many of Ambrosius' raw recruits such a cavalry charge would have given them their first blooding in battle against the Angles, seamen by tradition who chose to fight on foot, their weapons swords and axes that were no match for the lances and slicing swords of the young mounted warriors who pitched against them on strong battle-horses.

By giving each commander and his troop a period of duty at each of the front line fortresses, Ambrosius ensured that each soldier gained a working knowledge of the geography of each battle sector; furthermore, the fact that the two cavalry units nearest to an enemy incursion were able to combine forces to challenge a large war-band, was a great tactical advantage. Thus the army recruits who had been trained at Wroxeter would be posted to Lincoln for their first tour of duty; they would then ride south to Longthorpe for their second posting and thence to Camulodunum for their final period of duty, where they could compete in chariot races and enjoy the leisure facilities of the old Roman baths.

Ambrosius revived the structure of the Roman command of 'Britannia Prima' the area of central Britain protected by an outer ring of citadels from York in the north, Lincoln, Longthorpe and Colchester in the east, Winchester and Gloucester in the south, and Wroxeter and Chester in the north-west. Nennius refers to Ambrosius as '*Rex inter omnes reges*' or king among all the kings of the British people, whereas Gildas calls him '*Dux*' a reference to the Roman title of '*Dux Britanniarum*' the Duke of Britain. This was the title given to the supreme commander of British forces whose traditional headquarters was at York, eighty miles south of Hadrian's Wall, the Empire's northern frontier.

Second in command to the Duke of Britain came the Count of the Saxon Shore, the officer in charge of the shore forts along the invasion coast who commanded a mobile cavalry force trained to swiftly repel an enemy attack, and to maintain order and the rule of law. The Romans established ten naval bases around the south and east coasts of Britian, each garrisoned as a defensive fortress to harbour and re-victual the Roman fleet.

Portchester, Pevensey, Lympne and Dover guarded the south coast; Richborough and Reculver protected each end of the one mile wide channel that separated the Isle of Thanet from Kent; and the fortresses of Bradwell, Walton Castle, Burgh Castle, and Brancaster defended the east coast from the Blackwater estuary north to the Wash. Camulodunum, the first Roman capital of Britain, situated in a central position between Brancaster and Pevensey, was the ideal strategic base for coastal command and was chosen to be the headquarters of the Count of the Saxon shore.

As far as his limited resources allowed, Ambrosius emulated the Roman command structure in his revival of Britain's new army, but this fledgling force was not strong enough to garrison all the forts of Hadrian's Wall; moreover the old headquarters at York was too far north. With the main threat of attack along the east coast, Wroxeter provided a more central base that was secure and safe from enemy attack.

As Ambrosius' second in command, Arthur would have been appointed to the role of Count of the Saxon Shore. Now, with Arthur in command of a mobile cavalry force based at Camulodunum, or 'Camulud' as the Britons would have called it, the eastern front would be secure. Here then is plausible evidence to support the legendary story by Chrétien de Troyes that *Arthur's knights rode out from the many towered city of Camelot.* When this tale, most likely gleaned by Chrétien from an early Breton source, was written down in the twelfth century, the Roman name of Camulodunum had long since vanished from the map of Britain, and the abbreviated name of Camulod had evolved into the romantic 'Camelot,' the lost city of Arthurian legend.

Although Ambrosius had laid the foundations for Arthur's successful military campaigns, his achievements were not awarded the same accolade later given to Arthur, whose reputation as the greatest hero of his age became enshrined in legend centuries after his tragic demise at the Battle of Camlan.

The echoes of faint praise from Gildas and Nennius belie his great achievement, for it was Ambrosius who had rescued Britain from the brink of destruction in the second-half of the fifth century. Furthermore, besides re-forming the British army, it is claimed that he also established a new naval force; he certainly garrisoned the most important legionary forts for the defence of southern Britain and defined the front-line against Angles and Saxons. Soon after he had seized power from king Vortigern, Ambrosius assumed the role of *Dux Britanniarum* as supreme commander of British forces and welded together an alliance of the kings of Britain. At the same time he upheld the rule of law and in all probability re-introduced elements of Roman law that had lapsed under Vortigern's reversion to a nationalist regime. Similarly, Ambrosius re-affirmed Britain's loyalty to the true Christian faith encompassed by the Church of Rome by spurning the doctrine of Pelagianism encouraged by Vortigern and his followers. By strengthening and maintaining his military forces, Ambrosius succeeded in stemming the Anglo-Saxon advance into central Britain; and after thirty years of war, he achieved his life-long aim: a decisive victory in battle against Hengist and his Saxon cut-throats.

For such a distinguished commander it was exceptional to find that Ambrosius' death was not mentioned either by Gildas or Nennius, nor was the event recorded in the *Annales Cambriae* where the deaths of both Arthur and Maelgwyn are briefly listed; but surprisingly, Geoffrey of Monmouth told a legendary story of Ambrosius' last days, possibly from his own imagination, or even from his 'very ancient book in the Welsh language'.

According to Geoffrey, Ambrosius' Britons defeated Hengist at the battle of Maisbelli, a field near Kaerconan (Conisbrough). Perhaps Hengist, returning from Bernicia, had sailed up the Humber estuary as far as Goole, and then navigated his fleet along the river Don beyond the old Roman crossing at Doncaster with the aim of testing the British defences of South Yorkshire. Whether or not he realised that on reaching Conisbrough he would have been only eighty miles from Wroxeter is a matter for conjecture; but could he have been planning an audacious attack on Ambrosius' heartland of Powys from the north-east? Even if this had been his intention, he misjudged the British defences; Conisbrough was only thirty-five miles from Lincoln and was within easy striking distance of Ambrosius' cavalry detachment.

After a momentous and bloody battle, Hengist was captured and executed, beheaded by the sword of Eldol, Duke of Gloucester, who had survived the massacre on the 'Night of the Long-knives.' Ambrosius honoured his fallen adversary with a Saxon burial ceremony, covering his body under a mound of earth in the pagan tradition. The *Anglo-Saxon Chronicle* records Hengist's first landing in Britain, and his subsequent victories over the Britons; but the Saxons were reluctant to record the defeat and death of their most powerful leader. For a Saxon warrior, defeat in battle was shameful and the Chronicle makes a significant omission in not recording the death of Hengist. Nevertheless, his demise is confirmed by an oblique reference for the year 488:

*"Aesc* (Ochta, Hengist's son and heir) *received the kingdom and for thirty-four years was the king of the Kentish people."*

Vengeance for Hengist's death was administered with a treacherous blow by Vortigern's heir Pascent who, as Geoffrey of Monmouth claims, conspired with the Saxons to poison Ambrosius while he was recuperating from an illness at Winchester.

A more ignoble death cannot be imagined for such a statesman as Ambrosius: to be murdered on his sick-bed by the hand of his scheming enemy. Undoubtedly his compatriots, together with the few remaining kings of the states of Britain would have endeavoured to keep his death a secret. It was perhaps for this reason that the chroniclers of the day forbore to record his untimely death, for it also marked the end of a dark chapter in their troubled history.

Map 2   Possible locations for Arthur's Battles

Map of Britain, showing possible sites for Arthur's battles in the sequence listed by Nennius. The map reveals that Arthur's battle campaign was waged, not just in one local area, but throughout the whole island of Britain.

© C.M.Walmsley

# CHAPTER 4

# ARTHUR'S FIRST BATTLE 'AT THE MOUTH OF THE RIVER GLEIN'

*"The Battle of Britain is about to begin…*
*Upon this battle depends the survival of Christian civilisation"*
Winston Churchill, September 1939

Hengist was executed in the year 488, following his defeat by Ambrosius at the battle of Maisbelli in south Yorkshire. News of his death came as a shock to his compatriots in the Germanic homelands of Saxony, Friesland and Jutland, for his fame as the great leader of the Anglo-Saxon invasion of Britain was renowned through all of Gaul. Hengist's success in seizing control over a large part of south-eastern Britain, as well as establishing a satellite colony of Saxons in the north-eastern region of Bernicia (Northumberland) was due to his ruthless leadership and his cunning exploitation of British military and political weakness following the Roman exodus from the island early in the fifth century.

In Jutland, home of the Angles, king Icel of Angeln knew that Hengist's death would be a severe blow to the Saxon master plan to conquer the whole of Britain, and that his demise would create a power vacuum between his recently conquered territories; but his death also presented an immediate opportunity for another strong leader to take control of the middle lands of Britain. When this new leader had established a base that effectively bridged the gap between allies in the north and south, his force would act as the shaft of an offensive arrow-head aimed at the core of British defences in the south-west; Saxon forces to the south-east and north-east would form the barbs of the arrow-head and the advancing forces would be able to open up a war on three fronts against the enemy: it would split their forces and strike terror into the hearts of Britons.

The peninsula of Angeln formed a natural defensive site, jutting-out into the Baltic Sea on the east coast of Jutland some twenty miles from the town of Schleswig.

Steep cliffs made a chalk-white wall against attack from the sea; and the landward neck of the peninsula was defended by a construction of banks and ditches, with the innermost bank fortified with a strong timber palisade crowned with watch-towers. This fortified settlement was the home of the Angles, ancestors of the English; here on the high ground, not far from the sea, was king Icel's great hall, surrounded by the thatched dwelling houses of his seafaring warriors and the shipwrights, blacksmiths, artisans and armourers whose hard graft and honed skills maintained a fearsome fighting force of ships and men.

King Icel called his warrior chieftains to a council of war. The king took his place, enthroned in the great gabled hall, surrounded by his bodyguard and his chieftains in order of seniority. When all were assembled he explained his plan to establish a power-base in Britain by seizing the opportunity to reinforce Hengist's legacy of conquest; it was a bold endeavour that could win the prize of new land and wealth for his people. The council cheered their approval of the king's ambitious plan, but when the excitement of the moment had passed, the wisest of the elders sounded a note of caution, saying that it would be foolhardy to risk the loss of a large fighting force in an alien land against an unknown enemy:

*"For years we and our Saxon allies have despised the Britons as timid and worthless in war, but in the past decade the fame of their Roman leader Ambrosius has stirred the British to victory in many battles against invaders. It would therefore be wise to send no more than three warships on this expedition with the aim of exploring the eastern shores of Britain, both to assess the strength of our enemy and to find the most favourable part of this land in which to forge a new kingdom for our people".*

The king respected the wise advice of his sage and agreed to commission two new warships together with new shields, seaxes (long-knives) and spears for the expedition. If the new keels were laid immediately, the longships could be completed during the winter months when raging seas made navigation impossible. The new ships would be built on the shore of the natural harbour formed by the hook of land on the north-western tip of the Schlei Estuary, for this was the safe haven for king Icel's fleet. The third ship would be drawn from the existing fleet, and in order to avoid the hazardous five-hundred mile circumnavigation of Jutland from the Baltic to the North Sea, the boats would sail west to Schleswig, where they would be lashed to carts and wheeled twenty-five miles overland to the Husomer estuary on the west coast.

The ships would be made of oak, over seventy feet long by twelve feet wide, and clinker-built with nine broad strakes riveted together with iron-clench nails. A crew of thirty warriors would man the oars held by rowlocks lashed to the gunwales, and each ship, with its square flaxen sail rigged from a tall mast and a pennant streaming in the wind, would be steered by a long steering-oar or starboard. The tall curved prow and stern were distinguishing features of these ships that had been designed to pierce the waves and to weather the most storm tossed seas.

King Icel commanded a feast be prepared in the great hall to honour the chieftains and warriors chosen for the expedition to Britain. The banqueting hall was made ready, resplendent with old threaded tapestries, oak tables trestled and spread with an abundance of fare, and benches set in place. Torches were lit as the guests entered the hall, and after toasting one another with bumpers of mead, friends made merry and enjoyed the feast; accompanied by a harp, king Icel's poet entertained the company with songs, extolling the king's achievements and recounting the victorious battles of the past. When the feasting was done, the brave war-band paid homage to their king, swearing an oath of allegiance, and declaring a toast "To Conquest!" King Icel reciprocated the goodwill of his men by giving armlets and rings of fine gold as tokens of his bond, calling upon Tyr, the pagan warrior god and protector of champions and brave men, to augur a successful outcome for the expedition. Then at midnight the king retired to his sleeping quarters; in the great hall tables and benches were cleared away and bedding laid for the band of brothers-in-arms, for this would be their last night in Angeln.

At dawn the men were armed with bright silver shields, sharp axes, shining swords and strong ash spears. The new longships were launched and the warriors boarded at the prow, stowing their armour and provisions amidships around the mast; then, shouting their last farewells, each crew struck water with fourteen pairs of oars, pulling their boats through the harbour and out into the Schlei estuary. A fair easterly breeze caught the square-rigged sails as the three ships turned onto a westerly heading for Schleswig.

Five hours sailing bought the small fleet to the head of the estuary. With the sun in the south, the men beached their boats and dragged them forward to prepare for the twenty-five mile overland trek to the west coast of Jutland. Three pairs of oxen pulled each ship, now cradled and lashed onto long, low carts; it was an arduous eight-hour journey, with the men marching alongside, steadying their ships and coaxing the oxen forward over rough, narrow trackways. By nightfall this extraordinary convoy had reached the settlement of Husum, and the sight of the Husomer estuary cheered the crews after their toil: for by the end of this day they had sailed, dragged and wheeled their ships more than forty-seven miles from coast to coast.

At dawn the next day the ship's chieftains met to finalise their plan for the long sea voyage ahead. Olaf, the senior commander had gained invaluable experience sailing on coastal raids with a band of Saxons who had attacked the east coast of

Britain from their base at the mouth of the Rhine. He knew that the safest course to sail was south-west along the coast of Jutland, then, hugging the coast of Heligoland, to follow the islands for 280 miles to the Hook of Holland. From there the final leg, a distance of around 125 miles, would bring them to one of the estuaries on the east coast of Britain; with a favourable wind to fill their sails the voyage would take three days and nights at the very least, but if the wind dropped, the men would have to pull at their oars for hours at a time: this voyage of over four-hundred miles would test the mettle and endurance of commanders and crews alike.

Aware that a British force under Ambrosius was active in the south-east of the island, the leader of the Angles boldly suggested that they could save time by taking a shorter, more direct course; by steering just south of due west, or 'south by west', they would make landfall near the great inlet of the Metaris Estuary, the Wash. To achieve a covert arrival, the commanders agreed to make their landing, as far as wind and tide would allow, at dusk on the third day of their voyage; for if they could slip past Branodunum (Brancaster) the most northerly of the Saxon shore forts, without being detected, they would be able to find a small river estuary and make landfall under cover of darkness.

To meet the planned arrival time the Angles would need to embark at dusk, leaving the shores of their homeland to venture into the unknown of their first night at sea. As the sun sank below the western horizon the three warships pulled their oars rhythmically through the darkening channels of the Husomer estuary, heading for the open sea. Proud curved prows of king Icel's surf-fleet furrowed the foam-crested waves as the commander steered towards the afterglow of the sun; then as the stars began to shine through the darkness, he searched for Polaris, the north-star. Extending an imaginary line from the star to the northern horizon, he aligned the ship's prow with the western quadrant of his imaginary compass and trimmed the square sail for a long haul on the port tack.

Before midnight the south-westerly wind blew up into a storm force gale and the huge breakers threatened to engulf the ships. Each seafarer quickly forgot the pleasant memories of their homeland as their thoughts turned solely to surviving the relentless walls of foaming sea by baling out the swamped bilges through the night; mercifully the storm broke before dawn and in calmer seas each man had time to wonder what fate had in store for them on this long voyage: would they live to see their homeland another day, or would this be their journey to the other world beyond life's horizon? Only the bravest seafarers conquered their fear of shipwreck and drowning and put aside thoughts of a bloodier death in battle.

By day the helmsman looked to the sunrise to mark the eastern horizon, and at the sun's zenith to mark south; then, when the sun had completed the second

King Icel's warships approaching the east coast of Britain.
From a painting by Albert Seville. © photos.com

quadrant of its arc at dusk, he would fix the westerly course for the night. When the wind dropped and the ships were becalmed, commanders ordered their crews to pull: with fourteen pairs of oars each ship made good headway through the calmer waters. By nightfall, if the wind had not picked-up, half the crew would rest while the others rowed onward; and another helmsman would take the steer-board while the commander took a few hours rest.

After one night and a day at sea, Olaf was heartened to see the West Frisian Islands on the far southern horizon: he estimated that they had sailed about one third of the way to Britain and would soon be passing out of sight of land. They would then be at the mercy of the elements as they crossed the depths of the Oceanus Germanicus; but the sight of the Frisian Islands reminded him of the story of Hengist as a young warrior banished from his own land, and he related the tale to entertain his crewmen.

Hengist and Horsa were brothers in battle; they led a fearsome war-band from Friesland to Britain making landfall on the Isle of Thanet. Despite the fact that the Roman army had left Britain over twenty years before, the Britons were still weak and dispirited; they had failed to form an effective fighting force to combat the increasing threat of raids by the Scotti from Ireland and constant incursions by the Picts in the north. Seizing the opportunity, Hengist met with Vortigern, leader of the states of Britain and offered to do battle with the Picts in return for payment and supplies, as well as the gift of a secure base on the Isle of Thanet. Vortigern agreed, and thought that he had been extremely clever to pit Hengist and his band of rough-necks against the bloodcurdling Picts who had terrorised the northern Britons for so many years.

But Hengist was sharp-witted and cunning: after a skirmish with the Picts he returned south and demanded further payments and more land; but when the Britons refused to give in to his demands, Hengist made an alliance with the Picts and sent to Saxony for reinforcements. When sixteen keels of picked warriors arrived in Kent together with Hengist's beautiful young daughter Rowena, a feast was arranged for Vortigern and his nobles, who were accompanied by Ceretic the interpreter. When they were all seated for the feast, Rowena poured the wine and they all became exceedingly drunk. That evening Vortigern became so besotted with Rowena that he asked Hengist for her hand in marriage saying, *"ask of me what you will, even to the half of my kingdom."* Then Hengist, having consulted the elders of Angeln, agreed to ask for the country of Kent; this was granted and the girl was given in marriage to Vortigern, who slept with her and loved her deeply.

Hengist said to Vortigern, *"I am now your father, and will be your adviser: never ignore my advice and you will never fear conquest by any man or any people, for my race are strong. I will ask my son and his cousin, who are fine warriors, to fight the Scotti if you will give them lands about the Wall."* Vortigern agreed and Hengist invited his sons Ochta and Ebissa to come with forty keels; first they sailed north to waste the Orkney Islands and then occupied the north-eastern lands as far as the borders of the Picts; thenceforth Hengist called for reinforcements from his homeland to strengthen his hold on the prize of Kent.

Vortigern's entry to the enemy camp and sudden marriage to Hengist's daughter alienated him from his sons Vortimer and Cateyrn who strongly resolved to renew the war against the Saxons and beat them out of Kent. After four bloody battles, Vortimer pushed Hengist to an ignominious defeat on the shores of the Gallic Sea at Richborough; the British triumph was a bitter cup for Hengist who was angered and shamed in defeat. He vowed to take revenge and planned to strike back with a vicious blow conceived with cunning and delivered by stealth; but it would take him five years to recover from the British onslaught.

Vortimer's death was Hengist's cue to put his treacherous plan into action. With his battle force now strengthened with reinforcements, Hengist sent envoys to the Britons asking for a permanent peace treaty. Vortigern and his council agreed to discuss peace terms and at Hengist's invitation Vortigern and the nobility of Britain assembled for a peace conference. Laying down their arms, the Britons and Saxons sat down together at a magnificent feast; wine and mead flowed freely and the guests relaxed and enjoyed the entertainment. Suddenly Hengist rose and bellowed a command to his men: each Saxon drew a concealed knife, thrusting the blade into the nearest unarmed Briton. Thus Hengist and his crew murdered three hundred British nobles and their kin, in a ruthless and bloody attack that later became known as the infamous 'Night of the Long-knives.' Vortigern's life was spared, but the captive king was ransomed for more land.

At dawn on the second day of the voyage from Jutland the wind veered to the north, and the helmsman brought the great curved prow of the leading ship round to windward, setting a course to the north-west, and hauling the sail in close on the starboard tack, almost in line with the longboat's keel. With the wind, tide and waves beating against the long shallow-draught hull, making headway was arduous and the helmsman sensed nature's forces relentlessly pulling the ship to the south of his intended course. As darkness fell, the wind strengthened and the night turned into another battle for survival; the overcast sky obscured the stars and left the navigator without a single reference point: fighting the windswept breakers streaming over the starboard bow, he steered by intuition, looking fearfully into the eye of the storm and the black void of the ocean.

By sunrise on the third day the commanders and their crews were exhausted; now the wind had dropped and they would have to row all day long to reach the coast of Britain. It was well after mid-day when Olaf sighted land; realising that the fleet had been blown well to the south he turned onto a northerly heading to avoid the coastal defences at Gariannonum (Burgh Castle). As the sun slipped below the horizon the three ships of the surf-fleet turned towards the orange afterglow; they had reached the Wash, about five miles from each headland. A light wind caught the sails, spurring them through the Lynn Deeps; but when the wind dropped, the oarsmen were forced to pull slowly in a monotonous rhythm for the last twenty miles of the voyage.

The commander steered for the Welland estuary on the north-western shore of the Wash, aiming to keep as far as possible from Branodunum (Brancaster) the fortress guarding the coastal approaches. As they entered the estuary, the crews

Arthur's first battle: where the river Glen joins the river Welland at Surfleet, Lincolnshire.
Photo, © Kate Jewell

lowered their sails and rowed silently westward. Seven miles upstream the fleet reached the confluence of two rivers, the Welland and Glen; and just as darkness enveloped them, the commander beached his boat on the south bank of the river Glen, on what appeared to be a headland between the two rivers. His exhausted crews disembarked, pulling a few of their ships ashore and securing them with lines and anchors. After a meal of oats and dried fruit, washed down with beer to celebrate their unopposed arrival in Britain, some of the men went to sleep in the boats, others under awnings rigged from rolls of flax stretched out from the ships sides, their swords and shields to hand and their spears neatly stacked.

The Angles had neither seen nor heard any sign of the Britons. They knew Ambrosius' headquarters was somewhere in the west-country, and had heard that the eastern seaboard was only lightly garrisoned at the Saxon shore forts; their unchallenged landing gave them the confidence to plan for two days of recuperation before advancing upstream under cover of darkness. But the Britons guarded their coast with pride and fear: pride in the freedom of their country and fear of a Saxon invasion. A keen eyed watchman patrolling on horseback near Blakeney Point, fifteen miles south of Branodunum, had spotted the square-rigged longships on the horizon as they sailed in from the south-east. Riding to the fortress at the gallop, he raised the invasion alarm: messengers were immediately despatched, one to Viroconium, Ambrosius' military headquarters in the heart of Powys, the other to Camulodunum, the south-eastern garrison where Arthur, as second in command, held a cavalry troop on standby in readiness for battle.

News of the invaders reached Ambrosius late on the same day as the landing, just as the Angles were pulling ashore to make their encampment for the night. The enemy strength was estimated at between ninety and one-hundred and twenty men.

*"This will give the young warrior Arthur his first opportunity to lead his squadron into battle,"* Ambrosius declared to his senior commanders as they discussed the plan of action; *"and this will test his mettle as a leader!"* he exclaimed. Then, turning to the messenger, Ambrosius gave his battle orders: *"Alert the Longthorpe garrison commander to place thirty mounted cavalry at Arthur's disposal, and when you reach Camulod, tell Arthur that this is his battle, and his alone."*

Arthur did not wait for the messenger to return from Viroconium; as soon as he had been warned of the enemy incursion he called his young warriors to battle readiness and prepared to advance northwards to Longthorpe. A small crowd of citizens had gathered under the portico of the old Roman forum in the centre of Camulodunum, and they cheered as Arthur led his cavalry troop clattering to a crescendo along the cobbled main street, their flaming torches swirling in the wind until, two by two, they passed through the North-Gate and disappeared into the night.

Arthur and his squadron were given a warm welcome by the Longthorpe commander when they arrived before first light; after the seventy-five mile ride the men were ready for a hearty breakfast while new mounts were brought up from the stables. A flickering light from the bright flames of braziers revealed a hive of activity in the compound, with warriors arming for battle, grooms saddling up the battle-horses and armourers whetting double-edged swords for the final action. Ambrosius' messenger had arrived in the early hours, later joined by scouts from the fort at Branodunum who confirmed the enemy's last position. Arthur rallied his warriors for the final tactical briefing before the traditional *quaich of strong ruby wine was passed to each man to fortify them before battle.

*(a two handled wooden or silver drinking vessel)

Just before dawn Arthur led his two cavalry squadrons northward towards Bourne; then two miles north of Market Deeping he turned north-east along the old Roman road that cut across the Lincolnshire fens to Spalding. If the position reports were accurate, Arthur would locate the enemy at the confluence of the rivers Glen and Welland, about four miles upstream from Spalding. Here in the meadows on the north bank of the river Welland, Arthur gave his troops time to rest and water their mounts; then he gave the final order for battle: *"take up your formations and await my order to charge. Strike them hard and thrust to kill!"*

The Angles awoke from their deep slumber to the sound of distant thunder: confusion spread to fear as the thunder appeared as a storm of heavy battle-horses charging through the low strands of mist still clinging to the meadows along the river Glen. The night watchmen had fallen asleep from exhaustion and it was left to the commander to sound the alarm: a shrill staccato blast on his horn pierced the sound of the charging cavalry as it reached a crescendo.

Arthur led his first squadron into the attack at the head of an echelon-wedge formation of thirty warriors in three ranks of cavalry. Breaking through the mist they flew over the low embankment that shielded the headland, thrusting deep into the midst of the enemy encampment. The Angles were in disarray: grasping their shields and swords they fought where they stood. Caught off-guard by Arthur's surprise attack, they had no chance to form a defensive shield line, but instinctively a small core of warriors formed a barrier around Olaf, their commander, closing their shields together to protect him from the fray.

*"Set fire to their ships,"* Arthur commanded. In terror, some of the younger men who had survived Arthur's first charge ran for the longship moored on the embankment furthest from the battle, clambering aboard in a frantic attempt to escape the onslaught, as flaming spears set the flaxen sails alight. As the second squadron thundered into the melèe the Angles fought fiercely, wielding their swords and axes against the long sharp lances of the mounted Britons; but even the bravest of their warriors were cut to pieces, and as Arthur regrouped to make a final charge, only the leader and a few of his bodyguard were still fighting. Arthur came in fast and his bright steel-tipped spear found its target, pinning Olaf straight through his chain-mail tunic into the prow of his burning ship.

A pall of smoke drifted across the riverbank at the mouth of the river Glen, trailing from the longship that had escaped; the few survivors pulled furiously at their oars, heading downstream towards the open sea. For them it was a dishonourable retreat but as far as Arthur was concerned, those Angles who were lucky enough to escape this battle would return to their own land with news of the surprise, speed and ruthlessness of the British attack. It would be a fearsome warning to their compatriots to invade Britain at their peril.

Arthur seized the commander's magnificent sword, his first battle trophy; on the bloodied river-bank his warriors collected the enemy's weapons and took their gold and silver rings, the booty of battle. Some of the dead were dumped unceremoniously into the burning ships: the spirit of adventure of king Icel's surf-fleet was now fatefully transformed into a weird funeral pyre.

Arthur and his mounted warriors withdrew to Longthorpe where they toasted his first victory in battle, raising goblets of mead with a cheer, and celebrating late into the night.

The battle site at the mouth of the river Glen in Lincolnshire became known as *"Surfleet Seas End"* and the hamlet close by is so named to this day, in memory of Arthur's first battle.

Aerial photograph of the mouth of the river Glen at Surfleet: the narrow headland between the Glen and Welland would have made an ideal landfall for invading Angles, whose English descendants now moor their boats alongside the ancient battlefield.

Photo, © Google Earth

# CHAPTER 5

# ARTHUR'S FOUR BATTLES ON THE RIVER BLACKWATER

*"Qui desiderat pacem, praeparet bellum."*
*"Let him who desires peace, prepare for war."*
Flavius Vegetius Renatus c. AD 390

Nennius' historic battle-list describes Arthur's first battle *"at the mouth of the river Glein; the second, third, fourth and fifth battles were fought upon another river which is called Dubglas, in the region of linnuis."* It has been suggested that 'linnuis' may be derived from the Latin name 'Lindenses' meaning *'the people of Lincoln;'* in fact, it is in Lincolnshire that we find the river Glen winding across the fens in a north-easterly direction from the village of Bourne to the Wash, just a few miles from Spalding. Rivers like the Glen, Welland, Nene and Great Ouse offered easy access to the shallow-draught longships of invading Angles and Saxons intent on slipping undetected into the eastern fenlands under cover of darkness.

However, *'Dubglas'* is an early British name that translates as 'Blackwater' in English; but because there is no river of this name in Lincolnshire, the association of the word 'linnuis' with Dubglas may be mistaken. This apparent discrepancy could be explained by a simple scribal error where the cleric, in copying the original text, has transposed the descriptive phrase *in the region of linnuis* from the river Glein to the river Dubglas.

In fact there are several rivers in Britain named 'Blackwater,' one being in Scotland just north of Blairgowrie; another in Essex that rises at Braintree and flows to a wide estuary at Maldon; and another that runs along the Blackwater Valley which forms part of the border between Surrey and Hampshire. However, the rivers of south-east England are more likely to fit both historic and geographic profiles for the river Dubglas associated with Arthur's battles.

By the first century AD the Romans had colonised Maldon and were harvesting fish and oysters from the river Blackwater to feed the settlement, and to distribute as far as the garrisons on Hadrian's Wall. Recently, Saxon fish-traps have been found embedded in the river mud, clear evidence of later Saxon settlement in the area; no doubt the wide estuary nine miles south of Colchester made an ideal landfall for Saxons hoping to settle in Britain in the latter half of the fifth century.

If Arthur had established his south-eastern headquarters at the fortified city of Camulodunum, Colchester, it would have provided a secure base for a cavalry detachment whose role was to deter invaders arriving from the North Sea. However, Saxon foederati, or mercenaries, who had been allowed to settle in south-eastern Britain by king Vortigern, may not have been targeted as the enemy by Arthur's Britons; but there was clearly a different rule for new sea-borne immigrants: they were classified as enemy invaders and would be challenged as soon as they set foot on British soil.

Although there is a strong possibility that Arthur may have engaged in skirmishes along the river Blackwater near Maldon, there is little evidence to confirm it. However we can narrow the area of our search for the exact location of the river Dubglas by considering the question: "Who was Arthur's most dangerous enemy and where were they at this time?"

Not surprisingly it is Nennius who provides the answer in the *Historia Brittonum*: he relates that *"On Hengist's death, his son Ochta came down from the left-hand side of Britain to the kingdom of the Kentishmen, and from him come the royal line of Kent."* Nennius is evidently quoting from an early text when he uses the words *'transivit de sinistrali (left-hand) parte Brittanniae.'* Because the defending Britons were facing an enemy incursion from the east, the earliest battle line against the Anglo-Saxons was drawn from north to south; so the author, living in western Britain and facing east towards the front line, describes Ochta's move from Bernicia on his left (in the north of Britain) to Kent, in the south.

Finally defeated in battle by Ambrosius, Hengist died in the year 488. Despite his despotic reign, his lifetime achievements included the conquest of Kent, securing the settlement of Bernicia for his war-band north-east of the Wall, and forging military alliances with Pictish leaders in the north and Anglians in the east. But Hengist's death created a power vacuum in the largest of the new English kingdoms; it was therefore politically expedient for his son Ochta to take the reins of the kingdom of Kent, both to secure and consolidate this vast territorial gain, as well as to strengthen his battle forces for the future conquest of western Britain. Nennius confirms: *"at that time the Saxons increased their numbers and multiplied in Britain,"* and *'that time'* was thirty years or so after Hengist's treachery on the 'Night of the Long-knives,' when, to save his own life, Vortigern ceded Kent and other territories to the Saxons, including '*Est-saxum, Sut-saxum et Middelseaxan.*' (Essex, Sussex, and Middlesex).

Archaeological discoveries of weapons and jewellery from early fifth century Anglo-Saxon cemeteries confirm the migration routes of the invaders: Jutes and Frisians settled mostly in Kent, and Saxons predominated in the Thames Valley as far as Abingdon; from the east coast they followed the Icknield Way westward and settled alongside the Angles, who gradually populated the greater parts of East Anglia and Norfolk. Rivers and trackways gave the marauders access to the very heart of Britain: the Icknield Way leads from the east coast at Holm, fifteen miles north of King's Lynn, routing south-west via Thetford, Aylesbury, and Wallingford before linking with the Ridgeway along the Lambourn Downs by White Horse Hill, and ends at Silbury Hill near Avebury in Wiltshire: a distance of over 190 miles. From south-east Kent the North Downs Way leads from Canterbury and runs westward for 90 miles via Rochester, Caterham and Guildford to Farnham in Surrey, where it links with an ancient trackway running south-west through Andover and across Salisbury Plain to the Roman town of Ilchester in Somerset.

But it was Hengist's control of Kent that enabled him to encourage the open immigration of Angles, Saxons and Jutes from their homelands, to the extent that by the end of the fifth century, the whole region of Angel in Schleswig Holstein, and some parts of Saxony, had been completely evacuated. Half a century of settlement and regeneration had strengthened the Saxons' hold on south-eastern Britain: from a mercenary war-band first confined to a base on the Isle of Thanet, Hengist and his countrymen had expanded their new colony to become a political force and a military threat that the Britons could no longer ignore.

It was this position of strength that Ochta inherited, together with his father's ambitious plan for the future. Hengist's long-term strategy for the conquest of southern Britain was an allied spearhead of Angles attacking to the south-west along the axis of the Icknield Way, and his own Saxon force from Kent attacking to the north-west. The two war-bands would meet at Liddington Hillfort, where the ancient Ridgeway track meets the Roman road running north-west from Silchester; from here the combined and strengthened army would attack Cirencester and Gloucester, striking into the heartland of the British command.

Because the British strongholds of Londinium and Verulamium (London and St Alban's) kept the Anglian and Saxon forces apart in the south-east, any further expansion of Ochta's kingdom would have to be to the west. The British garrison at Rochester defined the northern frontier along the river Medway, forcing the Saxons to fight for the river crossing at Aylesford in their move due west from Thanet; but where was their final western border with the British? Ochta's kingdom of the Cantii was smaller than our present day county of Kent and bordered the tribal territory of the Regnesis to the west, an area equal to Surrey and Sussex combined, so the western border would most likely be defined by a river somewhere in this area.

Ochta aimed to push west into British territory as far as the natural river borders and his own supply route allowed. First overcoming British resistance at the river Mole near Dorking, then pushing forward across the river Wey at Guildford, he moved his army north-west towards the border with the Atrebates.

Just two miles north of Farnham in Surrey lies an iron-age fort known as Caesar's Camp; situated in an elevated position on the Surrey-Hampshire border, the fort has a steep double rampart to the south and holds commanding views over the forest to the west, and to the north towards Farnborough. Ten miles further north near Easthampstead, there was another Caesar's Camp, a fortified village occupied from the first century BC; it is said to be the best example of an Iron Age contour fort in Britain and as the name suggests, the defences carefully follow the contours of the hilltop. A timber palisade with watchtowers enclosed the settlement of round houses that were built from wattle and daub, whitewashed with lime, and their roofs thatched with local reeds; other rectangular buildings were used as animal pens, granaries and stores.

Caesar's Camp Iron Age Village now lies hidden in woodland near the 'Lookout' at Bracknell in Berkshire. The hillfort featured a single massive rampart and ditch that enclosed a settlement of more than 17 acres, with main entrances to the north and south.
© Bracknell Forest Council

Between these two forts lay ten miles of rough uninhabited heathland interspersed with pine-forest and gravel escarpments: it was the ideal landscape for military training and Ochta was quick to take full advantage of this new found location. Roughly half-way between the forts, he followed a fast flowing river as it curved to the north-west; this would provide the essential fresh water supply he needed for his troops. Advancing a few miles further, Ochta could not believe his good fortune when he saw that the river supported shoals of brown trout; the fish would supplement supplies from established Saxon farms that now yielded a plentiful harvest of grain from the weald of Kent. Ochta directed his men to the higher ground just to the east of the river valley. Here on the western border was the perfect location for a training camp where he could shape his rough and ready war-band into a forceful army capable of striking deep into the mainland of Britain.

The river flows through the Blackwater Valley in Surrey, with the village of Yateley to the south and Sandhurst just to the north. It must be more than coincidence that the area chosen by Ochta to train his fledgling army is now the centre of the British Military Establishment, from the Royal Military Academy at Sandhurst, to Deepcut and Pirbright Barracks, through to Farnborough and Aldershot, all operating within the ten mile strip of land between the original forts that were both known as Caesar's Camp. In all probability, Ochta's first military base became the traditional training ground for the earliest English army, for this ground was to become a springboard for the Saxon conquest of western Britain in the sixth century.

Within five years of his father's death, Ochta had pushed the western border with the British as far as the Blackwater Valley. By chance he had found the ideal place for a military base where he could recruit and train young Saxon warriors to battle readiness.

Here his army could act as a defensive buffer force against the Britons, and from this advantageous position he would launch a great attack to mark the beginning of a major campaign for the conquest of Britain.

As the setting sun appeared to set the river Blackwater ablaze, Ochta knew that his next objective lay just over the western horizon: it was the old Roman city of Calleva, Silchester, the tribal capital of the British Atrebates.

᪐᪐᪐᪐

News of Ambrosius' death stunned his close companions, and the shock reverberated from Winchester to the remotest realms of Britain. Uther Pendragon, the 'Head

Dragon' who ruled over western Britain from Castell Dinas Bran in the heart of Powys, trembled with foreboding as he called an emergency meeting of the Council of Kings. Arthur and his fellow commanders were immediately recalled from Camulodunum, Longthorpe and Lincoln to update the council on the latest military situation and to advise on a strategic plan for the continuation of the war.

Just as the death of Hengist had elevated Ochta to the throne of the Saxon kingdom of Kent, so Ambrosius' death thrust Arthur, his second in command, into the role of British Military Commander, or *'Dux Bellorum'* the leader of battles. Legend confirms that Arthur was still very young when he took command. In Malory's *Mort d'Arthur* published in 1485, an elaborate story taken from an original French book relates how Arthur, although just a boy, drew the sword from the stone, thus winning the right to rule the kingdom over all the other knights who had attempted, but failed to draw the sword:

*"But there afore them all, there might none take it out but Arthur; wherefore there were many lords wrath, and said it was a great shame unto them all and the realm, to be over-governed by a boy of no high blood born."*

But this magical element of the story may have arisen by a simple misunderstanding, for if the French author had taken the idea from an original chronicle of Arthur's exploits written in Latin, he may have found a line that read: *"Arturus gladium ex saxo eripuit"* meaning: *"Arthur drew the sword from a stone."*

These words ring true when we consider that over a thousand years before Arthur's time, swords were made by pouring molten bronze into a stone mould; this traditional method was still in use in Arthur's day, but iron was now the metal used to make swords, axes and spearheads. First cast as molten metal, then cooled and drawn from a stone mould, the iron blade was annealed to drive out the impurities of the metal and then tempered on the anvil by alternate heating and quenching to give the weapon greater strength. If Arthur had commissioned a new sword, he would no doubt have taken a great interest in its making, giving instructions to the smith on the exact size, and then drawing the blade from the stone himself, closely watching the final finishing work on the anvil.

But the commissioning of a new sword would not itself guarantee its owner the right to claim promotion to the highest military rank of Dux Bellorum. Perhaps after all, the French author had not only misunderstood the original text but also misinterpreted it. The phrase *"ex saxo,"* 'from a stone,' is very similar to *"ex saxono"* meaning 'from a Saxon.' If the cleric writing in Latin had followed the common practice of omitting the letter 'n' and putting a dash above the word to indicate the omission, then the words *"ex saxono"* would have read *"ex saxō"*; of course we cannot prove anything with guesswork, but this suggestion not only helps to explain the implausible magical events of the legendary story, but also makes it possible to imagine how the original text might have appeared:

*"Arthur was the bravest commander; in his first battle he charged courageously into the front line and routed the enemy. During the fight, Arthur seized the sword from a Saxon, a feat that not one of his warriors had achieved; and in this battle he was the victor."*

This victory, and the magnificent trophy, a sword wrested from his Saxon adversary, confirmed Arthur's prowess a warrior; he was young indeed, but he was also powerful, courageous and intelligent, all the attributes required of a great leader. But just how old would Arthur have been when he took command? If he had been born about 470 AD, then he would have been just sixteen years old when fighting his first battles alongside Ambrosius, and possibly eighteen when he achieved his first victory against the Angles at the battle of the river Glen, about the time of Hengist's death in 488. If Ambrosius had died around the year 490, then Arthur would have taken command when he was only twenty years of age; old enough to be a brilliant leader, but lacking the experience to take over Ambrosius' role as Duke of Britain. Until Arthur had gained more experience in the military arena, Uther Pendragon, brother of Ambrosius and Arthur's legendary father, would have assumed overlordship as leader of the Council of the Kings of Britain.

Despite the ever present danger of Irish raids to the west coast and bloody incursions by Picts in the north, Arthur's war began as Ambrosius' had ended: with a battle campaign in the south-east of Britain, where the greatest threat came from Ochta, the newly crowned Saxon king of Kent. British scouts had reported that Ochta and his warband had recently moved beyond the western border of their ceded territory to establish a new base-camp along the eastern banks of the river Blackwater. This audacious move by the Saxons put the city of Calleva Atrebatum, (Silchester) in immediate danger for it was only eight miles from the enemy encampment. If Ochta decided to break out to the west, Calleva would be his first target; then Caer Venta (Winchester) and Corinium, (Cirencester) would be the next on his list of British cities marked out for conquest.

Arthur explained his battle plan to the Council of Britain. He defined a second front along the valley of the river Blackwater that extended form Caesar's Camp in the south, through Sandhurst, then towards Spencers Wood and Arborfield where the Blackwater runs into the river Loddon; and from there northwards to the Thames at Wargrave. Along this twenty-four mile border the rivers form a natural barrier to an army that marched on foot; if Arthur made Calleva his forward base, he would be able to intercept a break-out anywhere along the border and launch an attack that could engage the enemy within a twelve mile radius of the city. This plan would enable him to employ short-range battle tactics to gain the advantage of surprise attacks with fast moving cavalry troops who were fit and ready for battle; and after the action his men could withdraw to safety within the Roman walls of Calleva.

The Council of Kings approved Arthur's bold battle plans but they were extremely concerned that the Saxons had increased their numbers by inviting more and more kith and kin from their homelands of Friesland and Saxony in northern Germania, enabling Ochta to recruit all the young men who were fit enough to become warriors in his new army, and to make good the severe losses suffered in recent battles with Ambrosius. At this time the British estimated the enemy force to be close to twelve hundred strong, including a small core of Hengist's battle hardened warriors; an army that was a serious threat to Arthur's smaller force of around five hundred cavalrymen, supported by three or four squadrons of recruits under training.

Uther Pendragon was concerned that Arthur should not throw himself and his men impetuously into the enemy ranks without being fully prepared for a major campaign; for this would be an altogether different challenge to his first battle on the river Glen. With this in mind, Uther suggested that Arthur should assemble his forces at Caer Venta, Winchester, making this city his rear-guard headquarters for the duration of this critical stage of the war against Ochta. Venta was only twenty-five miles from Calleva, far enough away from the Saxons to prepare for battle-group readiness in secret, but close enough to supply reinforcements of men, horses and provisions to the battlefront. Arthur would need time to assemble his support teams; armourers, blackmiths, and saddlers, as well as to organise supplies of food and grain for men and horses and to set up a field kitchen with cooks and bakers to supply hot meals for his army.

Caer Venta, the capital city of the Belgae tribe, was the fifth largest city in Roman Britain. The city's stone walls, built by the Romans in the third century, protected the army fortress, the forum, baths and temples, as well as shops and courtyard houses of wealthy Britons, enclosing an area of 144 acres. Set amidst the rich pastureland of the Itchen Valley, Venta grew from a small market settlement known as Oram's Arbour that was situated near the ford over the river. When Roman military engineers were building the city they cleverly reclaimed land from the flood-plain by diverting the river Itchen into a channel along the eastern wall of the town, at the same time providing an accessible and plentiful supply of water for the people. But the idyllic situation of Venta belied its major disadvantage, for it was built on the levels of a river valley and did not dominate its surroundings. Nevertheless, the nearby Iron Age hill-fort to the south of the city compensated for the weakness in defence: the magnificent and imposing fortress of St Catherine's Hill towered above the Itchen, providing a defensive refuge for the citizens of Venta in times of strife, and it was here that Arthur chose to make his headquarters for the coming conflict.

Originally occupied by an Iron-Age settlement in the fifth century BC, this formidable natural hilltop was later fortified in the third century BC with a single ditch and bank rampart completely enclosing the oval-shaped hilltop. Massive ramparts towered twenty-five feet high, flanked by a ditch six feet deep and topped by a timber palisade and platform that would have given the defenders a height advantage of more than thirty feet over their enemy. It was a truly monumental fortress, with earthworks constructed on a massive scale defending an area of twenty-two acres across the summit, four acres larger than Cadbury Castle in Somerset.

The defenders commanded extensive views across the horizon from Bitterne in the south, over the city of Venta to the north, and to the north-east towards Avington; further south, the long escarpment of Twyford Down obstructed their view but also concealed the fortress from the eyes of a potential enemy approaching along the old Roman road from Portchester Castle. As a precautionary measure, a satellite fort just beyond the escarpment to the south-east could be occupied, and look-out posts were established on nearby hilltops to warn of approaching danger.

The natural elevation of the main hilltop rises to the north-east and forms a saddle to Twyford Down; in turn, the saddle links the fort to a causeway used for centuries by drovers and their cattle, known traditionally as the 'Dongas.' (Sadly, the building of the M3 motorway cut a mile long scar into the hillside and this important link with the past was severed; it has been replaced by a steel bridge over the motorway). Where the Dongas meets the eastern approach to the saddle, significant earth-works indicate the early existence of a complex defensive structure or outer main gateway. This was the key position for the first-line defence of the fortress and it was situated almost a quarter of a mile from the fort's main entrance.

But it was the natural contour of the landscape that offered the defenders the optimum position for their single entrance to the fortress, for the saddle gave the causeway direct access to the north-east wall of the fort. The original wide entrance that led through in-turned ramparts was revetted with timber and protected by guard-houses set in bays on either side of the ramparts. During the second century BC the entrance passage was narrowed and the revetment strengthened with chalk blocks, alterations that greatly improved the security of the inhabitants.

Arthur arrived at Venta with a small detachment of newly trained cavalry after a two-day chariot drive from Wroxeter. Breaking his journey at Gloucester to rally more young men to the cause, his route took him onward to Cirencester and through Andover, before he reached Venta on the evening of the second day, having covered well over 125 miles. He was saddened to find the city in a state of disrepair, with public buildings and town-houses falling into ruin, and it was evident from the unhealthy smell, that the Roman drainage system had collapsed. With the water supply polluted, most of the people had moved out of the city to encampments on higher ground.

Arthur and his small band of warriors rode on through the city and turned towards the sunset, climbing up to join the Dongas and heading for the fortress. Prince Cadwy and his battle-troop from Caer Cadarn, the 'strong fortress' by South Cadbury, had already pitched camp, erecting their tents in the orchard on the fort's lower terrace, and lighting fires for the evening spit roast. They cheered Arthur and his men as they rode up to the main entrance and into the safety of the fortress.

The next morning Arthur called all the citizens together in the fort's compound where his men had already begun to prepare for battle:

*"People of Venta, we are now at war. As you well know, for many years the Irish have been raiding our western shores, and the people of our northern lands have suffered endless attacks by the barbarian dog-heads who steal their cattle and ravage their homes; but it is the Angles in the east and the Saxons to the south that have now become the greatest threat to our freedom in Albion's fair island.*

*Not content with the land granted to them by Vortigern in return for their services fighting the Pictish invaders, now they themselves have turned invader, and seek to conquer even more of our island. We have inherited the scourge of Hengist's kith and kin: as I speak his son Ochta is training an army to break even further into Britain, and his compatriots across the sea threaten to invade our eastern coast with fleets of galley-slaves.*

*If we are to save our land from conquest by these ruthless, destructive and murderous war-bands…even to save our homes, and to save ourselves, we must all stand firm together. I assure you all, that wherever the enemy strikes, we will be there speedily to meet him: to face him with our keenest weapons, and to repel him from our land with deadly force and determination. We shall deal the enemy seven times the death and destruction that they have meted-out to us, and with God's help we will repel the heathens from this, the land of our inheritance.*

*But if we are to win this battle for our country we will need the help of everyone from countryman to statesman, even to our kings! Every man, woman and child must make a sacrifice; every state and province of Britain must contribute towards the establishment of a strong army and bear the cost of battle campaigns that will be fought across the length and breadth of the country. The Roman army, once the great protector of our island civilisation, is now long gone; but we are not defenceless, for I am Arthur, your Leader of Battles. I command a growing army of warriors, strong and courageous men who spur their horses into battle striking swiftly, their swords glinting, their spears thrusting at their enemies.*

*But for now, I can only promise you years of strife ahead: for Britons there will be toil and sweat and tears; and for Britain's warriors there will be bloodshed on bloodshed: the warriors' sacrifice for the freedom of their country. And when the battles are done, we shall prevail! With God's help we shall prevail! And we shall bring peace once more to this glorious land of Britain.*

*I therefore command you all: go now and serve your country; and if you find that you have nothing to give, then at the very least, remember us in your prayers."*

With only three months to prepare for war, Arthur galvanised the people of Venta into action. He organised a supply chain, purchased wheat to provide flour for the bakeries, and grain for the battle horses; found blacksmiths to shoe, and stable-hands to groom the horses, and women to weave and make clothes for the soldiers. Arthur commandeered premises and sent his armourers to set up smelting workshops to enable craftsmen to make swords, spears and shields. He set up a field kitchen and planned for a field dressing station to prepare for battle casualties. In the space of a few weeks he had transformed a run-down and deserted city into an industrial enclave; but the greatest change was shown by the people of Venta, whose enthusiasm and hard work was inspired by a new sense of purpose.

Over the weeks Arthur's army continued to grow in strength. Prince Cadwy had arrived at Venta with one hundred cavalry from Caer Cadarn. Arthur brought fifty newly trained recruits from Wroxeter and called in his own squadron of warriors from Camulodunum. Cei, Arthur's second in command, would draw troops from the eastern front to complete the battle group. Arthur's aim was to emulate the Roman *'comitatenses'*, cavalry units of 500 men, originally the companions or *'comites'* of the emperor.

But after twelve weeks of preparation, Arthur was still fifty men short of his target. Fewer men had volunteered for service, and those now at Wroxeter would have to make their way to the front when their training was complete; they would form a reserve squadron at Venta to hold the fortress secure. Nevertheless, Arthur had established all the support teams capable of supplying the army for a long campaign, perhaps as long as three or four years. With all the battle plans complete, Arthur moved his army eastwards under cover of night.

As Arthur's cavalry moved silently from the turf covered entrance of the great hill-fort of Venta into the moonlit landscape, they appeared through the mist as if they had galloped straight out of a cavern in the depths of the fortress. It was this illusion that later gave rise to the legendary claim that Arthur and his knights had sojourned in a cave deep underneath the castle.

Within five hours the army's move from Venta to Calleva was complete; every man moved into the battle zone with great stealth, for their arrival at Calleva was to be kept secret at all costs. Arthur's best tactical move was the surprise attack that took the enemy off-guard; with their ranks in confusion his mounted warriors could deliver mayhem. There would be no delay, every man was at battle readiness, every mount champing at the bit, sensing tension in the air. Arthur called his commanders together in the old forum in the centre of Calleva. He explained that the first battle of the river Blackwater would be a night attack: three troops of cavalry, each one hundred strong, would advance at midnight and move east along the Roman road towards London. After fording the river Loddon near Swallowfield and Riseley, Arthur's cavalry would follow the Blackwater Valley moving through the pine-forest for cover, until they reached the heathland close to the hamlet of Yateley.

It would be a hit and run attack on the Saxon camp that now straddled the eastern bank of the river, near the rough heathland of Sandhurst. Arthur's squadron would move first, attacking right into the heart of the Saxon camp. The second and third cavalry squadrons would take up their positions on the north and south flanks; they would attack then the enemy from the rear as Arthur confronted them with a bold frontal assault across the river Blackwater.

River Blackwater near Farley Hill, Berkshire. The river valley defined Arthur's battlefront against Ochta's Saxon army. Four battles waged over the Blackwater show that Arthur was facing a determined enemy, and that for many years he succeeded in preventing the Saxons from breaking into southern Britain. Photo, © Helen White

Arthur's squadrons delivered their three-pronged attack with perfect timing, storming into the centre of the camp, unleashing firebrands, with swords flashing and lances thrusting at the enemy. The Saxons were caught off-guard; half asleep or drunk they staggered around cursing, grasping for their swords and shields and running around in disarray. Before they could mobilise in any shape or form, Arthur and his warriors had disappeared into the night, leaving a trail of death and destruction; flames from the burning tents lit up the surrounding forest and reflected eerily in the dark waters of the river.

It was a daring attack that left the Saxons stunned; but for Arthur it was an invaluable battle experience that enabled him to test the enemy defences and assess their strength. It was clear that he was now up against the full complement of Ochta's new army, for it was a much larger force than the few dozen Angles he had fought at the river Glen. The first battle of the river Blackwater was a tactical victory for Arthur; he had inflicted serious loss to the enemy's number for only light British casualties. He had stung the Saxons, but had stirred a hornet's nest. Ochta was seething with anger and vowed to avenge his losses; but his first priority was to find a more strongly defended position. He promptly abandoned the burned-out encampment by the river and moved three miles north to seize the palisaded village of Caesar's Camp near Crowthorne.

Before the year was out, Ochta made good his losses, trained and armed more recruits to bring his war-band up to full strength. The Roman road to Calleva was less than a mile south of his new base. It was a gift to Ochta, for it ran through a pine forest straight to the east gate of Arthur's stronghold. This stretch of road is known as 'nine mile ride' and further west runs into 'the Devil's Highway' most probably so named by Britons of Arthur's day who thought that the pagan Saxons were the sons of the devil. Perhaps Ochta, as their leader, was regarded as the Devil incarnate, for it was Ochta who led his army along this highway to do battle with Arthur.

The Saxons were not short of men, with their swords and shields clattering as they marched four abreast in an extended line along the Devil's Highway; but they were short of tactics. They lumbered into battle, fanning out to present a wide front line before an engagement, then charging forward en-masse, shouting blood-curdling curses as they closed in to clash with their enemy. Arthur had anticipated a revenge attack and had sent out scouts to warn of a Saxon break-out. By the time Ochta had advanced four miles to the west, two of Arthur's cavalry squadrons had been scrambled to attack. Eight miles west of Caesar's Camp and half-way to Calleva, the Roman road fords the river Blackwater; Arthur knew that the Saxon army would be constricted at this river crossing and it was here that he planned to attack.

Arthur advanced rapidly eastward along the Devil's Highway as far as Swallowfield. Here the squadrons divided: Arthur led his troop north-east towards the Blackwater, then followed the river south towards the ford, while the second troop carried out a reciprocal manoeuvre to the south-east. It was a perfect pincer movement. Ochta's straggling war-band was half way across the ford when Arthur signalled the advance: the pincer attack split the enemy into two groups on each side of the ford. The force of the attack scattered the enemy: with no time to form a shield line, they were forced to fight where they stood, pinned down by British chargers, speared on the spot, hacked into the river where they either drowned or bled to death.

Arthur called his squadrons out of the battle, allowing the remnants of the enemy to form a defensive corps. At that moment Arthur's third squadron, fresh and now fully mobilised, charged straight from the Devil's Highway and into the battle. Ochta and his stalwart commanders put up a brave fight, but his army was decimated by Arthur's mounted warriors, and the survivors fled eastward into the forest. Ochta's attempt to lay siege to Calleva had been forestalled by Arthur: he had been rebuffed not by a larger army but by a much smaller cavalry force directed by a young intelligent commander who had employed tactics and timing to deliver a crushing blow to the enemy. This, the second battle of the river Blackwater, was an overwhelming victory for Arthur.

The Saxons had suffered serious losses. Arthur had also lost a number of the younger, less experienced warriors; horses too had fallen from sword and axe wounds inflicted in close quarter fighting with enemy foot-soldiers. For the first time Britons needed the field dressing teams that had accompanied the soldiers to the front line. After the experience of this, the bloodiest battle of his career, Arthur realised that his men needed time to recuperate. Now certain that he had incapacitated the Saxons, he withdrew two squadrons of cavalry from the front at Calleva, and despatched them back to Venta, where the injured would be cared for and given time for their wounds to heal; and in the security of the great fortress, his weary soldiers could rest their minds from the trauma of battle.

The onset of winter precluded plans for another battle, but Cei's squadron remained at Calleva to maintain a vigilant guard along the Blackwater front, and to act as a deterrent to further Saxon incursion. Arthur returned to Wroxeter to train more young men for the battles to come.

❧ ❧ ❧ ❧

Although Nennius' battle-list credits Arthur with twelve victories, Gildas is more circumspect in his comments on the war: *"from this time, now our citizens and now the enemy were victorious"*… Evidently, battles won were lauded and recorded, battles lost were glossed over, best forgotten. One such battle of Arthur's, clearly omitted from the victory list, is revealed in an early Welsh poem, the *Elegy for Geraint,* a lament for the loss of a young British warrior prince who fought alongside Arthur to repel the Saxon invasion of Portchester Castle:

> *"Before Geraint, the enemy's scourge*
> *I saw white stallions red shinned*
> *and after the war cry, bitter death.*
>
> *At Llongborth I saw the clash of swords,*
> *men in terror, bloodied heads*
> *before great Geraint, his father's son.*
> *At Llongborth I saw spurs*
> *and men who did not flinch from spears,*
> *who drank wine from glinting glasses.*
>
> *At Llongborth I saw Arthur*
> *his heroes would cut with steel;*
> *the emperor, strife's commander.*
>
> *At Llongborth Geraint was slain*
> *brave soldiers from Dyfneint,*
> *before they were slain, they slew.*
>
> *Swift chargers under Geraint's thigh,*
> *long-shanked, raised on wheat.*
> *Roans, swooping white eagle's assault.*
>
> *When Geraint was born, Heaven's gates were open,*
> *Christ granted all our prayers.*
> *A wonder to behold, the glory of Britain."*

Winter passed and Arthur, with the core of his cavalry, returned to Venta to prepare for a spring offensive on the Blackwater. The unexpected arrival of a Saxon fleet in Portsmouth harbour, followed by an attack on Portchester Castle was an unpleasant surprise for Arthur; he called on Geraint to muster his Dumnonian squadron. The Saxons had landed on their doorstep only seventeen miles from Venta and Arthur decided to take immediate action to repel them: *"We will attack before they have time to erect their tents,"* he shouted to his men.

Alongside Geraint, Arthur led the cavalry squadron south from Venta's great fortress. Fortified by a glass of strong red wine the warriors were eager for action, but their only barrier to battle was the great main gate of Portchester Castle that the Saxons had barred shut against them. Arthur quickly improvised a battering ram to force the gates, allowing his cavalry to sweep into the castle and engage the enemy in hand to hand combat; but in the confinement of the inner compound the mounted chargers came to an abrupt halt as both horses and men became targets for Saxon axes and seaxes, the short-shafted long-knives that gave the Saxons their fearsome reputation.

Arthur hacked his way through a mass of thrashing warriors to the south gateway, but he saw Geraint's stallion hemmed into the melèe: forced to a standstill he became an immediate target for the enemy. Suddenly, with a ghastly cry, he fell, victim to a Saxon axe. The shock of seeing his companion in arms fall to the ground, mortally wounded, prompted Arthur to call the retreat. Many of the enemy had been killed in the first attack, but Arthur too had lost more men than he had expected in the ferocious fighting. Neither side could declare a victory and Arthur withdrew Geraint's heroic troop to Venta while the Saxons looked to their wounded and prepared a funeral pyre for the dead.

The sudden loss of Geraint shocked Arthur to the core of his being. They had charged into battle side by side, Geraint's golden circlet glinting in the sunlight; but now this gallant warrior was resting in a cold grave beneath a mound in the grassy dunes close to Portus Ardaoni. The death of this young nobleman was a tragic loss to Arthur and all his compatriots.

In Venta's fortress the soldiers were in sombre mood. More than thirty of the squadron had lost their lives in the battle. A few of the blood-stained bodies, strapped to their mounts, had been brought back to the fort; with a simple ceremony, they were buried in the verge of the north-east rampart, in sight of the orchard with its apple blossom in full array. Arthur rode away, descending the steep escarpment towards the river Itchen that ran through the valley close to the fort. He sought solace in a small monastic chapel that stood alone in a meadow by the stream. In his grief, Arthur knelt before the small stone altar and prayed for the soul of Geraint. His mixed feelings of guilt for leading him to his death and the overbearing responsibility of his role as Commander in Chief in a bloody and unrelenting war on all fronts, overwhelmed him; but in his heart Arthur knew that he had been chosen to champion the cause of Christian freedom and to save his country from heathen invaders. Arthur prayed aloud:

*"Dear Lord, give me the strength to bear this cross; for this cross I bear for Britain."*

As Arthur came out of the chapel the sun broke through rainclouds and a wide rainbow arched brightly across the eastern sky. Arthur's spirit lifted: if this was a sign that God had heard his prayer, then he would give his life, his all, to the battles ahead and to the Christian cause.

᠅᠅᠅᠅᠅

Calleva Atrebatum, Silchester, the 'woodland town' of the Atrebates was listed by ancient writers and named on an inscription found in the ruins of the Roman city. Soon after Caesar had conquered their Belgic homeland around Arras, the Atrebates people emigrated from northern Gaul to Britain. Under the leadership of Commius their king, they chose to settle in a fortunate place that had a natural defensive advantage and a plentiful supply of water; here they established a thriving agricultural community and maintained their prosperous trading links with Gaul.

But eventually, by the third century, the Romans caught-up with the Atrebates and embarked on a massive project to re-fortify their town, building a stone wall defence that enclosed the central area of the original settlement. The city walls were over nine feet thick at the base and along the inside face, projections were built at intervals to locate wooden steps up to the parapet-walk some twenty-five feet above the ground. At the cardinal points, four main gates gave access to the city. The more important gates to the east and west had twin arched portals with guard-rooms on each side, for through these gates ran the main road from London to the west-country and Wales. The road north to Dorchester, beyond Wallingford, and south to Winchester and Chichester had gateways with only a single arched portal, but they were deeply recessed to give a defensive advantage.

Compared to Wroxeter, at less than half the area, Calleva was a Roman city in miniature, yet it had all the features and facilities attributed to the greater civitates; these included a forum and basilica, baths and temples, as well as an amphitheatre designed to seat over 3500 people, where bear-baiting, wrestling and seasonal festivals entertained the people. The forum became the hub of the city, having an open square lined with porticos, shops and offices on three sides with an impressive main entrance designed as a triumphal archway. The basilica, or town-hall, enclosed the fourth side of the square; its great hall featured raised tribunals at each end for the dispensation of Roman justice, and on the west side was the marble-lined curia, or council chamber.

In the Temple Precinct close to the east gate were derelict temples of the old Roman pantheon that had fallen out of use following Constantine's full recognition of Christianity as the official religion of the Roman Empire in 313 AD. Confirmation of Christian worship at Calleva was revealed in the late nineteenth century, when archaeologists unearthed the foundations of a small church close to the south-east corner of the forum; measuring only 42 x 32 feet, the church fulfilled the Romanesque design with a nave, a western apse featuring a chequered mosaic pavement, and a wide entrance hall. Perhaps this very small church reflected the limited resources available to its builders and the fact that Christians were still very much a minority in fourth century Britain; even so, in common with other early churches, Calleva's tiny church faced west, paying obeisance to the holiest sanctuary of St Mary's Church at Glastonbury.

By the mid-fifth century the dwindling population of Calleva was accelerated by the threat of being overwhelmed by the Saxons, so that by the end of the century the town had been practically abandoned; only the stalwarts remained, reluctant to leave their farms and houses, assets gleaned from a lifetime of hard work and sacrifice. Arthur's unexpected military occupation of Calleva would have given some reassurance to those who had remained firmly attached to their smallholdings, for the army's presence not only guaranteed their security, but also gave employment and income for those willing to serve the army and provide for the needs of horses and men.

The forum and basilica became the centre of military activity, while Arthur established his headquarters in the council chamber. A large inn by the south gate was re-commissioned to accommodate soldiers, although most of the men pitched their tents in the open. Arthur, Cei and Cadwy requisitioned a large abandoned courtyard house and made the best of the deteriorating accommodation.

For Arthur, the new year brought nothing more than the prospect of a renewed battle campaign against the Saxons in the south-east of Britain. Ochta and his war-band had been severely punished at the last battle of Blackwater, but to remove the threat of their recovery Arthur needed to mount an offensive that would take the war to Ochta's doorstep and rout the fox in his lair. British scouts returned from their reconnaissance of the enemy's position, reporting that Ochta had secured and refortified Caesar's Camp and continued to train young recruits who had recently arrived from Friesland and Saxony.

Siege warfare required a different tactical approach to the open battlefield warfare for which the British cavalry were so well trained. To attack a fortified camp with strong gates and a timber palisade some twenty feet high, Arthur would have to break into the fort with battering rams before his cavalry could be effectively employed against the enemy within. The Roman army's siege strategy demanded the use of heavy weapons including horse-drawn siege-engines or wheeled towers that enabled soldiers to reach the height of the enemy battlements; catapultii, huge catapults that projected stone missiles and fireballs; and horse-drawn battering rams that were employed to break through iron-barred city gates.

Arthur rejected the idea of using siege engines and catapults, for his battle-plan depended on a swift attack; these out-dated instruments of war were too slow and cumbersome to combine with a fast cavalry advance. But Arthur would need battering rams to break into the fort. At Calleva preparations for battle were in full swing, with every available carpenter and wainwright set to work on the manufacture of mobile battering rams to a simple design based on a four-wheeled chassis, with a timber frame to hold the ram that arrived in the shape of a pine trunk cut from the nearby forest, mounted in the centre and lashed securely with rope. Pulled by a pair of strong horses, the rams could be moved quickly to the battlefront and manoeuvred into position for soldiers to make their final assault.

Arthur held fast to his belief that the element of surprise would give him the best tactical advantage in open warfare. His greatest concern for the next battle was to bring the battering rams into position without alerting the enemy, and for this reason he decided to attack Caesar's camp before dawn. At his soldiers' suggestion, the horses' hooves and the wheels of the rams would be bound with sack-cloth and leather to make their approach along the roughly cobbled road as silent as possible. Then, turning north, the final mile would take them through forest and open heathland to the gates of Ochta's compound.

In the early hours of the morning, Arthur moved his three cavalry squadrons through the city's east gate and onto the Devil's Highway towards the river Blackwater, then silently into the forest that surrounded Ochta's stronghold. Arthur led the attack, charging out of the forest from the east, having anticipated that Ochta would have prepared his defences for an attack from the west. Arthur's unexpected arrival caused panic in the Saxon camp as Ochta sounded the alarm and ordered his warriors to mount the ramparts to repel the British troops; but as Arthur's squadron took the brunt of the Saxon's spears, battering rams broke through the south gates of the fort allowing Cadwy's troop to burst through into the compound.

Just as Arthur had planned, his bluff attack from the east had drawn the full attention of the enemy, whose backs were now exposed to the spears of the second cavalry troop. Then Cei's squadron swiftly followed with the next onslaught: spears found their targets, swords swept away heads and flailing limbs of young Saxon foot-soldiers desperately challenging their mounted assailants, whose powerful battle-horses charged and trampled the defenders before disappearing into the forest. Arthur regrouped his squadron and charged through the south-gate to make a final sweep through the camp, torching their tents and the thatched roofs of dwelling houses and military workshops.

Compared to the first battle, Arthur's third attempt to dislodge Ochta and his war-band from their encampment by the river Blackwater delivered a more powerful blow that crippled the Saxon army for many months. Once again Ochta had been taken by surprise; Arthur had successfully broken into his fortified stronghold and brought to bear upon the enemy the full might of his fast and powerful British cavalry.

In the days that followed Arthur's third victory on the Blackwater front, Ochta had no way of knowing whether or not Arthur was present at Calleva, for the city walls were so secure that they kept secret the number of soldiers and citizens within. Thus by maintaining a garrison of one squadron of cavalry to patrol the Blackwater valley during the day, and guard the city at night, Arthur was able to effect a strategic withdrawal with Ochta none the wiser; he returned with his own troop to Camulodunum and Cei moved his squadron to Lincoln. This move, albeit a temporary measure, restored a military presence to the eastern front, while Cadwy maintained the garrison at Calleva.

But Ochta was now beginning to match Arthur's clever tactics with his own Germanic cunning. Unknown to Arthur's scouts, Ochta had concealed a detachment of recruits in the rough sandy scrubland only three miles south of Caesar's Camp; here at Sandhurst his embryo army had been training secretly during the day and digging-in for the night in shallow sandy trenches covered over with pine branches, the forest's natural camouflage. Within twelve months, these young men would be fully trained and ready for battle.

༄ ༄ ఌ ఌ

To make a significant advance into Britain, Ochta would have to overcome Arthur's forward base at Calleva Atrebatum, for the city stood directly in his intended path to the west; but Ochta's options were limited: he would either have to take Calleva by force, or route-march north or south of the city. He realised that to lay siege to Calleva would be to invite disaster, for his army was not strong enough to blockade a fortified city and he feared the swift vengeance of British cavalry troops, who would charge in to decimate the flanks of his force. But whichever route he took, Ochta knew that he would eventually have to face Arthur for a decisive battle. If the Saxons were to conquer Britain, they would have to beat Arthur first, challenging his powerful equestrian warriors with their own axe-wielding soldiers.

After three battles in as many years, Ochta again needed to rebuild his army. He had suffered serious losses of three to one against the Britons; for the remotest chance of victory he would need to muster at least nine hundred men. It would take him another year to recover. Survivors of the last battle formed an experienced core of warriors who would train the diminishing number of recruits coming in from Saxony, and to boost numbers further, Ochta appealed to Aelle, leader of the south Saxons who had settled in the region of the South Downs in East Sussex.

At first Aelle was reluctant send his warriors to reinforce Ochta's army because he had secured a settlement treaty with the British overlord of Noviomagnus Regnorum, the city of Chichester. A warlike act against Arthur would bring vengeance upon his small southern kingdom; but Ochta's determination to win new territory and his promise to reward Aelle with new lands proved a persuasive argument. Aelle agreed to send ninety warriors to reinforce Ochta's army, but they would have to travel north in small groups at night to avoid alerting British scouts.

Ochta had learned from the bitter experience of the Blackwater battles: he was now wary of marching his men in one large war-band into a constricted area before fording a river; moreover he had also realised the folly of billeting his force in one military base. He therefore decided to establish three separate camps: first his battle headquarters would remain at Caesar's Camp, secondly, the training squadron would be based at Sandhurst, and Aelle's men would make the third encampment in the rough heathland two miles east of the river Blackwater in the area known as Deepcut.

Ochta's battle-plan called for each unit to advance directly to the west, crossing the Blackwater at three separate points. Each troop would then advance five miles to converge at a rendezvous position in open ground to the west of the river. From here, Ochta planned to advance in a south-westerly direction, steering his army to the south of Calleva to avoid Arthur's cavalry, and then turning north-west towards his primary target, Roman Corinium, the city of Cirencester. It was an ambitious plan, but to take this city as his prize, Ochta would have to cut a swathe fifty miles deep into hostile territory in a high-risk campaign that would be more of a gamble than a well-considered military strategy, for he faced a mobile enemy who would not be sitting on their haunches, nor patiently awaiting his arrival at the gates of Cirencester.

In fact, Arthur's men were far from idle. Cadwy's squadron patrolled the Blackwater front from the Loddon Valley in the north to Caesar's Camp, by Farnham, in the south. Vigilant scouts had observed signs of activity near the Blackwater ford in the area of Chobham Ridges: smoke from evening camp fires was seen rising where before the air had been clear, and small numbers of young Saxon men had been seen fishing and swimming in the river Blackwater.

Arthur reckoned that it would take Ochta more than a year to recover from the last battle, but these apparently insignificant signs of increased activity on the Blackwater front alerted him to the possibility that the Saxons were once again close to launching another strike into British territory. Arthur decided that it was time to bring Calleva's garrison up to full strength: he immediately re-called the squadrons from the eastern front and moved the reserve troops from Venta to Calleva, replacing them in turn with fifty newly-trained recruits from Wroxeter.

The fourth battle of Blackwater began by chance, when a British cavalry patrol moving north from Farnham ran into Aelle's small band of young warriors as they were advancing towards the ford at Blackwater. The British troop commander promptly ordered a scout to Calleva to warn Arthur; then, dividing his cavalry into two sections of fifteen horse, he charged towards the Saxons. The opposing forces clashed in mid-stream; heavy battle-horses met the enemy ranks as they waded across the fast flowing stream. Britons wielding cold-steel swords and thrusting elm-shafted spears with brutal force pierced the first wave of warriors. Aelle's men put up a valiant fight, over-confident in the knowledge that they out-numbered the British by three to one. In the close quarter fighting horses were felled, their riders plunging headlong to their fate, dispatched by Saxon axes; but when the second wave of cavalry charged into the flanks of the skirmish, British horsepower prevailed and Prince Cadwy's men beat the Saxons into retreat, leaving the bodies of their comrades ebbing into the blood-stained stream-water. A few battle-shocked surviviors dragged the seriously wounded back to their Deepcut camp.

Unknown to Ochta, in the time taken to march his men from Caesar's camp to the river Blackwater, his South Saxon allies had been intercepted and disabled; but as he ordered his war-band to wade across the Blackwater on a wide front near Warbrook, his newly trained recruits were crossing the river four miles to the south.

At battle-readiness, Arthur's squadron was the first to gallop through Calleva's eastern gateway, cutting across country by the hamlet of Stratfield Saye into the Bramshill pine forest, following rough tracks that led towards the river Blackwater. Cei's squadron followed, moving fast along the Devil's Highway to the north, while Cadwy followed Arthur, heading towards the river Blackwater with a squadron of recruits.

As Ochta wheeled his army south towards the rendezvous point near the Blackwater, Arthur's squadron charged out of the pine-forest, appearing out of the early morning mist as if by magic. With a sharp battle-cry Arthur charged into the enemy host's right flank, cutting, thrusting, killing every opponent in his path; he held the momentum of the charge as his cavalry swept through the floundering ranks of Saxons. Suddenly finding himself in the centre of an enemy throng over five-hundred strong, Arthur realised that his impetuous charge could end in disaster: his single troop was seriously out-numbered by a seething mass of axe-wielding infantry, and in order to survive he had to keep his cavalry moving at all costs. Calling his men to regroup, he cut a swathe through the host towards the edge of the pine-forest.

Arthur's gallant charge and swift reprise cut a trail of wounded and dying men through the Saxon host; but this skirmish with the British cavalry spurred Ochta to push further south to join his reinforcements and bring his army to full strength; but just as Ochta moved his vanguard towards the river, Cei appeared from the north, ploughing his troop into the rearmost ranks of the Saxons: fear showed in their faces as the rear-guard turned to defend their leader against Cei's cavalry attack. Then, to Ochta's great relief he saw that his corps of young recruits had crossed the river and were moving towards the meeting point to the west; but there was no sign of Aelle's warriors, and Ochta cursed, swearing because he thought they had deserted him at the last minute.

Suddenly the sound of charging horses filled the misty morning air as Prince Cadwy led his squadron in from the south for their first encounter with the enemy. Petrified by the onslaught of heavy battle-horses the Saxon recruits, some only fifteen or sixteen years of age, fell back towards the river. Sadly their short period of training had not equipped them for close quarter cavalry warfare and many of them succumbed to their fate at the hands of Cadwy's young lancers. The second wave of Cadwy's cavalry devastated the corps of Ochta's recruits, some of them even cut-down as they reached the reeds by the riverbank. The dead and dying lay strewn across the battlefield. With a shrill horn-blast, Cadwy called his men away, allowing a small remnant of the enemy band to swim to the safety of the eastern shore, where they disappeared into the reeded thickets, thanking Woden for sparing their lives.

Ochta's army had been split in two: the rear-guard fell to the ruthless attack of Cei's battle-hardened warriors; even the Saxons who escaped from the field were hunted down, their bodies shafted from behind as they ran for the cover of Ravenswood and Crowthorne where they were left to rot, pickings for ravens and crows, the vultures of battle.

Ochta was horrified to see his recruits decimated before his eyes, but his horror turned to shock as he found himself suddenly surrounded by British cavalry, with Cadwy confronting him, Cei to his rear and Arthur on his right flank; Ochta had no option but to stand and fight.

On Arthur's signal all three squadrons advanced together, first at the trot, then at the gallop, reined in only when the cavalry were confronted by Ochta's semi-circular wall of Saxon shields and spears more than three rows deep, that appeared like a writhing monster before the dark waters of the Blackwater.

As the first wave of cavalry was rebuffed, the second line charged into the massive shield wall that shivered from the shock of thrusting lances. Arthur, now repositioned for another attack, led the third wave of mounted warriors in a powerful charge that pierced the centre of the shield wall, opening a pathway into the heart of the Saxon battle monster, and as more and more of the heavy horses broke through, the shield formation disintegrated: now it was every man for himself in the fierce hand to hand fighting that followed. Suddenly, Arthur came face to face with Ochta in the very centre of the battle arena. Ochta fought like a devil, slashing angrily at Arthur with his sword in his right hand, his axe in the other. Arthur deftly parried his blows, but was swept forward in the swirling throng of horses and blood-stained men. Slowly, relentlessly, the Britons pressed forward until the ranks of Saxon dead outnumbered the ranks of the living; as they gave ground, Ochta and his men were forced back to the very edge of the riverbank.

By noon the battle was won. The remnant of the enemy host was forced into the bloody waters of the river; some swam for their lives, others ran towards the cover of Sandhurst forest. The Britons recovered the wounded and took their rightful spoils of war: dead warriors were stripped of their gold and silver rings, their swords and shields now trophies of the victors. Arthur, for his second battle trophy, drew a maginificent sword from a fallen Saxon commander.

Arthur thanked God for his victory, for not just a battle, but a war had been won on this day. He led the weary survivors of his army back to Calleva in triumph and called for a feast to be prepared to celebrate this great British victory over the Saxons. In the courtyard of the old Roman forum, spit-roasts were readied and with a plentiful supply of mead, all made merry into the night. In celebration, his warriors, some still bloodied from the battle, carried Arthur shoulder high around the square, then with a great cheer, they presented him with a simple torque of bright twisted gold. "For this treasured gift, for your loyalty, your courage, and your love, I thank you most sincerely" replied Arthur, proudly securing the gold band around his neck.

## CHAPTER 6

# A ROMAN WEDDING

*"Shall I compare thee to a summer's day?*
*Thou art more lovely and more temperate:*
*Rough winds do shake the darling buds of May,*
*And summer's lease hath all too short a date:*
*Sometime too hot the eye of heaven shines,*
*And often is his gold complexion dimm'd;*
*But thy eternal summer shall not fade*
*Nor lose possession of that fair thou ow'st."*
William Shakespeare

The citizens lined the streets of Venta, Winchester, to welcome Arthur and his warriors on their return from Calleva Atrebatum; the people had all played a part in helping Arthur to win four battles against the Saxons at Blackwater and they joined in the victory celebrations with new-found pride. All the town and country-folk had gathered for the festivities in the market-square, where home-made fare was displayed on trestle tables that had been overhung with brightly coloured awnings for the occasion; hungry soldiers were soon mingling with their hosts, the people of Venta, enjoying spit-roast pork and game, and quaffing strong Celtic ale.

Arthur, Cei and Prince Cadwy joined in the celebrations, honoured to have received such a warm welcome from the people; but for Arthur, the jollity of the occasion was tinged with sadness, for he could not forget that it was at Winchester that Ambrosius Aurelianus had been taken ill. Rumours still abounded that he had been poisoned by a Saxon infiltrator, but it was just as likely that he had contracted an infection from the city's polluted water supply. Concerned for the safety of the populace, Arthur set his recruits to work to repair the drains and sluice gates during their tour of duty at Venta.

Victory celebrations went on well into the night, until all the food and ale had been consumed by the revellers. Arthur found himself leading a disorderly procession of inebriated soldiers, singing at the top of their voices and brandishing their flaming torches at the moon as they climbed the steep track to the summit of the hillfort.

Early next morning Arthur roused his weary troops and gave the order to break camp: he intended to return to Wroxeter with Cei, where he would reward his warriors with a period of recovery leave, and ensure the continued training of new recruits who would eventually replace the soldiers lost in battle.

But prince Cadwy had other plans for Arthur: "Come back with us to Dumnonia where you can enjoy our hospitality; come fishing and forget the war for a while."

"I wish I could come with you," replied Arthur, but military affairs demand my attention; we must keep our guard."

"Go Arthur," shouted Cei, "go with Cadwy while you may. This peace may be short-lived, but while it lasts I will keep guard at Wroxeter on your behalf."

"Very well," said Arthur, "Cei, my stalwart friend, you are right; and I am battle weary."

"Enjoy your fishing!" exclaimed Cei as he wheeled his mount around to lead the troops back to Wroxeter.

South Cadbury Castle, Somerset. Renowned for centuries as the legendary site of King Arthur's Camelot, this bastion of Arthur's Britain protected Dumnonia from marauding Saxons attacking from the east. Refortified in Arthur's lifetime, the fortress was defended by four formidable ramparts with steep escarpments and deep ditches, and boasted a feasting hall large enough to accommodate a powerful military leader with a cavalry force of skilled warriors.

Photo, © Jim Eastaugh

The massive defences of Caer Cadarn's ramparts were silhouetted against the western sky when prince Cadwy and Arthur led their weary warriors up the steep track towards the eastern gateway. *"Who goes there?"* shouted the gate guardian.

*"It is Cadwy with Arthur and a brave company of warriors returned from Calleva."* *"Welcome my lords,"* replied the guard; suddenly the great oak gates swung open, allowing the commanders and their cavalry into the spacious compound of the fortress.

The noon-day sun greeted Arthur when he emerged from Cadwy's spacious roundhouse, having spent a long night locked in an endless nightmare of unrelenting pitched battle. *"Come Arthur,"* called Prince Cadwy, *"our mounts are ready, and now we shall go fishing for our supper."*

Cadwy and Arthur mounted their chestnut stallions and cantered down the narrow cobbled street to the western gateway. On Cadwy's command the gate-guards swung open the outer gates, and as the riders passed through the gate-tower they reined in their mounts, anticipating the sudden steep descent down to the level ground several hundred feet below the fortress.

In the distance they could see the river Camel meandering through meadows, but as they turned west towards the river, a young noblewoman approached on horseback, accompanied by her maidservant and a groom, crossing Cadwy's path as she took the bridleway to Caer Cadarn.

*"Come and join us for a dip in the cool stream waters!"* Cadwy taunted. *"I cannot,"* replied the young lady, *"for my father has called me to the fortress to tend your wounded soldiers."*

Arthur caught her eye and smiled, admiring her dedication to duty; then, in an instant, he caught his breath, transfixed by her golden hair and her perfect features; she was a vision of natural beauty. For a moment Arthur was unsure whether he had encountered a real person or a goddess. Without further hesitation the young lady turned from Arthur's gaze, spurred her dappled grey mare, and with a cursory *"Good day, my lords,"* cantered away towards Caer Cadarn.

Cadwy and Arthur rode off in the opposite direction until they reached the hamlet of Chilton Cantelo; close by, they found a calm stretch of the river Yeo shaded by willow trees. *"This is the best spot for miles; here we can spear salmon as they leap upstream,"* Cadwy shouted.

But Arthur was lost in a world of his own thoughts. *"Who was the beautiful young lady who crossed our path?"* he asked, unable to hide his interest any longer. *"She is the youngest daughter of my surgeon Ambrose who lives over at Sutton Montis, just half a mile from the fortress,"* replied Cadwy. *"And her name?"* enquired Arthur, persistently. *"I will introduce you at our festivities this very evening,"* promised Cadwy, *"but first you must gaff a salmon for our supper."*

Woodsmoke from the camp-fires greeted Cadwy and Arthur when they returned to Caer Cadarn with their catch of salmon and brown trout; the fish were well received by the cooks who had already prepared venison and wild pork for the feast. At dusk the youngest warriors lit the torches that hung from the walls and timber pillars of the great feasting hall; sturdy oak table-tops were set upon trestles, and benches were brought out for the guests.

Prince Cadwy invited Arthur to take the seat of honour on his right hand side, next to Ambrose and his wife Celemon, and their eldest daughter Gwenhwyfach, while his commanders and their wives took their places in turn. Then as Cadwy's warriors entered the hall, jugs of ale and mead were passed around, while roast meats and steamed fish were served to each table. When all were seated, a young woman with golden tresses sang to the accompaniment of a cittern:

> "Universal mother, famed Demeter, august, the source of wealth,
> great nurse, all bounteous, blessed and divine, who joyest in peace;
> to nourish corn is thine, Goddess of seed, of fruits abundant, fair,
> harvest and threshing are thy constant care.
> Nurse of all mortals, who gave to men what nature's wants require,
> with plenteous means of bliss which all desire.
> Hail Goddess! Come with summer's rich increase,
> swelling and pregnant, leading smiling peace.
> Come with fair concord and keep this people in harmony and prosperity,
> and in the fields bring us all pleasant things!
> Feed our kind, bring us flocks, bring us the corn-ear, bring us harvest!
> And nurse peace, that he who sows may also reap."

Arthur was entranced, for the songstress was none other than the young lady who had crossed his path that afternoon. Her song stirred the hearts of the assembly, and when the applause had faded, Cadwy called her to take her place on the dais; he showed her to the vacant chair, opposite Arthur.

*"Come Guinevere, Arthur has been longing to meet you,"* he called, *"Arthur, here is Guinevere, our delightful songstress."* Arthur took Guinevere's right hand and lightly kissed it. *"You have the voice of an angel,"* he said softly. *"You honour me, sire,"* she replied.

Ambrose turned to Arthur, *"Today I have repaired the wounds of nine battle-scarred soldiers,"* he said, *"and now Guinevere has the task of nursing them back to health."* *"Ready for the next battle?"* asked Arthur.

*"Yes,"* replied Guinevere, *"but this war has been relentless, and we so long for peace."*

*"Will your victory secure a lasting peace?"* asked Ambrose.

*"Perhaps,"* said Arthur, with a non-committal gesture; *"at least until our next enemy rears his head. God willing, a year or two without a battle would give us all a chance to recover,"* added Arthur, looking deeply into Guinevere's eyes.

*"Prince Cadwy tells me that you live in a Roman villa,"* said Arthur. *"Yes, at Sutton Montis, where we are surrounded by orchards. In the spring we enjoy the heavenly blossom and* in *the autumn we reap a harvest of rosy apples,"* Guinevere replied.

*"Have you lived there long?"* asked Arthur. *"The villa has been in our family for well over a century,"* Ambrose replied. *"We come from a Roman family,"* said Guinevere.

*"And we have escaped the scourge of the Saxons because we are hidden amongst our apple trees,"* Ambrose added. *"You have been fortunate,"* said Arthur, *"for so many of our beautiful villas have been destroyed."*

*"Please come and visit us while you are here,"* suggested Ambrose. *"It would be a great pleasure,"* Arthur replied, as he gazed admiringly at Guinevere's radiant beauty.

The next morning, nineteen of Cadwy's wounded warriors arrived from Venta, where they had rested for a while after the battle of Blackwater. Cadwy and Arthur went out to the eastern gate to greet the wounded and to help them from their carts into the infirmary, where Ambrose cauterized and stitched their wounds; Guinevere and her young nurses applied healing ointments and bandages, and gave each weary warrior a helping of meaty broth and freshly made oatmeal bread.

While Cadwy gave words of encouragement to his men, Arthur watched Guinevere's every move, admiring how she galvanised the nurses into action and carefully tended the seriously wounded soldiers.

*"Arthur, help me please!"* cried Guinevere suddenly, *"Hold this tourniquet for me. This young man is bleeding profusely and we'll lose him if we don't close his wound."* Arthur twisted the linen tourniquet tightly around the soldier's upper arm while Guinevere bandaged his open wound. *"Thank you for saving me!"* cried the young warrior. *"You'll live to fight another day,"* said Arthur, encouragingly.

Ambrose caught Arthur as he was leaving the infirmary, *"Come and join us for supper. Guinevere will ride with you down to the villa."* *"That's very kind of you Ambrose,"* said Arthur, *"I shall look forward to this evening; thank you for asking me."*

At sunset Arthur and Guinevere rode together towards the south-western gateway of Caer Cadarn: as they approached, four soldiers ran from their small guardroom to open the inner and outer gates of the fortress. Passing through the gate-tower, Guinevere turned sharply to her right, reining-in her mount to descend the steep trackway between the ramparts. Arthur held back until they had reached the open fields below the fortress; he drew level with Guinevere as she allowed her mount to drink from a clear freshwater spring that flowed freely over the ripening corn.

This illustration shows a reconstruction of the south-west gateway to South Cadbury Castle as it would have appeared after the complete rebuilding of the defences in the Arthurian period.                                                                        © Eric Walmsley

*"That's our villa,"* said Guinevere, pointing ahead, *"just beyond the orchard."* *"So you are only a stone's throw from the fort!"* exclaimed Arthur in surprise, *"and you are so close to the chapel."*

Guinevere cantered ahead of Arthur, fording a small stream and scattering chickens, sheep and cows that were grazing peacefully in the orchard; but as she turned onto the lane that led through the small hamlet of Sutton Montis, Arthur caught up with her, and together they rode through the gated archway of the villa. Bridling their mounts in the courtyard, they dismounted and passed the reins to the stable boys.

*"As you can see from the old barns and stables, it's more of a farm than a villa,"* Guinevere explained, *"my father employs most of the villeins to gather the wheat and apples at harvest time."* *"So who buys your corn?"* asked Arthur. *"Prince Cadwy,"* Guinevere replied, *"most of it goes up to the fortress to make bread for the soldiers and to feed the battle-horses."*

Ambrose and his wife Celemon welcomed Arthur to the villa with a glass of fine Burgundy wine, while their cook prepared the trout caught by Ambrose from a stream that ran through the meadows beyond the orchard. Soon the appetising smell of fish grilling over a charcoal fire wafted through the villa; when supper was ready the cook rang a small bronze bell and the housemaid served the trout with a fish sauce together with freshly picked peas and cabbage from the vegetable garden.

Ambrose waited for Guinevere and her sister Gwenhwyfach to join them in the dining-room before saying grace, "*Benedictus benedicat,*" he said, asking the Blessed One to bless their food, before serving Arthur his honoured guest.

"*In the summer we enjoy the plentiful benefits of the countryside,*" said Ambrose. "*Indeed,*" said Arthur, "*I see that you have a well tended vegetable garden; and you are surrounded by cornfields.*"

"*With God's grace we shall have a good harvest,*" said Celemon, "*and enough grain to store so that Cadwy's warriors can enjoy their daily bread through the winter months.*"

"*Some of the old grain-pits in the fort have gone sour,*" said Guinevere. "*And they keep having to dig new pits to store the emergency supplies,*" added Gwenhwyfach.

"*So this must be a quiet time for you, before the harvest,*" Arthur remarked. "*Yes it is,*" agreed Ambrose. "*Except for all the wounded warriors who come back from your battles,*" interjected Guinevere, sharply.

Arthur was surprised by her outspoken remark, but he answered her promptly. "*That is the high price that some of our soldiers have to pay for fighting for the freedom of our country.*" "*Sadly,*" said Guinevere.

"*Sadly,*" repeated Arthur, "*some of our brave warriors pay the highest price: they sacrifice their lives to Saxon swords and axes for the people of Britain!*" exclaimed Arthur, looking sternly at Guinevere as he spoke.

"*I'm so sorry Arthur,*" said Celemon, "*I'm sure my daughter did not mean to make you angry. Guinevere has been overwhelmed with so many wounded after the recent battles.*"

"*Arthur, you must count yourself lucky to have survived five battles,*" Ambrose remarked. "*Yes, you are lucky!*" exclaimed Gwenhwyfach, echoing her father's words.

"*It's not just luck!*" Arthur exclaimed sternly. "*Most of a battle is brute force and bravado; but at the same time you have to keep your wits about you. It was our great commander Ambrosius Aurelianus who taught me to outwit the enemy before the battle began,*" explained Arthur. "*Above all, it is intelligent strategic planning applied with intuitive tactics on the battlefield that wins the day.*"

"*And your stamina,*" added Guinevere, with an admiring glance at Arthur. "*Of course,*" agreed Arthur, "*every warrior has to keep fit and ready for battle.*"

Celemon invited Arthur to try some fresh plums followed by home-made cheeses; and when they had finished the meal, Ambrose gave thanks with the closing grace, *"Benedicto benedicatur,"* *"Amen,"* they responded in unison.

*"And now Ambrose and Celemon, my kind hosts, I thank you for a delicious supper, and I drink to your health and good fortune."* Arthur raised his glass, *"And to you young nurses, I wish you patience and fortitude in your arduous, but very necessary task of helping our soldiers recover from their wounds."*

*"And now I must return to Caer Cadarn,"* said Arthur. *"But it is late,"* Ambrose replied, *"please stay with us tonight."* *"Very well Ambrose, I will accept your kind offer,"* said Arthur.

*"Gwenhwyfach, please show Arthur to our guest-room,"* said Celemon courteously.

*"I will,"* said Guinevere briskly, taking hold of a nearby oil-lamp and leading Arthur up the stairs to his bed-chamber. *"I'm sorry if I made you angry,"* she said softly to Arthur.

*"Only Saxons make me angry!"* Arthur exclaimed, with a warm smile; then gently brushing aside her hair, he kissed her softly on the cheek, *"Goodnight Guinevere."* *"Sleep well, Arthur,"* she replied.

That night no-one slept more soundly than Arthur; still weary from battle, and enveloped in a soft duck-down palliasse, Arthur was locked in deep slumber until the afternoon sun shone through his window and broke his dreams.

It was Sunday, and Ambrose had attended a simple service of prayer and thanksgiving with his family in the small chapel next to the villa.

*"We didn't wake you this morning as we thought that you deserved a good rest,"* said Guinevere when Arthur appeared at the kitchen doorway. *"Have some breakfast,"* she said, offering Arthur a bowl of fruit and a small loaf of freshly baked bread from the hot oven. While Arthur broke a generous piece of bread, Guinevere used the kitchen water-pump to draw some fresh springwater from the storage tank below the floor-boards.

*"Is the water pure?"* asked Arthur. *"Yes,"* replied Guinevere, *"we have a natural spring in the orchard, and we fill our tank with its pure water; do try some,"* and she offered Arthur a glass of clear water. *"I'm sorry that I could not join you for your Sunday thanksgiving service,"* said Arthur apologetically, *"is there time for me to have a look inside the chapel?"* *"Come with me,"* said Guinevere, *"and I will show you our little church."*

*"Father is very proud of his chapel,"* said Guinevere, as she ushered Arthur into the porch and opened the sturdy iron-studded oak door that was framed with a simple Romanesque arch made from local sandstone. *"Did the villagers help to build the chapel?"* Arthur enquired. *"Yes, but Prince Cadwy took a great interest and even sent a team of his warriors to help with the building work."*

Arthur followed Guinevere into the nave where a circular stone font containing hallowed water stood upon a chequered mosaic floor. A simple wall painting that depicted the head of Christ caught Arthur's attention; framed with a roundel that had a carefully painted scroll pattern, the portrait made a focal point behind the altar.

*"Who painted this?"* asked Arthur. *"Well, it was my idea,"* Guinevere replied, *"but I must admit, I took the centre-piece from a beautiful mosaic floor in a friend's villa at Hinton Saint Mary. You wouldn't believe that the original Roman mosaic is over one hundred and fifty years old, because it looks as pristine as the day it was made."*

*"I think you are very talented,"* Arthur remarked, *"but what are all these apples doing in the painting?"* *"They're meant to be pomegranets!"* exclaimed Guinevere, laughing at Arthur; *"pomegranates are associated with Persephone in Greek mythology; she is the daughter of Demeter, goddess of fruits and the corn harvest. Persephone is the seed of corn that spends one third of the year in the ground; she rises to meet her mother at harvest-time, bestowing the fruits of the earth upon mankind."*

*"Isn't the pomegranet a pagan symbol?"* asked Arthur. *"Yes, but its symbolism is understood by Christians to represent the resurrection of Christ,"* Guinevere paused for a moment's thought, *"and the pomegranet also symbolizes chastity,"* she added wistfully.

*"So the painting shows Christ blessing the harvest,"* observed Arthur. *"And it reminds us to pray for a fruitful harvest,"* added Guinevere.

A ray of afternoon sunlight beamed through the small circular window in the western apse, reflecting in the Celtic silver cross that stood on the altar. *"It is very peaceful here,"* said Arthur. *"It is a very special place; and in our quiet moments we feel God's presence here,"* said Guinevere sincerely, looking into Arthur's eyes. He took Guinevere's hand and led her back to the porch.

*"You are a very special person,"* said Arthur quietly, *"I am so glad that we met here at* Caer Cadarn." *"So am I,"* said Guinevere, her voice trembling, as Arthur pulled her closer and kissed her cheek; and as she succumbed to his strong embrace, they kissed each other, softly at first, and then passionately, until Arthur whirled Guinevere around in his arms, *"I love you deeply Guinevere,"* he said softly in her ear." *"And I love you, Arthur,"* she replied, *"and I seal it with a kiss."*

Arm in arm they walked from the chapel through the adjoining orchard and along a pathway that led through a natural avenue of apple trees to the pasture-land on the western edge of the village. *"Look at those magnificent hills!"* Arthur exclaimed. *"That is Corton Ridge, between the two peaks, it's my favourite ride; let's saddle the horses and I'll take you there,"* Guinevere suggested with excitement.

Exhilarated after the steep climb to the top of the ridge, Guinevere raced into the sun, with her golden tresses streaming in the wind; with Arthur chasing alongside her at the gallop, she was elated and happy. Together they rode along the crest of the ridge, spurring their mounts for almost a mile; they felt as if they were on top of the world. Guinevere pointed towards Glastonbury on the north-western horizon: *"Look Arthur, you can see the Tor!"* she exclaimed. *"It seems to be pointing to the place where the sun will set,"* said Arthur. And Guinevere quickly responded, *"Let us stay here for a while and watch the sun set on our wonderful day."*

They returned to the villa at dusk. Arthur bade farewell to Ambrose and Celemon and thanked them for their kind hospitality. *"Come and stay with us again soon,"* said Ambrose. *"Thank you! I will, replied Arthur, but military matters call for my attention and Price Cadwy and I have much to discuss before I return to Powys,"* said Arthur.

*"Will I see you tomorrow?"* asked Guinevere. *"Hopefully,"* Arthur replied, and then spoke softly into her ear, *"Guinevere, thank you for a wonderful day."*

The next morning Arthur and Prince Cadwy walked round the perimeter of Caer Cadarn, inspecting the ramparts, observation towers and parapets; Cadwy then put several teams of soldiers to work to strengthen the defences, carry out repairs and clear the rubble that had accumulated in the deep ditches between the ramparts. By mid-day the camp was alive with activity: sparks flew from the blacksmith's anvil as he hammered and twisted a rod of red-hot iron that he was shaping into a new sword-blade. Grey smoke from his forge wafted through the compound where experienced craftsmen were busy making new shields and spears, and tanners were immersing animal hides in a pungent mixture of cow-dung and urine to produce leather pelts for saddles, bridles and tough leather jerkins that would protect soldiers in combat.

Cadwy, always keen to encourage local craftsmen and women, had provided small workshops where they could make everyday artifacts from local materials; potters turned earthenware jugs and cooking pots from Dumnonian clay, weavers made cloaks and winter clothing from local wool, and metal-smiths made ornamental shield bosses, brooches and clasps that were embellished with traditional Celtic scrollwork.

Cadwy and Arthur walked through the camp giving words of encouragement to the artisans whose hard work sustained this detachment of British warriors in their formidable fortress. Suddenly, short blasts on a hunting horn announced an arrival at the north-east gate of the fortress, and the two commanders returned to Cadwy's round-house to await their guest. It was a cavalry scout from Wroxeter who approached, his horse foaming at the mouth after the long ride, and Arthur sensed that his recall to duty was imminent.

The messenger brought ill tidings: the Picts had carried out a devastating raid on the borderlands to the north of Carlisle; enraged by this news, king Uther had demanded a reprisal attack against their leader Heuil and his rebellious war-band. Arthur and his commanders were summoned to Castell Dinas Bran to plan a battle campaign in the north.

*"Our battling for this year is done!"* exclaimed Arthur. *"There's nothing to be gained by marching north in winter,"* added Cadwy. *"You're right,"* agreed Arthur, *"We'll aim for an offensive in the spring, when the weather is favourable."* *"And when we have all fully recovered from Blackwater,"* Cadwy concluded.

Arthur thanked the scout and Cadwy showed him the way down to the stables and the soldiers' billets. At that moment, Arthur's heart jumped when he saw Guinevere approaching and he ran forward to greet her. *"Arthur!"* she exclaimed in surprise. *"Come inside,"* he said, taking Guinevere by the hand and pulling her into the seclusion of Cadwy's round-house.

*"Sadly I must leave Caer Cadarn,"* he said, *"the Chief Dragon has asked me to plan our next battle."* *"How long will you be away?"* asked Guinevere. *"Perhaps a month or more,"* he replied. *"I will miss you,"* said Guinevere softly. *" I lay awake all night thinking of you,"* Arthur whispered, *"I love you Guinevere, and I want you to be my wife,"* he said in ernest. *"Will you marry me?"*

*"Should you ask me on bended knee, my lord, as a true warrior would, I may consider your request,"* she replied.

Then Arthur knelt before Guinevere and cupped her hands in his own; *"Guinevere, will you marry me, and make me the happiest warrior in the kingdom?"* He looked deeply into Guinevere's eyes, *"for I truly love you."*

*"Arthur,"* she paused for a moment and smiled, raising Arthur up and drawing close to him: *"I will, I will,"* she declared, *"for I am truly in love with you."* Guinevere fell into Arthur's arms, and they embraced, locked together in a betrothal kiss that they wished would last until the end of time.

☙☙☙☙

When Arthur returned from Wroxeter one month later, he found Caer Cadarn like an island citadel towering over a sea of mellow golden corn, its shimmering surface rippled by gusts of late summer wind. Prince Cadwy had already started to gather in the harvest, and his villeins were busy shearing wheat with their sharp sickels, while children gathered sheaves of corn into stooks ready for the haycarts.

Prince Cadwy came to greet Arthur at the gateway, and they rode together into the fortress where strong mead, a hearty meal and a comfortable bed, the hallmarks of Cadwy's hospitality, awaited Arthur after his long journey. Their conversation inevitably turned to military topics; Arthur explained how he had pacified king

Uther's anger by promising to mount a reprisal attack against Heuil in the spring. This would give Arthur six months to plan for a campaign in the north, and would allow him to spend more time on matters of a romantic nature; since first meeting Guinevere he had held a vision of her radiant beauty continually in mind, and he could not wait to see her again.

Arthur and Guinevere had vowed to keep their betrothal secret until Arthur returned from Wroxeter, when he would seek Ambrose's approval and formally request his daughter's hand in marriage.

Ambrose was pleasantly surprised by Arthur's unexpected arrival at the villa so soon after his last visit, and he embraced Arthur warmly, leading him through to the garden and into the orchard beyond. When Arthur asked for Guinevere's hand in marriage, Ambrose was delighted for them both, saying that it was his privilege to welcome Arthur into his family, and that he would, in due course, negotiate the settlement of a dowry in the accepted Roman tradition; but Arthur raised his hand, politely declining Ambrose's kind offer. *"Guinevere to me is priceless,"* he said quietly. *"We will simply exchange gifts as a token of our love for each other."* *"Then we shall arrange a celebration,"* declared Ambrose.

It was Guinevere's wish to have a Roman Wedding in the true tradition of her family. At the Betrothal Ceremony, Arthur duly made a promise of marriage, and Ambrose, as the father of the bride, promised on his daughter's behalf in the presence of Prince Cadwy and Guinevere's family and friends.

Gifts were exchanged. Arthur presented Guinevere with a beautiful silver hand-mirror exquisitely etched on the reverse side with with a Celtic scroll pattern, and Guinevere gave Arthur a small black bear, cleverly carved from a piece of Newby jet. Then Arthur took Guinevere's left hand and gently placed a silver ring on her third finger, and in return, Guinevere gave Arthur a gold ring. The giving of rings sealed their betrothal, and Ambrose called on his guests to drink a toast to "Arthur and Guinevere."

*"Let me be the first to congratulate you both,"* said Prince Cadwy, embracing Guinevere and Arthur in turn. *"And have you chosen a day for the happy event of your wedding here at Sutton Montis?"* he asked.

*"Our villa will be too small to entertain all the guests,"* declared Celemon, with some concern. *"Then you are most welcome to hold the wedding feast in my hall at Caer Cadarn,"* said Cadwy, with a reassuring smile.

*"Perhaps it would be best to have the wedding when the harvest is gathered in,"* suggested Ambrose, *"when we can all relax and enjoy the occasion."*

*"At the Harvest Festival,"* Guinevere proclaimed. *"That would be perfect,"* said Celemon.

*"Then we are all agreed,"* confirmed Arthur. *"We'll look forward to the harvest moon."*

*"And where will we live when we are married?"* asked Guinevere.

*"The commander's villa at Viroconium will surprise you,"* said Arthur, *"it overlooks the river Severn on the western edge of the city and is surrounded by green pastures; and on a clear day you can see for miles across the plain to the distant mountains of western Powys." "It sounds truly wonderful,"* said Guinevere, with an admiring glance at Arthur.

ઈઈઈઈ

Arthur, Cei and Bedivere accompanied King Uther, and Prince Cadwy escorted Queen Ygerna as the wedding party rode from Caer Cadarn to the small chapel at Sutton Montis where Arthur and Guinevere would solemnize their marriage vows. When all the guests had assembled by the western porch, Arthur looked expectantly towards the gate where an archway formed the entrance to the churchyard; he noticed that the trellis arch was interwoven with honeysuckle, the flower of true love.

Then, a moment later, Guinevere appeared. She was a vision of perfection, framed by the archway, wearing a long yellow silk dress that fell in simple classical folds over her lithesome form, drawn together at the waist with gold braid tied in a lovers knot. Her golden hair had been carefully divided into six plaits that were then twisted together to form a crown, interwoven with a garland of flowers.

Ambrose took Guinevere's arm and led her to join Arthur by the porchway. As they joined hands, Arthur could see Guinevere's radiant smile through her veil; he had never before seen her looking so happy.

Then Prince Cadwy's priest came from the chapel to welcome the distinguished guests to the wedding ceremony. He began with the prayer of St Peter:

*"Blessed be God, father of our Lord Jesus Christ, who in His great mercy has enabled you to be born again, in the hope of eternal life through the resurrection of our Lord to an incorruptible heritage, never decaying, unsustained, which is preserved in heaven for you who are guarded by the Power of God."*

The priest took the gold ring from Arthur and the silver ring from Guinevere for the Blessing of the rings,

*"Heavenly Father, we pray for your blessing upon these precious rings of gold and silver, so that, sanctified by your grace, they may be presented to bride and bridegroom as symbols of their pledge of fidelity to one another; and in the presence of God, and of all the witnesses here present, I call upon you Arthur, and you Guinevere, to exchange rings and to solemnize your vows to each other."*

117

Whereupon Arthur took the gold ring to give to his beloved, *"Guinevere, with this ring I thee wed, and promise before God and angels to love, honour and cherish you always."*

Guinevere looked into Arthur's eyes and spoke softly, *"Arthur, I give to you this silver ring as a token of my love, for where you are Arthur, I Guinevere will be by your side, and promise before God to love, honour and cherish you always."*

The priest concluded the ceremony with the crowning of the bride and bridegroom, placing a simple gold coronet first upon Guinevere, then another upon Arthur; and with arms outstretched he placed his hands upon both of them for the Blessing, *"May the Lord bless you both and keep you always in His care, in the name of the Father, Son and Holy Spirit."*

Arthur kissed his bride, to the delight of all present, who gave a rousing cheer in unison; and the priest opened the church door, inviting Arthur and Guinevere to celebrate the Nuptial Mass, together with as many of their family and friends who could fit into the tiny chapel.

❧❧❧❧

Woodsmoke from an open fire drifted up through the rafters of Caer Cadarn's great feasting hall as the guests took their places at the Wedding Feast. Prince Cadwy, with a detachment of warriors bearing flaming torches, escorted king Uther and his consort, the lady Ygerna, into the hall, where they received a warm welcome from Ambrose and Celemon their hosts.

A great cheer went up from the whole assembly when Arthur and Guinevere appeared; Cei and Bedivere escorted the bride and bridegroom to their seats of honour at the high table. Guinevere was pleasantly surprised by the appearance of the hall, for that afternoon the villagers had transformed it from a well-used hall-barn into a rustic palace.

Decorated with wall-hangings that had been woven on hand-looms by soldier's wives, the hall now looked resplendent with bright shining swords, spears and shields on display. Every one of the hall's oak posts had been entwined with spiral garlands of ivy and oak leaves, and all around the hall, torches secured in iron wall-brackets cast a warm glow of flickering light over the assembled guests and the armed warriors who stood guard over them.

Prince Cadwy rose to welcome Uther and Ygerna, his royal guests. He then addressed the whole assembly extolling Arthur's prowess and praising Guinevere's virtues, proposing a toast to their health and happiness.

*"But before our celebrations, it is just and right to honour God first, from whom we*

receive our plentiful harvest; therefore we give a sheaf of the first fruits of our harvest to the priest, in thanks to our Heavenly Father." As he spoke, Prince Cadwy uplifted the first sheaf gleaned from his fields, and passed it to the priest; the grain from this sheaf would be made into small loaves of bread that the priest would place on the chapel altar as thanksgiving for the first fruits of the harvest.

"Now let the festivities begin," announced Cadwy. Young maidens poured mead, and the sons of warriors served roasted meats to every table; pork, lamb and venison was the fare for the feast, and there was more than sufficient for every guest to enjoy a plentiful portion. While minstrels played, tumblers entertained the company, juggling, dancing and performing somersaults to the rhythm of the music.

Celemon presented Arthur and Guinevere with a traditional cake that she had baked from spelt wheat grains harvested form the cornfields of Sutton Montis. Arthur broke the small loaf in half, giving an equal share to Guinevere, and as the bride and groom enjoyed their wedding cake, Gwenhwyfach sang a song to wish them good fortune.

Arthur thanked Gwenhwyfach for her good wishes; he turned to thank Ambrose and Celemon for providing such a magnificent Wedding Feast, "And I thank my wonderful wife Guinevere for making me the happiest man alive!" Arthur exclaimed, as the whole company gave a great cheer of approval with a final mead toast.

Guinevere rose to bid farewell to her parents, but as Celemon embraced her, three young girls pulled her away from her mother's arms and dragged her down from the dais to join Arthur for the torchlit procession to the groom's house.

On this special occasion, Cadwy had invited Arthur to reside in his own round-house, and his warriors, now armed with flaming torches, escorted Arthur and his bride from the feasting-hall to the house, with all the wedding guests joining the procession as it beat the bounds of Caer Cadarn to the sound of merrymaking and a few inebriated old soldiers who shouted jocular taunts at the bridegroom.

Finally, the procession arrived at the bridegroom's house, and Arthur lifted Guinevere into his arms and carried her over the threshold. Alone at last, they fell into each other's arms, and in the soft glow of candle-light enjoyed their first night of conjugal bliss.

CHAPTER 7

# THE BATTLE OF BASSAS

*"Pictland's men, deadly war-bands;*
*Like waves harsh roar upon the shore*
*I saw savage men in war-bands:*
*And after the morning's fray, torn flesh.*
*Strong and angry the shout until*
*I saw border-crossing forces dead."*
From a sixth-century battle-poem by Taliesin

Nennius' *Historia Brittonum* is written in Latin; however, after listing Arthur's seventh battle '*in filia celidonu*' Nennius adds the original British description '*cat coit celidon*' the battle of the Calidonian Forest. His use of Brithonic words suggests that he is translating from a text written in the early Welsh language, a document that may even have been penned in Arthur's lifetime listing his battles in chronological order as a true historical record.

Some historians locate this battle in the Borders region that lies to the north of Hadrian's Wall; but it is more likely that 'Celidon' refers to Caledonia, the Roman name for Scotland, where in the highland forests between Stirling and the Grampian Mountains, Pictish war-bands made their refuge. This heartland of the Picts was not beyond the reach of Arthur's retribution, for he was determined to rout them out of their forest lair and destroy them.

History and legend conjoin to provide supporting evidence for Arthur's northern campaign. One story in particular relates how Caw, the king of Strathclyde and father of Gildas, whose realm extended from Dumbarton to Stirling, is said to have been driven from his kingdom by the Picts in the late fifth century; at Arthur's behest he took refuge in the kindred principality of Powys. But his son Heuil, who became king at the beginning of the sixth century, opposed Arthur. Angered by this upstart, Arthur marched his army north to track down Heuil and challenge him to battle.

Another legendary story claims that Arthur killed the sons of Caw in a battle at Cambuslang near East Kilbride, a site associated with Arthur's sixth battle on the river Bassas; the same source claims that Arthur, having conquered Strathclyde, made his headquarters at the fortress of Alclywd, and presided over the 'Round Table' in Stirling Castle.

Recent archaeological evidence has revealed that Hadrian's Wall was re-defended by the British in the fifth century after the Romans had withdrawn legionary troops and cavalry from the Empire's northern border. Abandoned forts that had once been under the command of the Roman *Dux Bellorum* were re-occupied under Arthur's control in the late fifth and early sixth centuries. At South Shields and Vindolanda fortifications were strengthened, and at Birdoswald, Roman Banna, a large timber hall and out-buildings were constructed on top of the derelict Roman granaries.

If Arthur had planned and personally supervised the reconstruction of the defences along Britain's northern border as part of his northern campaign, then it would make sense to consider that his sixth battle on the river Bassas took place somewhere in the rugged and inhospitable territory north of the Wall against Picts or Saxons, whose long-term intent was to raid, steal cattle, and conquer land in the Borders and northern regions of Cumbria.

But the exact location of the river Bassas has never been found. Clearly a name of Roman or Spanish origin, it has completely disappeared from the map of Britain. Possibly at some time over the past fifteen hundred years the name was corrupted when old or illegible maps were carelessly copied; or perhaps the original Latin name was changed because its meaning was no longer understood by later generations who spoke only Welsh or English.

It was the Emperor Hadrian who drafted Spanish legionaries into Britain to build the great Wall. Cohors I Aelia Hispanorum Militaria Equitata was a cavalry unit raised in Spain about 119 AD, and the men of this unit built Alavna, the supply fort at Maryport on the west coast of Cumbria. They formed the first garrison on the Wall and later took part in the campaign to conquer Caledonia.

Then in the third century, Cohors II Asturum Equitata, a Roman cavalry brigade raised from the Astures of northern Spain was posted to garrison Aesica, Great Chesters fort on Hadrian's Wall; their commander was a distinguished general named Munatius Aurelius Bassus who deployed his cavalry force as a reconnaissance unit to garrison the small forts north of the Wall. These vexillation forts were outposts of the main garrison, usually manned by a maniple of 120 legionaries on a temporary basis, to give advance warning of enemy raids. In the year 222 AD General Bassus posted a detachment of his men to Castra Exploratorum, at Netherby, a Roman fort ten miles north of Carlisle, with instructions to build a cavalry drill-hall. Here his mounted soldiers would be able to exercise their mounts within the safety of the fort, maintaining the peak of fitness in preparation for their next sortie against enemy marauders.

Perhaps the appearance of General Munatius Bassus riding to inspect the outposts of the Empire in his horse-drawn chariot, would not have been very different from the illustration of the Roman Consul Junius Bassus, who was depicted in a fourth century mosaic leading a triumphal procession. Naturally our search for the river Bassas gives rise to the question: "Did General Munatius Bassus give his name to a river somewhere near Netherby, or close to one of the other vexillation forts in an area where he had become renowned for a distinguished victory over the Picts?" Another Latin word 'basarse' meaning 'to be based on' is similar to the Spanish word 'basa' meaning 'foundation;' if all the word clues point to a legionary base close to a river, then perhaps the cavalrymen of the 'exploratores' shared the joke that they had been ordered by General Bassus to basarse at the fort on the river Bassas!

More to the point, Basso, Bassus and Bassas are traditional Spanish surnames that are still in existence, and the fact that the surname Bassus has virtually the same meaning as the river name Bassas reveals a significant clue in our search for the location of Arthur's sixth battle. 'Bassas' means 'low' or 'lowest' just as the English word 'bass' means low when used to describe an instrument that plays the lowest range of notes; but it is interesting to note that the Spanish dictionary gives the alternative meaning of Bassas as 'shallow'. Perhaps we should be looking for a shallow river running in a valley at the lowest point in the surrounding countryside?

Three miles north of Netherby the small town of Canonbie marks the confluence of two important rivers; here Liddel Water runs into the river Esk before its estuary meets the Solway Firth. The point where the valleys of Eskdale and Liddesdale meet could truly be described as the lowest locality in the area, marked by the Roman fort of Broomholm and surrounded by highland hills: Calkin Rig to the north-west reaches a height of 1478 feet; Black Edge to the north-east climbs to 1464 feet, and the lowest, Earnshaw Hill just south of Langholm is just 920 feet high. The fort at Broomhill guarded this low-point between the Dales: it was the outermost sentinel sixteen miles from the garrison headquarters at Carlisle, and the first line of defence to face an enemy approaching from the north.

Broomholm fort overlooks a shallow stream called Tarras Water. This river rises high on Hartsgarth Fell and runs ten miles south to Broomholm where it becomes a tributary to the river Esk; but Tarras Water is not a gentle stream, as the Gazetteer for Scotland reports: *its course is impetuous, and so obstructed by rocks, that any person swept away in the fast running stream is less in danger of being drowned than of being dashed to pieces.*

Here we believe, runs the river Bassas, disguised by a more recent derivation of its original name. If we closely compare the names 'bassas' and 'tarras' it is evident that the letter 'b' of bassas could easily have been mistaken for a letter 't' where an original early map had been spoiled or corrupted; again, if we look closely at Nennius' original script, in which river and place names are penned without initial capital letters, the similarity between the letters 'r' and 's' is clearly evident, particularly if the top flourish of the 's' had faded.

But there may be a much simpler explanation for the name change: over the centuries the Roman fort of Broomhill became derelict; the timber billets rotted away leaving only the level terrace of the original site and the Roman name Bassas was forgotten. With the coming of the English the river was given a new name that suited the location: as it appeared, it was the river than ran below the terrace of the old fort, literally 'terrace water'. The word terrace is the Latin root for the abbreviated form 'tarras', thus the name evolved from the original Roman 'Bassas Fluvius' to the new English 'Tarras Water'.

⊱⊰⊱⊰

It was early January when Arthur arrived at Castell Dinas Bran to attend the round-table war conference with Uther Pendragon and the Kings of Britain. The countryside of Powys was embedded in deep snow. Icicles appeared like dragons' teeth from the clefts of a sheer slate-grey mountain that towered above the rugged and narrow valley of the river Dee; high above, almost in the clouds, appeared the impregnable fortress of Dinas Bran, crowning the mountain's summit with massive ramparts and a gilded roof that glistened pure gold in the afternoon sunlight. For the peasant folk of the hamlet of Llangollen the castle was an awe inspiring sight, and when Arthur was present there was an air of excitement and great expectation, for the warrior had returned victorious, and everyone would take part in the celebrations and feasting.

Now the war-council had the Pictish bit between its teeth: the threat of invasion from the north had become their great concern, but a greater threat was the possibility of the Picts forging an alliance with the Saxons of Bernicia and combining their forces into an indefatigable army that would destroy the northern kingdoms of Strathclyde, Rheged and Cumbria. By his sheer stubbornness, dogged persistence and refusal to be beaten, Arthur had finally overcome the Saxon enemy in the south. His next challenge was to eliminate the threat of the Picts in the north; but to achieve this, Arthur knew that he would have to seek-out and pierce the heart of the Pictish war-band; if this meant an expedition as far as the Grampian Mountains and the forests of Caledonia, then Arthur would need to establish his headquarters at Stirling, as Roman generals had done when campaigning against the same northern enemy; but his first objective was to strengthen the long abandoned garrisons on Hadrian's

Wall in an attempt to prevent further enemy incursions into northern Britain.

When winter had passed, Arthur, Cei and Bedivere marched north with their trusty battle-hardened warriors, taking with them a troop of newly trained recruits from Wroxeter. Arthur would need to muster three more squadrons of cavalry from the kings of northern Britain before he reached Stirling. Arthur's planned route took him first to Camulodunum, present day Slack in south Yorkshire, where he was joined by a small group of Sarmatians, grandsons of the renowned Sarmatian cavalry who had come to Britain with the Roman Army; by tradition they were skilled horsemen and fierce fighters, and more than a match for the Picts.

The Roman fortress of Brougham Castle, long associated with the round-table legend, may well have been chosen by Arthur for a war-council with the king of Rheged, a firm ally of Powys who had pledged his support for Arthur's campaign. Rheged was one of the wealthiest and most powerful principalities of Britain, well able to equip Arthur with a troop of armed mounted warriors who would come supplied with victuals to sustain them on their journey north.

This fledgling army clattered its way through the great Roman gateway of Carlisle. With a dramatic flourish the young Arthur spurred his fine white stallion, proudly leading his cavalry forward with their pennants flying in the wind and their rowan cloaks cutting a dash of colour against the motley crowd that had turned out to welcome them. As they wheeled round inside the safety of the fortified city, the setting sun glinted like fire on their chain-mail tunics: they appeared invincible, bright and armed like sentinels of the gods.

*"The Emperor Caesar Traianus Hadrianus Augustus, son of his divine ancestors, decided on the advice of the gods to set the boundary of the Empire in the second consulship. The barbarians were scattered and the province of Britannia freed."*

Arthur pondered on the inscription of Hadrian's memorial. It was no surprise that the people of his day looked upon Hadrian's Wall as a wonder of the world and the work of giants; but in fact it had been Hadrian's great idea to build a wall from sea to sea spanning seventy-three miles of the natural isthmus between the river Tyne and the Solway Firth that would mark the northernmost frontier of the Empire; not only would the wall provide a military barrier against barbarian incursions, but it would also give the army a secure base from which to conquer the tribes and territories of the north.

The idea of linking a line of defensive forts with a solid barrier was the latest concept in Roman military thinking at the start of the second century. The idea had been tried and tested by Hadrian in northern Gaul, where he built palisades between forts that allowed him to successfully block and repel barbarian attacks from the east. Fortunately, the line of forts built by Agricola in the early eighties between Carlisle and Corbridge was a great gift to Hadrian, for it gave him a base-line on which to develop his ambitious plan.

Somewhat surprisingly the idea of building the wall had originated from Hadrian's decision to consolidate the borders of the Roman Empire following Trajan's extravagant campaigns in Dacia and Mesopotamia; by abandoning these territories Hadrian was able to redirect both financial and military resources to the new province of Britain. Furthermore the enormous expense in money and manpower would be justified if the new barrier succeeded in keeping the rebellious tribes at bay; this would allow Hadrian to curtail exploratory expeditions into the highlands, where four decades earlier Agricola had drawn the Caledonians into a pitched battle at great cost to the Roman treasury.

As Emperor, Hadrian exercised his power, privilege and Divine Right to commission three legions, a force of around fifteen thousand men, to build and subsequently garrison the new wall; on the completion of this great project Hadrian crowned his achievement by striking a new coin, a sestertius that depicted Britannia guarding the Wall. Now Hadrian's Wall had become a visible manifestation of the Roman concept of uniting the separate tribes of Britain under the banner of 'Britannia.'

Ironically however, within four years of his death, Hadrian's stupendous achievement was made redundant when his successor Antoninus Pius decided to build a new wall ninety miles further north linking the Forth-Clyde forts. But Antoninus' motive for a new war against the barbarians was determined by his personal need, as the new Emperor, to prove himself in battle; for only with a victory on the battle-field would he be able to claim the time-honoured title of *'imperator'* traditionally accorded to victorious Roman generals. But the success of the Antonine Wall was shortlived: abandoned by the Romans in the year 162, they burned the forts to the ground before retreating back to Hadrian's Wall. It was a significant turning point, for the unconquered Caledonians had secured their independence from Rome and the northern border of the Empire had suddenly contracted, verifying the wisdom of Hadrian's original decision to draw the line between the Tyne and the Solway Firth.

Yet even the subsequent re-fortification of Hadrian's Wall did not deter the Picts who, despite the fact that they could neither read nor write, demonstrated their ability for lateral thinking by sailing round the land barriers in coracles to attack south of the Tyne. Even Gildas was moved to comment on the brutal vengeance of the Picts:

*"As the Romans went back home, there eagerly emerged from the coracles that had carried them across the sea-valleys, the foul hordes of Scots and Picts, like dark throngs of*

*worms that wriggle out of narrow fissures in the rock when the sun is high. They were to some extent different in their customs, but they were in perfect accord in their greed for bloodshed: and they were happier to cover their villainous faces with hair than to cover their private parts with clothes. No sooner had they heard of the Romans' departure than they became more confident than ever, and seized the whole of the northern part of the island right up to the Wall. A force stationed on the high towers was too lazy to fight and too unwieldy to flee; foolish and frightened the men sat about day and night, rotting away in their folly. Meanwhile there was no respite from the barbed spears unleashed by their naked opponents, who tore our countrymen from the walls and dashed them to the ground."*

Gildas must have known that the events he described continued through to the later years of the fifth century when his own father, king Caw, was himself defeated by the Picts and forced to appeal to Arthur for help. In the central region of the Wall close to Great Chesters fort, a Roman milecastle overlooks the landscape of Cawfields and the valley of Caw Burn, the most likely site of king Caw's last battle with the Picts. Just seven miles further east, two rocky outcrops known as King's Crags and Queen's Crags have a legendary association with Arthur and Guinevere, who according to an ancient local legend lie enchanted in a vaulted hall below the nearby castle of Sewingshields: asleep on their thrones, the King and Queen are surrounded by the knights and ladies of the court, their hunting dogs lying asleep at their feet. There they will remain forever enchanted until someone takes up Arthur's sword to cut a nearby garter and blows a hunting horn to break the spell. One afternoon, while seeking a ball of yarn that he had dropped into an underground passage, a lone shepherd discovered the wondrous scene: as he drew the sword from its scabbard, the king and his company awoke to witness the cutting of the garter. Then, as the shepherd sheathed the sword, the ancient power of the spell overcame them once more; but not before the King had time to exclaim:

> *"O woe betide that evil day*
> *On which this witless wight was born,*
> *Who drew the sword, the garter cut,*
> *But never blew the bugle-horn!"*

We do not have to look very far to find a plausible explanation for the origin of this legend: five miles east of Sewingshields, the fort of Chesters held a strategic position guarding the bridge that took the Wall's route over the North Tyne river. The fort was designed to accommodate a Roman cavalry unit five-hundred strong and in the third century was garrisoned by Cohors II Asturum, commanded by our old friend

General Munatius Bassus. Outside the fort the '*vicus*' or military town boasted several important houses as well as one of the best military bath-houses in Britain. Within the spacious headquarters building a central '*sacellum*' housed the regimental colours and a statue of the Emperor; from here the officers gained access to an underground strong-room or '*aerarium,*' where the regiment's money and valuables were secured. Before its accidental discovery in 1803, a local tradition held that the fort had once been occupied by a cavalry regiment with its stables underground! An iron-studded oak door secured the entrance to a dark chamber that featured a triple arched vaulted-roof; but of the original contents only a few denarii were found, dating to Flavius Severus, Caesar from 305 to 306 AD.

Ravaged by enemy assaults, weather-beaten and neglected, most of the wall-forts would have become derelict a century after the Roman legions departed. When Arthur made his tour of inspection, he would have visited the strategically positioned fort at Chesters, situated mid-way between Carlisle and South Shields. Finding the fort and its headquarters deserted, it would have been logical for Arthur and his cavalrymen to seek shelter for the night in the safety of the underground strong-room. Later, local hearsay reported that *"Arthur and his men had slept in the vaulted underground chamber of the fortress"* a simple truth that, over time, was embellished into a magical legend.

Another medieval ballad links Arthur with Carlisle:

> *"King Arthur lives in merry Carlisle*
> *And seemly is to see;*
> *And there with him is Queen Guinever*
> *That bride so bright of blee."*

So did Arthur bring his newly wedded bride Guinevere with him as far as Carlisle before setting-off on his northern battle campaign? It was certainly the custom for Roman generals and legionary officers to bring their wives and families with them on a posting to Hadrian's Wall; so it would not have been unusual for Guinevere to accompany Arthur at least as far as the safe citadel of Carlisle, and even risk a short excursion along the Wall to the east. Perhaps they ventured as far as the fort at Banna, Birdoswald, with its imposing view over the river Irthing, where Arthur had commissioned a new timber hall large enough to house a commander and his cavalry brigade. This fort guarded the Willowford Bridge over the Irthing and controlled the Roman road leading to the outpost vexillation fort of Bewcastle six miles to the north.

When news reached Arthur that Heuil had mustered a war-band of rebellious Picts and was moving south towards the Wall, he assembled his cavalry at Banna and prepared for battle. Forwarned, Arthur planned to intercept Heuil's march south, but he could only make a guess at the route his enemy would take. However, one thing was certain, that the Picts would be bound to follow one of the river valleys that led south towards Carlisle: Eskdale and Liddesdale converged at Canonbie, and the vale of Ewes Water converged with the Esk at Langholm. With this area now the focus of his attention, Arthur moved his army north towards the old Roman fort at Bewcastle. Long derelict, the fort occupied a plateau, an area of six acres with an unusual six-sided embankment that gave a measure of protection for over a thousand soldiers. In this isolated position Arthur's force was within a ten mile radius of Canonbie and Liddesdale yet well hidden from the approaching enemy. With an advance scout patrol Arthur moved forward five miles to a vantage point on the southern edge of Kershope Forest where he could overlook Liddel Water towards Langholm: it was the perfect observation position for Arthur to await Heuil's arrival. Situated five miles east of Canonbie this location is now known as 'Arthur's Seat.'

But Arthur did not just sit there admiring the view: first he sent out scouts to Black Edge, a lookout peak with an uninterrupted view over Teviot Vale to the north; he then sent a second section of scouts to Earnshaw Hill a mile south-west of Langholm that afforded a commanding view of Eskdale; and the third reconnaissance patrol was dispatched to map out the area around the old Roman fort of Broomholm, where General Bassus' legionaries had once defended the Esk Valley below Earnshaw Hill.

With a roughly drawn map delivered by his scouts, Arthur called his commanders Cei and Bedivere together in the makeshift tent that would be his battle headquarters. Now in the dim light of an oil lamp he looked more closely at the position of the fort; with his experience as a military tactician, Arthur saw instantly how he could trap the enemy. Rather than make the obvious move to occupy the fort and defend it with his own men against an enemy attack, Arthur decided to hold back and allow Heuil the advantage of occupying the fort; it would offer some protection for an overnight encampment, a place where his men could rest after their long march and prepare for the next day's attack on Carlisle.

The track that followed the river Esk forded the river Bassas just below the fort and at this point the rebels would be constricted as they forded the river. Arthur drew a large arrow on the map, its point centred on the ford: this was the target, and he decided to split his cavalry force into three squadrons for the ambush.

The view from Tarrasfoot Hill overlooking Tarras Water. The distant grass plateau marks the site of the Roman fort of Broomholm, an outpost twenty miles north of Hadrian's Wall that was designed to give warning of Pictish war-bands approaching from the north. All the historical clues point to this area as the location for Arthur's sixth battle, on the river Bassas.

Photo, © Walter Baxter

By late afternoon on the third day, the scouts at Black Edge spotted the vanguard of Heuil's war-band tramping down the vale of Ewes Water in ragged formation, warriors on chariots drawn by short-legged horses leading the way, foot-soldiers following them along the dusty trackway. One scout galloped back to headquarters and Arthur promptly dispatched a rider to Bewcastle to call the other squadrons forward to the edge of the Kershope Forest. Then Arthur briefed his men: Cei's troop on the left flank would attack first, sweeping in from the west to draw the enemy's attention. Arthur's squadron, in the centre, would then cut into the rebels left flank; Bedivere's squadron would remain hidden in woodland to the east until Arthur signalled them to attack. If Heuil decided to rest his army at Broomhill fort Arthur would hold-off the ambush, but if they pushed forward towards the ford, he would attack at once.

The three squadrons moved swiftly and silently to their battle positions, taking advantage of woodland cover to avoid detection by the enemy, each man sweating with the anticipation of battle. But time passed, and there was no signal from Arthur, for it appeared that Heuil had decided to make camp at the fort: some of his straggling war-band had already refreshed themselves in the river, while others had pitched their tents on the plateau and were now imbibing strong honey-coloured mead from pig-skin bladders. Heuil's decision to halt for the night was a godsend for Arthur: it meant that he could go for his preferred plan of action, to gain the advantage by surprising the enemy with a dawn attack. According to plan, his troops withdrew a mile or so into the woods, out of enemy earshot; that night, the cold forest floor would be their bed, the clear night-sky their canopy. For most of the young warriors it was a fitful night; to a man they were fearful of the morrow's battle, wondering whether they would live or die; but the veterans who had fought against Saxons under Arthur's banner reassured them, "If you *put your trust in God… and Arthur, you'll have nothing to fear!*"

Before dawn the two front-line squadrons moved stealthily forward through the woodland valley of the river Esk; at the wood's edge Arthur paused, allowing Cei's squadron on the opposite river bank to sweep out to the north-west and move into position for the first assault; breaking cover less than half a mile from the fort, Cei charged, leading his cavalry into the attack. As Heuil's lookout sounded the alarm on his rams-horn, bewildered Picts staggered from their tents, grasped their weapons and ran to their chariots. Then, while Cei's troop waded across the river Esk, Arthur advanced, charging out of the wood line-abreast to ford the shallow river Bassas; the two squadrons hit the fort in a well-timed simultaneous attack, Cei's troop mounting the ramparts head-on, with Arthur's warriors charging up the embankment to cut into the enemy's left flank. The Picts were taken completely by surprise: the few who had formed a ragged line of resistance were cut down where they stood, while the charioteers were speared to death before they could reach their horses. Heuil was nowhere to be seen.

Before the sun had broken through the morning mists, Arthur and his men, fighting fiercely in the thick of the enemy, had forced the remnants of the war-band out of Broomholm fort and down to the meadow-bank of the river Bassas. While Cei's men whirled around the camp with firebrands torching tents, Heuil, together with a few of his horsemen, fled to the north using the pall of smoke to cover their escape.

Panic stricken, fearing for their lives, the straggling survivors floundered across the river Bassas, climbing for the cover of a wooded hillside to the east. Arthur paused and regrouped his two battle squadrons. He had to remind himself that he was fighting fellow Britons, not Saxons; yet the Picts were no less a foe. In fact, Arthur was now fighting a civil action against rebellious Britons, descendants of the warlike Maeatae tribe who controlled the land of Fortrenn between Stirling and the Grampian Mountains; but no love was lost between Arthur and the Maeatae, for he was related to the Votadini whose royal seat of power was Edinburgh Fortress, and whose king held sway over the Manau Gododdin, a wealthy principality that reached from Yeavering Bell to Stirling.

The Red Dragon of the Cymri unfurled in the breeze as Arthur's standard bearer raised his pennon; sounding his battle-horn, Arthur gave three short blasts signalling Bedivere's squadron to attack. The enemy escapees had almost reached the wooded cover of Bruntshiel Hill when, to their sheer horror, they found themselves facing Bedivere's chargers head-on. The stragglers who were not cut-down in the first charge fell back to the river in the hope of escaping to the north, but Arthur and Cei were there to greet them, their spears and swords glinting in the morning sunlight.

Arthur had played out his battle-tactics like a game of chess, taking the advantage with a surprise attack that had wrong-footed his enemy from the start: now he declared 'check-mate' to the wretched remnants of Heuil's war-band who were sandwiched between his warriors and the river Bassas. They fought ferociously as the cavalry onslaught drove them backwards into the river, their lives cut short by sharp steel; their abandoned shields floated away in the fast stream of the river Bassas, its clear waters now running stained with blood.

The name given to Bruntshiel Hill may well relate to the time of Arthur's sixth battle on the river Bassas, for 'bruntshiel' interpreted from early English means: *"a temporary refuge from the full force of the attack."*

Seventy-five years after the Picts had been defeated at Bassas, the English king Aethelric followed in Heuil's footsteps in an attempt to attack king Urien of Rheged at Carlisle; but Urien was well prepared and drew Aethelric into an ambush at the Battle of Argoed Llwyfain, a woodland near Langholm that was not far from the site of Arthur's battle of the river Bassas on the northern border of Rheged.

# CHAPTER 8

# THE BATTLE OF THE CALEDONIAN FOREST

*"Heuil, a proud and distinguished warrior, submitted to no king, not even Arthur."*
Caradoc of Llancarfan

Heuil fled to the north after his catastrophic defeat at the hands of Arthur's warriors in the battle of the river Bassas: he fled as far as his short-legged horse would carry him, until he reached the safety of the Maeatae fortress of Dumyat, Dunblane, just north of Stirling, and at least one hundred miles from Arthur and the burning encampment at Broomholm.

Arthur buried the few of his brave warriors killed in the battle at the foot of Bruntshiel Hill; the wounded were mounted on spare horses and escorted back to Carlisle. The enemy dead were left where they fell, pickings for ravens and kites. For Arthur, there was no turning back: he was now more than ever determined to catch Heuil, to track him down for a final battle that would end his rebellious game and teach the Picts a lesson that they would not easily forget. Arthur marched north, following the vale of Eweswater to Burgh Hill fort, a safe refuge where his soldiers could recover from the fatigue of battle; he gave them three days respite, then pushed forward through Teviot Dale towards Dere Street, the main Roman road that linked Corbridge with Edinburgh.

Peniel Heugh, an iron-age hill-fort with a natural strategic advantage, overlooked the Roman bridge that took Dere Street across the river Teviot; situated just a mile north of the bridge, the fort held a commanding position with magnificent views over Teviot Vale and across the Tweed Valley four miles to the north. As a British stronghold that had been frequently attacked by Pictish war-bands coming by sea, and then forcing their way up the river Tweed to raid inland targets, it was a defensive position of great interest to Arthur. Climbing the ramparts, he was relieved to find the fort manned by a small force of Votadini, who gave Arthur and his warriors a hospitable welcome and a night's rest.

By noon the following day Arthur and his troops had advanced as far as Newstead fort, situated on the south-bank of the river Tweed. Called Trimontium, 'the place of three peaks,' by the Romans, who took the name from the nearby Eildon Hills, the fortress served as a base for legions in transit to Caledonia and as a secure headquarters for the commanders who controlled the Borders region. Long abandoned and derelict, only the fort's lower stone ramparts remained as evidence of the Roman occupation; yet the dilapidated walls gave Arthur's army a measure of protection for their short stay. Once across the old Roman bridge that spanned the river Tweed, the troops would have a good day's march ahead of them to cover the thirty-five mile trek to Edinburgh.

As commander of the British army, Arthur was now the custodian of the history of the Roman Conquest of Britain; under the instruction of Ambrosius, he had studied the campaigns of Caesar and Claudius, and come to admire the achievements of Hadrian and Agricola, whose battle against the Caledonian tribes at Mons Graupius was renowned as an epic victory. Arthur now found himself following in the footsteps of Agricola, marching to challenge an elusive enemy in Caledonia; to lift the spirits of his men before the inevitable clash with highlanders, and to give them a lesson in battle-tactics, Arthur related the story of Agricola's great battle of Mons Graupius.

By the year AD 80, the tenacious Roman general Julius Agricola, Governor of Britain, had subjected Wales to the suzerainty of Rome and mustered his legions in preparation for the conquest of Scotland. Having consolidated his gains in the north by building a line of forts from Carlisle to Corbridge, Agricola hungered for further conquest; he marched north, leading the IX Legion from Corbridge to Inveresk on the Forth estuary, where he established a base. At the same time he was joined by the XX Legion who had marched up the Annan Valley from Carlisle. From Inveresk Agricola launched a co-ordinated attack north of the Forth with naval and land forces, marching his legions through Stirling, Dunblane and Ardoch to join the fleet at Carpow on the Tay estuary, where he established a legionary fortress and headquarters.

But Agricola's presence at Inveresk had not gone un-noticed by the tribesman of Fife; in preparing his own forces he had given the northern tribes a year to rally and strengthen their own forces. Suddenly confronted by the Caledonians on his left flank and the Venicones on his right as he marched towards Strathallan, Agricola hastily split his army into three divisions, two to counter the flanking attacks, with one division held in reserve. But his enemy held-off until nightfall, combined forces and mounted a surprise attack on the IX Legion, cutting deeply into their vanguard near Dunblane; only by moving in quickly to reinforce the hard-pressed IX, did Agricola succeed in averting a major disaster.

The Picts had drawn first blood, but Agricola was determined to gain the upper hand. During the winter of the year 83 AD he set his troops the challenging task of building a line of small forts from Doune near Dunblane, to Bertha on the outskirts of Perth; linked by a supply road with look-out posts between forts, this defensive network gave Agricola control over the lowlands from Strathallan to the Tay. Pushing a further ten miles into the Caledonian hinterland, Agricola established a number of out-post vexillation forts that would give him control over a fifty mile frontier that extended from Drumquhassie Ridge on Loch Lomond as far as Cargill, where the river Isla joins the Tay. Mounted reconnaissance scouts dispatched from the frontier forts penetrated deep into the valleys of the Grampian foothills, their mission to locate the enemy's forts and assess their strength; but the Romans were frustrated by the Caledonians canny ability to disappear into the surrounding forest, occasionally leaving a sheep's carcass in the path of the scouts who would be tempted to give up the chase in favour of a spit-roast.

Fearful that he would soon lose the Highlands to the Romans, Calgacus, leader of the Caledonians, made his own preparations for war. Secure in his fortified village overlooking Inverness, he called the tribal leaders of the Highlands together to forge a battle plan. Eleven chieftains gathered around the winter fire in the centre of Calgacus' spacious iron-age roundhouse, lamenting their earlier losses; but Calgacus inspired each chieftain to pledge their bond to the Caledonian alliance, to train every able-bodied man for battle, and to forge new weapons, armour and war-chariots.

In the early summer, when Calgacus gave the order to march into battle, war-bands from every region of the Highlands rallied at the great hill-fort of Dun da Lamh, close to the northern shore of Loch Laggan. From there, Calgacus planned to lead his war-band through Glen Garry to Dunkeld, the fort of the Caledonians, then onward to his prime target, Agricola's legionary headquarters at Carpow. But Agricola was one step ahead of Calgacus: having spotted the gathering enemy host his scouts had raised the alarm, reporting the Picts' strength at thirty thousand men. Agricola brought his legions to battle-readiness; reinforced with eight thousand auxiliary infantry and five thousand auxiliary cavalry, he advanced towards the Forest of Atholl with a full complement of twenty thousand soldiers.

Calgacus, leading his chariots towards Glen Garry, pulled-up sharply when he was suddenly faced with the awesome sight of serried ranks of Roman legionaries in full battle array advancing towards him. The shock of this unexpected confrontation with Agricola's formidable battle force struck fear into the hearts of the Caledonians. Calgacus, realising that discretion was the better part of a suicidal head-on clash, withdrew his warriors to a defensive ridge of high ground on the eastern edge of the Grampian Mountains, and prepared for battle.

Holding his legions and their cavalry support in reserve, Agricola dismounted and led his auxiliary cavalry cohorts into battle; employing the basic tactical formation known as the 'simplex acies,' a single extended battle-line, he ordered the auxiliary infantry to advance line abreast, supported by three cavalry squadrons on each wing. Marching as vanguard, Agricola led by example to encourage his men to excel in close combat. In a co-ordinated uphill attack, the cavalry charged into the Caledonians chariots, overcoming them before turning to support the auxiliaries who had advanced so far into the throng that they were surrounded; Agricola ordered four reserve troops of cavalry to cut through the enemy ranks and attack them from the rear, a tactical manoeuvre that put the highlanders into disarray and gave Agricola the upper hand: the enemy were routed.

The Roman historian Tacitus reported the event: *"some ten thousand of the enemy had fallen; our losses were three hundred and sixty, among their number was Aulus Atticus, prefect of a cohort, whose youthful keenness for battle and the ardour of his horse had carried him deep among the enemy."* Speaking in praise of Agricola, his father-in-law, Tacitus had the final word, *"You would have readily believed him to be a good man, and gladly to be a great one."*

Overnight Calgacus and his surviving warriors withdrew to the safety of their hillforts, fearfully reflecting on the awesome might of the Roman military machine and realising that their only option was to run the gauntlet of the Roman advance; but for Agricola, the battle of Mons Graupius marked the pinnacle of his career. Celebrated as the victory that completed the Roman conquest of Britain, the reward for Agricola and his legions was lasting fame.

Arthur admired how Agricola had held his highly trained cavalry in reserve until the critical moment of the battle, a tactical move that demonstrated how an uphill cavalry charge against an enemy holding the more advantageous position, had the power to change the course of the battle in his favour. Arthur's small army bore no comparison to the mighty legions of Agricola, but what he lacked in manpower and resources was compensated by the mobility of his highly trained cavalry, a fighting force that could move like the wind and strike with devastating effect. As he marched on through Lauderdale towards Edinburgh, Arthur realised that the success of his Caledonian campaign would depend both on the goodwill of his allies in the north, and on his own ability to track down and destroy his enemy in a swift punitive attack.

King Kynvelyn ordered a feast to be prepared in the great Royal Hall of Din Eidyn to celebrate Arthur's arrival. Chandeliers were lit and hung from the gilded beams of the high arched roof, while poets sang in praise of the prowess of Votadini kings and warriors. Mead made all merry and king Kynvelyn rose to welcome Arthur, Cei and Bedivere, and to greet his neighbour king Dyfnwal of Dumbarton. As he raised a toast *"To Arthur!"* his warriors roared in response: *"To Arthur!"* With a great fire kindled and spit-roast venison carved for the feast, Arthur took the seat of honour between the two great kings of the north, for this meeting of allies was a cause for happiness and celebration: the meeting of minds and talk of battle would be reserved for another day.

Kynvelyn's wealthy kingdom of Lothian extended as far south as the river Tweed; north of the Forth he ruled over Manau Gododdin with its imposing citadel at Stirling crowning a natural outcrop of volcanic rock, and his fortresses at Traprian Law to the east of Dunbar, and the Votadini Royal Palace of Yeavering Bell, gave him effective control over a wide area of north-eastern Britain. To the west, Dyfnwal ruled the Britons of Strathclyde from his impregnable fortress of Alcluid, Dumbarton Rock, a natural defensive mount on the north bank of the river Clyde. Both kings shared a common enemy: the Caledonian Picts, whose war-bands were a constant threat to the northern borders of their territory; but they also shared Arthur's concept of Britain as one nation whose people would be united by their Christian faith. Kynvelyn and Dyfnwal reaffirmed their alliegance to Arthur with the promise of cavalry and supplies to be marshalled at Stirling Fortress, Arthur's chosen headquarters for the campaign.

The Pictish Tribes of Caledonia were proud of their independent status having escaped overall domination by the Romans: they remained the original unconquered Britons who viewed the submission of the southern British tribes to the Romans as traitorous collusion. Furthermore, almost a century after the Romans' exodus, they saw Arthur as the equivalent of a Roman Governor and as such, a direct threat to their independence; because Arthur had assumed military authority over the whole of Britain, he was, in their eyes, a tyrant neither to be trusted nor welcome to rule over them.

The bitter enmity between Heuil, the rebellious leader of the Picts, and 'Arthur the Tyrant' had been enflamed by Heuil's humiliation and defeat at the battle of Bassas: with his enemy recouperating at Din Eidyn, Heuil took the opportunity to wreak vengeance on Arthur while he was off-guard. Mustering a band of his wolf-heads at Dunblane, Heuil advanced towards Mynedd Eidyn, Edinburgh's Mount, under cover of night. This volcanic peak, now known as Arthur's Seat, rises dramatically from the surrounding plain to form a natural fortress where Arthur and his troops made their temporary encampment; it gave them a secure defensive position overlooking Edinburgh and the surrounding countryside.

It was a mark of bravery for a Caledonian warrior to have captured and killed a wolf single-handed in the forest; the wolf-skin was worn as a trophy, with the wolf's head above the warrior's head to terrify his enemy, and the pelt draped over his shoulders to provide natural camouflage when hiding in open heathland or forest. Heuil and his wolf-men marched more than forty miles through the night, reaching the lower slopes of Mynedd Eidyn before dawn.

Before first light Heuil's warriors stealthily climbed the rugged escarpment to reach the rock-faced ramparts of the hill-fort; but before Heuil had time to give the signal to attack, one of his men slipped from his precarious position on the rock-face and fell to his death. The commotion alerted the British sentinel who promptly sounded the alarm: Cei's squadron, already armed for the dawn patrol, was the first to reach the ramparts and as Heuil's wolf-heads appeared above the rampart they were hacked down into the gorge hundreds of feet below.

Arthur was not with his men; as the guest of king Kynvelyn at Din Eidyn he had devoted several days to planning the next stage of his campaign to rout the Picts; but as he watched the flames of the distress beacon at the peak of Mynedd Eidyn, he realised that he had underestimated Heuil's capacity for revenge. Angered by the fact that, this time, he had been taken by surprise, Arthur called upon Kynvelyn for help. With a squadron of Votadini warriors at his disposal, he seized his sword and shield, mounted his great white battle-horse, and charged towards the besieged fort.

Heuil's wolf-pack was renowned for its ferocious fighters, but as they mounted the ramparts they came face to face with a shield wall of Cei's men: then came the shock of sharp steel thrusting to repel them. Charging up the lower slopes of the mount, Arthur and his Votadini troop dismounted as the going became too steep for their horses; climbing on foot, they cut into the rear ranks of the enemy until wolf-men's blood flowed freely down the black igneous rock-face of the mountain. Heuil and his men fell back into retreat as Arthur climbed to the topmost rampart to join his own men, who gave a rousing cheer. Bodies of the wolf-men who had fallen at the shield-wall were unceremoniously thrown over the ramparts, tumbling headlong down the jagged rock-face, coming to rest splayed-out in contorted heaps, food for foxes.

This unexpected attack sharpened Arthur's focus on his plan to pin-down Heuil for a final decisive battle. Within a week Arthur had marched his army north to Stirling Fortress. King Dyfnwal's squadrons from Dumbarton joined forces with the Votadini troops from Din Eidyn at Camelon, Agricola's old supply fort where blacksmiths had forged horseshoes and weapons for his legionaries. Camelon would also make a good supply base for Arthur, as the Roman road ran directly from here to Stirling, less than ten miles to the north; victuals and provisions would be sent forward daily to maintain his new army at full strength.

Heuil's scouts had seen reinforcements arriving at Stirling and estimated Arthur's force to be about three-hundred mounted warriors, not even the equivalent of a cohort of Roman cavalry. Nevertheless, Heuil decided that this military build-up only five miles from Dunblane was too close for comfort, prompting him to abandon his headquarters for the relative safty of Strathyre Forest twenty miles to the north-west; from here he would rally support from Dundern and Dunkeld, the old Fortress of the Caledonians.

Stirling was now a hive of activity as nine troops of cavalry prepared for battle, with one troop held in reserve: horses were shod and groomed, spears sharpened, swords whetted; mail tunics damaged after the last skirmish were repaired and round shields coated with lime-wash that dried in the sun to give a hard protective finish of gleaming white. As soon as the Votadini reconnaissance scouts had returned to the fortress, Arthur called his commanders together for the final briefing before battle. The scouts had followed Heuil as far as the Pass of Levy where his ragged band had disappeared into the thick forest bordering Loch Lubnaig. Arthur trusted the advice of his scouts for, although in enemy territory, they knew the lie of the land and were also familiar with the locations of Roman forts and the Picts' strongholds. On their suggestion Arthur agreed to advance to the old Roman fort at Bochastle, a strategic position at the head of the Pass of Levy: less than a half-day's

Loch Voil near Balquhidder, where the Calair Burn, a fast flowing stream, runs down into the valley below Mount Benyane.

Photo, © Stuart Low

march from Stirling, this would be an ideal base-camp for the first stage of the campaign.

The following morning Arthur rode out with the Votadini scouts, accompanied by a troop of cavalry for protection, to search the Strathyre Forest for Picts. The advance party took the rough track along the eastern bank of Loch Lubaig, and then followed a fast flowing stream along Strathyre until they came to a small settlement of huts and round-houses at Balquhidder, almost twelve miles north of Bocastle. Here Arthur called a halt, not just to rest the horses, but because he found the place enchanting: smoke from the settlement drifted lazily acros the meadow towards a loch that stretched far into the distance. Trees on a small islet were reflected in the still waters of the loch, and a torrent of water that tumbled from the eastern shore of the loch was joined by streams from adjacent hills on each side of the settlement.

Just across the old wooden bridge on the river's south bank, smoke poured from a timber-framed hut where a blacksmith was hammering a shaft of red-hot steel over a huge anvil. Arthur, curious to see a blacksmith with flowing red hair, spurred his horse towards the forge, and as the smith turned to greet him with a red-hot sword shaft, his eyes met the rugged beauty of a swarthy young woman, her face and arms blackened with soot, her bright red hair complimenting her angry defiance at Arthur's intrusion. Dismounting, he reassured her that he meant no harm, and that, despite his fearsome appearance as a fully armed warrior, he came in peace.

But Arthur made the mistake of suggesting that her weapon would be no match for his own sword that had been made by a Saxon smith. With an angry look, and to prove the quality of her work, the blacksmith challenged Arthur to a duel, to test her well tempered steel against her opponent's sword. Arthur smiled at her audacity, but flinched as she wielded the first blow, then parried with a counter stroke that shook her frame: as they thrust and parried, the ring of steel echoed across the valley until Arthur closed in and locked their swords together at the hilts. *My name is Arthur,* he said softly. *Katrine,* she replied. When they examined each blade it was clear that Arthur had a few more notches in the keen edge of his sword whereas Katrine's blade was pristine, its cutting edge like new. *I concede defeat,* admitted Arthur, *you have truly made the strongest blade in Britain. Now you must make me a new battle-sword that will be unmatched in quality and strength,* he declared.

While Arthur dispatched his scouts to scour the forest for signs of the enemy, Katrine drew several ingots of iron from her basement store and fed them into the melting pot in the heat of her furnace; keen to help in the making of his new sword, Arthur pumped the huge bellows that fanned the furnace to a white heat until the rough ingots slowly fused into a mass of red-hot molten metal. Sweating from the heat, Katrine deftly swung the pot of molten iron from the furnace, scuffing off a layer of impurities before pouring the liquid metal into a cylindrical stone mould; then, opening a sluice gate in a wooden trough that ducted water from a fast flowing mountain stream, she quenched the red-hot metal to the sound of hissing steam as the metal solidified within the mould. The drop-forging complete, Katrine released the binding that held each half of the mould together, and invited her guest to draw the shaft from the stone.

Arthur drew the sword from the stone. He was pleased to find that the moulding and annealing of the molten iron had produced a fine blade, and he proudly handed it to Katrine for the finishing treatment: the blade would have to be re-heated, twisted and tempered on the anvil before the strengthening process was complete; each time the blade would be annealed in the mineral rich waters of the mountain stream.

By the time the scouts had returned from their mission, Arthur had moved his cavalry squadrons from Bocastle to Balquhidder, and Katrine had finished the new sword: it was a masterpiece of craftsmanship, bright-bladed steel whetted sharp as a razor, the hilt carved with two serpent heads intertwined in a traditional Celtic pattern and finished in bright silver-gilt.

*"A sword fit for a king,"* said Katrine as she presented Arthur with her gift. *"I am no king,"* replied Arthur as he took the sword, *"but this most certainly is the king of swords, and I will treasure your gift always."* Arthur looked deeply into her eyes, *"Katrine, in your honour I shall name this sword after the mountain stream that quenched the fire of its blade."*

*"The name of this stream is Calair Burn,"* replied Katrine. *"Then it shall be called Ex Calair Burn,"* declared Arthur, adding the Latin word 'from' to the name of the stream.

*"And our beautiful loch is known as Loch Voil, because its secrets are forever veiled in mist."*

Katrine said softly. *"Then I shall call you my Lady of the Loch,"* replied Arthur as he kissed her rough and blackened hand.

Arthur knew that the Caledonians prized iron as other tribes prized gold; now he too would prize this new sword as if it had been made of gold; but suddenly, battle plans drew Arthur from his enchantment with Katrine and Loch Voil into the real world of war, for his scouts had at last located Heuil's refuge at Dundern, the Picts stronghold that commanded the eastern shores of Loch Earn. From here it appeared that Heuil was attempting to reinforce his depleted war-band, appealing for reinforcements from Dunkeld and the Picts' royal fortress at Castle Law by Bridge of Earn; but Heuil's record as a battle leader had failed to impress the Caledonian war-lords. Recent losses had been severe and they were now reluctant to volunteer more men to face another defeat.

Arthur bade farewell to Katrine, the lady of Loch Voil, brandishing his bright

The River Ledrock cascades out from a rocky gorge in the misty and verdant amphitheatre known as the De'ils Cauldron, near Comrie, Scotland.          Photo, © Tom Parnell

new sword Excaliburn aloft as he led his cavalry towards Loch Earn. Arthur took three squadrons of cavalry to the north of the loch, Cei's three squadrons headed along the south bank, and Bedivere's cavalry followed Arthur at some distance, holding back as the reserve troop. In the dim light before dawn Arthur charged from the cover of the forest, leading his warriors in a full frontal attack on Dundern. Simultaneously Cei and his cavalry attacked from the south, smashing into the hillfort's defences, while Bedivere's troop formed a second wave of attacking cavalry. Now Arthur had the advantage over Heuil, who was quickly pushed onto the back foot, cornered in his own compound. Despite outnumbering Arthur's men, Heuil and his wolf-heads were now fighting for their lives: unable to mount their horses they were trampled by a wall of oncoming battle-horses and most of their number speared to death.

Heuil realised that the battle was lost and charged into the forest in a bid to escape; but Arthur rallied his men and gave chase: after a four mile dash through the pine forest Arthur's strong stallion drew level with Heuil as he sought to hide in the rocky gully of the Devil's Cauldron. With one powerful thrust of his spear Arthur struck Heuil in the right shoulder, spinning him to the ground. Dismounting, Arthur drew his bright new sword and dealt a crushing blow upon Heuil's shield, splintering its surface; the sound of clashing swords pierced the air above the roar of the stream's torrent as it poured over a waterfall into the dark pool below. Heuil cursed Arthur and vowed that he would never bow to a tyrant's rule.

Arthur replied with an angry scowl, swinging his sword at full length, slicing deeply into his opponent's neck armour, drawing blood: Heuil shuddered from the mighty blow, his body crumpled, his life-force gushing from a mortal wound; the tall, proud warrior fell against the glistening rock-face, moistened by the spray from the waterfall. At the last moment, as his spirit waned, Heuil bowed to Arthur: *"See how the proud rebel pays obeisance to Excaliburn!"* shouted Arthur, pressing the bright blade momentarily upon Heuil's helmet before his bloodsoaked body plunged into the deep crevasse of the Devil's Cauldron.

Spurring his mount, Arthur led his cavalry troop back towards Dundern to claim victory in the battle of the Caledonian Forest. Bloodstained and weary, his men withdrew to a small loch less than a mile to the north of Dundern, where they refreshed themselves in the cool waters, washing away the enemy blood that stained their swords, shields and mail tunics. After a day's rest the commanders and their troops returned to Stirling, but Arthur and his squadron returned along the southern shore of Loch Earn, moving steadily towards the setting sun.

The afterglow of sunset reflected in the still waters of Loch Voil as Arthur and his warriors rode into Balquhidder. When Arthur approached the forge, he found Katrine quenching steel and she appeared from a cloud of hissing steam to greet Arthur: *"I knew you would return,"* she said quietly. *"I have come to thank you,"* said Arthur, *"and to celebrate Excaliburn's first victory."*

Soon the warriors had camp fires burning brightly with enough spit-roast deer and wild pig to make a feast for the villagers; mead flowed freely and there was much joyfulness while Katrine sang to the accompaniment of her cittern until drowsiness overcame them all. Full of admiration for her playing, Arthur came up to speak with her. *"I have a small gift for you,"* he said, pulling a fine gold torc from his tunic and placing it round Katrine's slender neck. With her red hair flowing free and the embers of the fire reflecting in the bright gold neck-band, she looked more like a warrior queen than a blacksmith. Katrine shed a tear as she turned to Arthur. *"I thank you my lord Arthur, for this fine gift and for your kindness to me."*

# CHAPTER 9

# OUR LADY'S ISLAND

*"It is she who helpeth everyone in danger;*
*It is she that abateth the the pestilences;*
*It is she that quelleth the rage and the storm of the sea.*
*She is the Queen of the South;*
*She is the Mary of the Gael."*
St Brigid of Kildare, from *The Book of Lismore.*

On the western seaboard of Powys a south-westerly breeze dispersed the strands of early morning mist that shrouded a tall-masted sailing ship moored alongside the old Roman quay at Aberdyfi. A guilded dragon's head thrusting from the prow peered through the mist; then *Prydwen* appeared, a fine Gallo-Roman sailing barge with a large square sail made from thin leather hides, and a streaming pennant atop the mast that boasted the symbol of the Cymri, the fellow countrymen of Britain: '*Y Ddraig Goch*' the Red Dragon.

Arthur and six of his trusted warriors had pushed their mounts hard all morning. Leaving Wroxeter at dawn, they had travelled west towards the Roman fort at Llanfair Caereinion, following a mountain track beside the river Banwy; then onward through a narrow, rugged mountain pass to the point where the river Dugoed runs into the river Dyfi at Mallwyd. Once across the Dyfi they followed its fast flowing stream towards the wide estuary, galloping along the northern shore. By the time they had reached Aberdyfi, the mist had cleared, and the ship's crew were making ready to sail.

Arthur had arrived none too soon, for the tide was ebbing and the narrow channel to the harbour mouth would soon be too shallow to navigate. *"Let the Red Dragon lead the way,"* shouted Arthur, as he signalled captain Barinthus to cast-off. The ship's crew hoisted the great square mainsail and *Prydwen* slipped slowly from the quayside into the stream, catching the breeze across her port bow, sailing gently to windward with the helmsman pointing the prow towards the harbour entrance. Arthur's ship had, as her name *Prydwen* implied, a 'fair form' combining the features

Arthur's ship sails for Ireland. In this composite picture, Prydwen is shown as a traditional Roman sailing barge with a square mainsail and a smaller stunsail at the bow. The helmsman steered the ship with two long steerboards at each side of the stern, and the shallow draught allowed easy access to coastal harbours and estuaries.

Photo, Roman Merchant Ship, © Science&Society. Photo, Stormy Sea, © photos.com

of Roman vessels that had a large square mainsail and a small foresail rigged from a boom on the fore-deck, with the traditional Gallic design that featured a high curved prow and stern; she was well fitted for battering through heavy seas and violent gales and could withstand all the rough weather the Atlantic Ocean could throw at her. With dimensions measuring seventy-six feet in length and eighteen feet abeam, but having a shallow draught of only four feet, *Prydwen* was carvel-built entirely from oak with long planks of timber butted together and caulked, all laid on heavy ribs at least one foot thick and fastened with iron bolts as thick as a man's thumb. The sixty-foot pine mast was stepped through the deck and jointed at the base to secure it to the keel; and at the stern Arthur had built a low poop-deck to improve the forward view over the high prow. Twin steering-boards, or 'starboards' as they were commonly known, served as effective rudders, with a helmsman apiece responding to the commands of the captain. The ship's cockboat was lashed to the deck just aft of the mast, straddling the hatch-cover to the hold, and two huge bronze anchors were secured to the fore-deck, their coils of thick rope ready for use.

As *Prydwen's* bow sliced into the crests blown up by the south-westerly breeze, Arthur looked back beyond Aberdyfi to admire the seven peaks of Cader Idris; the summit dominated the skyline of western Powys and overlooked the Mawddach estuary that met the sea at Barmouth. Arthur had also found a safe anchorage here for *Prydwen* but the shifting sands and the narrow channel at the bar made navigation difficult at low water tides. Barmouth, Aberdyfi and Gloucester were all roughly sixty miles from Arthur's headquarters at Wroxeter; all were safe-havens for British warships patrolling the Irish Sea.

Arthur was enjoying his first sail for many months; freed for a while from his military campaigns, he found this an opportunity to reflect on his recent achievements. In the north he had suppressed the Caledonian revolt; he had extinguished Heuil's proud flame and routed his rebellious war-band. In the south, he had stemmed Ochta's incursion into Britain; and in the east, Arthur had drawn the line of his frontier defences from the river Tyne to Camulodunum, a line to be crossed by Angles and Saxons at their peril.

Following six distinctive victories that confirmed Arthur's success as Britain's military leader, there appeared for a moment to be a prospect of peace between the warring factions. On his return from Caledonia Arthur had received a letter from the powerful Irish king Muirtach Mac Erca, with an invitation to visit his royal court at Din Rig to discuss the possibility of his young warriors completing their military training with Arthur at Wroxeter. Aware that the notorious king Illan, who ruled over Leinster in the south-east of Ireland, was a confirmed enemy of Britain, Arthur looked favourably upon king Mac Erca's offer of friendship and agreed to meet near Waterford, where he could make a safe landing.

By mid-day the south-westerly breeze had strengthened and *Prydwen* began to make headway; with Aberystwyth off the port bow, the captain gave the order to steer to starboard, tacking to bring the wind onto his port quarter, and heading due west for Wexford. If the wind held constant and the weather fine, holding the ship on course with reference to the sun from mid-day to sunset would not tax the captain's navigation skills; but at night his only reference was the north-star, fixed in the firmament until obscured by cloud: then all hope rested on the prevailing wind remaining constant until sunrise gave the captain his eastern bearing.

Fortunately the weather held fair, and at dawn the lookout found the Wexford coast on the bow: after a twenty-four hour crossing *Prydwen* was on course for Waterford. Passing abeam Carnsore Point the captain held a westerly course for the last twenty-mile leg of the voyage to Hook Head and the entrance to Waterford Harbour. As *Prydwen* rounded the headland, Arthur could see the monks of Dubhan's small community tending the cliff-top lighthouse; with this unusual addition to their monastic duties they had become like their Master, a true light in the darkness, much blessed by the sailors whose lives they safeguarded through the night.

At the harbour entrance the strong outgoing tidal stream met the oncoming westerly wind and the sea cut up rough; but the captain steered *Prydwen* into the white horses and sailed towards the sheltered haven, coming alongside Kings Bay Quay just after high tide, when he could safely berth. The crew had barely lowered the sail when, suddenly, twelve mounted warriors appeared: their commander rode forward to greet Arthur in the name of king Mac Erca. *"We come in peace!"* shouted Arthur. *"Welcome to our beautiful island of Hivernia,"* replied the commander, as he beckoned Arthur and his six warriors towards their mounts. *"The king has come from Din Rig to meet you here, so we ride only a few miles north to the Abbey of Moyarney."*

The Abbey, founded by Bishop Ibar in the early years of the fifth century, nestled in luxuriant pastureland to the east of the river Barrow, where the monks fished for trout and salmon. The king welcomed Arthur and his companions, ushering them into the great hall that served as a refectory for the Abbey. As guest of honour Arthur took his place on the great top table to the right of his host the king; abbot Iban was seated to the right of Arthur and the king's guards alternated with Arthur's warriors. Jugs of mead were passed around the company, and the king raised a toast to Arthur who reciprocated his host's goodwill. Lamb from their own pastures, and vegetables grown in the Abbey gardens had been prepared by the monks for this special occasion; a jovial monk served this wholesome food from a great cauldron that hung over a roaring log fire laid in the hearth of the hall's great fireplace.

King Mac Erca ruled over the UiNeill from his fortress at Arlech on the Inishowen Peninsula in the north-west of Ireland. With a combination of strategic alliances and the use of military force he had succeeded, more than any other ruler, to weld the five rival states of Ireland into one realm. His most recent alliance with the king of Leinster had enabled him to combine forces to subdue the disparate rulers of Munster in the south-west; rejecting subservience to Mac Erca, these rebels had abandoned their territory and sailed to join their compatriots in Demetia, south Wales, and Dumnonia in south-western Britain.

Arthur acknowledged the migration of the Dal Raida people of north-east Ireland, who, together with Fergus their king, had crossed the sea to settle in Kintyre; by joining Britons of the Clyde in their fight against the Caledonian Picts, they had shown their loyalty to Arthur, as had the Laigin people from Leinster who had settled peaceably in the Lleyn Peninsula at the southern tip of Caernarvonshire; but the Irish rulers of Dyfed and Brecon were arrogant despots whose demands threatened the stability of western Britain.

King Mac Erca was aware that Arthur was no friend of Illan of Leinster, whose piratical raids on the western coasts of Britain had terrified the population: with hit and run tactics he stole gold and silver from wealthy villas, even from churches, escaping by sea before British forces could catch him. The love of gold ruled king Illan, for when he was not stealing Britons' gold, he was extracting the precious metal from the Wicklow Mountains, and even panning for golden grains in streams that tumbled down the rocky mountainsides. His natural good fortune had made Illan a rich and powerful king, and he traded gold for soldiers, ships and brigands to further his rewards from piracy.

Just as Arthur feared the growing power of the kings of Brecon and Dyfed, so king Mac Erca feared the power of his ally king Illan; secretly he envied Illan's control over the Wicklow Mountains and the source of gold, but his own war-band was not powerful enough to defeat king Illan in open battle. Arthur was quick to read the king's thoughts: by an unexpected twist of circumstance, king Illan had become their common enemy. Here was an opportunity for Arthur to forge a secret alliance wth Mac Erca that would secure the ultimate demise of king Illan and his pirates.

King Mac Erca offered Arthur a corps of young recruits to be trained at Wroxeter, accompanied by two experienced commanders who would later be able to lead them into battle. Together they devised a strategic plan that would draw Illan to a target in Britain: Mac Erca's men would povide a rear-guard, while Arthur's vanguard struck Illan's pirates with a piercing ambush. The two great military leaders raised their goblets and drank a toast to seal their alliance; if their master plan succeeded, Arthur would have destroyed a feared enemy of Britain, at the same time allowing king Mac Erca to take control of Leinster and become High King to rule over all Ireland.

As a reward, Arthur would receive payment in gold from Mac Erca's new source of wealth in the Wicklow Mountains, together with a settlement of land. Extremely pleased with the generous terms offered by the king, Arthur suggested that he could make good use of a site close to the quay at King's Bay, where a base camp would be needed to marshal recruits prior to their embarkation for Britain. Not only did this location offer a commanding view over Waterford Harbour but also afforded good fishing upstream towards Dunbrody. King Mac Erca agreed wholeheartedly with Arthur's suggestion.

The abbot of Moyarney and his monks were none the wiser concerning the king's secret plans when he departed for Ailech in the north, leaving his commanders to muster the first fifty young recruits scheduled to sail on *Prydwen's* return voyage. This gave Arthur and his guards a few days respite before returning to their ship. The next day, just before noon, a horsedrawn carriage pulled up sharply in the courtyard of the abbot's house; as Arthur appeared in the doorway, a dishevelled woman stepped down from the chariot, her white gown covered in mud. Abbess Brigid of Kildare had been travelling south to attend a pilgrimage when her chariot had unexpectedly overturned: she had been thrown clear but had suffered cuts and bruises to her hands and face. Seeing her in distress, Arthur ran forward to help and escorted Brigid into the hall; he poured some water for her to drink, and cleansed her wounds with a white linen cloth. *"You've had quite an accident,"* declared Arthur. *"Yes,"* replied Brigid, *"the farm track we often use had been fenced off by the farmer; it took us completely by surprise."*

When Abban realised that his unexpected guest was Brigid of Kildare, he invited her to rest at Moyarney until she had recovered from the shock of her accident. When Brigid had retired to the guest room, Abban took the opportunity to extol her virtue as the greatest and most loved evangelist since Patrick, and to tell Arthur the story of her life.

Brigid's father Dubtach was a pagan chieftain of Leinster; her mother Brocseach was his Christian bondswoman whom he sold to a druid living near Dundalk. Brigid was born in the hamlet of Faughart in the year 452 and baptised a Christian. When she was old enough, her mother put her in charge of the dairy, but having a kind and generous nature, Brigid gave away her mother's store of butter to the poor people of the village. In her childhood Brigid was taken to hear St Patrick preach; she was overwhelmed by the power of his message of love and hope for all who put their faith in Jesus Christ, the living God.

From that moment Brigid resolved to follow Patrick's example: when she reached marriageable age she rejected her father's choice of husband and instead pledged her heart to Christ. With seven friends robed in white, she left home for Meath, where Bishop Macaille received the girls into his church at Crogham; when they had completed their novitiate, Brigid travelled with her friends to Ardagh to make their final vows before Bishop Mel, a nephew of St Patrick. Later Brigid returned to her home province of Leinster, where she decided to make her foundation at Druim Criadh, close to the river Liffey, building a small oratory on an old pagan site beneath a large oak tree: 'Cill Dara,' the church of the oak tree, soon became known as a centre of consolation where Brigid helped the poor, healed the sick, and gave solace to those in sorrow. As a patron of the arts, Brigid founded a school of art where metalwork and illumination were perfected. An excellent example of this work was the Book of the Gospels, illuminated for Kildare scriptorium: every page was beautifully illuminated with interlaced designs and radiant colours that gave the impression that the work had been accomplished by the hand of an angel.

By the time the sun had set, Brigid had recovered from her fall and joined Abban and Arthur for supper in the abbot's house. Arthur felt honoured to be in the company of this renowned lady of the Church; but Brigid was not in awe of Arthur, even though she had heard of his military exploits in Britain, for she would sooner have men lay down their arms for the sake of peace. Brigid explained to Arthur that this was not her first visit to Moyarney. It was Abban's uncle, Bishop Ibar, who had founded the Abbey and he had always given Brigid his loyal support. On the day they met, Ibar was surprised to see that Brigid was the very image of the Virgin Mary who had appeared to him in a dream the previous night, and from this moment on, Brigid had become known as *Mary of the Gael.*

"*God has blessed you with many gifts,*" said Arthur, "*In battle I have taken many lives, but you, Brigid, were born to save lives.*"

"*With my gift of healing, through the power of the Holy Spirit I have healed many lepers, and given sight to the blind,*" replied Brigid, "*but on one unusual occasion I was asked to save the life of a king's servant. At a feast near Ardach the king of Teffia was drinking from a jewel encrusted goblet when a clumsy servant took it from his hand, but it fell to the floor and was smashed to pieces. The king seized the servant and condemned him to death; but Bishop Mel interceded, asking the king's permission to take up the goblet, which he then brought to me to repair. In a while I restored the vessel, and when it was returned to the king, he could not believe that it was as good as new, and he pardoned his unfortunate servant. Then Bishop Mel turned to me and said, 'Not for me hath God wrought this miracle, but for you, Brigid'.*"

"*Our land of Britain is like your broken goblet,*" said Arthur, "*for we face enemies on all sides that threaten to break our kingdom to pieces, from the dogheads of the north to the Saxon devils in the south, we are over-run with godless pagans.*"

"*I will pray for you,*" said Brigid, "*that the good Lord will give you the power to overcome your enemies and bring peace to your land.*"

"*We will not find peace until our bishops spread the Word of God amongst the Saxons!*" exclaimed Arthur, "*Sadly our churchmen flinch with fear at the very mention of the word Saxon.*"

"*Then perhaps we should undertake this mission on their behalf,*" volunteered Abban, "*but where would we start?*"

"*There is a small settlement of friendly Saxons by the river at Abingdon,*" said Arthur: "*they are descendants of the Roman foederati, German auxiliaries pressed into military service to swell the ranks of their conquering legions.*"

"*I will sow the seed of Christ's word amongst them,*" declared Abban, "*and with God's grace some of them will spread the holy word to their pagan sea-dog cousins, in their own language.*"

"*You are a brave man,*" said Arthur, *and I give you my full support.*"

"*I have not seen your Saxon devils,*" said Brigid, "*but I must tell you that I have seen*

149

*the Devil himself in the company of a young virgin called Brigit, daughter of Congaile, who had worked many miracles. During supper one evening I made the sign of the cross over the virgin's eyes so that she beheld Satan beside her: I demanded the demon to answer to me, but he replied, 'I cannot, Oh nunn! be without conversing with you, for you keep God's commandments, and you are compassionate to His poor and to His family.' 'Then tell us why you are so hurtful in your deeds to the human race?' I asked, and Satan answered, 'That the human race may not attain Paradise.' 'Why have you come amongst us?' I asked, 'A certain pious virgin is here, and I am in her company,' he replied. When I made the sign of the cross over the virgin's eyes, she was overcome with fear as she saw the demon beside her and I commanded her to banish the fosterling she had been cherishing for many seasons. The young virgin repented and was healed of the devil of gluttony and lust that had dwelt in her company."*

"*I too have seen the Devil amongst my monks,*" said Abban, "*but I have not been half as successful as Brigid in banishing him from our presence.*"

"*Tomorrow I will pray for you all,*" said Brigid, *for I must continue my journey to the new chapel on Our Lady's Island where we shall celebrate the feast of the Birth of our Lady.*"

Before the dying embers of the great log-fire, Arthur offered to escort Brigid safely to her destination, saying that he would be honoured to join the pilgrimage on this special occasion.

The next morning Brigid and Arthur thanked Abban for his kind hospitality, and the abbot bade them both farewell and a safe journey. Arthur took the reins of Brigid's chariot, setting off in a south-easterly direction towards Bridgetown, with Arthur's bodyguard as their escort. As they sped through the autumnal countryside, Brigid told Arthur of her dream during her stay at the Abbey:

"*I saw a vision of four ploughs in the south-east, and they ploughed the whole island of Hivernia; and before sowing was finished, the harvest grew and clear well-springs and shining streams came out of the furrows, and white garments were upon the sowers and ploughmen. Then I saw four other ploughs in the north, and they ploughed the island from one side to the other, and before harvest time the oats grew at once and ripened, and black streams came out of the furrows and the sowers and ploughmen were draped in black garments: and that made me truly sorrowful,*" said Brigid.

"*Please don't be sad,*" said Arthur sympathetically, "*for there is cause to rejoice in the first part of your dream: it seems to me that the first four ploughs are the four gospels that you and Patrick have sown with the seed of faith; and the harvest is the perfect faith of your followers. As to the four ploughs of the north that ploughed athwart your island, they must represent the false teachers and liars who will try to overturn your teaching, for they will reap only strife and death,*" Arthur explained intuitively, "*but do not be fearful my lady, for this will not happen in our lifetime: your dream is a warning to the future generations of Hivernia.*"

"*Arthur, you are indeed a man of true vision,*" observed Brigid, "*and I thank you most sincerely for interpreting my dream.*"

By mid-day Brigid and her military escort had almost reached the south-eastern tip of the island; here, just two miles north of Carnsore Point, Brigid had recently founded a small oratory on a natural peninsula jutting into a beautiful freshwater lake that was separated from the sea by the long ridge of a sandbar. The oratory appeared pristine with a thatched roof made of local reeds, and walls made from wattle and daub that had been limewashed peak white, with narrow arched windows and a small bell-tower; the single bronze bell had been cast in the foundry of Brigid's metalworkshop in Kildare. A small bothy adjoining the oratory provided accommodation for the nuns, whose livelihood depended on a few sheep and goats, some dairy cattle, and fresh fish from the lake.

Arthur reined in the horses and brought the chariot to a halt outside the oratory; but when Brigid saw a bloodstained cart by the door, she approached with foreboding and turned to Arthur for reassurance. Drawing his sword, Arthur kicked open the door. No enemy opposed him: instead Arthur was confronted with a scene reminiscent of a battlefield, with wounded men lying on makeshift beds of straw overlaid with flax-cloth to soak up the blood from their wounds. Sister Morgen and eight maidens attended the seriously wounded soldiers, applying linen bandages and comforting those in severe pain with true care and dedication.

Arthur and his men moved as one to help the young nuns, finding makeshift timbers that could be used as splints for twisted and broken limbs; then they pulled out the unfortunate few who had died from their wounds. Sister Morgen explained to Brigid that the cause of the bloodshed had been a skirmish when the Deisi warrriors had fallen foul of a band of king Illan's men: the bloodthirsty pirates of Leinster had hacked their way through the young Deisi soldiers showing no remorse, killing most of them, then leaving the wounded to the mercy of a farmer who had brought them by horse and cart to the sisters' oratory.

"*It is God's will that my sanctuary is now a hospital for wounded warriors,*" Brigid announced to Arthur, "*but now the day draws to a close, it would be best to celebrate Our Lady's Day with a simple service for these poor souls.*"

Arthur and his men knelt alongside the wounded and their nurses while Brigid presided over the service, praying to Saint Mary for her blessing and for the power to heal the wounded through the Holy Spirit; Brigid concluded with a blessing for Arthur and his warriors, and a prayer for peace in the world.

Brigid poured wine into a magnificent silver chalice; made to her design in the

The Derrynaflan Chalice. This beautiful silver chalice was unearthed by Michael Webb at Derrynaflan Church in 1980. Now fully restored and displayed in the National Museum of Ireland, this Christian communion vessel is one of the finest examples of 9th century Celtic design and follows the high standard of craftsmanship set by St Brigid's workshop at Kildare in the early 6th century. It is no small wonder that a vessel as magnificent as this became the focal point for the medieval legends of the Holy Grail.

Photo, © National Museum of Ireland

workshop at Kildare, it was decorated with gold filigree and studded with amber, an object of great beauty. Arthur was the last to drink from the chalice, and he returned it to Brigid.

*"Arthur, this is for you,"* said Brigid softly, *"for all your help and kindness to me, a token of thanks from Mary of the Gael."* Arthur was amazed by Brigid's generous gift, and taking the chalice he thanked Brigid most sincerely, *"Your priceless gift will honour our king's Royal Chapel at Castell Dinas Bran, the strongest fortress in Britain, where it will be cherished always."*

As Brigid said farewell, she handed Arthur a beautiful cloth with the image of the Virgin Mary embroidered in the centre, *"Take this Holy mantle, and let it be your armour in battle, for in faith, Our Lady will protect you from harm."*

By nightfall Arthur and his warriors had returned to King's Bay Quay, only to find *Prydwen* sitting unceremoniously in the mud where the ebb tide had left her high and dry. Before dawn the next day Arthur rode down to his newly acquired land where king Mac Erca's commanders had marshalled the recruits in a temporary encampment. Arthur welcomed them to his command, and in return for their dedication and commitment promised to turn them into the best warriors in the world.

By the time the troops had embarked, *Prydwen* was fully afloat on the morning flood tide. Captain Barinthus gave the order to sail, steering the great barge through the wind onto the starboard tack, and out towards the main channel for the eight mile run downstream to the harbour mouth; rounding Hook Head *Prydwen* turned due east, running with the wind on the long voyage to Aberdyfi. As soon as the coastline of Hivernia had dipped below the western horizon, one of Arthur's men ran forward with a small scroll of parchment: "Sister Brigid asked me to deliver this to you when we were under sail."

Arthur broke the seal to find a short poem, penned perfectly by Brigid herself:

> *"I long for a lake of great ale;*
> *I long for the meats of belief and pure piety;*
> *I long for the flails of penance at my house;*
> *I long for them to have barrels full of peace;*
> *I long to give away jars full of love;*
> *I long for them to have cellars full of mercy;*
> *I long for cheerfulness to be in their drinking;*
> *And I long for Jesus too, to be there among them."*

Arthur was deeply moved.

# CHAPTER 10

# THE BATTLE OF CASTELL GUINNION

*"The eighth battle was fought in Castell Guinnion in which Arthur*
*carried the image of St Mary, ever virgin, on his shoulders."*
The Historia Brittonum, compiled by Nennius.

The location of Arthur's eighth battle, listed by Nennius as "Castello Guinnion" has never been found; perhaps the original Latin name 'Guinnion' may have been confused with the Welsh 'Gwynion' meaning 'white' in English, and leading naturally to the assumption that Guinnion was 'a white castle somewhere in Wales.' Not surprisingly, there are a number of ancient hill-forts in Wales called 'Gwynion' all possible contenders for the site of Arthur's battle.

Cerrig Gwynion, or 'White Stone' lies on the lower slopes of Tal-y-fan, a mountain that rises to a peak of 2000 feet, three miles to the south of Conwy in Gwynedd. Seven miles south-west of Llangollen, Clwydd, there is another hill-fort of the same name in the upper reaches of the Ceiriog Valley; and two miles south-west of Denbigh in Clwyd there is a castle mound at Caeugwynion Mawr. Finally, just one mile north-east of Llandysil, we find Castell Gwynionedd located in the heart of Dyfed, a stronghold controlled by the Welsh baron Llywelyn ab Owain, following King Edward I's conquest of Wales in the year 1283.

Nothing but the ridges of the castle foundation remains to be seen, but evidently it once commanded a favoured rural position that overlooked the river Teifi. This remote and beautiful place, historically renowned for its seclusion, is also the site of two important iron-age fortresses: to the north a steep escarpment rises to the crown of Pencoed-y-foel, an imposing hill-fort with a single ditch and bank fortification; and just over a mile to the south, we come across Craig Gwrtheyrn, said to be the fifth century fort of Cair Guorthigern, built by the powerful British king Vortigern as his last refuge.

But before we can confirm the location of Castell Guinnion we must look for further clues in Nennius' text that may help to identify the site of the battle. The unknown author of the battle-list transcribed by Nennius devoted seven lines to his detailed description of the battle, amounting to almost one third of the complete text, showing the importance that he attached to the event:

*"The eighth battle was fought in Castell Guinnion*
*in which Arthur carried the image*
*of St Mary, ever virgin, on his shoulders*
*and that day the pagans were put to flight;*
*and a great slaughter was upon them*
*through the virtue of Our Lord Jesus Christ*
*and through the virtue of St Mary the virgin, His mother."*

Gildas, writing of Britain's enemies the Picts and Saxons, made a similar reference to enemies 'being put to flight,' *the old enemies of Britain re-appeared, they came relying on their oars as wings, on the arms of their oarsmen, and on the winds swelling their sails."*

And again, when describing the advance of the Roman Cavalry against the invaders:

*"They hurried the flight of their horsemen like eagles on the land and the course of their sailors on the sea, and planted in their enemies' necks the claws of their sword points: and they caused among them a slaughter like the fall of leaves in the autumn. This was the way our worthy allies the Romans instantly 'put to flight' across the sea the columns of their rivals, such as could escape."*

If the pagans who opposed Arthur at Guinnion had sailed across the sea from Jutland or Saxony, they would have attempted to secure a foothold somewhere along the south or east coast of Britain. Furthermore, in Arthur's day the word 'Castello' would have applied to a Roman fortress built of flint and stone, combined with bricks and mortar, rather than a British hill-fort with a turf rampart and timber palisade. Just as the Saxons had earlier succeeded in overcoming the lightly defended forts of Pevensey and Portchester, it is therefore highly probable that the battle of Castell Guinnion resulted from an audacious attack on another of the Saxon shore-forts further to the east.

The suggested link to a Welsh 'Castell Gwynion' may therefore have no foundation in fact; Nennius quotes British names such as Glein, Dubglas and Celidon together with Latin names like Bassas, Guinnion and Badon; with his understanding of both languages as well as a reasonable knowledge of the geography and place-names of North-Wales, he would have realised that the name Guinnion was distinctly 'un-Welsh' and was certainly not to be confused with 'Gwynion.'

Allowing for a period of delay from the time Arthur's battles actually took place, to a bard's memorisation of the verbal record of events, and taking into consideration the natural errors that would have occurred from the first verbal account to the first written record, it is not surprising that most of the names included in Nennius' list are as incomprehensible to us today, as they may well have been to Nennius and his contemporaries when they were first copied from the original texts in the early ninth century. It is certain that at least three of the battles, Bassas, Guinnion and Agned, have suffered this identity problem in transmission, so that their original names have become disguised beyond recognition. However, if we compare the complex spelling of some English place-names with their much simplified local pronunciations, for example Leicester is pronounced 'Lester,' Shaftesbury, affectionately shortened to 'Shaston,' and Wymondham, pronounced 'Wyndham,' then it may just be possible to identify the lost battle names by searching for the more complex names from which they have originated.

In the case of 'Guinnion' we find a helpful clue in the use of the double letter 'n' which is distinctly different from the Welsh 'Gwynion' with only the single letter; in order to match the clues we have uncovered so far, we need to look for a Roman fortress with a name beginning with 'G' featuring the double 'n' in the middle, and ending with 'on.' If we examine the list of Saxon Shore Forts from Portchester, the Roman Portus Ardaoni in the south, to Brancaster, Branodunum, in the north at the entrance of the Wash, we find Roman Gariannonum in a strategic position guarding Bredon Water and the River Waveney estuary just a few miles from Great Yarmouth.

Evidently the Angles, the first English people, to settle in this part of Britain, found the Roman name 'Gariannonum' unpronounceable, and promptly changed it to 'Burgh Castle.' There is no doubt that the local Britons would also have found the name too much of a mouthful; they would have certainly dropped the 'um' at the end of the word, and softened the first part to something like 'Gwiannon.' It is not difficult to see how this word could have evolved naturally into 'Guinnion;' if it did not, then we should forgive the scribe who, when struggling to translate the vernacular Brithonic into Latin heard 'Castello Gariannon' and wrote down 'Castello Guinnion.'

Castell Dinas Bran, North Wales. The stone ruin of the medieval Castell Dinas Bran crowns a summit that towers imposingly one thousand feet above the town of Llangollen in the Dee Valley. Set in the heart of the ancient kingdom of Powys, Dinas Bran was the seat of the Princes of Powys, whose Iron Age fortress was encompassed by massive earthen ramparts topped with a wooden palisade that protected their feasting hall and round-houses within. The castle is named after Bran the Blessed, a heroic deity of Welsh and Irish mythology. According to legend, Bran travelled to Ireland to recover a magical vessel of plenty, a Cauldron of Rebirth whose pagan attributes were later echoed in the Christian symbol of the Holy Grail. This legendary association has survived to the present day, for many still believe that Dinas Bran is the Castle of the Grail.　　　　　　　　　　　　　Photo, © Gareth Houghton

Arthur's first duty on his return from Hibernia was to report to King Uther at Castle Dinas Bran. Uther was pleased to hear that Arthur had secured a secret alliance with king Mac Erca and was intrigued with the idea of enticing the renegade king Illan into battle. The offer of three hundred young Irish recruits in return for the elimination of a mutual enemy in a staged battle was an acceptable bargain. That very night, Uther arranged a feast to celebrate Arthur's successful mission, and when Guinevere arrived to welcome Arthur he told of his fortuitous meeting with Brigid and bishop Abban at Moyarney. Later, as the evening's celebrations drew to a close, Arthur revealed the beautiful chalice; calling for everyone's attention he presented Brigid's gift to the king: *"I am honoured to present you with this treasured chalice, with the blessing of Mary of the Gael,"* said Arthur. *"Indeed, I am greatly honoured to receive this holy gift,"* replied king Uther, *"this fine chalice will have pride of place in our chapel. Together we shall celebrate and give thanks to God for His Divine Love and Protection."*

The next day Arthur returned to his headquarters at Wroxeter to welcome the Irish recruits and their commander. They would receive intensive training during the winter months: first they would undergo weapon training, and all who reached the high standard required would progress to the equestrian school for mounted battle-training. Every successful cadet would be given their own horse as a reward from Arthur. Within six months, these aspiring warriors would be ready for their first battle.

That evening, Arthur and Cei retired to the Commander's Villa overlooking the banks of the river Severn to discuss defence plans and review the need to bring the garrisons up to strength, now that Arthur's campaign in Caledonia had been successfully completed. Squadrons drawn from Lincoln, Longthorpe and Camulod would return to defend the eastern front; looking closely at his military map of Britain, Arthur suggested that it would make good sense to hold a reserve garrison at Guerensis, now Warwick, the strategic centre of southern Britain.

*"From Warwick, an operational range with a radius of eighty miles would encompass Chester, Brough to the north, the estuaries of the Wash, Londinium, Venta; Cadbury Castle in the south-west, and Caerleon and Caersws in the west,"* declared Arthur, whilst sweeping his right hand over the map in a great circle around Warwick. Cei thought it would be an excellent idea to have a troop of warriors at readiness, able at very short notice to re-inforce a battle-front over such a wide area; together they agreed this strategy and resolved to establish a military base at Warwick by the spring of the new year, when the weather would allow a new season of open warfare to begin. *"Until then, we shall enjoy this fragile peace!"* exclaimed Arthur.

The sudden appearance of five square sails on the eastern horizon of the Oceanus Germanicus heralded the start of the new battle season. Cerdic, the Saxon war-leader, and his son Cenric, together with an invasion force of two hundred warriors, were set to strike the east coast of Britain. Their westerly heading would lead them straight to the estuary of the river Gariannus, now called the river Yare. Cerdic planned to slip unseen into the southern channel of the estuary at dusk, when the high tide would give him enough water to sail over the sand-bar and into the deep, wide lagoon of Breydon Water beyond: this course would steer his fleet well clear of the coastal fort at Caister, and hopefully allow him to sail upstream undetected by the British. On the voyage from Saxony the fleet had ploughed through rough seas for over four-hundred miles, and Cerdic and his crews were exhausted; they were more than happy when he gave the order to pull ashore on the south bank of Breydon Water, allowing them to make camp just before nightfall.

The Roman Fortress of Gariannonum. Re-named Burgh Castle by the English, Castell Gariannonum was built by the Romans on a terrace overlooking Breydon Water and the Waveney Estuary. The castle, with walls eight feet thick made of flintstone and tiles that enclosed an area of almost six acres, formed part of a chain of coastal defences from the Solent to the Wash that were known as the Saxon Shore Forts. Photo, © Mike Page

When the morning mists began to clear, Cerdic set sail towards the southern reach of the estuary; then, suddenly, above the strands of thinning mist, the huge towering wall of the old Roman fortress of Gariannonum appeared before the Saxons like an apparition. Cerdic was shocked, expecting an assault from the castle at any moment; but when no attack came, he quickly realised that luck had presented him with an opportunity that was too good to let slip: the capture of a British fortress on his first day ashore would be a fortuitous prize with a great strategic advantage.

Gariannonum, built in the late third century by the Romans at the mouth of the river Gariannus, overlooked the wide natural harbour of Breydon Water; the fortress provided a safe anchorage for ships that plied their trade between Britain and Gaul, and guarded their merchandise and supplies from Saxon pirates. But the Roman sailing barges had long since departed, leaving only the weathered oak quay below the west wall of the castle as a reminder of more prosperous times.

Cerdic's crews deftly manoeuvred their shallow-draught longships, and moored line-astern along the quay; then, grasping their weapons, they disembarked and prepared to attack. To the Saxons, the walls of Gariannonum, eight feet thick at the base and towering almost twenty feet above them, appeared impenetrable. Massive rounded bastions at each corner of the castle had supported Roman artillery platforms that fired stone balls and rocks at invaders; but the Roman weaponry had been dismantled years before, allowing Cerdic to approach the castle unopposed. Baffled by the fact that the long west wall facing the estuary had no gateway, the Saxons pushed forward, only to find the north and south walls just as impenetrable: finally, as they reached the east side of the fortress, they discovered a large arched gateway in the centre of the east wall.

Despite the formidable appearance of the massive oak gates, Cerdic realised that this was the fort's weakest point; an intensive battering would soon shatter the timbers and give him access to the castle. The small garrison of local Britons were cut down by Saxons wielding long swords and seaxes as they stampeded through the splintered gateway. Scant mercy was shown to the few villeins who had taken refuge in the castle: the men and older women were put to the sword: bloody Saxon axes split children's heads like logs for firewood; only the young women were spared, bound and held as unwilling slaves for Saxon soldiers. The ravagers seized everything they could lay their hands upon, swords, shields and the gold and silver rings and brooches of the dead; but in their greed for the pickings of war, they failed to notice a young girl partly hidden beneath an old haycart, burying a few treasured pieces of glassware that she had placed in a bronze bowl and hastily covered with loose soil and straw.

Before sunset the invaders brought out the bodies of the dead: then as the sun dipped below the western horizon, flames from a great funeral pyre licked skywards leaving the east wind to scatter the ashes of those unfortunate Britons over the gloomy expanse of Breydon Water. Cerdic and Cynric congratulated themselves on their seemingly effortless conquest. *"Where is the renowned Arthur and his valiant army?"* Cerdic asked his men. *"In the land beyond the sunset,"* suggested one. *"Too far away to care about this place!"* shouted another.

Cerdic mused on the irony that the so called "Saxon Shore Fort" of Gariannonum was now truly in Saxon hands: it was not just the practical prize of a headquarters from which he could attack the British while strengthening his warband with reinforcements from Saxony; but it was, more significantly, a political prize and a great snub to Arthur, for Cerdic had succeeded in taking one of the important chess-pieces off the battle-board of Britain. Now it was Arthur's move.

News of the Saxon assault on Gariannonum reached Arthur at Warwick later the following day. Whilst riding out from a nearby hamlet a farmer had witnessed the last stages of the Saxon attack: turning around, he rode through the night to the British garrison at Camulod, seventy miles away to the south-west. Without delay, the garrrison commander dispatched a messenger to Warwick, where Arthur and Cei had just completed a large timber hall and barracks to accommodate the reserve squadron.

The couriers who delivered the Imperial post were expected to achieve a distance of fifty miles in one day, but Arthur's military messengers had been trained to cover one hundred miles or more in a day, with the authority to commandeer fresh mounts wherever they were available. The messenger from Camulod reached Arthur's encampment at Warwick by nightfall on the day following the attack; after riding across country for over one hundred miles, he was exhausted. Arthur was shocked and angered to hear of the Saxon's remorseless slaughter at Gariannon, and vowed to avenge their deaths.

Arthur and Cei worked through the night to devise a battle-plan for a reprisal attack against Cerdic and his marauders; marshalling a force strong enough to repel the Saxons would take some time, and Cei suggested that they allow five days to prepare for battle. Responding later rather than sooner would hopefully lull the Saxons into a false sense of security when they could be taken off-guard. Arthur agreed, and proposed to call forward fifty newly trained warriors from Wroxeter to Longthorpe where they would meet, together with a hundred men from the new garrison at Warwick. On the day before the battle, Cei would lead his troop of one hundred cavalry from Camulodunum; an additional troop of fifty from Longthorpe would give Arthur a battle force of three-hundred mounted warriors, most of whom, with the exception of the Wroxeter squadron, were men experienced in battle.

Cei knew that the commander at Camulod would have alerted Longthorpe, so that both garrisons would be at battle readiness. At dawn, Arthur dispatched riders to Wroxeter and Longthorpe with his troop requirements, together with the battle-plan, and Cei departed for Camulod to prepare his men for battle. An enemy incursion along the eastern seaboard of Britain presented Arthur with the serious logistical problem of moving his cavalry into position as quickly as possible over the long distance to the coast. Arthur had always imagined that his march north to Carlisle was much further than any of his journeys to the eastern parts of Britain; but in fact Gariannonum was further from Arthur's headquarters at Wroxeter than Carlisle; over one hundred and ninety miles to the east, it was as far as he had marched to the battle of Bassas the previous year.

The experience of his first battle on the River Glen in Lincolnshire had shown Arthur the advantage of using Longthorpe as a rendezvous point: just one hundred miles from Wroxeter, and eighty miles from Gariannon, Longthorpe fort offered the ideal staging post where his men could break their journey and recouperate for a day before continuing their march eastward. From Longthorpe Arthur would take the old Roman road as far as Swaffham, then route across open country to Wymondham before heading to the coast. Cei would march north from Camulod along the Roman road to Norwich, and then move north-east to meet Arthur at Geldeston. Here, only nine miles from Gariannon, the two forces would meet in the water meadows that reached down to the north bank of the river Waveney; and when his men and their mounts had refreshed themselves in the cool waters of the stream, Arthur would deliver his final battle briefing.

The charcoal grey clouds of an impending storm hung ominously over Breydon Water at dusk as Arthur gave the signal to attack. A sudden flash of lightning momentarily shocked the castle walls into a dazzling whiteness; then the accompanying rumble of thunder muffled the trampling of soft turf as the British cavalry charged towards its target.

The unexpected storm had not deterred the Saxons from their evening festivities in the open keep of the castle, where sparks from spit-roasts flew high above the walls and Cerdic's merry crew quaffed strong Saxon ale to celebrate a feast that marked their sixth day of unopposed conquest in Britain.

Arthur came in from the east, leading two columns of fifty cavalry, followed closely by Cei, at the head of his squadron in the same formation. To the rear, and on each flank of the main attack force, the two reserve squadrons followed at a distance: on the right flank the commander and a troop of fifty cavalry had orders to follow-up the main attack to prevent the enemy escaping from the fortress; and on the left flank, the troop of inexperienced young warriors from Wroxeter had instructions to push around the south wall of the fortress to attack and set fire to the Saxon's boats.

Arthur could not believe his good fortune as he closed in on the fort's east wall, for the broken and splintered gates had been left unrepaired and were wide open. With a sharp battle-cry Arthur charged through the open archway leading his cavalry swiftly into the centre of the keep. Cei followed with the second wave of cavalry breaking to the left and right of Arthur's squadron. Faced with the sudden appearance of two hundred mounted British warriors, the Saxons did not know which way to turn: drawing their swords they flailed and slashed at the horses, but already half drunk from their own strong ale, Cerdic's men were now at the mercy of Arthur's expert spearmen.

Those who were not speared to death by Arthur's warriors were hacked into submission by Cei's swordsmen; suddenly their shouts of merriment were turned to shrieks of pain as their blood mingled with the froth of spilt ale. A few of the enemy dashed to the parapets, abseiling to the open ground on ropes hastily flung from the battlements; then, running to their boats to escape Arthur's wrath, they came face to face with the Wroxeter squadron torching their ships. Cerdic and Cynric, in a desperate bid to escape, led a straggling band of men to fight their way aboard the nearest flaming ship, slashing the mooring lines with their swords and taking flight towards the open sea.

Arthur's white stallion reared up in the centre of the fray as if sensing victory: in the light of the fierce fires now burning within the walls of the mighty Castell Gariannon, Arthur's helmet glinted, reflecting the flames. As he turned to survey the scene of battle, the fire's bright glow illuminated the image of Saint Mary the Holy Virgin, peaceful and resplendent upon Brigid's embroidered cape that Arthur wore across his shoulders.

*"and that day the pagans were put to flight*
*and a great slaughter was upon them."*

# CHAPTER 11

# THE BATTLE IN THE CITY OF THE LEGION

*"All that glisters is not gold."*
William Shakespeare: *The Merchant of Venice*

By the end of the first century the Romans had established permanent fortresses in Caerleon, Chester and York, key strategic centres that would play a vital role in securing their long-term conquest of Britain.

Julius Frontinus established a base for Legio II Augusta at Isca, Caerleon-on-Usk; from here the Romans controlled the fertile land of the Silures in the Vale of Glamorgan, receiving supplies and reinforcements from ships of the Roman fleet based in Cardiff Harbour. In the later years of his governorship, Frontinus began the construction of a new fortress at Deva, Chester, with a turf wall and timber palisade built by Legio II Adiutrix in 78 AD; this original wooden fort was later rebuilt in stone by Agricola as a permanent base for Legio XX, following a swift battle campaign in North Wales to crush the recalcitrant Ordovices and to spearhead an attack on the Druids who had taken refuge on the holy island of Anglesey.

When Petillius Cerialis, the new Governor of Britain, arrived with reinforcements, he stationed Legio II Adiutrix at Lincoln before moving north with his own ninth Legion to establish a new fortress at York. From the legionary bases of York and Chester, Cerialis launched a coordinated campaign to conquer northern Britain: as Agricola struck north from Chester towards Carlisle with Legio XX, Cerialis advanced from York, engaging in bloody battles with the Brigantes as he marched up the Stanhope Pass to join Agricola at Carlisle.

From these early beginnings, the three legionary fortresses maintained their status as military headquarters throughout the Roman occupation of Britain; and although the army's presence at Caerleon was gradually reduced, Chester remained an active legionary base for over three hundred and fifty years. In the final years of Roman rule, York became the capital city of northern Britain and the headquarters of the Dux Britanniarum.

Of the three legionary cities, both Caerleon and Chester became known as *'Cair Legion'* or the 'City of the Legion.' Both cities would therefore be eligible to claim the site of Arthur's eighth battle as listed by Nennius; however in the year 616, just over a century after Arthur's battle, another battle of Chester was recorded in the *Annales Cambriae* as 'Cair Legion' and was also referred to as 'Urbe Legionis' the 'City of the Legion.' It was an epic battle between Aethelfrith, the English king of Northumbria and king Iago of Gwynedd, with his allies from Rhos and Powys. The great Roman citadel of Chester now became the Britons' bastion of defence against the English invaders. Believing in the power of God, the king of Gwynedd called upon the monks of Bangor-on-Dee to pray for victory; but when more than a thousand monks formed a vanguard to the British army, the pagan king Aethelfrith

Illustration of Deva, the Roman city of Chester. Home to the Twentieth Legion for over two hundred years, Chester became known as the 'City of the Legion.' The strategic advantages of Chester as a military base were fully appreciated by the Romans from an early date: a large harbour at the highest navigable point on the river Dee, a river crossing, and a defendable position close to a valuable natural supply of salt. A new amphitheatre, built early in the second century, seated 7000 spectators, and in the late third century, a unique elliptical building was completed, possibly to house the Roman Pantheon. The city took its Roman name from the river Dee, Deva, meaning 'the holy one.'

Illustration by kind permission of the artist, © David Swarbrick shouted his derisory verdict on their presence: *"If these men invoke their God against us, they fight against us, even though they come unarmed to battle."* Whereupon the pagans slaughtered the monks as they knelt in prayer on the field of battle, and then ploughed into the British line wielding swords and axes in a most barbaric attack.

This battle of Chester was renowned as Aethelfrith's infamous victory, because of his merciless slaughter of the innocent monks; but the historical clue in the chronicles points to the fact that, by the sixth century, the name 'Cair Legion' was understood to refer to the city of Chester.

The withdrawal of the twentieth legion from Chester in the early years of the fifth century left a military vacuum in the city; this, and the loss of Roman garrisons in the south and west of Britain opened the floodgates to a mass of Irish settlers whose arrival along the western seaboard went unopposed. In time, the foothold settlements of Irish immigrants from Cornwall to north Wales expanded gradually into major colonies. The Ui Liathain from Munster in southern Ireland migrated to south-west Wales, colonising Dyfed, and the Brychan kings, pushing eastward from their landfall in Cardigan Bay, took control of the old Roman fort at Llandovery before finally establishing their royal centre at Brecon. Further north, the Leinster Irish sailed across the Irish Sea to colonise the Lleyn Peninsula; and hostile forces from Meath and Airgialla invaded Anglesey and the coastal regions of North Wales.

When Vortigern, the High King of Britain, finally realised that he was virtually surrounded by powerful Irish colonies whose kings and leaders were eager to secure and expand their settlements by force, he acted with an urgent sense of purpose to restore the balance of power in his own favour. From his central state of Powys he sent a contingent of the local Cornovii to repel the Irish occupation of Dumnonia. He then engaged the services of the most powerful war leader in Britain, Cunedda, a military leader of the Votadini, who ruled over the Manau Gododdin from his fortress at Stirling. A few lines of verse have survived to celebrate his prowess in the north:

*"Splendid he was in battle, with his nine hundred horse, Cunedda the lion, the son of Aeternus."*

With a mandate from the Council of Britain to expel the Irish from Venedotia in return for a generous part of the re-conquered territory, Cunedda moved south with his army and prepared for battle; but in seeking a new base for his cavalry, he was spoilt for choice, for both Chester and Wroxeter had originally been equipped to accommodate Roman cavalry and were now only lightly garrisoned. But Chester, with the security of its imposing stone walls and its strategic position close to north Wales, offered Cunedda the ideal headquarters for his campaign.

Cunedda's first attacks on the coastal settlements of Gwynedd and Anglesey sent a shockwave through the Irish colonies in Wales: without warning, his mounted warriors had appeared in force. Unprepared, and mostly unarmed, the Irish were either pushed into the sea or massacred close to their homesteads. Nennius confirms the story in his *Historia Brittonum:*

*"Cunedda, ancestor of king Maelgwyn the Great, came from the north with his eight sons, from the region called Manau Gododdin, and expelled the Irish from these countries with great slaughter, so they never returned to live there again."*

Cunedda's mission to expel the Irish from western Britain was not a short-lived campaign: it would take him over a quarter of a century to re-conquer Gwynedd, Anglesey and Cardigan, before he was able to give his attention to South Wales, where his presence in the kingdom of Ystrad Tiwi is marked by the small town of Cynheidre on the east coast of Carmarthenshire. He regained control of Kidwelly (Cetgueli), only nine miles south of Castell Dwyran near Carmarthen, where a powerful Irish dynasty known as the Deisi ruled as the protectors of Dyfed.

In the last decades of the fourth century, the Irish Deisi tribe from the Waterford region of southern Ireland were allowed by the Romans to settle in Demetia; in return their leader Aed Brosc agreed to protect the coast of western Britain from attacks by Irish pirates; from this time onwards the Deisi rulers of Dyfed used the Roman title of 'Protector' rather than the British title of 'King.' Aed Brosc's eldest son Urb moved eastward to found the kingdom of Brycheiniog, or Brecon, around 420 AD, while his youngest son Triffyn Farfog married Gwledyr, the heiress of the Demetian leader Clotrius, thereby securing their Irish regal heritage in both Dyfed and Brecon.

Between these territories the land of Ystrad Tywi extended from the Gower Peninsula on the coast to Llandeilo where the northern border followed the river Teifi; the eastern and western borders were defined by the rivers Tywi and Duad respectively; and to the north, the Black Mountains formed a natural border between Dyfed and Brecon. By striking at the settlements on the coast of Ystrad Tywi, Cunedda was pushing the boundaries of his mandate close to the limit, but whether or not his attack on Kidwelly had been sanctioned by the Council of Britain, the presence of his warriors so close to the heart of Dyfed would have served as a shock warning to Triffyn Farfog and his brother Urb Mac Aed. The very real threat of retribution from Cunedda's army would have made them think twice about attempting to extend their territories to the north and east.

However, the degree of Cunedda's overall success in expelling the Irish from western Britain was measured by the wide extent of re-conquered territory inherited by his sons. Cunedda granted land to his son Ceretic that included over fifty miles of the western seaboard of Wales, and this new kingdom was named Ceredigion (Cardigan) after him. In turn Ceretic gave the northern part of this land to his own son Marianus, who gave his name to Merioneth; a much smaller kingdom, it extended northward from Machynlleth to Dolgellau.

Cunedda's son Ennuaun Yrth inherited Powys and Gwynedd, together with the wealth and political power assumed when he took over his father's role as the supreme commander of Venedotia. In due course, these lands were passed down to Ennuaun's sons: Gwynedd to Catwallaun Longhand, and Powys to Ewein Ddantgwyn. Eventually, these powerful kingdoms were inherited in turn by their sons, Maelgwyn and Cuneglassus, first cousins who shared the great warrior Cunedda as their great grandfather.

But what was Arthur's position in the heirarchy of Britain? Was he just *"Arthuri Militi, Arthur the Warrior?"* as Nennius describes him in *De Mirabilibus Britanniae;* or was he also a Prince of Powys, the rightful heir to one of the royal kingdoms of Britain?

Geoffrey of Monmouth's legendary story of Arthur's birth from the liason of Uther Pendragon, the Chief Dragon of Britain, with Ygraine, Duchess of Cornwall, links Arthur to the royal line of Gwynedd. Dark Age genealogies compiled about 950 AD from the earliest records and preserved in the *Annales Cambriae*, confirm that it was Cunedda's eldest son Ennuaun Yrth who became 'Chief Dragon' in the second half of the fifth century, and this title inferred that he held sway over all the kings of Britain.

If Uther Pendragon's real name was Ennuaun Yrth, and the legend of Arthur's birth is true, then he was Arthur's father; but which of his two sons was called 'Arthur' the Bear? For the vital clue that leads to the true identification of Arthur we need to look at the succeeding generation of Ennuaun's descendants: Catwallaun's son Maelgwyn, also known as Maglocunus, became the 'great king of Gwynedd' described by Gildas as the "Dragon of the Island" whose life of misdeeds finally earned him the reputation of the most evil king in Britain.

But his cousin Cuneglassus was also included in Gildas' list of reprobate kings: in the course of his diatribe Gildas reveals that Cuneglassus was, in his youth, *"the charioteer of the bear."* This statement confirms Arthur's true identity, for although Gildas uses the Latin word *'ursus'* for 'bear' we know that the name 'Arthur' is a combination of the British word for bear, *'arth,'* and *'ursus,'* meaning 'bear' in Latin.

Furthermore, Gildas first addresses Cuneglassus calling him *"you bear"* implying that he is of the same family as 'the bear,' or in other words: *"you are now the bear, the son of Arthur."*

If Cuneglas was Arthur's son, then Arthur must be Ewein Ddantgwyn, the eldest son of Ennuaun Yrth, and grandson of Cunedda, the founder of the dynasty of North Wales that lasted over eight hundred years. The fact that Ewein Ddantgwyn was related to Maelgwyn was of great significance, for it meant that Maelgwyn was Arthur's nephew.

First and foremost Arthur was renowned as a warrior, the 'Dux Britanniarum' or military commander of Britain, but as the rightful heir to part of his father's kingdom he was lawfully the 'Prince of Powys.' This meant that on Uther Pendragon's death, Arthur would become the king of Powys.

☙ ☙ ❧ ❧

Ynys Mon, later called Anglesey from the old Norse word '*ongull*' meaning 'strait,' was a prize worth fighting for. For Britons, the island was both a shield from their seaborne enemies from the west and a refuge from enemies approaching overland from the east. For centuries the island had been held sacrosanct by the Celts as a centre of pagan power and human sacrifice, until the Druid priests and their followers were massacred by the Romans.

For the Irish, however, Ynys Mon was regarded as an easy stepping stone into Britain: sailing barges bringing gold from the Wicklow Mountains in Leinster disembarked passengers at the port of Holyhead and traded their precious cargo for livestock, as well as copper from the Roman mine at Parys Mountain near Amlwch. Avaricious pirates took their share of the precious metal by force; then, for good measure, they enchained a human cargo to be sold in the notorious slave market at Clontarf, Dublin, on their return.

In the latter half of the fourth century the emperor Valentinian appointed Theodosius, as Count of Britain, to supress invasion by Picts, Scotti and Irish pirates. In the west, Theodosius established a base for the Roman fleet at Holyhead, where he built a strong cliff-top fortress and appointed a garrison commander to act as the new guardian of Anglesey; but a century later, long after the Romans had gone, the Holy Island with its port and fortress became a strategic target for the king of Leinster.

Without a male heir to inherit his piratical principality, king Illan of Leinster appointed his son-in-law Serach as his second in command; Serach's first task was to recruit warriors and prepare his war-band for an attack on Britain. Illan had vowed to avenge the deaths of his countrymen who had been murderously swept aside by Cunedda's purge of Irish settlers in Mon, and his bitter retribution was aimed at the princes of Powys.

Illan's invasion fleet sailed from Dun Laoghaire at dusk heading due east across the Irish Sea. At dawn king Illan launched his attack on the port of Holyhead, while Serach and his warriors besieged the Roman fort. The pirates quickly overpowered the lightly defended garrison, putting their military captives to the sword but sparing the women and children for slavery. His expeditious conquest of Holyhead confirmed king Illan's suspicions that Ynys Mon was the weakest link in the British chain of defence: it was clear that Arthur was fully engaged battling with enemies elsewhere in Britain and that he was unable to spare more than a handful of troops to garrison distant coastal forts. Now, with the Roman fort of Caer Gybi as his headquarters, Serach would be free to strike into the heart of the island, knowing that any British response would be hampered by the Menai Strait, a natural feature that was renowned as an obstacle to the speedy movement of troops.

Nevertheless, one future event was certain, for as soon as Arthur heard that Serach was roaming across Mon creating havoc wherever he went, there would be a British counter-attack: in fact, king Illan depended on the action of this counter-attack for the success of his own battle plan. Guessing that Serach's foothold on Ynys Mon would so infuriate Arthur that he would call on every soldier garrisoned at Chester to join a rapid response force to counter the invasion, Illan planned to strike a deadly blow at Chester while the British were battling with Serach's war-band. The king of Leinster not only yearned to torch the city in a final act of retribution against the kings of Gwynedd, but ever since king Mac Erca had jokingly dared him to steal Chester's heart of gold, he had secretly lusted after Uther Pendragon's treasure hoard that was rumoured to lie within the vaults of the fortress.

When Uther Pendragon heard that Serach had invaded Ynys Mon he flew into a rage: *"How dare the Irish set foot on my Holy Island?"* he shouted, swearing to God that they would reap his vengeance before the next full moon. *"May a lightning bolt strike Serach off the face of the earth."* he growled; *"Where is my army? Where is Arthur?"* he demanded, knowing full well that Arthur was far away to the east battling against the Saxons at Gariannonum.

In desperation, Uther Pendragon ordered his son Catwaullan to muster an emergency battle troop to repel the Irish invaders from Mon. Catwaullan did not dare to call out the small Chester garrison without Arthur's permission; instead he decided to draw on the reserves at Lincoln and Warwick, and dispatched riders to command a troop of fifty cavalry from each garrison to report to Chester within three days. Riding in haste to Wroxeter, Catwaullan mobilised fifty of Arthur's Irish recruits, explaining that expediency demanded they complete their training on the battlefield.

With his battle force assembled at Chester, Catwaullan led his troops sixty-five miles along the north coast of Gwynedd to the Roman fortress of Caernarfon. The following day he assembled his men on the headland spit at Traith Melynog; then, as the receding tide revealed the sand-bar, he marched his troops over the natural causeway across the Menai Strait and onto the sand dunes of Ynys Mon. Reaching the north coast before dusk, Catwaullan decided to make camp at Brwdd Arthur, Arthur's Table, a natural rocky plateau on high ground overlooking Red Wharf Bay, where large slabs of limestone had been erected to form the walls of a small fort; it was a good twenty miles from the enemy stronghold at Caer Gybi and made a safe refuge for his men as they prepared for battle.

The advance reconnaissance patrol sent forward under cover of darkness to investigate the enemy's position and strength reported back to Catwaullan before dawn: they had discovered a detachment of Serach's war-band at Parys Mountain where they had over-run the copper mine and were seen loading carts with as much metal and unsmelted ore as they could get their hands on. The scouts estimated that there were a hundred or more of the bandits at the mine, and the local villeins reported that Serach and the rest of his crew had been unloading supplies at the port during the day, and barricading themselves into the fort at dusk.

Catwaullan led the attack on the mine: three waves of cavalry thundered out of the morning sun, cutting into the enemy with a ferocious assault, scything through ranks of pirates still half-drunk and staggering from their night's revelry; some scurried like rats down the narrow mineshafts, hoping to escape in the maze of tunnels that pierced the mountain, but the British dismounted and went in after them, ferreting the pirates to the edge of a subterranean lake by sword-point, where one by one they were despatched to the underworld.

Catwaullan had to restrain his warriors after their successful strike: he saw the battle-lust in their eyes and heard their calls to press home the attack on Serach, but the experienced commander knew that it was time to put discretion above valour, for he was not equipped for the siege of a Roman fort full of cut-throats. Serach would be stung by the loss of his crew at the mine and his instinctive reaction would be a reprisal attack against the British. Indeed, Catwaullan was so sure of his prediction that he selected a site for the battle half-way across the island: about three miles west of Llangefni a wide expanse of level pastureland would give free range for his cavalry to charge into the enemy's footsoldiers and then regroup for a second attack.

By mid-day a cloud of dust rising from the Roman road running east from Holy Island gave Catwaullan warning of his enemy's approach; it was time to move his force to a forward position one mile north of the highway, with two flanking squadrons of cavalry to his left and right, but further back and out of sight of the enemy.

When Serach spotted the British cavalry he counted a line of fifty horse, a small force that was outnumbered by at least four to one of his own men; even though his foot-soldiers would be fighting mounted warriors, Serach felt confident of a swift victory. With spearmen to the fore, Serach's ragged band of pirates advanced towards the Britons. Catwaullan held back his men until the enemy were well into the chosen field. When the enemy had closed to a distance of three hundred yards he gave the order to charge, hitting Serach's front line at full force, spearing and trampling opponents as his cavalry flew through the motley mass of infantrymen.

Just as Catwaullan's chargers reformed to confront their enemy, Serach saw the two flanking squadrons racing towards his war-band at full gallop; Serach realised that he had been caught in a trap from which there was little chance of escape; this encounter would be a fight to the death. Three squadrons of cavalry hit the pirates simultaneously, reaping a bloody harvest of mutilated men; after the charge, Serach lay wounded amidst the carnage of the battlefield. With Catwaullan's sword at his throat, he pleaded for mercy, and in a moment of Christian compassion the Prince of Gwynedd spared his life; but he would be held hostage at Caer Gybi for a king's ransom, to be paid in Irish gold.

❧❧❦❧

Before news of Catwaullan's victory had reached Dinas Bran, Arthur himself had returned to the castle, bruised and blood-stained after his battle with Cerdic at Castell Gariannonum. Uther Pendragon thanked God for Arthur's safe return, but he expressed great concern for Catwaullan, explaining the emergency measures that he had taken to raise a fighting force for the re-conquest of Ynys Mon. Arthur was angered that Catwaullan had taken some of the Irish recruits who were still training for the campaign against king Illan, and he demanded their immediate return to Wroxeter. *"You are asking the impossible,"* replied the king, defensively. *"They will return in due course, when they have defeated Serach and his pirates."*

Before Arthur could make any further objections a messenger arrived with an escort from the Chester garrison: he had sailed from Dundalk with a letter addressed to Arthur, to be delivered in haste. Arthur broke the seal and opened the parchment scroll: *"Illan's fleet prepares to sail from Dun Laoghaire. I have asked him to help himself to the gold you are hoarding in Cair Legion."* The letter was signed, *"Mac Erca of the Ui Neill and Hibernia."* Arthur smiled, his anger cooling as he imagined king Illan searching for gold in Chester's great fortress. *"Thank your king,"* said Arthur, *"the message is understood and we will act upon it without delay."*

Weary from the recent battle, Arthur had just one night to rest and recuperate before planning the next; but he was already mulling over some ideas for Illan's reception at Chester, and as he sat down beside the roaring log fire to a hearty serving of venison stew, he revealed his plan to king Uther.

News of Catwaullan's victory reached Dinas Bran the next day. King Uther was overjoyed that Ynys Mon had been re-conquered and once more belonged to Gwynedd. Arthur was also pleased, for he could now put his Irish recruits to their

*172*

intended purpose. With some urgency he dispatched a rider with sailing orders to the captain of *Prydwen* at Aberdyfi and a second sailing barge moored at Barmouth, to sail immediately for Holyhead, there to embark as many of Catwaullan's warriors as they could carry, and to follow Illan's fleet at a discreet distance, as it sailed towards Chester.

At most, Arthur would have three days to prepare for battle: at his Wroxeter headquarters he called his commanders together and briefed them with the details of his plan. He mustered the remaining Irish contingent together with a detachment of his own battle-hardened warriors and marched north to Chester. For the people of Heronbridge, a small settlement on the south bank of the river Dee, it was a stirring sight to see Arthur and his cavalry charging through their village. *"Lock your doors against pirates!"* shouted Arthur as he galloped towards the Roman Bridge, its massive stone piers and oak superstructure silhouetted against the sunset. With a deafening clattering of hooves on cobblestones, Arthur led his cavalry through the south gate of the great legionary fortress of Deva into the headquarters that was situated in the central insula of the fort. Here, a unique Roman building known as the Oval Pantheon would play a key role in Arthur's strategy to defeat the pirate king.

This remarkable building, designed when Gnaeus Agricola governed Britain, was planned as an integral feature of the original fortress built towards the end of the

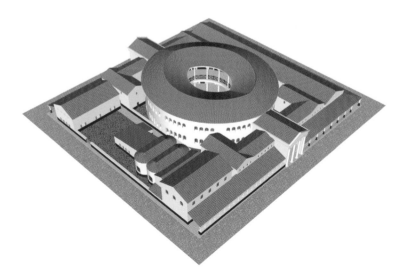

The Roman Elliptical Building at Chester, by kind permission of Julian Baum.

first century by the second legion; but as soon as the outer defences had been built to secure the officers' headquarters and the soldiers' barracks, Agricola's military priorities turned to the conquest of northern Britain, and the plans of the Oval Pantheon were locked away when Legio II Adiutrix marched north. More than a century and a half later, the plans were re-discovered by the emperor Septimus Severus, and he commissioned the oval building as part of the reconstructon of Deva's fortress, now to be built in stone.

The twelve major gods of the Roman Pantheon were known as the Dei Consentes and they were highly honoured by the Romans; in all probability, each of the twelve chambers in the oval building would have contained a shrine dedicated to one of the gods or goddesses of the Dei Consentes: Jupiter, Juno, Minerva, Vesta, Ceres, Diana, Venus, Mars, Mercury, Neptune, Vulcan and Apollo. In the central courtyard, a fountain played a constant spray of water into an oval pool surrounded by a colonnade, and natural sunlight streamed in through the open atrium. With such a unique and special place dedicated to the gods, Deva would surely be favoured with prosperity and good fortune; and indeed it was.

But under the new emperor Constantine, the power of Christianity, the new religion, gained ascendancy over the old gods; so their power waned, until at the end of the fourth century the emperor Theodosius summarily dismissed the Roman Pantheon altogether. In compliance with this sweeping religious change, the function of the Oval Pantheon changed from a place of worship to a market forum where the people of Deva could meet to barter goods, gossip, and exchange ideas.

But in time of war, military expediency took precedence over civil amenities, allowing Arthur to requisition the Oval Forum for use as a strong-room; a secure store with twelve bays that could be used to hold weapons and supplies for his army: wheat and grain, the staple foods for men and horses, copper, tin, lead and iron for the armourers, and on rare occasions, gold bullion in transit to the king's vaults.

A fierce storm in the Irish sea had battered the five ships of king Illan's fleet: from the moment he set sail from Dun Laoghaire there had been no respite from the south-westerly gale blowing in from the Atlantic Ocean, and the pirate crews had suffered a tortuous thirty hour crossing before sighting the river Dee estuary; there they would find calmer waters in the lee of the mountains of north Gwynedd. Illan was no stranger to the strong tides and wayward channels of the Dee estuary, for he had made more than one successful raid on Chester in the past; employing 'hit and run' tactics, he had carried off sack-loads of grain and salt as well as ingots of lead and copper.

The south-westerly was favourable to Illan's fleet as he sailed with the wind abeam towards the head of the wide estuary, fourteen miles or more upstream; then beyond

Connah's Quay where the river narrows, he took advantage of the rising tide to sail the last eight miles to Chester. On the spring tide, the seaward entrance of the Dee estuary had a huge tidal range of twenty-eight feet, with a period of six hours from flood to ebb; but the same tide at Chester had a much reduced range of nine feet, with only three hours of flood tide. This limited tidal window gave Illan just two or three hours to carry out his mission and set sail for Ireland before the ebb tide left his boats stranded.

As the sun reached for the western horizon, the pirate fleet slipped silently into the wide sheltered pool of Deva's old Roman harbour, each ship in line astern turning through the eye of the wind to bring them up to the long wharf on a northerly heading, ready for their departure. As each ship berthed the pirates disembarked shouting oaths and waving their swords in the air. Illan ordered one crew to guard the ships as he moved towards the western gate of the fortress with a war-band of two hundred men. As they pushed through the gatehouse unopposed, Illan reassured himself that the rumours of Arthur's absence were true, and he surmised that Arthur had taken the Deva garrison with him to fight on the eastern battle-front. Now, with the run of the fortress to himself, Illan split his force into two: one half to ransack the warehouses and take what booty they could find back to the boats, the other half under his command to break into the Oval Pantheon and take the gold.

Axing their way into the narrow corridor of the western entrance the pirates scrambled into the inner courtyard of the oval building: king Illan shouted with joy to see boxes of bullion stacked in front of him and with one stroke of his axe, hacked open the nearest case to reveal the gold: *"Welcome to the Oval Treasure Trove!"* bellowed Arthur, appearing suddenly from the eastern entrance. Illan was so shocked to come face to face with Arthur that he dropped the gold ingots to the floor, and as he reached for his sword, Arthur's warriors appeared: armed men hidden behind loose hessian draped over the twelve shrines of the old Roman Pantheon, moved forward as one body to surround the pirates.

As fast as a flash of lightning, Arthur's sword was at Illan's throat: he drew back, then parried, but Arthur attacked with brutal force, spinning his adversary and forcing him to retreat with each blow of his bright steel blade. A throng of warriors and pirates were engaged in a hand to hand battle: swords clashed, axes split shields, young men shrieked as their blood was spilt over the worn marble floor tiles. Half of Illan's men were trapped in the narrow entrance corridor as Arthur's soldiers sprang their attack from inside the Forum, and as the hindmost turned around to make their escape they ran straight into Arthur's second battle squadron who had wheeled around the outside of the Oval Pantheon, to cut off the pirates' retreat. The king of Leinster fought back ferociously, but under the welter of blows from the great warrior,

Illan's strength was almost spent: as he tripped backwards over a bar of gold, Arthur thrust forward, piercing his black chain-mail tunic through to the heart, and forcing the pirate king's body over the base of the oval fountain into a pool of bloody, stagnant water.

Arthur called his fighters back from the macabre scene of the battle, away from the revolting carnage of the dead, the dying and the wounded, and the stench of congealing blood. This part of the battle for Deva was done; the Oval Pantheon had become a mausoleum for king Illan and his war-band.

Arthur assembled his battle weary men in the parade ground of the military headquarters just as his reserve squadron thundered past, cutting into the remnants of the pirates who had ransacked the stores and were carting their booty back to the quayside. *"Into the fray!"* cried Arthur, as he called upon every man fit enough to mount a horse and charge into battle. As they sped towards the west gate, Arthur saw a pall of smoke rising from the harbour: three of the pirate ships were on fire, their flaxen sails burning fiercely, shooting long tongues of flame into the dusk sky, forcing the guards to launch the ships' cock-boats and row for their lives. Two other sailing barges had hurriedly slipped their moorings and were drifting slowly out of the port, making their escape.

Suddenly, Catwaullan appeared out of the smoke, leading his men across the burning deck of Illan's barge, and leaping ashore through flames and sparks from the burning sails. By commandeering the pirates' supply ship from the port at Holyhead, Catwaullan had embarked all his men and horses in the three available ships, and had sailed for Chester just in time to engage in a rear-guard action that would block the pirates escape, and seal their fate.

The British reinforcements charged headlong into the fracas on the quay, and as the last of Illan's men were chased out of the warehouses, a full-scale battle began in the midst of the fire and smoke from the burning ships. As the pirates' losses mounted, some survivors ran for cover, while others dived into the harbour, swimming desperately towards their boats. Then, as the clashing of swords fell silent, Arthur led his battle-worn army along the wide embankment towards the great Roman amphitheatre. No more the crowd of eight thousand citizens and legionaries being entertained with gladiatorial duels to the death; the silent arena now encompassed just Arthur's few hundred warriors, elated and victorious.

Slowly and steadily the people of Chester appeared from their humble wattle and daub dwellings, bringing simple gifts of food: meat, bread, and home-brewed ale for Arthur and Catwaullan and their steadfast warriors; sharing too their joy at Arthur's victory over the notorious pirate king, and expressing their hope for the prospect of peace.

# CHAPTER 12

# ARTHUR'S RUBICON AND THE BATTLE OF TRIBRUIT

*"The tenth battle was fought on the shore of the river called Tribruit"*
Nennius: *Historia Brittonum*

By the time Nennius had translated the battle-list from the original Brithonic language into Latin around the year 800 AD, many of Arthur's battle sites would have fallen to the enemy; and it is certain that by the beginning of the ninth century most of the Romano-British towns and rivers of central and southern Britain would have new English names, as the Angles and Saxons secured their conquest of Kent, Essex, East Anglia and Mercia.

In his mission to write down some of the historical extracts *that the stupidity of the British cast out, for the scholars of the island of Britain had no skill, and set down no record in books,"* Nennius clearly did his best to translate the original texts into Latin, recording place names as he found them, even quoting the British name for the battle of Celidon Forest as *"Cat Coit Celidon"* alongside his Latin, for the sake of clarity.

In all probability Nennius encountered difficulties when he found parts of the original documents corrupted by damp and mould, or where fading ink may have obscured part of a word or place-name, making it unintelligible to the reader. For example, by comparing later copies of the original *Historia Brittonum,* where Welsh scribes have added explanatory notations or 'glosses' to Nennius original text prior to the publication of each handwritten copy of the book, we find that the battles of 'Tribruit' and 'Agned' have glosses that give the names of these locations in the original Welsh: Tribruit is called *"Traht Treuroit,"* and Agned is revised to *"the mountain called Bregion, which we call Cat Bregion,"* or the 'battle of Bregion.' The fact that the scribes found it necessary to add these names to the text may well indicate that 'Tribruit' and 'Agned' were as meaningless to them as they are to us in the present day; but it also shows that the British names, if not the locations of these battle sites, were known by Britons some two hundred and seventy years after Arthur's time.

One other reference that associates Arthur with the battle of Tribruit is found in *Pa Gur?* an early Welsh poem preserved in the *Black Book of Carmarthen* that mentions two of Arthur's warriors: *"Manawyd returned from Tryfrwyd with a shattered shield;"* and Bedivere the hewer is depicted *"Ar traetheu Tryvruid"* on the shores of Tryfrwyd in battle with the dog-man, *"furious his mien with sword and shield,"* when he fought against Gwrgi Garwllwyd, the renowned killer of the Cymri.

One possible translation of 'Tribruit' could be 'three rushing rivers' but this meaning is contradicted by the literal translation of the Welsh word 'Tryfrwyd' as 'the pierced shore.' However, the 'tri' or 'three' is the significant part of the name because it has a link to a known river: 'Trisantona Fluvius' was named by the Romans as they advanced into central Britain, and this important river remained the outermost frontier of the Roman Empire until 79 AD. 'Trisantona' means "three pure streams" that are identified today as the river Soar that rises just to the east of Hinkley in South Leicestershire, and the rivers Derwent and Trent that spring from pure sources in the Peak District of South Yorkshire and North Staffordshire. The Derwent and Soar flow into the river Trent as tributaries a few miles south-west of Nottingham, to form a wide and powerful waterway that flows north to the Humber Estuary.

In the first century the Trent became the natural border between the conquered and unconquered tribes of Britain, and its value as a navigable waterway that ran for eighty miles or more was soon realised by the Romans. To protect the new frontier they built a line of fortresses along the river, supplied from two great arterial roads, the Fosse Way and Ermine Street.

Over several centuries the Roman name 'Trisantona' became shorter and its pronounciation was softened by years of colloquial use; the original "Trisanctimonia" soon became 'Trisantona,' and that was later shortened to 'Trisante' until, by the Middle Ages, the name had changed to 'Treonte,' finally evolving into 'Trent' as it is known today. By comparing the early medieval Welsh spelling of 'Treuroit' with the early English word 'Treonte,' we can see that the similarity between the two supports the suggestion that both names apply to the river Trent; and the 'Tryfrwyd' of *Pa Gur?* falls into place as a later variation of the 'Tribruit' that we find in Nennius' text.

It was an ironic twist of fate that by the beginning of the sixth century, almost one hundred years after the Roman exodus from Britain, the river Trent once again became a frontier line of great importance. Before, the river had marked the battle front between the Britons and Romans; now, in Arthur's time, it marked the front line between the Romano-British and the Anglo-Saxons. The Trent was a natural physical barrier that divided the countries of Powys and Elmet to the west, from the flat coastal plain of Lincolnshire to the east; for Arthur, the river became his last line of defence against foreign invaders intent on conquering the central heartlands of Britain.

Reading between the lines of Sir Thomas Malory's legendary tale *Le Mort d'Arthur,* published in 1485, we can detect a faint echo of truth in an early chapter where Arthur prepares for a great battle against an alliance of eleven kings, *"but there was made such an ordinance afore Merlin that there should no man of war ride nor go in any country on this side of Trent Water but if he had a token from King Arthur, where-through the king's enemies durst not ride as they did to-fore to espy."*

So the river Trent became Arthur's Rubicon, for here Arthur drew the line; and from this time onward spies seeking Arthur's military emplacements, or enemy warriors and war-bands crossing the river to the west did so at their peril: this would now become the land of no return. However, this positive retrenchment by Arthur may well have been the result of a peace treaty between the East Angles and the Britons, an agreement that would have allowed the new immigrants to settle peacefully in an area of ceded territory along the eastern seaboard of Lincolnshire and East Anglia in exchange for vows to cease hostilities against the Britons and to relinquish all ambitions of further conquest. Such an agreement may have been the beginning of a long and friendly alliance between the middle Angles, or Mercians as they were later known, and the Britons of Powys, who were the 'heirs of Arthur.'

In return for the ceded territory, Arthur would have demanded tribute from the lands newly settled 'beyond the Trent,' and this tax would have given Arthur much needed additional revenue to pay for the army and to fund his campaigns. Perhaps Nennius had this idea in mind when translating the original battle-list, coining the word 'Tribruit' from the Latin 'tribuit' or tax that had been paid to Arthur by the Angles who settled to the east of the river.

For as long as the Angles kept faith with the terms of the treaty Arthur would treat marauders plundering west of Trent Water as new enemies who would reap the hurricane of his anger; but as much as the Trent was a physical barrier to a land army, Arthur was well aware that the river offered an arterial waterway to his sea-borne enemies. The Humber Estuary extended an open invitation to friend and foe alike to visit the heart of Britain; in the not too distant past Roman barges had sailed into the river Humber, navigating a further twenty mile stretch of the river Ouse with military supplies for York. Furthermore, supply ships could use the upper reaches of the Trent to gain access to Foss Dyke, a man-made waterway that linked the river to Lincoln, just thirty miles south of the estuary.

Under moonlight and with a favourable wind, an ambitious commander would be able to navigate fifty miles or more inland, perhaps as far as the Roman fort of Margidunum, Castle Hill, just east of Nottingham; venturing upstream another thirty miles would bring the enemy fleet close to Lichfield and the nearby Roman town of Letocetum, at Wall near Lichfield, dangerously close to Arthur's headquarters and stronghold of Viroconium. Naturally, it was this tactical approach by an enemy using the river Trent as a back-door route to the heartland of Powys that Arthur most feared, and it was for this reason that he maintained the garrison at Lincoln with an alert commander and a troop of cavalry at battle-readiness.

Who then was Arthur's enemy at the battle of the river Tribruit? In the poem, *Pa Gur?* the name of Bedivere's opponent is revealed as 'Gwrgi Garwllwyd' the killer of the Cymri, an enemy associated with the dog-men from the land of the Picts. If the Picts had planned an audacious raid to knock on Arthur's front door by sailing up the Humber Estuary and thence into Powys by way of the river Trent, then Arthur's real enemy at Tribriut was not known by the garbled name of Gwrgi Garwllwyd, but as Galanan Erilich, king of the Picts.

࿔ ࿔ ࿔ ࿔

Drest Gurthinmoch ruled over the northern Picts from his royal fortress of Craig Phadraig, a mighty bastion of the Pictish kings set high on a rocky crag, with a commanding view over Inverness and the upper reaches of the Moray Firth; for thirty years, Drest had ruled the Highlands with a rod of iron, forging a strong alliance between the eleven tribes of northern Britain.

Fearing that the military supremacy he had achieved would fade with his own demise, Drest chose a strong warrior chieftain to succeed him: Galanan Erilich, whose skills as seafaring commander matched his lust for battle, would inherit the highland kingdom. When Drest Gurthinmoch died the tribal chiefs honoured his passing, travelling from their distant kingdoms to attend the funeral. Ten chieftains joined the royal bodyguard to escort the chariot carrying the king's body from Craig Phadraig to his chosen burial place in the vale that lay between the mountains of Croc Na Gaoithe and Doire Mhor; in this wild, heather clad valley overlooking Loch Ness, his spirit would guard the southern approaches of the kingdom. Each warrior chieftain carried a flaming torch to illuminate the king's last earthly journey and to present the sacred elements of fire and water. As Drest was laid to rest in a stone sarcophagus, pagan priests sprinkled holy spring water over his head to purify his soul.

The warrior king lay resplendent, dressed for battle, with his sword and shield beside him. Gifts of small carved stones, carefully incised with drawings of the sacred symbols of the Pictish pantheon that included fish, birds, bulls, boars and deer, were place by his side; and for his good cheer a jug of mead was placed close to his head. When the chief priest performed the final act of the ceremony by laying a small pot of incense at the king's foot, the wind fanned the charcoal to a bright glow, wafting scented smoke into the night sky, accompanying the spirit of Drest Gurthinmoch to the Otherworld.

Galanan Erilich seized the opportunity presented by the king's funeral to call the assembled chieftains together for a council of war; but first he arranged to show them the great iron foundry at Culduthel a few miles to the south-east of Craig Phadraig, where a settlement of seventeen round-houses dedicated to making arms and armour clustered around a circular grass enclosure. No fewer than five smithies had been established to factor iron and copper, using small furnaces constructed with large edging stones that formed containers to collect slag and bloom from the molten metals. The largest and most important foundry, a round-house with walls over sixty feet in diameter, was built of wattle and daub, with timber posts supporting a thatched roof; here the chieftains were shown the full range of weapons in various stages of manufacture: war chariots, iron daggers, spear-heads, shield bosses and swords, and an ornamental sea-monster cast in a stone mould, all proudly displayed by the skilled craftsmen who had made them. Galanan proudly presented each tribal chieftain with a bright new sword, a token of his pledge to be a trustworthy leader for which, in turn, he would demand loyalty and military support from the eleven tribes of Caledonia.

Duneidion, the Fortress of the Bulls, was Galanan's greatest asset, a masterpiece of fourth-century Iron Age military technology; the fort's builders had transformed the headland of Burghead on the Moray Firth into the strongest bulwark in Caledonia. At the landward end of the natural promontory a series of three sets of ramparts and ditches guarded the entrance to the fort. Massive walls, over twenty-five feet thick and twenty feet high, were interlaced with rows of oak timbers along the front face, all nailed together, with transverse beams running deep into the walls to form a strong internal framework for the ramparts. The central area of the fort was divided into two enclosures, separated by a high partition wall: soldiers barracks, smithies, carpenters workshops and servants quarters were all concentrated together in the eastern compound, all serving the separate royal residence to the west. Built on a promontory of solid rock, the outer walls, topped by a wooden stockade towered over the sea on three sides; and to the south the triple vallate formed the defence against landward attack.

This formidable fortress was the undisputed jewel i
inherited by the young Galanan, who had deter

residence and military headquarters. Without delay he convened the first war council of his reign, addressing the senate of chieftains with a speech that revealed his political awareness and his determination to bring about a new era of conquest and reward for the people of the north.

*"One battle begets another until the killing is avenged!"* he declared, *"ten thousand Caledonian warriors slaughtered by the Romans at the battle of Mons Graupius will never be forgotten."*

A deep thorn in the side of Pictish pride, the memory engendered a hatred of Rome, the servitude of overlordship and the sting of taxation that was the inevitable price to be paid for imperial civilization. To Galanan and his warrior chieftains, Arthur had become the personification of Rome: despite the fact that Arthur had no mandate of authority from the Emperor, in their eyes he had become a tyrant whose quest to unite the separate states of Britain under one banner posed the same threat to their freedom and independence as the Roman generals who had advanced beyond the Antonine Wall in the distant past.

Yet Arthur was not the only enemy to be feared: the Dal Raida Scotti, pushed out of their own territory in the north-east of Ireland by the belligerent king Mac Erca, had settled in large numbers on the west coast of Kintyre. When Fergus, their erstwhile king, was finally forced to join his people in the early years of the sixth century, he established a new powerbase at Dunadd, building a great fortress on a rocky plateau overlooking the floodplain of the river Add where it reaches towards Jura Sound. Boat-builders and seafarers by tradition, the Dal Raida Scotti gradually expanded their small naval force to gain firm control of the western islands and coastal shores of Kintyre.

The first Dal Raida settlers had arrived as scattered groups of refugees and their landfall over one hundred miles south-west of Craig Phadraig was not considered to be a threat to the Caledonians of the north; but as soon as king Fergus had marshalled his people into a naval fighting force capable of reinforcing the military strength of his allies, king Dyfnwal of the Clyde and king Kynvelyn of Edinburgh, the Dal Raida Scots became a serious threat to the balance of power in northern Britain.

Although he was aware, as well as somewhat envious of king Fergus' naval force, Galanan turned a blind eye to the Dal Raidans gathering on his western doorstep, for his great bone of contention was with Arthur. The recent humiliating defeat suffered by Heuil and his Caledonian warriors at the battle of the Caledonian Forest b a bitter blow to Pictish pride that Galanan had become obsessed with loody reprisal. He planned a daring sea-borne raid that would take prise and score an overwhelming victory for the Picts; but expensive military expedition with revenge as his sole motive for war: he would need to offer his allies some reward, a significant material gain that would complement the restoration of Caledonian pride.

His proposal to the assembled chieftains was imaginative and practical, born of necessity, for the iron-ore that the Picts depended upon for the manufacture of weapons was in extremely short supply: local sources of iron-ore from open rock seams and bog deposits were all but finished, and iron bars traded by the southern Caledonians from their fortress at Clatchard Craig on the Firth of Tay, had become prohibitively expensive.

Galanan, with his native cunning, planned to attack and conquer one of Arthur's iron mines in the south. Depending upon the strength of the enemy, he would keep his options open for a swift hit-and-run attack on the chosen mine, seizing as much iron-ore and as many ingots as he could lay his hands on. At the same time he would assess the possibility of taking over the mine and claiming the site for the long term. Rumours were abroad that Arthur had allowed Angles to settle south of the river Humber; perhaps Galanan could force Arthur's hand and gain some southern pastureland for the Picts.

With one accord the council of chieftains agreed Galanan's daring plan of attack. Within six months, each chief would supply one warship with a trained crew of thirty warriors together with victuals and arms. Galanan would lead this fleet of eleven ships and over three hundred warriors south to the Humber Estuary, a voyage of almost five-hundred miles, even further than the Angles had sailed when crossing the North Sea from Jutland.

To celebrate the end of the old year, king Galanan prepared a feast for his guests, inviting the chieftains to join festivities at Duneidion before they returned to their own countries. As night fell, soldiers and servants joined the villagers for the Hogmanay fire festival. Many believed the pagan Celtic tradition that at the end of the old year the dead would rise and wander the land in search of an earthly soul to repossess. Fire was considered the only element that could scare away the spirits of the dead and the ancient tradition decreed that a barrel of fire should be escorted round the settlement to keep evil at bay and to ensure good fortune for the coming year. The ceremony of 'The Burning of the Clavie' was no more than an old half-barrel filled with wood-shavings and tar, nailed to a carrying post shouldered by one of the local men; set alight, the Clavie was carried first by the elected Clavie King, then in turn by ten fishermen who processed around the settlement pausing at houses to present a smouldering ember that would bring each household good luck for the new year. Finally, when the flaming barrel reached the fortress of Duneidion it was set on high as a flaming beacon visible for many miles; and while some saw fiendish faces in the flames, others caught the flaming embers for luck.

Under the midnight moon the king's prized Highland bull was sacrificed: when the flames of the Clavie died, the bull's blood was spilt into the earth as a sacrifice to the god of fertility; the carcass was buried, but the image of the bull was carved into a sandstone plaque that was mounted on the outer wall of the fortress to ensure protection from enemies, and to grant a fertile harvest of livestock and grain.

At the appointed time, Galanan's battle fleet assembled in the harbour of Beauly Firth under the watchful eye of the guardian of Craig Phadraig, and sheltered from the elements by the surrounding highlands. Three warships sailed in from the north, two newly built at Thurso and one from the seafaring base at Portmahomack; another two warships, built by the king's shipwrights at Inverness from materials supplied by the northern tribes were joined by two ships of the king's fleet. All the ships had been made to the traditional design of the Celtic curragh using tanned animal skins stretched over a light wooden framework secured with glue and nails to a strong oak keel; amidships, lateral timbers formed rigid plates to secure the base of a pine mast. Fourteen pairs of oarsmen pulled the ship forward in calm seas, with a helmsman at the aft steer-board, his chieftain the skipper and navigator. Each boat carried a crew of thirty, so that, if one man went down with sickness, his crew-mate had the onerous task of pulling the oar on his own; but when the wind blew fair, with the square sail set, the oarsmen could take a well-earned rest from their exertions.

The fleet of seven warships made a magnificent sight as they sailed up the Moray Firth catching the north-westerly wind and reaching towards the open sea. Soon, Galanan's ship was leading the fleet and bearing away with the following wind as they sped along the coast. Passing Duneidion, Galanan turned onto a south-easterly heading towards Kinnaird Head; then, as they approached the Pictish naval base at CullyKhan, a solitary ship crewed by the warriors of Buchan sailed out to join the fleet; rounding the headland, Galanan took a south-westerly course towards Aberdeen, where he would rest his crews for a day, take on fresh water and supplies, and welcome another ship to his battle force.

With his men refreshed, Galanan sailed south to reach Loch Tay, where, at the great fortress of Clatchard Craig, two more warships awaited his arrival. Pulling his ships ashore by South Deep, where the inlet was overlooked by the Roman fortress of Carpow, Galanan congratulated his stalwart seafarers on completing the first two-hundred mile leg of the voyage south; as a reward for their efforts he granted the crews two days to recuperate.

Galanan's warriors returned in high spirits after two nights of feasting at Clatchard Craig to find their ships well stocked with oatmeal bread, dried meats and mead; they were all keen to set sail for the final leg of the voyage, but to their chagrin the wind had dropped, leaving them to row the full length of the Firth of Tay. With the open sea more than twenty miles away, it was an unwelcome start, but the men were eager for battle and they pulled steadily towards the sea, until it turned into a race to see whose ship would be first to reach Buddon Ness.

At sea the wind picked up, a north-westerly blowing strongly from the direction of Glen Clova across the fertile Strathmore plain, filled the eleven square sails of Galanan's Pictish fleet. In contrast to Saxon ships that were built from solid planks of oak and pine, the Picts' boats were much the same as Irish coracles in construction: made with animal hides stretched over a sturdy wooden frame, they were both light-weight and strong. With a fair wind behind them they could speed through the water at ten knots or more, easily out-running the heavier Saxon and British boats.

By nightfall the fleet had passed thirty miles south of Berwick, and making fair headway they reached South Shields by midnight. Then a resounding cheer went up as the boats crossed an imaginary line in the sea that marked their passing of

Galanan's Pictish fleet cresting the waves in a stormy sea. Image of Pictish Boats from *Pictish Warrior AD 297 – 841* by Paul Wagner, illustrated by Wayne Reynolds.

Hadrian's Wall. For centuries the Picts had regarded Hadrian's great wall as something of a joke: an expensive defensive barrier once manned by ten thousand centurions to keep them out of Britain, when all they had to do to raid southern Britain was to sail past the Wall with the coast on their western horizon, then attack the lowland regions of the Tyne and Humber at will.

By dawn the following day, the wind had strengthened and backed to the west. In the distance, Galanan recognised the old Roman lookout tower at Scarborough. He estimated that they would have about another sixty miles to sail to the Humber; then a further thirty-mile sail upstream would see them to their target under cover of darkness, hopefully undetected by the enemy.

Dark grey and purple clouds threatened the western horizon with an oncoming storm, and soon the wind was gusting up to gale force, filling the square sails full stretch and sending the light curroughs full pelt into the white-horses cresting over the storm-swept waves. It was a magnificent sight: eleven ships coursing through the spray, each flaxen sail displaying the symbol of the Pictish Beast, a dolphin-like creature that was worshipped by their sailors as a marine deity, the watch-keeper and bringer of good-fortune to all Picts who sailed the high seas.

Even the coastal watchman, perched atop the old castle at Flamborough Head, could scarcely believe his eyes when he saw a fleet of sails scudding across the distant horizon as if they were flying: he knew that no Saxon or British boat could move at that speed, and Irish vessels were not known to frequent this part of the Oceanus Germanicus. Pictish boats had not been seen this far south for years, yet this fleet was heading south towards Gaul. The bemused watchman suddenly realised the possibility that if Gaul was not their destination, these ships would be about to pay an unwelcome visit to the eastern shores of Britain.

Raising the alarm, he dispatched a rider to Lincoln to warn the garrison commander of the danger of imminent invasion. The messenger took the Roman road to Brough where the river ferryboat crossed the Humber to Winteringham; from there the Fosse Way ran straight as a die to Lincoln. Alarmed by the threat of an enemy fleet on the eastern horizon, Bedivere called his garrison to battle-readiness and sent riders to warn Arthur at Wroxeter; he then alerted Gawain, commander of the Longthorpe garrison, and ordered scouts to the coast to look out for the enemy ships. Hopefully, by the time Arthur arrived, Bedivere would have a clear idea of the enemy's position.

But time was short, for it had taken the best part of a day for news of the Picts' fleet to reach Lincoln; even with a change of horses it would take most of the night for a messenger to cover the one hundred miles to Arthur's headquarters. No offensive action would be taken until Arthur had reached Lincoln later the following day: he would only brief his commanders when the enemy's position was known for certain.

The westerly gale had played havoc with Galanan's battle fleet: when the storm hit, his boats either shortened sail or lowered them to the decks to avoid them being ripped from the masthead by the wind's powerful blast; with huge waves cresting over their bows it became impossible to row, leaving two men to wrestle with the steer-boards in an attempt to point their bows into the eye of the wind. Now they were at the mercy of the elements. The storm eased as the sun went down, but Galanan realised that they had been blown well to the east of their intended course, perhaps by twenty miles or more, and that would make his final westward leg back to the Humber a long sail into the wind. The fact that his square-rigged ships would not sail close to the wind meant that he would have to zig-zag, tacking across the wind all the way to the estuary, and unless the wind changed direction, his men would have to row many miles upstream to their destination.

Galanan was not far out in his reckoning, for they reached Spurn Head an hour or so after midnight, gliding silently into the river Humber on the port tack, navigating by moonlight. The storm had shaken them all to the point of exhaustion, as well as delaying their arrival; but the delay would be fortuitous if it helped them

This aerial photograph shows the confluence of the river Ouse and the river Trent (on the right), flowing into the Humber Estuary that reaches towards the eastern horizon. The ploughed field to the west of the Trent is the most likely site for Arthur's battle on the shores of the river Tribruit.                    Photo, © Richard Lee

to reach their landing place in the early hours, when the Britons were still asleep. Steering due west into the upper reaches of the river Humber, sails were close-hauled and aligned fore-and-aft as they came into wind: now the crews would have to row the last fifteen mile leg of the voyage.

When the early twilight revealed reeded marshland along the river-bank, Galanan suddenly realised that the salt-marsh on his bow was a headland at the confluence of two rivers, the Trent and the Ouse. Just here the shoreline was pierced by a narrow inlet: it would make the ideal hiding place for his fleet, surrounded on either side by tall reeds and reaching almost a mile inland, his boats would be completely hidden from the mainstream of the river Trent. Moments before dawn the fleet came to rest; the crews shipped their oars, and collapsed on the spot from utter exhaustion. Only Galanan remained standing, keeping watch over his men.

By mid-day the chorus of snoring from the fatigued sailors was loud enough to give away their position: Galanan woke his men and ordered them to re-position the boats with their sterns pulled ashore and prows angled to the east to allow them the chance of a quick get-away. It was evident that his men were not fit for battle, so Galanan allowed them to relax for the rest of the day while he called a battle meeting with the commanders. He was uncertain of the exact position of the iron-mine, and briefed two commanders to take their boats across to the eastern bank of the river Trent that night, and to send out a reconnaissance patrol to look for the mine. Early next morning, Galanan and seven crews would attack and secure a small settlement just two miles south of their beach-head, leaving ninety men in reserve to guard the boats. The possession of the village would give the Picts a tactical land base with fresh water and provisions; from this forward position, Galanan could plan his attack on the iron-mine when his scouts had located its exact position.

While the Picts were asleep in their boats, Arthur had already mobilised two hundred warriors from Wroxeter and was marching eastward along Watling Street towards Lichfield. At the break of day he had sent riders to Cei and Gawain, the commanders at Warwick and Longthorpe, with orders to marshal their troops, and in all haste, to meet him at Lincoln.

Arthur turned north-east along Ryknild Street, crossing the river Trent by the old Roman bridge at Alrewas; then, riding across country, he followed the west bank of the river as far as Ad Pontem, East Stoke. As darkness fell, Arthur was surprised to see a dispatch rider galloping across the oak-timbered bridge towards him: a message from Bedivere confirmed the enemy's landfall at the mouth of the river Trent. Eleven Pictish boats were hidden in a creek on the western bank: the enemy force was estimated at around three hundred and fifty strong.

With this essential information, Arthur could plan his next move. Crossing this part of the river Trent with an army at short notice was a major problem because there were only two bridges available: one at Ad Pontem, and the other, twenty miles to the north at Segelocum, Littleborough, which carried the Roman road from Lincoln to Doncaster across the Trent. Arthur was relieved that his main force was already on the same side of the river as the enemy's last reported position, and he ordered his men to advance to Osmanthorpe, five miles north-west of Ad Pontem, where they could make camp for the night in the derelict Roman fort on the very edge of Sherwood Forest.

At dusk, Arthur watched as Cei turned off the Fosse Way towards Ad Pontem, leading his squadron of fifty cavalry from Warwick, their horses steaming from the sixty mile ride. Arthur galloped across the bridge to join Cei and his warriors for the march to Lincoln, where Bedivere's troops had already retired to their barracks for the night.

Before dawn the Lincoln garrison was alive with the activity of soldiers preparing for action. With a sense of urgency Arthur called his commanders together to plan for battle. If the enemy attacked from the south during the day, then Arthur's combined forces from Osmanthorpe and Lincoln, would advance to Segelocum and hold their line of defence along the Roman road; but if the Picts remained at their landing site, then Arthur would hold his army at Segelocum until nightfall, advancing the last twenty miles under cover of darkness: this would give him the advantage of a surprise attack at dawn the following day.

But Cei wanted to know what the Picts were doing so far to the south. If they had come for vengeance he would be happy to give them a taste of his sword, as he had before at Din Eidyn and in the Forest of Caledonia; but if they had come to wreak havoc and steal, what were they after?

"*Perhaps it's the iron mine,*" suggested Bedivere. "*Indeed,*" said Arthur, "*you could be right, for as we know, the Picts prize iron more than gold.*" "*Then we need to guard the mine,*" declared the Lincoln commander. Arthur agreed and suggested that Gawain advance with his squadron to guard Dragonby, but charged him to keep out of sight of the enemy who were on the other side of the river, only four miles from the mine.

"*And if the enemy sails across the river to attack the mine?*" asked Bedivere. "*Then we will have to return to Segelocum to cross the Trent, regroup and advance along Ermine Street to do battle at Dragonby,*" replied Arthur. "*One thing is certain,*" he said, looking at Bedivere, "*we will need regular reports of the enemy's position by day and by night.*"

As Arthur, Cei, and Bedivere led the British cavalry north from Lincoln, Galanan, with two hundred Picts, sprang from their reeded hiding place and advanced across the marshland towards the village settlement. Wading across a shallow stream that ran eastward to the river Trent, the Picts found firmer ground and quickened their advance; but as they approached the settlement, one of the villeins' children heard the clash of their armour and shouted in alarm. Women and children scattered away from their huts as fast as they could run; some of the menfolk ran for their horses and galloped away to the south. By the time Galanan's raiders had broken into a run for the final attack, only a handful of men and the elderly remained in the village. The men prepared for a fight, shouting and brandishing their swords and axes as Galanan's war-band came in for the kill. Galanan could not understand what they were shouting, but suddenly realised that they were Angles. *"Where is the mine?"* he shouted back in Gaelic, but they did not understand him either. *"I have no quarrel with Angles or Saxons,"* he shouted, waving his sword at them to clear a path for his men. But one man lunged at Galanan with his axe, and in a flash, Galanan's sword sliced across his neck, despatching him in an instant. The remaining Angles drew back, allowing Galanan and his warriors to occupy the village without further bloodshed.

Now, with the village as a land-based headquarters, Galanan could intensify his search for the mine and finalise his plan of attack. Overnight the reconnaissance patrols had explored two miles or more to the east without locating the mine; Galanan ordered them to continue searching further east and sent another crew to explore to the west. Three scouts were detailed to follow the river south to look out for British forces.

By mid-day Arthur and his commanders had crossed to the west bank of the river Trent at Segelocum where his own troops had assembled. Now at full strength, Arthur's army of three hundred cavalry made an impressive sight as they straddled the Roman road awaiting battle orders; but Arthur had no intention of dashing into battle, and took the precaution of sending two mounted scouts forward to check the lie of the land about Epworth and the Isle of Axholm, where he planned make his final encampment before the battle. Later the scouts returned, reporting no sign of the enemy, but they had run into the Angles who had escaped from the Picts' attack on their village, and they had confirmed seeing a force of about two-hundred 'wolf-men.'

Arthur gave the order to advance fifteen miles north to Axholme, making camp on the flat windswept plain just eight miles from the enemy. Without tree cover or shelter, his men lay silent under the stars.

Galanan's crew had settled into the village, celebrating their conquest with a spit-roast and helping themselves to the Angles' home-brewed ale. Their scouts had reported no sighting of British activity to the south; but by nightfall the other crews had not returned, leaving Galanan concerned for their safety and still without a strategic target. He decided that, at sunrise, he himself would lead the search for the iron-mine.

Galanan was woken at first light by the shrill staccato sound of a hunting horn accompanied by the thundering of hooves. The lookout shrieked the alarm: "*To arms! To arms! Shield line forward!*" As Cei charged towards the outer huts with his squadron in close formation, followed by Bedivere and his cavalry, the Picts staggered from the village round-houses, grasping their swords and shields: Cei's cavalry troop swept through the village compound, cutting and thrusting, severing heads and limbs as they went, despatching any of the enemy foolish enough to stand in their path. The Picts tried to group into a battle line, but Bedivere's troop thundered down on them, breaking their ranks, swift steel spilling blood, spears piercing enemy flesh.

While Bedivere's squadron galloped through the village, Cei's warriors had turned around to make a second charge, but they held back while Bedivere's troop turned to form a second rank of cavalry. Then they charged together, one hundred strong, fierce in formation; shrill their battle cry, fearsome their weaponry. Charging back into the village they wreaked havoc with the enemy, spearing, dealing death to the wolf-men of the north.

Galanan called on his chieftains to evacuate the village, and made an attempt to form a defensive line that would allow him to fall back to the boats; but he was short of men. With one crew guarding the boats, as well as the two crews still out searching for the mine, he was at least ninety men under strength. For a moment, while the British re-grouped to the south, there was a lull in the onslaught, and Galanan took the opportunity to move his men towards the creek as fast as they could run. Then, to his relief, he saw the commander and his crew returning from their scouting mission to the west of the river; having searched for miles, they had become disoriented when night fell.

But now they were eager to reinforce the shield line against the next cavalry attack. It appeared to Galanan that his war-band outnumbered the British force and he felt confident as he watched Cei and Bedivere preparing for another attack. Then, in an instant, he paled with shock as another cavalry troop appeared from the south-west: a vanguard carried the standard aloft, its long pennant streaming in the wind. It was the Red Dragon of Arthur.

"*Now we shall see how these northern Britons can fight!*" exclaimed Arthur, as he led the cavalry charge in three arrowhead echelons towards the enemy. With one hundred and fifty of Arthur's mounted warriors charging at their right flank, and one hundred troops led by Cei and Bedivere charging into their left flank, the Picts braced their shield wall for the brunt of the clash. Suddenly the thundering war-horses were upon them, crushing their defence, splintering shields, splitting skulls, trampling bodies and tearing limb from limb. It was a murderous onslaught, yet somehow, when the cavalry had passed over them, brave men were still standing, dazed, bloody and dishevelled. Five of the hardened battle commanders had speared the youngest of Arthur's men from their mounts and taken their horses: now they could do battle with Arthur's commanders on equal terms.

Galanan unhorsed a young warrior and took his mount, pushing into the fray towards Arthur: this was his chance to engage his enemy hand to hand. Rearing his white stallion, Arthur turned to engage Galanan whose quick spear thrust thudded into Arthur's shield: Arthur parried pari-passu, his sword slashing within an inch of his opponents neck, his second thrust slicing through chain-mail, wounding. Angered by the pain, Galanan summoned all his strength, thrusting his spear with such force into Arthur's shield that he shuddered with the shock and recoiled, falling from his mount onto the soft marshland turf. In a moment, Bedivere was by his side, reining Arthur's foaming horse so that he could remount, while another warrior fought off Galanan's attack.

Arthur was stunned, but regained control of his mount; thanking Bedivere for his rescue with a wave of his sword, Arthur thrust forward once more into the battle. The combined cavalry attack had pushed the Picts back to the stream that ran right across the field of battle, most of them dousing in the cool water to wash their bloody wounds as they waded to the far bank. When Galanan made a defensive shield-line along the shallow riverbank, the crew who had been guarding the boats moved forward to reinforce the new battle-line, but to his dismay, a detachment of Cei's squadron moved in behind them, intent on setting fire to their curroughs.

The stream gave Galanan's front line some respite, but, undaunted, Arthur's warriors charged through the water, challenging the wall of shields that were now locked together in defence. But with Cei's troops attacking his rear, Galanan pressed his reinforcements into a second shield line: his men were now back to back, fighting their enemy on both sides; they fought bravely, fighting for their lives. While Bedivere speared his way through the enemy's left flank, Cei was in the thick of the fray, a strong giant of a man, hacking at heads, parrying spears and sword blows, proving his reputation as the great killer of Picts, the despised dog-heads of the north.

Charging up and down the shield-line to encourage his embattled men, Galanan saw some of his men running towards him from the western bank of the river Trent: to the fore was the commander of one of the reconnaissance crews that had ventured across to the east bank to look for the mine. *"We found the mine,"* he gasped, *"but in the darkness we could not see much. Suddenly the British sprung an attack: it was like a hornet's nest. Most of our men fell to the swords and spears of Gawain's warriors."*

*"Back to the boats!"* shouted Galanan. *"Form a shield-wall in front of the boats!"*

Staggering back in retreat, his men pushed back several hundred paces through the fracas of the battlefield, running towards the inlet, fighting as they went. Several ships were already on fire, and the acrid grey smoke began to drift across the battlefield.

Arthur was covered in blood, almost unrecognisable, his white horse stained deep red up to the fetlocks: it was a gruesome battle, and he felt suddenly sick to think that this was a battle of Briton against Briton: it was civil war. *"Too many Britons have lost their young lives this day,"* exclaimed Cei, as Arthur pulled his warriors back beyond the stream that was now crimson with blood. *"Regroup in your battle formations!"* shouted Arthur, while Galanan and his commanders drew their horses up in front of the straggling shield-wall, their last line of defence. *"Let us agree to stand-fast to the end!"* Galanan shouted to his chieftains, *"but let us allow our brave warriors, who have fought so fiercely in this day's battle, to take their freedom."* All agreed with Galanan's call and moved to close formation, anticipating Arthur's final onslaught.

*"Brave king! Brave men!"* said Bedivere as Arthur wheeled around to face the enemy. *"Have we not shed enough blood this day?"* he asked. *"Enough is enough!"* echoed Cei. *"Yes,"* agreed Arthur, *"you are right. Enough bloodshed for one day!"* shouted Arthur. *"We see the brave king Galanan with the golden torque around his neck, ready to die for his men and for his courage we will show him mercy. As the Lord our God is merciful to us, so shall we show mercy to our enemy."*

*"We declare this battle won!"* Arthur shouted to his troops: *"Make to the village with the wounded!"* was the last command that day. Arthur and his warriors withdrew silently into the pall of smoke that had fallen like a veil over the blood-soaked field.

By the time the sun had dipped to the west, and the southerly wind had gradually cleared the smoke from the battlefield, king Galanan and his wolf-men had vanished. Away in the distance, five square sails could be seen, reaching downstream to the Humber estuary and heading for the open sea.

This was the Battle of Tribruit, fought between Arthur's Britons and Galanan Erilich's Picts on the western shores of the river Trent. Manawyd, one of Arthur's warriors, took the shattered timbers of his shield home to Powys, as a personal memento of this violent battle that would be long remembered by the bards:

*"By the hundred they fell*
*To Bedwyr's four-pronged spear*
*On the shores of Tryfrwyd."*

# CHAPTER 13

# THE BATTLE OF MOUNT AGNED

*"Undecimum factum bellum in monte qui dicitur agned."*
*The eleventh battle was on the hill called Agned*
Nennius: *Historia Brittonum.*

At the southern tip of the Lleyn Peninsula, the sheer, rugged cliffs of Porth Neigwl meet the shingle beach of a great bay several miles wide. Aptly named "Hell's Mouth" the bay is set like the rim of a great crucible that takes the brunt of south-westerly storms, rebuffing angry seas that shatter ships timbers and thunder ashore, relentlessly threshing rough rocks and eventually grinding them down to smooth pebbles.

Arthur craved the desolation and the solitude of this place; after the carnage of the Battle of Tribruit, the blood-stained swords, shields and chainmail, the crimson field and the stream running with blood, Arthur needed desperately to refresh his mind and soul. Now his battle would be with the wind and spray as he braced himself against the storm. Staggering forward towards the cliffs, Arthur knelt into the shingle embankment, the salt spray mingling with his own tears as he began to build a tower of stones from the shingle: one stone for each life lost on the field of Tribruit, for his Britons, and for the Britons of the north. It was Arthur's own personal act of remembrance as well as his acceptance of the tragic loss of so many young warriors.

When darkness fell, Arthur placed a capping stone to his tower of over three hundred smooth pebbles: *"Dear Lord, I plead, receive their souls. May heaven honour them for evermore,"* cried Arthur. Rising slowly, he turned to climb the steep and jagged cliff that towered high above the crashing waves. Striding forcefully into the raging storm, Arthur forced his way along the cliff-top towards the western headland, climbing up to the crown of a rocky outcrop where great bastions of granite guarded the ancient fortress of Cregiau Gwineu. Long deserted, the old compound provided Arthur with a perfect refuge from the storm; here he would banish all thoughts of battle and sleep soundly under the stars.

The freak summer storm had abated overnight leaving the air fresh and clear. Arthur rose at dawn to walk the ramparts. The south wall overlooked a small bay

194

that curved southward towards Ynys Enlli, Bardsey Island, the burial isle of Celtic Saints; in contrast to the raging seas of the previous night, the sea was now flat calm and Arthur could see for miles. On the western horizon he could clearly see the peak of Lugnaquilla Mountain, the highest of the Wicklow Mountains: snow-capped in winter, but having a heart of gold in all seasons. The thought reminded Arthur that king Mac Erca was even now in his debt; it would be expedient to pay another visit to Ireland to collect the gold promised as due reward for the victory over king Illan at Cair Legion.

Climbing to the north wall, Arthur found himself atop a sheer rock-face that towered sixty feet above the heathland of the Lleyn Peninsula, and as he looked towards the horizon he was uplifted by the magnificent sight of Mount Snowdon in the heart of Gwynedd. He recalled the happy days when, as a young warrior he had joined Ambrosius at Dinas Emrys, climbing the great mountain and fishing in the nearby lakes and streams.

Riding out a few miles from Cregiau Gwineu, Arthur came across a stream, the Afon Horon, and he followed its winding course through fields of ripe corn as far as the old Roman mill-house near Llandegwn. It was an idyllic spot, shaded by overhanging branches where the stream ran clear, and Arthur enjoyed the late summer afternoon spearing trout, his mind now far from the field of battle. As the sun went down Arthur followed a group of harvesters to the nearby farmstead, their carts full to the brim with stooks of corn. The friendly farmer gave the soldier a warm welcome, inviting Arthur to join the evening festivities to celebrate their fruitful harvest.

Arthur kept his identity secret, introducing himself as Owain, one of Arthur's warriors; he willingly exchanged his trout for a large flagon of mead, and relaxed in the company of the villagers as they enjoyed mutton stew served by the farmer's wife from a huge cauldron suspended over an open fire. A trio of local musicians arrived to accompany the dancing, with pipes, drums and tambourines; they soon encouraged the shy young farm boys to dance with the village girls who twirled ribbons through the air as they laughed in merriment. At midnight Arthur bade farewell to his hosts, thanking them for their kindness. *"Come and stay with us whenever you wish,"* said the farmer. *"Indeed, I will,"* shouted Arthur, as he rode off towards the fort.

For Arthur, the simple pleasures of rural life helped him to recuperate from the physical exhaustion and the mental stress of battle; once more he had been lucky enough to come through a fierce and bitter clash suffering only superficial cuts and bruises, but the less fortunate had been dragged from the battlefield with severe injuries; most of the warriors whose limbs were severed by enemy swords and axes, bled to death before they could be rescued.

Guinevere, for her part, made a significant contribution to the war effort, and took an active role setting up a working hospital in the military base at Wroxeter, recruiting physicians and nurses to tend wounded warriors after battle. Guinevere also took on the dolorous task of talking to the families of loved ones who had not returned from battle, whose only solace was that their sons had given their lives for Britain.

Guinevere was taken by surprise when Arthur's charioteer arrived at the commander's Wroxeter villa: *"Arthur asks you to join him at Cregiau Gwineu,"* he called. *"But I have so much to do here with the wounded,"* she replied. *"Arthur insists that you take a day or two of rest by the sea!"* *"Very well,"* replied Guinevere, *"but only for two days."*

When the chariot pulled up the steep rampart leading to the fort's gateway, Arthur came out to greet them, catching Guinevere in his arms as she jumped down from the chariot. *"You must come and see this sunset"* said Arthur as he led Guinevere past a roaring fire to the vantage point overlooking the bay. It was a breath-taking sight as the sun's great golden disc sank slowly towards the horizon beyond Bardsey Island, the still brilliant rays of light brushing the evening sky with strands of gold and deep orange that seemed to set the sea on fire. *"It is truly beautiful!"* said Guinevere, as she gazed in wonderment at the view, *"thank you for bringing me to this special place."*

*"Come,"* said Arthur, with a smile, *"this windy old fortress is no place for a lady"* and he pulled Guinevere back to the chariot and raced down the rough track-way towards Llandegwn. When Arthur reached the cobbled courtyard of the farmstead he found the farmer and his family threshing wheat in front of the barn. *"May we take up your kind offer of a guest-room for a night or two?"* asked Arthur. *"Most welcome to,"* replied the farmer, dropping his flail as he came forward to bridle the horses. Arthur introduced Guinevere to his new friends. *"Pleased to meet you m'lady,"* said the farmer, introducing himself: *"Gwyn, and this is my dear wife Olwen. Come inside and join us for supper."*

When the children had been fed and packed off to bed, Olwen served a wholesome stew of pork with suet dumplings and freshly grown vegetables, and Gwyn produced a jug of his home-made elderberry wine for the occasion. Guinevere complimented Olwen on her home-baked wholemeal bread, saying that it was the best she had ever tasted. *"Do you grind your own corn?"* asked Arthur. *"No,"* replied Gwyn, *"apart from the tithes we set aside in kind for the king, and the oats we use to feed the cattle, all our grain goes down the lane to the miller."*

*"Grumpy old Gryfudd!"* exclaimed Olwen, *"and what's more, he won't pay us a fair price for it either,"* she admitted, wincing as she spoke. *"I don't remember seeing him*

*at the harvest festivities,"* said Arthur. *"No, he keeps himself to himself,"* replied Gwyn, *"he's not best liked in the village."* *"Especially not since he got young Gwladys in a family way,"* Olwen remarked, *"and then refused to have anything to do with her."*

*"Does he not know the law?"* exclaimed Arthur, *"A man who sleeps three nights or more with a maiden must give her three oxen as his forfeit for deserting her."* *"At the very least,"* added Guinevere, *"a child begotten in the bush must be maintained and provided for by the father."*

*"He's not only ruined the girls' chance of an honourable marriage, but he's also bribed the magistrate to keep himself out of court,"* said Gwyn; *"and rumour has it that he doesn't pay his fair dues to the king either."*

*"To cap it all!"* shouted Arthur in disbelief, *"we surely have an old scoundrel here."* *"I may be able to find a buyer who will give you a fair price for your grain,"* said Arthur, reassuringly. *"And who might that be?"* asked Gwyn. *"Arthur, our Commander of Battles,"* said Arthur, winking at Guinevere, *"he needs bread for his warriors and oats for his horses."* He looked steadfastly at his host, *"if you are willing to deliver your harvest to Wroxeter, I will talk to him on my return to headquarters."* *"That would be a miracle!"* said Gwyn and Olwen in unison, and they all laughed heartily.

It was Sunday morning and Arthur and Guinevere rose early to join their friends for the service at the chapel of St Tegonwy; built of wattle and daub with a thatched roof, this tiny chapel was set on its own at the edge of a country lane, yet at most was only three or four fields away from the surrounding farmsteads of Trewen, Pen-y-bont and Neigwl Uchaf.

A shaft of morning sunlight streamed through the clerestory windows as if it was a manifestation of God's blessing on this humble assembly; Arthur prayed for forgiveness for all the killing, all the bloodshed, and for the fortitude and strength of spirit to save his country and his people from pagan conquest and oppression. Then the words *"Come unto me all who are heavily laden, and I will refresh you,"* echoed in his mind and struck a chord in his heart, so that when he received the Sacrament, he felt the clear stream of the Holy Spirit washing his own spirit clean. Guinevere prayed for Arthur, and for the healing of his wounded warriors, and for peace.

The young parish priest Tegonwy ap Teon blessed his motley congregation and gave the Lord's absolution to rich and poor alike: for whether they were freemen, bondmen, soldier or serf, all were equal in the sight of God. Hoping to remain unrecognised, Arthur passed no more than the time of day as he led Guinevere quickly through the small group of parishoners who had gathered outside the west door of the chapel, to greet each other and gossip after the service.

Following a farm track to the west that cut through stubble fields towards a distant wood, Arthur confessed to Guinevere how shocked he had been by the audacity of Galanan's attack on the iron mine at Dragonby. *"It's not so surprising when you consider the value of iron,"* said Guinevere, *"A good sword is worth fifty cows; and a good sword together with an embroidered cloak can be exchanged for a whole estate."* *"True,"* said Arthur, *"but now we must safeguard our iron mines; all the more so as we have already lost the weald mines to the Saxons: now we must plan to defend the mines of Gwent, as well as those to the east of Leicester; and most important, Pen y Gogarth, our copper mine that is the great secret source of the wealth of the kings of Gwynedd."*

Arthur followed a shallow stream that ran through a woodland grove and into a miniature lake: *"What a beautiful place! It's so peaceful here,"* said Guinevere, softly, *"and look, Arthur, you can see the mountains through the trees."* *"Enchanting,"* agreed Arthur, *"this is the perfect place for a summer villa!"* he exclaimed. *"It would be wonderful,"* said Guinevere as she embraced Arthur, *"promise me that we will come here again."* *"When the battles are done and we have won the war: until then we shall call this our enchanted grove, our Celliwig!"* exclaimed Arthur.

At dawn the following day Arthur and Guinevere thanked their new friends Gwyn and Olwen for their kindness and homely hospitality, and set off in their chariot towards Cregiau Gwineu. Arthur's charioteer had made a fire from driftwood washed up on the beach, and was preparing a piglet for the spit; by mid-day the dripping fat was spitting over the fire and when the crackling had crisped to perfection, they gathered round the fire to enjoy tender pork ribs with farmhouse bread and mead.

They were interrupted by a courier who charged unexpectedly through the open gateway, his mount foaming at the mouth, *"I come from Viroconium with a message for Arthur,"* he announced, *"Seneschal Cei has some good news for you sire, and he asks you to return to headquarters."* *"We'll come at once,"* Arthur replied, *"but you can stay and help yourself to some ribs."*

Cei was waiting on the veranda of the commander's villa when Arthur's chariot raced through the timber-towered gateway of Viroconium's fortress and sped along the dusty track that led to the western edge of the city; the chariot wheeled through the villa's arched gateway and onto the oval driveway that led to the main entrance. Cei came forward to help Guinevere down from the chariot as the charioteer reigned in the exhausted horses. *"Seventy miles in an afternoon!"* shouted Arthur, *"We drove full pelt to hear your news."*

Arthur and Cei walked straight to the Battle Operations Room in the south-wing of the villa, where Arthur had built a map-table of Britain with castellated wooden blocks to represent major cities and fortresses, and had marked the major Roman roads and strategically important rivers on the map; the ceded territories of

Kent, Anglia and east Lincolnshire were painted white, bordered by the a bold red line that defined Arthur's eastern front. Old Roman dinari mounted on tesserae marked the most important working mines, the iron, copper, lead, tin and gold mines representing the source of the nation's wealth that sustained the kings and warriors of Britain. Enemy positions were marked with black pawns taken from an old chess-set, opposed by Arthur's own squadrons and forts that were represented by pawns painted in bright rowan.

Cei took a pawn from the box of symbols and moved round to the south-west corner of the plotting board, placing the rowan pawn in the Colne Estuary, close to the fortress of Camulodunum. *"We have a new naval force,"* he announced to Arthur, *"Clovis the Frank has attacked western Gaul in great strength and has beaten the Visigoths into submission: but some of their warriors escaped over the Pyrenees Mountains into Spain, and Theodoric, the commander of the Goth's Atlantic fleet, has brought his surviving ships to Britain."*

*"Incredible! A godsend!"* exclaimed Arthur, *"Did you speak with him?"* *"Most certainly,"* replied Cei, *"his crew rowed the ship's cock-boat right up to the quay at Camulod, for Theodoric expected to find you at the Garrison."* *"And his terms?"* asked Arthur eagerly. *"In return for a safe harbour and victualling, five ships under his command are placed at your service,"* said Cei, with a beaming smile.

*"But they are too far away to the east at Camulod,"* said Arthur. *"We need Theodoric's force closer to our command headquarters here in the west. I fear for the safety of our iron mines in Gwent because the kings of Dyfed and Brecon succour raiders from Ireland and strengthen their own war-bands at every opportunity: they play our tune to keep the peace but in their hearts they covet our mineral wealth, and when their greed is ripe, they will combine their mercenary forces and strike us here,"* explained Arthur, thrusting his dagger into the plotting map, piercing the Roman fortress of Gobannium, Abergavenny, in anger. *"Invite Theodoric to bring his fleet to our safe port of Gloucester,"* said Arthur, *"we can victual him there and keep his ships secure; and then, with only sixty miles between us, we can quickly join forces to oppose these dissident kings of Dyfed and Brecon."*

*"But we must give him leave to put in at Portsmouth or Plymouth if the weather turns foul,"* pleaded Cei. *"With six-hundred miles of sea ahead of him, we should not hope to see his ships at Gloucester within eight or nine days,"* replied Arthur, *"but when he does arrive, we'll be there to meet him."*

The late summer weather was kind to Theodoric, and once he had turned onto a north-easterly heading beyond Land's End, his square-rigged ships ran with a steady south-westerly breeze for the long leg of the voyage to the Severn Estuary. Every sailor knew that the Bristol Channel was the last place anyone would want to be in a south-westerly gale, with the ships wallowing awkwardly for hours in the troughs of huge following waves, and battling with the swirling currents that swept around the estuary mouth when the tide ran against the wind; fortunately for Theodoric the weather remained fair, and he steered his fleet into the Severn, following the river's meandering stream for nine miles through water meadows before reaching the long Roman quay at Gloucester.

Arthur and Cei gave their new allies a warm welcome, and as Theodoric and Marcellus, his second-in-command, stepped ashore, they were cheered by the crowd that had gathered on the dockside to watch the fleet berth. Commanders and their crews were invited to the Roman Fortress where Arthur had laid on a feast to celebrate their arrival and to welcome them to their new shore garrison.

Arthur was champing at the bit to plan his next campaign, and a soon as the festivities were over, he escorted his new commanders to Viroconium. In a formal ceremony, Theodoric and Marcellus took an oath of allegiance to king Uther, pledging their support to the British cause and giving an assurance of loyalty to Arthur and the king. They adjourned to the Operations Room where Arthur recounted his recent battles and explained to Theodoric how Britain was surrounded by enemies on all fronts: but his battle for Britain was not yet won, for the Saxons were a constant threat in the south, and the burgeoning power of the so called 'protector kings' of Dyfed and Brecon posed an immediate threat to the valuable mining area of Gwent in the west.

Theodoric suggested that his ships could patrol the western seaboard of Britain in order to stem the incursion of Irish marauders, and Arthur agreed that a token force of two ships could be assigned to that role, with the proviso that Theodoric's main force would spearhead the landward advance into Brecon, while Arthur himself took his army south to intercept the enemy in Dyfed. Arthur was the first to acknowledge that he could not instantly turn Theodoric's sailors into cavalry, but he could train them to become effective infantrymen who would be able to reinforce his own mounted warriors in battle.

As a Christian, king Uther had made it clear that he would not sanction a repeat of Cunedda's massacre of the Irish migrants of Gwynedd that had taken place in the early years of the fifth century. The prime objective of Arthur's campaign would be to remove the rulers of the Irish dynasties of Brecon and Dyfed with the least bloodshed, and replace them with British protectors whose allegiance to Gwynedd and Powys would strengthen Arthur's control over the states of western Britain.

For Arthur, the timing of the campaign was critical: on the one hand, if he were to make a pre-emptive strike on Brecon and Dyfed he would for ever be accused of acting like a tyrant for starting a civil war and murdering his enemies without justification. On the other hand, he could play the waiting game, allowing the dissident kings to marshal their war-bands and make the first move to attack; then Arthur could not only trap their forces but remove their leaders at the same time.

King Uther and his commanders agreed that this was the best course of action, and while Theodoric's men trained for the land-battle, Arthur's scouts moved into Brecon and Dyfed to assess the strength and position of the enemy forces.

❧ ❧ ❧ ❧

Echoes of Arthur's presence in South Wales are embedded in several different stories recorded by medieval authors almost six hundred years after his lifetime. In the epic poem *Culhwych and Olwen,* written around 1095, Arthur's enemy is depicted as the evil and destructive boar *Twrch Trwyth* who had already laid waste to one third of Ireland from his lair at Esgair Oerfel in the heart of the Wicklow Mountains. Later in the poem, when Arthur sailed to Ireland, his warriors demanded to know the story of the boar: *"He was a king and for his wickedness God transformed him into a swine,"* explained Arthur.

Seizing the opportunity to attack Britain while Arthur was trying to pin him down to a pitched battle in Ireland, the cunning Twrch Trwyth sailed with his war-band to South Wales to make as much mischief as possible before Arthur could catch up with him. Landing at Porth Cleis by the mouth of the river Alun he marched west, ravaging the lowlands between the rivers, east and west Cleddau, before moving north to the high ground of Mynedd Preseli. While Twrch secured the mountain peak of Foel Cwmcerwyn, Arthur positioned his army along both banks of the river Nevern and prepared to attack.

In the ensuing bloody skirmishes with the enemy, several of Arthur's champions were reputedly killed, including his own son, named Gwydre in the story. Then, with Arthur's forces moving in for the kill, Twrch escaped westward to Aber Tywi, following the river upstream towards Llandello, where he took refuge on Mynedd Amann, a western peak of the Black Mountains in Dyfed. Here, in a hand to hand fight, Arthur and his warriors killed five of Twrch's pigs, forcing him to run another thirty miles to the safety of Ewyas Vale, close to Castell Dinas and the protection of the king of Brychan.

At this critical stage of the great boar-hunt, Arthur was forced to muster a large army from the Cornovii and the men of Dumnonia, with orders to report to Arthur at the mouth of the river Severn. Twrch Trwyth was then forced out of Ewyas into the river Severn, where Arthur and his army fell upon him: yet even after a near drowning, the wily Twrch escaped to Cornwall, where Arthur finally cornered him and drove him into the sea.

The story of Twrch Trwyth mentions many real locations and gives the names of warriors who fell in the course of the hunt, but it is only Arthur's force that opposes the Irish raiders in their rampage through Dyfed, and the fact that there is no mention of the forces of Dyfed or Brecon opposing them, or coming to Arthur's aid, suggests that the rulers of both those countries were in league with the invaders. Twrch's refuge in the Vale of Ewyas, only a few miles from the king of Brecon's headquarters at Castell Dinas, gives credence to the suggestion that Twrch was acting in allegiance with the Irish king Brychan, whose ambition to conquer the wealthy iron resources of Gwent would have been well served by an armed force from Ireland.

Evidently, the immediate threat to Arthur's iron supplies had become so serious that he was forced to declare a national emergency and to call a large force of men to arms. The great Roman fortress of Gloucester, at the mouth of the river Severn, became Arthur's rallying point for a counter-attack against the Irish enemy and the rebellious rulers of South Wales.

Llifris, a monk of Llancarfan, writing the *Life of Saint Cadog* around 1100 AD tells the romantic story of the saint's father king Gwynllyw, who fell in love with Princess Gwladus, the eldest daughter of his neighbour king Brychan of Brycheiniog. When Gwynllyw sent messengers to the king, demanding her hand in marriage, Brychan became indignant and resolutely refused to bestow his daughter upon him. This rebuttal put Gwynllyw into a fury, and he resolved to take the princess by force.

With a war-band of three hundred men, Gwynllyw made a daring raid on Castell Dinas by Talgarth, seized the beautiful Gwladus, and eloped with her on horseback. King Brychan, outraged by the loss of his daughter, mustered his army and chased the abductors, killing two hundred of Gwynllyw's men before they could reach the fort of Boch Rhiw Carn near Fochrin on the southern border of Brecon.

When Gwynllyw reached the fort, safely securing Gwladus in his own territory, to his surprise he found Arthur, Cei and Bedivere sitting on the hill-top playing a game of dice. Seeing such a beautiful girl, Arthur was inflamed with desire and wished to take Gwladus for himself; but his companions restrained him, and reminded him that their mission was to help the needy and distressed. Arthur needed to confirm that Boch Rhiw Carn belonged to Gwynllyw because that would make king Brychan's attack an unlawful invasion of his territory, thereby justifying Arthur's retribution. Gwynllyw reassured Arthur that, "*God being my witness, also all who best know of the Britons, I avow that I am the owner of this land.*"

On hearing this declaration, Arthur and his companions, being fully armed, rushed into battle against king Brychan's soldiers, who turned their backs and fled in great confusion. Thus, through Arthur's intervention and rescue, king Gwynllyw returned in triumph and brought Gwladus safely to his own residence at Allt Wynllwy in Casnewydd, Stowhill in Newport.

In another chapter of *The Life of Saint Cadog,* Llifris relates the story of Ligessauc, a brave chieftain, who, having killed three of Arthur's warriors, sought sanctuary within Cadoc's church. After seven years, when the legal period of sanctuary had expired, Arthur came to claim rightful compensation for the loss of his men, arriving at the river Usk *"with a very great force of soldiers."* In this instance, although the author clearly draws on the tradition that *"Arthur brought his army to the Usk"* he uses the occasion to show that Arthur held authority over rights and privileges granted to Saint Cadoc's monastery at Llancarfan.

By seeking out the plausible facts from the more fabulous elements of these legendary texts, we find evidence that relates to a major military campaign culminating in Arthur's eleventh battle at "Mount Agned." First, the tale of *Culhwych and Olwen* tracks Irish invaders from their landfall near Mynyw, St David's, and follows their rampage through Dyfed and Brecon to the Vale of Ewyas, close to the northern border of Gwent; in this location, and in alliance with the king of Brychan, they would have posed a serious threat to the mineral resources of Gwent and the security of western Britain.

Furthermore, by drawing on the earliest Glamorgan tradition, the monastic author Llifris revealed Arthur's strategic position on a hill-fort beside the Roman road that ran from Cardiff to Brecon, close to the forts of Gelligaer and Penydarren, Merthyr Tydfil. When Arthur attacked the enemy host they retreated to the north and took up a position on high ground near Llangynidr. Then, as Arthur advanced, the stage was set for a fearsome battle.

Finally, texts from early Brecon manuscripts help to complete the story of Arthur's campaign against his enemies in South Wales, for they reveal evidence of a military expedition that swept the invaders out of Brecon and into the south-western tip of Dyfed, killing them by the hundred as they went; yet ultimately allowing the remnant to escape by ship from Porth Mawr.

&&&&

King Thuibaius, ruler of the Ui Dunlaing of Leinster, and none other than the Twrch Trwyth of legend, sailed from Ireland with his war-band to reinforce the king of Brychan's army. His land-fall in South Wales was a wake-up call for Arthur, who could see the scales of the balance of power tipping away from the ruling dynasty of Gwynedd and Powys in favour of Brecon and Dyfed. Arthur had no need to second guess king Brychan's next move, for it was widely known that he coveted the iron mining area to the east of his kingdom, and was determined to help himself to some of the wealth on his doorstep.

Sensing that an invasion of Gwent was imminent, Arthur marshalled the forces of Dumnonia and Cornovii to reinforce his experienced and highly trained cavalry squadrons from Wroxeter; his good fortune in securing the services of Theodoric and his battle-hardened men could not have come at a more opportune moment, for Arthur would need a large army to defeat the combined forces that were now ranged against him. Another fortuitous string to Arthur's bow came from his good friend and ally, king Gwynllyw of Gwynlliog, whose small country bordered Gwent and Brycheiniog (Brecon). Gwynllyw, ever true to the British cause, had pledged his allegiance to Arthur, and offered his small force as a token of his loyalty.

Altogether, his cavalry units, Theodoric's militia, and rural infantrymen combined to give Arthur an impressive fighting force of around one thousand men: a powerful army that would enable him to develop an ambitious battle-plan, the crux of which involved drawing the enemy into rough terrain to the west of Abergavenny, then trapping them in a triangular battle zone by initiating a three-pronged attack. Just as Arthur and his commanders were racking their brains to find a way of getting king Brychan's army to move south into the designated battle zone, king Gwynllyw suggested that he could sting Brychan into action by abducting his beautiful daughter Gwladus from the royal residence at Castell Dinas. Arthur laughed, for it was the most novel idea for starting a battle that he had ever heard, but although it sounded a risky operation, he thought it worth a try. King Gwynllyw was thus assigned to steal the king of Brecon's daughter and to hold her hostage in Gwynlliog.

In the headquarters of Gloucester Castle, Arthur unrolled a rough parchment map on which he had drawn the key Roman forts and the roads linking Gloucester with Gwent, Brecon and Dyfed. Then, in the presence of his battle commanders, he drew the triangular battle-zone onto the map, marking a line south from Llangynidr to Beaufort, then east to Abergavenny and back again to Llangynidr: *"Within this triangle,"* Arthur explained, *"here we trap the enemy."* He then briefed each commander with their individual roles for the battle.

First, Theodoric and Marcellus would march from Gloucester to a holding position at the old fort of Clyro, two miles west of Hay-on-Wye. As soon as Brychan's army marched south, Theodoric's company would follow them at a safe distance, and block their return at the river Usk. At the same time, Marcellus' troop would advance from the north along the Vale of Ewyas, and sweep the Irish war-band south towards Abergavenny.

Prior to this action, Arthur planned to march his main army from Gloucester to the Roman fortress at Usk. Bedivere, commanding his own cavalry troop and the Dumnonian company, would join Arthur at Usk and then move north as far as Abergavenny. Arthur and Cei would then march south-west with their cavalry, reinforced with the Cornovian infantrymen, to take up their holding position at Gelligaer fort. Arthur gave the commanders two days to reach their respective positions and prepare for battle. Clyro and Gelligaer were at least forty miles from Gloucester, and that would mean a long day's march for the foot-soldiers. Finally, Arthur emphasized the importance of moving into position as covertly as possible: the element of surprise would be the key to victory.

Accompanied by king Gwynllyw and his warriors, Arthur, Cei and Bedivere advanced from Usk to Gelligaer where the army made camp. Early the following morning, Arthur and his commanders moved forward to climb Mynedd Fochriw, an excellent vantage point high above the Rhymney Valley that gave them a clear view of the main highway between the forts of Merthyr Tydfil and Abergavenny. From here, Arthur could spy upon enemy troop movements and detect Dyfed forces moving east, and Brecon forces moving west. Arthur pitched his temporary camp on the hill-top, while Gwynllyw and his men encamped in the river valley below, pitching their tents on the edge of the pine forest and keening their weapons before nightfall in readiness for battle. As the sun went down, and with time to relax, the three commanders entertained themselves with a jovial game of dice.

At sunrise the following day, Arthur put his battle plan into action: Gwynllyw rode north towards Talgarth at the head of three-hundred men; Bedivere returned to Usk to mobilize the Dumnonians for the march to Abergavenny; and Cei returned to Gelligaer to marshal the Cornovii forward to the forest near Fochriw, where they would stay hidden until Gwynllyw's return. Crossing the Usk at Llangynidr, and keeping to the west of the enemy garrison at Pen-y-Gaer, Gwynllyw moved north along the Llynfi valley towards his target. The king sent a detachment of thirty warriors to seize princess Gwladus, while he held fast at the head of his war-band, prepared to order the attack should Brychan's guards put up a fight; but the castle had been posted with a light guard, and the few armed men were quickly overpowered by the attacking warriors, who captured Gwladus and brought her to meet the king.

Gwynllyw, struck by the young girl's great beauty, immediately apologised for the inconvenience of being taken hostage, explaining that it was essential for the security of Britain. Alarmed by her sudden abduction, and with her heart racing with fear and excitement, Gwladus was re-assured by the handsome young king and agreed to go with him willingly. Whereupon two warriors lifted the princess onto the back of Gwynllyw's horse, and he galloped south, leading his men back towards the river Usk.

King Brychan was enraged when he discovered that his eldest daughter had been abducted; he called his men to arms and galloped after Gwynllyw and his raiders, catching them and cutting down more than one hundred warriors as they crossed the river Usk. Gwynllyw spurred his men forward towards the safety of Mynedd Fochrw, but as they raced for the border his brave soldiers turned to do battle with their enemy. More men lost their lives as Brychan's onslaught continued: then, as they reached the Rhymney Valley Arthur raised the alarm from his look-out post on the hill-top. Three short, shrill blasts from Arthur's horn gave Cei the signal to attack: he led the cavalry charge from the pine-forest into a head-on clash with Brychan's advancing army.

Brychan was flushed with pride after the retribution he had meted out to Gwynllyw's men, but as his front line reared-up in disarray, his face turned a pale shade of grey with the shock of seeing the Red Dragon of Arthur's cavalry unfurling before his eyes. With brutal force he wheeled his mount around, barking at his troops to retreat to the high ground to the north where they could take refuge from Arthur's assault.

In the momentary calm after the first clash with the enemy, Arthur rode back to the Rhymney Valley to greet Gwynllyw, but when he first set eyes on Brychan's daughter, he was overwhelmed with her beauty and secretly wished that he had gone to Talgarth to capture her himself. Arthur congratulated Gwynllyw on successfully gaining an invaluable prize, but commiserated with him on suffering the costly loss of over two hundred warriors. Arthur released the young king from the battlefield to secure the princess who was now his prisoner; and when Gwynllyw returned with Gwladus to his own fortress at Allt Wynllyw, his people gave him a hero's welcome.

As the day drew to a close, Arthur's forces had begun to close-in on the enemy. Theodoric's company had moved south from Clyro, keeping a cautious distance from Brychan's cavalry as they chased after Gwynllyw; the few guards remaining at Castell Dinas and Pen-y-Gaer were swiftly despatched by Theodoric's warriors. The natural hill-fort of Myarth gave Theodoric an excellent defensive position overlooking the river Usk, with a clear view of the bridge at Llangynidr, and he decided to pitch camp and await Arthur's signal to advance.

Brychan's Irish allies, without having the advantage of horses, had taken most of the day to mobilize and march south along the Vale of Ewyas, crossing the Usk at Llangattock, and following Brychan's track towards Beaufort. However, Marcellus' company reached the Usk without making contact with the enemy, and from Llanbedr they marched along the riverbank to join Theodoric's camp at Myarth.

Mynedd Llangynidr, Brecon.
Situated on the eastern edge of the Brecon Beacons ten miles from Abergavenny, Mynedd Llangynidr rises majestically to its peak some 1700 feet above sea level. Although the rocky limestone outcrop at its peak offered little shelter to an enemy on the run, the command of the mountain peak would have given them a major tactical advantage, for it would have forced their adversary to undertake an exhausting climb prior to the final uphill charge into battle.

Photo, © Gordon Scammell

Brychan's exhausted troops were now running the gauntlet of Cei's cavalry charge as they staggered up the steep mountain track from Blaen-y-cwm to the peak of Mynedd Llangynidr: the summit plateau gave Brychan the highest defensive position for miles, where he could hold at bay, rest his men, and re-form his battle-lines.

At sunset Arthur called-off the attack, and Cei returned to Blaen-y-cwm to make camp for the night and to discuss with Arthur the final battle-plan. Brychan seized the opportunity of this lull in the fighting to dispatch a rider eastwards to Mynedd Llangattock with orders to locate Thuibaius and persuade him to march his Irish war-band up to the summit of Mynedd Llangynidr to reinforce the defensive position.

As soon as Arthur's scouts had reported that the Irish troops had moved west to join Brychan's men on the summit, Arthur realised that the enemy were outside his original target triangle; although they were now only two miles further west, they had presented Arthur with the challenge of fighting an uphill battle to the very summit of Llangynidr, one thousand, seven-hundred feet above sea level.

As darkness fell, Arthur sent two of his trusted cavalry riders with battle orders for Theodoric and Bedivere. Before dawn, Theodoric would cross the river Usk at the village of Llangynidr and then march two miles south to the head of the Cwm Claisfer Valley: at dawn his force would begin the steep ascent towards the eastern plateau of Mynedd Llangynidr and await Arthur's signal to attack. Marcellus' company would cross the Usk at dawn, but hold off a mile or so east of Llangynidr, acting as a strategic reserve force that would block the escape of the enemy from Arthur's battle zone on the mountain.

Bedivere's brief, apart from having the earliest call well before dawn, was to move his cavalry and infantry troops eight miles west of Abergavenny to the lower slopes of Mynedd Llangynidr at Cefn Ownnau, where he would hold his position on Theodoric's right flank.

At first light Arthur broke camp at Blaen-y-cwm, leading his cavalry squadron to Garnlydan, where he turned north along the rugged track that made a steep ascent to Cefn Pwll-coch, less than a mile from the eastern plateau that he had chosen as his rallying point. In turn Cei, with cavalry and infantry troops, followed the route of his earlier attack, climbing the steep ascent past Cwyn Bryn-march toward the summit.

Arthur paused his troop by a small stream that crossed the mountain track, giving his men and their mounts a chance to refresh themselves before the battle; but just as they re-mounted, king Gwynllyw appeared out of the mist with fifty of his warriors: they had returned, in loyalty to Arthur, to reinforce his army.

*"How is your princess?"* asked Arthur, surprised by Gwynllyw's unexpected presence. *"She is very happy,"* Gwynllyw replied, *"for we are to be joined in wedlock."* *"You do not surprise me!"* Arthur quipped, *"Gwladus is indeed the fairest maiden in our land."* *"But she has a favour to ask of you, Arthur,"* pleaded the young king, *"she begs you to spare her father's life."*

*"If you and your men descend from here and guard the western valley at Flos-y-wern, then Gwladus' plea is granted, and we shall spare old king Brychan… when we have brought him to his knees."* Arthur spurred his horse forward towards the eastern plateau and vanished into the mountain mist.

Arthur had planned to attack at dawn, but the early morning mists swirling across Mynedd Llangynidr obscured the sunrise, and he lost the advantage of this precise time signal; but the enforced delay would give his men and their mounts time to recover after the exertion of climbing the mountain.

King Brychan and his Irish allies recoiled with shock as the mists cleared, gradually revealing the massive force of Arthur's army ranged against them in a great semi-circle from north to south: six companies of warriors in alternating corps of cavalry and infantry, poised with drawn swords and elevated spears, their mounts champing at the bit, ready to strike.

The enemy, already shivering with cold after a night in the open on a windswept peak, were now shaking with fear at the formidable force confronting them. Brychan posted his allies to defend the northern sector of the hilltop while he formed his war-band into three ranks of shield-lines on a natural terrace towards the south, holding back a small bodyguard to muster round his command position on the peak.

Then, as the strands of early morning sunlight outlined the craggy outcrop of limestone rock that defined the edge of the summit, Arthur's shrill horn-blast broke the eerie silence that had fallen over the assembled host: with a battle-cry that resounded to the heavens, cavalry squadrons charged across the rough heathland towards the enemy. Bedivere led the assault from the north-east as Arthur charged over the level plateau from the east, racing ahead of Cei's squadron as they wheeled in from the south-west. Arthur was the first to cut through the front line, striking his foes in a powerful head-on attack that swept the enemy off their feet. Pincer attacks by his flanking squadrons cut into Brychan's defensive lines and scattered his men: they recoiled from the shock of the assault and the overwhelming power unleashed by Arthur's skilled warriors.

As the cavalry assault followed through to re-form on the western ridge of the summit, Arthur's horn signalled three companies of infantrymen to advance. Theodoric and his Goths from the steep ridge above the Cwm Claisfer valley, the Dumnonian troops spread across the eastern plateau, and the Cornovii assembled on the southern slopes, moved forward en-masse; it was a motley army of citizens brandishing axes, knives, staves and pitchforks, beating their shields to accompany the battle-cries that reached a fearful crescendo as they closed-in on the enemy. Arthur's three separate companies now closed together to form a wide, crescent shaped battle-line, prepared for the final assault. Theodoric's well-trained warriors were first into the fray, taking the advantage of a natural incline in the landscape to advance rapidly onto the enemy terrace; but the others were forced to fight their way to the top of a natural rampart where a bunch of Brychan's men had been coerced to form a battle line three-hundred yards long, with orders to defend the ridge.

Proud to be fighting for Arthur and the British cause, the Dumnonians, their faces flushed with the adrenalin of battle, hacked their way forcefully to the top of the rampart, piercing the shield wall and breaking into the enemy ranks. On their right flank, Theodoric's men were cutting into the Irishmen, forcing them back against an outcrop of rock that formed the defensive cliff-face of the mountain summit, where Brychan was still shouting orders to his unruly and recalcitrant soldiers. The sight of Brychan's obese figure flailing around on his stocky grey mare roused Arthur's anger and strengthened his resolve to bring this proud tyrant to the ground, to deliver swift retribution for his treachery.

Three short shrill blasts signalled the second cavalry charge: Bedivere's troop targeted the north terrace, Cei's the south, and Arthur, leading from the centre, charged towards the summit of Mynedd Llangynidr. As he galloped fast over the rough, rock-strewn heathland the words of David's psalm gave him a flash of inspiration: *"Thou preparest a table before me in the presence of mine enemies."* This summit was Arthur's table, and here were his enemies. Spiritually elated, Arthur charged full force into king Brychan's bodyguard, venting his anger in the fury of the attack, cutting into the enemy's front rank and spearing Brychan off his mount and pinning him to the ground. While Arthur's warriors engaged in a hand to hand fight for the hill-top, Cei's squadron charged once more from the south, cleaving limbs and skulls, driving a pathway through the enemy as they fell from Arthur's table, their bodies tumbling from the summit down the steep cliff face onto the rocks below.

Arthur dismounted, pressing his sword into Brychan's throat as he writhed in the dust, pleading for mercy. *"Grovel you traitorous bastard!"* shouted Arthur; *"Give me a good reason why I should spare your miserable, gluttonous life,"* Arthur demanded. *"For my daughter's sake,"* pleaded the king. *"Then kiss the gritty soil of Brecon!"* shouted Arthur, forcing Brychan's head into the dust. *"Once for your life; once for your beautiful daughter Gwladus; and once for me!"* ... *"Now, Brychan, you owe your life and allegiance to me, Arthur, Dux Britanniarum."*

This moment marked Arthur's victory in the Battle of Mynedd Llangynidr, but although his mounted warriors had taken the mountain peak, and Cei with Bedivere had swept most of the enemy off the surrounding plateau, the scrap between the Britons and Brychan's men, and between Theodoric and the Irish pirates continued as the remaining enemy soldiers were pushed towards the steep escarpments of the mountain.

Gwynllyw looked up with amazement when he saw the bodies of enemy soldiers falling from the rocky cliff-face of Clo Cadno, and while Theodoric thrust his sword in to the nearest of the remnants, a few fortunate survivors fell sprawling towards the valley below; some of the wounded threw themselves into the stream that cascaded into a waterfall above Flos-y-wern, and as Gwynllyw and his warriors watched the macabre scene taking place on the north-west ridge of the mountain, the waterfall gushed incarnadine with blood.

Now, in the aftermath of battle, Gwynllyw's lust for vengeance had cooled, and in an act of mercy he gathered the enemy wounded and took them down the valley to be cared for at the camp by Blaen-y-cwm; they were, after all, his neighbours; and as a Christian king, he showed them mercy.

But it was evident that king Thuibaius, the commander of the pirate war-band, valued his own life more than his erstwhile allegiance to the king of Brecon; in battle he was certainly a brave fighter, but he was also a master of the art of tactical withdrawal. Shocked to see Brychan downed to the ground, and seeing death's approach with the final onslaught of Arthur's mounted warriors, he feared the ominous outcome of the battle. The northern plateau of Llangynidr was now unguarded, and Thuibaius seized the opportunity to make a run for the safety of Cwm Claisfer.

His escape from the battlefield did not go unnoticed, but Arthur let him go: he had already planned the end-game for the Irish pirates. Just as Thuibaius was congratulating himself on achieving a masterful escape, he ran straight into Marcellus' troops who were guarding the bridge over the Usk at Llangynidr. A few of his men engaged the guards, just long enough to allow the king and his battle-scarred gang to take evasive action by heading towards Brecon.

The pirates had gained a head-start along the old Roman road to Brecon, but this was the opportunity Marcellus had been waiting for, the chance to lead his own military action as the commander of a company of well-trained warriors: he was determined to track-down the enemy war-band, and if they refused to stand and fight, he would chase them back the one hundred miles through Dyfed to their boats, and run them out of the country for good.

Before noon that day Arthur had raised his banner on the summit: the long pennant unfurled in the breeze and the Red Dragon, glinting with gold, declared Arthur's victory on the battlefield of Mynedd Llangynidr. King Brychan was dragged back to his own dungeon at Castell Dinas near Brecon, accompanied by Arthur's guards, to do penance at king Uther's pleasure.

After the toil of battle, Arthur, Cei, Bedivere and Theodoric, together with their exhausted men, refreshed themselves in the cool waters of Lyn y Garn-fawr, a natural lake close to the summit, dousing the blood and sweat from their armoured mail tunics and cleansing their blood-stained weapons. Sadly, during the first battle-charge, several horses had fallen unexpectedly into shake-holes concealed by the rough highland heather; now the unfortunate mounts with broken and twisted limbs were despatched by the sword, and spared further suffering. The defeated troops were ordered to gather the fallen from the battlefield and to carry them down the mountain to their final resting place, a meadow beside a stream called Nant Trefil that runs through Blaen-y-cwm.

Five days after the battle, news reached Arthur from Marcellus at Porth Mawr, where he had finally booted Thuibaius and the remnant of his war-band back to their ships and out into the Irish Sea. By all accounts, the chase had not been easy, for Marcellus and his warriors had scrapped with the enemy at the end of each day's march as they pushed them west from Brecon to Llandovery, then through Carmarthen to the western coast beyond Mynyw, St David's. There had been bloody clashes with the enemy at Llan Maes near Brecon, Lan Semin near Llandello, and a full-scale battle at Meidrum, seven miles west of Carmarthen, where Marcellus had slaughtered half the enemy, but suffered severe losses to his own company.

Arthur was truly pleased with his young commander's success and on his return to Wroxeter appointed Marcellus to the honourable post of "Protector of Dyfed." He would be directly responsible to Agricola, the military commander recently promoted by king Uther to act as tribune over the wayward dynasties of Brecon and Dyfed: Arthur's victory at Llangynidr extinguished their power and brought peace to South Wales; Britons celebrated and king Gwynllyw and Princess Gwladus were happily joined in holy wedlock.

King Uther breathed an unmistakable sigh of relief as he counted Brychan's gold, and assigned his new wealth to the royal vaults that were secured with iron-clad doors of oak, deep in the cavernous rock beneath Castell Dinas Bran.

‹›‹›‹›‹›‹›

Many years later, the last survivor of the battle related the campaigns of Arthur to a young monk attending him in the last moments of his life: "*And where was Arthur's eleventh battle?*" asked the young cleric. "*Mynedd Llangynidr*" replied the ancient warrior softly … "*Mount Agned*" wrote the scribe; "*and where exactly was that?*" enquired the young monk. "*Brychan!*" gasped the warrior, almost with his last breath … "*Bregoin*" wrote the scribe; thus unwittingly confiding the true location of Arthur's eleventh battle to mystery and conjecture for fifteen hundred years.

# CHAPTER 14

# THE BATTLE OF BADON

*"The action of the Battle of Badon was shown in the day of the victorious dragon's anger: a track of shield-cleaving and shattering, a path of hewing-down with red blades."*
Cynddelw (1155-1200)

The Battle of Badon gave Arthur the final victory in his thirty year fight for the freedom of Britain: it was indeed Arthur's Battle for Britain, a campaign against foreign invaders that culminated on Mount Badon, where the Saxon king, Ochta and his war-band of galley-slaves were beaten. The few who survived limped away to the east, as far from the battlefield as their legs could carry them, to tend their wounds and hide their shame; the strongest staggered slowly back to their country of Kent, each with their own sad tale of the horror of the battle, the wanton bloodshed, and the tragic loss of life on that day at Badon Hill.

Thenceforth *"Bloody Badon"* as it was called, became famous for the day the Saxons were beaten. Such a catastrophic defeat was beyond record, and Saxon pride precluded any admission of defeat: in future years the battle of Badon became conspicuous for its absence from the Anglo-Saxon Chronicle; but for the Britons, the Saxon defeat was a cause for celebration: *"the war was over!"* and the battle of Badon became renowned as Arthur's final victory in his battle for Britain.

Considered in its true historical perspective, Badon ranks in importance with the great British victories of more recent times: Nelson's victory at Trafalgar; Wellington's at Waterloo; Montgomery's at El Alamein. The names of these famous battles will be remembered for all time; but today, the average Briton, the 'man or woman in the street' would most likely have some difficulty if asked to pin-point the exact location of these battles. So it was with Badon, the most famous battle of sixth century Britain, fought hand-to-hand against the country's most reviled enemy on a remote hill-fort somewhere in southern Britain. Possibly off the beaten track, but more than likely close to a Roman road that would take the Saxon war-band from their newly conquered homeland of Kent, straight to Arthur's doorstep "*somewhere in the west*;" and if not to his secret stronghold, then to one of his cities, perhaps Cirencester or Gloucester, that were known to be of strategic importance in the military defence of western Britain.

There is no doubt that Arthur and his warriors, together with the Saxon survivors of Badon, had good cause to remember exactly where the battle had taken place; but in time, perhaps some decades after Arthur's death, the site of the great battle was lost, leaving only the name to resound down the centuries, locked into history in the manuscripts of Gildas, and Nennius, and the entry for the year AD 518 in the *Annales Cambriae*.

But if the evidence from these early sources is combined together as one report, we can reveal a much clearer picture of the circumstances of the battle:

"*After the death of Ambrosius the British battle commander, there was a long struggle against the invaders, with victory going sometimes to the British, sometimes to the Saxons, until the battle of Mount Badon in the year 518. During the three day siege of Badon Hill, Arthur, the Leader of Battles, wore a tunic over his shoulders, a holy emblem that was emblazoned with the cross of Christ.*"

"*Arthur and his warriors fought this battle on their own: there was no time to enlist the help of any other British king because they had to take immediate action against an enemy that was already on the march. On the day of the battle, following Arthur's great cavalry charge, nine hundred and sixty of the enemy were killed, and the Britons were victorious.*"

In contrast to these contemporary reports, occasional references are made to the battle of Badon in early Welsh poetry and prose, reaffirming the epic status of Arthur's victory and offering curious clues, some stranger than fiction, that reveal historical details of the battle. One unusual tale, *The Dream of Rhonabwy* found in the early medieval collection of Welsh stories known as the *Mabinogion,* links Arthur to Camlan and Badon; the author refers to Arthur as '*the emperor,*' and mentions that cavalry troops from different parts of the country assembled prior to the preparations for the battle of Baddon, pronounced '*Bathon,*' which he describes as a fortress. Furthermore, in an extraordinary comment, the author actually gives the time of the battle: "*Then a proud and handsome man of bold and eloquent speech said that it was a wonder how a large force could be contained in such a confined area, the more so as they had promised to be at the Battle of Baddon by noon in order to fight against Osla Big knife.*" In other words, it would appear that Arthur had anticipated the confrontation, and had actually set a time for his troops to muster for the battle.

But where was Badon? Geoffrey of Monmouth understandably took the German word '*badon*' to mean '*bath*' in English; thus in his story, he set the great battle in the city of Bath in Somerset; and if by chance he had come across the reference to Bath as 'balnea Badonis' in *Wonders of Britain* by Nennius, this would have certainly confirmed his opinion of the location of Badon. Many historians have since concurred with this view, despite the fact that the city is set in a valley, and in Arthur's day would have been known as '*Aqua Sulis*', the original Roman name for Bath. Furthermore, the recent tenuous link with the nearby hill-fort of Little Solsbury lacks conviction because the fort has revealed no evidence to support fifth century occupation.

Breidden Hill to the west of Shrewsbury, Breedon hill near Evesham, Badbury rings in Dorset, and Liddington Castle near Badbury, are all possible contenders for the site of Badon; but of all the suggested sites, Liddington Castle is perhaps the strongest candidate. Situated on the ancient Ridgeway track half-way between Silchester and Cirencester, it would have been directly in the line of fire of a Saxon army advancing from Calleva Atrebatum, Silchester, towards Cirencester or Gloucester.

The great Iron Age forts of the Ridgeway, namely Segsbury Camp, Uffington Castle, Liddington, and Barbury Castle to the west, were built by the ancient Britons not only to defend the Ridgeway from the north, but also to protect their equestrian territory on the Lambourn Downs, and ultimately to defend the hallowed ground of Avebury where the Silbury monument and Megalithic Stone Circle marked the religious centre of southern Britain.

These forts formed part of a defensive chain that for centuries defined a buffer zone between Britons and their enemies. Even after the English had conquered most of southern Britain, the *Annales Cambriae* recorded a second Battle of Badon in the year 665, fought, not between Britons and Saxons, but between Wulfhere the Anglian king of Mercia, and Aescwine, the Saxon king of Wessex; these two powerful kings were engaged in a power struggle centred on the north-eastern borders of Wessex.

Just over a century later, Alfred and his brother king Ethelred opposed the Danes as they advanced westward through the Thames Valley; after a skirmish near Hungerford, Alfred retreated to the north along the Lambourn Valley. Then, as the Danes gave chase, their war-band split into two, unexpectedly confined by the narrow valleys beyond Lambourn. Alfred and Ethelred sprang an ambush, and after a bloody clash a mile south of the Ridgeway at Ashdown, the Danes were routed: they had fallen into a natural trap, a geographical blind alley.

But of all the Ridgeway forts, Liddington was the most formidable, standing guard on the highest point of the Lambourn Downs: at a height of just over 900 feet, it commanded the western approach to the Vale of the White Horse. This fort's strategic position was prized by the Britons and envied by the English: situated as it was, just a mile and a half to the west of the cross-roads where the Roman road to

Cirencester cut straight through the Ridgeway, the fort enabled the military commander of Liddington to exercise control over all movement in the area, east to west along the Ridgeway, and north to south along the Roman road.

Liddington hill-fort was originally known as Badbury Castle, or *'Baddanbyrig'* in old English, meaning 'the fort of Badda,' hence the traditional association with Badon; but despite its commanding position in the area most likely to have encompassed Arthur's great battle, Liddington, even as 'Baddanbyrig' does not ring true to the name 'Badon.'

However, there is an alternative way of finding the most likely site for the battle of Badon: by comparing the logistics of the opposing armies, one comprising cavalry, the other infantry, advancing towards each other on the same day, along a pre-determined route, it should be possible to estimate their point of contact.

Referring to the map of Roman Britain, Arthur's most direct route from his headquarters at Wroxeter via Droitwich, Tewkesbury and Cirencester to Silchester, was a distance of about 120 miles. Having taken Silchester by force, Ochta and his Saxon foot-soldiers would have advanced along the Roman road west towards Liddington at an average speed of around three miles an hour, achieving a total distance of about twenty-five miles over an eight-hour march. Arthur's cavalry, on the other hand, capable of moving three or four times faster than infantry at an average speed of twelve miles an hour, would have advanced 90 to 95 miles in the same time. Assuming that both armies set out towards each other on the same day, this would bring Ochta's war-band as far as Membury, a place named after the nearby Membury Estate, but now well-known for the service station on the M4 Motorway two miles south of Lambourn in Berkshire.

Meanwhile, Arthur's cavalry would have certainly made it to Liddington Castle, giving him an excellent defensive position from which to mount an attack further to the south. By this estimated reckoning, with Arthur at Liddington, and Ochta at Membury, the opposing armies would have been within seven miles of a head-on confrontation.

If Liddington gave Arthur a secure base for his army, what did Membury have to offer Ochta? Apart from the motorway service station, there is more to Membury than meets the eye: during the Second World War the Royal Air Force found the long level hill-top the ideal position for an airfield, and in 1942 built a new bomber base that was scheduled for use by the United States Army Air Force. Several thousand American troops embarked from RAF Membury to engage in historic missions, including Operation 'Overlord,' the 'D Day' Invasion of Normandy in September 1943, and Operation 'Market Garden,' the campaign to take Arnhem and establish bridgeheads in Holland during September 1944. In its hey-day, the

Insignia of 436 Troop Carrier Group, USAAF, based at RAF Membury. This unique example of American military wall art was rescued by the Ridgeway Military & Aviation Research Group and transported to the museum at RAF Welford. By kind permission of the Chairman, Donald Summers. Photo, © Eric Walmsley

airfield could accommodate over 2300 personnel, but at the end of the war in May 1945 the U.S. forces left in a hurry to get home, abandoning and even burying some of their equipment.

Some years ago, a local landowner was surprised to discover a complete Willys Jeep that had been buried in the corner of the airfield; more recently in 1995, members of the Ridgeway Military and Aviation Research Group found the well-preserved insignia of the 436th Troop Carrier Group in an old Maycrete hut. The insignia shows a stylized painting of Pegasus, the Flying Horse, carrying airmen over the clouds and into battle, an idea taken from the story of the Greek legendary hero Bellerophon who rides Pegasus to defeat the monster Chimera; and everywhere the winged horse struck his hoof to the earth, an inspiring spring burst forth.

For the American airmen of Membury the metaphorical Pegasus of their insignia represented the stark reality of their own sturdy war-horses of the air, the Douglas Dakotas that towed Waco and Horsa gliders loaded with thousands of troops into battle over Europe to fight against the monster of Hitler's Third Reich.

Wartime photograph of RAF Membury Airfield, Berkshire. © English Heritage

An aerial photograph, taken in August 1944, clearly reveals an ancient hill-fort nestling in seclusion just to the west of the main runways, and shows that Membury Airfield shares a military past with its close neighbour, Membury Hillfort. Re-fortified in the Iron-Age, this double-vallate fort has revealed evidence of a long period of occupation from the Mesolithic period through to the Romano-British settlement in the late fifth and early sixth century.

Whether by accident or design, from the air the outline of the fort's ramparts resemble the shape of a shield, wider at the northern end and curving to a point at the southern tip; but it was a very large shield, covering an area of thirty-four acres; this was almost twice the size of Cadbury Castle in Somerset and large enough to support the local populace in times of trouble, or to happily accommodate a legion of the Roman Army. More to the point, if Ochta had stumbled across Membury fort at the end of a hard-day's march, it would have offered his army an ideal stronghold for a night's recuperation.

The name 'Membury' reveals an ancient meaning that tells us something very interesting about the fort: the first part *'mem'* comes from the Ancient Egyptian hieroglyph for water: this was originally represented as a continuous wave form that was simplified by the Phoenicians to the symbol *'m'* and named after their word for water *'mem.'* Mem is the thirteenth letter of many Semitic abjads, including Phoenician, Aramaic, Hebrew and Arabic, and its application at Membury points to contact with these eastern Mediterranean regions, either through trade or migration, from the earliest times.

The second part of the name *'bury'* comes from the Old English, or more appropriately, the late Saxon word *'burh,'* (later *'burgh'*) meaning *'a fortified place.'* So in Membury the ancient word for water is linked with the Saxon word for fortress to give the combined meaning *'a fortress with water.'*

Coincidentally, the word *'Badon'* is also associated with water; it is derived from the German word *'baden'* meaning *'bath,'* or *'to bathe'* as in the name of the German spa town of Baden-Baden, so called because it is the town of Baden in the state of Baden. The springs of Baden-Baden were known to the Romans, and the foundation of the town and establishment of the Roman baths are attributed to the emperor Hadrian. From Gaul, Hadrian and his German recruits sailed to Britain, where he initiated the building of new cities as he advanced through the country: St Alban's, Silchester, Cirencester, Wroxeter and Chester all benefited from Hadrian's generosity and architectural vision.

Membury was originally a British hill-fort, and to the Romans it was a gift for the taking. Exactly half-way between Silchester and Cirencester, with strong ramparts and large enough to accommodate a legion of five thousand soldiers, this fort

The steep north-eastern ramparts of Membury Hillfort, Berkshire. Photo, © EricWalmsley

crowned the flat top of a high ridge almost two miles long; at a height over 660 feet above sea-level it commanded the Aldbourne valley to the west and the Lambourn Valley to the east. For Hadrian and his Legio XX the fort offered a secure resting place after a day's march along the Ermine Way; but to cap its strategic advantages, Membury had a surprise for its Roman conquerors: tucked away between the northern ramparts they found a natural spring that gushed with cool, clear water that ran into a clay-lined pool. Now they would have fresh water to drink and be able to refresh their supplies for the next day's march; but they could not conceal their joy at finding this small bathing pool: here was their new Baden!

If the Romans had re-named Membury as '*Baden Fort*,' and later referred to the surrounding high ground as '*Mount Baden,*' then it is plausible to suggest that the fort would have retained this name from Hadrian's day until the time of Arthur's battle early in the sixth century; the variation from '*Baden*' to '*Badon*' over a period of six centuries would be perfectly understandable, as would a further variation of the name over the following centuries.

Although the Roman name for Badon Fort has been forgotten and Membury has reverted to its original British name, echoes of the Roman occupation remain close by; just three quarters of a mile to the west of the fort we find Baydon Manor, and two miles north-west of the fort lies the early settlement of Baydon village, both recorded in the Domesday Book of AD 1086. This early medieval variation of the original name belies the fact that, if the village and the manor took their name from the old fort of Badon, then Badon, the Romans' 'bathing fort,' and Membury, the ancient 'water fort,' must be one and the same!

⊱⊰⊱⊰

Ochta inherited the kingdom of Kent from his father Hengist, the great Saxon warrior, who, by threat of force, cunning diplomacy, and ultimate treachery, contrived to seize a major portion of south-east Britain. To further his gains on a wider front, he also established a foothold on the east coast, to the north of Hadrian's Wall; but Hengist's most significant legacy was his ambition to conquer, an ambition that did not fade with his death, for he had pledged his son to the Saxon cause, the conquest of Britain.

Ochta's commitment to the role of Britain's arch enemy was revealed following a decade of apparent peace that had allowed him time to consolidate his hold on Kent and rebuild the Saxon army: he then pushed westward and unleashed his new force across the river Blackwater in an outright challenge to Arthur, the new, young leader of the Britons. But in Arthur, Ochta met more than his match, for not only was Arthur's highly trained cavalry corps a devastating force when ranged against his foot-soldiers, but Arthur's intelligent battle-tactics had out-witted him on the field. With his new army decimated, Ochta had been forced to retreat from the battles at Blackwater, angered in defeat, his pride injured.

Nevertheless, Ochta's ambition did not die with his men on the battlefield; with his confidence shaken, he paused to reflect on the heroic age of Beowulf and Widsith, whose heroes had battled with giants and monsters. For inspiration he looked to those empire builders of an earlier age whose lust for power and conquest had turned them into obsessive tyrants, feared as much by their own people as by their enemies.

One such hero of the Saxon kings was Eormenric, mighty emperor of the Ostrogoths, whose empire reached from the Baltic Coast to the Black Sea. Held in awe by his subjects yet in high esteem by lesser kings and aspiring tyrants, Eormenric secured his lands with military might and ruled with ruthless force. He was killed while fighting valiantly against the Huns in 375 AD, and became the hero of his age.

In an act of sheer defiance Ochta named his own son Eormenric after the famous emperor; born at some time between the defeat at Blackwater and the turn of the century, 500 AD, the young Eormenric grew to manhood alongside the sons of warriors who had survived the last battle of Blackwater. The message to the Britons was clear: should Ochta be killed in battle by chance, before he had conquered another tranche of Britain, then Eormenric would champion the cause of Saxon conquest.

Suddenly, the inevitable facts stared Ochta in the face: first, it would take the best part of two decades to grow an army from the cradle to manhood: secondly, he would need to lie low, exercising great patience while he trained and nurtured a new army. Then, when the time came for the inevitable battle, he would need allies to guarantee the decisive victory over the Britons that he so strongly craved; but in the meantime, he would have plenty of time to contemplate the best formula for success: it was no secret that wealth created military strength, and this, combined with his ruthless leadership, would eventually bring the rewards of victory and conquest.

❧❧❦❦

Calleva Atrebatum was the first British city to fall to Ochta's new army. The years that had passed since Blackwater had not diminished the bitterness of the defeated Saxon king, nor his determination to deliver Arthur a crushing blow by axing his way deep into western Britain.

Early one spring morning in the year 518 AD, Ochta moved quickly to take his first objective, for Calleva lay directly in his path en-route to Liddington Castle, where he had planned to join his allies. Invitations, with the promise of shared rewards of conquered territory, had been sent to all concerned: king Icel of the Angles, Cerdic, who ruled the South Saxons, and king Aelle of Sussex. For the English allies, all roads led to Liddington, at the point of Ochta's strategic arrowhead: Aelle's war-band would join Ochta's army at Calleva and together they would form the main shaft of the arrow advancing north-west along the Ermine Way. Cerdic, closing to the target along the Roman road from Marlborough would form the left barb of the arrow; and Icel's Angles, pushing down the Icknield Way from the east, would complete the right-hand barb of the arrowhead.

If fortune favoured Ochta's plan to meet his allies at Liddington Castle, he would have a mighty force at his command; it would be strong enough to storm Liddington and sweep onward to attack Cirencester and Gloucester. Despite the fact that he had never set eyes on these cities, Ochta knew from all reports that they were strategically important to the British, and he imagined that they formed the outer defences of Arthur's stronghold further to the west.

When the Saxons battered their way through the worn oak doors of Calleva's east-gate, two cavalrymen who were armed and ready for the dawn patrol, galloped for their lives through the west-gate and into the early morning mist. Their

222

commander and the rest of the garrison troops were axed to death by the onrushing Saxons before they could even give the call to arms.

Ochta had announced his invasion by fire and sword; by nightfall Calleva was a flaming beacon in the sky, and as his men torched the city they threw as much debris as they could find down the city's well-shaft to choke off the water supply, depriving the few survivors of drinking water and any means of dousing the raging fire. Ochta was pleased with his day's work: this was part repayment for the defeat he had suffered at the hands of Arthur at the last battle of Blackwater, twenty years before.

The Irish cavalrymen who escaped from Calleva reached Cirencester by noon. Then, with fresh mounts from the garrison, one departed for Gloucester, the other to Warwick to raise the alarm. By late afternoon on the day of the attack, Theodoric and Cei had ordered their troops to battle readiness; but the rider dispatched by Theodoric to Wroxeter to alert Arthur was faced with a seventy mile ride: he would be unlikely to reach his destination before midnight.

Arthur flew into a mighty rage when he heard that Ochta had once again broken out of Kent to attack Calleva Atrebatum: the Saxon king had finally betrayed the peace treaty established between them after Blackwater. Arthur imagined how his old enemy had marched out from Caesar's Camp at the head of a large war-band, stirring up the dust along the Devil's Highway to engage in the devil's work: and he knew that he would need the Lord's help to challenge and overcome the pagan host when their forces clashed in the final duel of dragons.

That night the troops of the Wroxeter squadrons would be lucky to get any sleep at all; Arthur had called for battle-readiness by first light. As the alarm was trumpeted though the streets of the old Roman city of Viroconium, soldiers and citizens sprang to life as Arthur's well-rehearsed military machine geared-up for action. Grooms saddled the war-horses, soldiers donned their chain-mail armour; swords, spears and shields were brought to hand while supply waggons were loaded with weapons, victuals and water, together with sacks of grain for the horses. While soldiers' wives baked small oaten loaves of bread, their men sharpened steel blades ready for battle.

Not yet fully armed, Arthur and his brother Catwallaun, accompanied by their troop commanders, retreated to the operations room in the east wing of their headquarters to plan for battle. Arthur quickly chalked-out a plan on the battle-table, marking the garrisons and their troop numbers, then triangulating the Roman highways between the cities of Wroxeter, Gloucester and Warwick, marking-off distances in Roman miles; he completed his improvised sketch-plan with a final spur to the south-east, from Liddington to Calleva, a distance of thirty miles along the Ermine Way.

Arthur focussed on the immediate question: "*How long would it take Ochta to march from Calleva to Liddington?"* He could not read Ochta's mind but he could second guess that Liddington Hillfort was the obvious target for Saxon allies converging from the south and east of Britain. It was therefore vital that Arthur's vanguard, possibly comprising one or two squadrons of cavalry, secured Liddington fort for the British by noon, in anticipation of Ochta's arrival sometime between noon and sunset.

Not long after midnight a rider from Warwick arrived with a message from Cei confirming that he had responded immediately to the alarm, mobilizing his cavalry and riding south to Cirencester, where he would hold his force overnight. Sensing the seriousness of the situation, he had, on his own initiative, taken expedient action by calling upon Theodoric to move his troops from Gloucester to Cirencester, and sending a rider south to Caer Cadarn to alert Prince Cadwy, and to request his urgent advance to Liddington at the head of his cavalry troop.

Arthur thanked the messenger and ordered an escort to see that he was well-fed and given a comfortable palliasse for a night's stay in Wroxeter's old basilica. He also thanked God for Cei's quick reaction to the alarm: the idea to garrison Warwick with a squadron of cavalry ready for battle had paid off, for Cei's troops were within a two-hour ride of Liddington fort. If Cei and Theodoric could occupy and hold the fortress by noon, before the Saxon war-bands arrived, it would give Arthur the chance to marshal all his troops in a strong defensive position from which he could seek-out and destroy the enemy.

Allowing him time to arm and ride fifty miles across country, Arthur reckoned that Cadwy's squadron would reach Liddington by mid-afternoon, but his own troops had the prospect of trekking the best part of one hundred and ten miles, a march that would take from dawn 'til dusk, routing south along the Roman road to Worcester and Tewkesbury, but by-passing Gloucester and cutting across country via Chedworth to Cirencester. There he planned to rest and feed his troops before completing the last leg of the march to Liddington.

The sun was moving towards the first quarter of its daily orbit of the southern sky before Ochta's men had overcome the reluctance to emerge from their tents and resume their march westward. By the time they had turned their backs on the smouldering ruins of Calleva, Ochta's troops were joined by Aelle's Saxons from the south, a small war-band of about one hundred and fifty young warriors led by Cymen and Wlencing. Because of his advancing age, and fearing Arthur's retribution for breaking their peace agreement, Aelle had declined Ochta's invitation to lead another campaign against the Britons; but as a measure of his support for the Saxon cause, he had sent a token force, led by his eldest sons.

Well before mid-day, Ochta's dishevelled war-band had advanced more than ten miles along the Ermine Way towards Liddington hill-fort. Reaching the confluence of the rivers Kennet and Lambourn, Ochta was presented with a choice of three routes that would take him to his target destination: the Roman road followed a ridge of high ground between the river valleys: this would be undoubtedly the most obvious route to take because it made an easy march north-west to the Ridgeway crossing, then moving west for two miles along the ancient track-way to reach the fort. But Ochta was no fool: he knew that the British cavalry would use the Roman roads to position their forces for a reprisal attack. A river valley would offer a less conspicuous route for his advance, and would also provide water for his men.

The river Lambourn ran two miles north-east of the Ermine Way, whereas the Kennet ran three miles to the south of the highway; by following the Kennet as far as the hamlet of Chiltern Foliat, Ochta could then take the old track-way along the Aldbourne Valley that would lead him straight to Liddington. Taking the advice of his scouts, Ochta marched along the north bank of the Kennet; by mid-afternoon he turned north-west to follow the stream towards Aldbourne, where he called a halt to rest the troops. Having advanced twenty-five miles from Calleva, they were now only five miles from their objective, and the prospect of an imminent clash with the Britons weighed heavily on Ochta's mind; it was clear that the long march had jaded the enthusiasm of his men for another battle so soon after Calleva.

The local inhabitants fled as the Saxons appeared on their doorstep, scouring farmsteads for food, stealing bread, piglets and any other livestock that they could lay their hands on to provide the night's feast for the whole army. To earn their keep, Ochta sent twenty-five of Aelle's men forward on a reconnaissance patrol to locate the forces of Cerdic and Icel, who were due to reach Liddington before sunset; he warned Cymen to keep a low profile and to keep a sharp look-out for the British cavalry: they were to report back as soon as it was safe for Ochta to advance.

Cymen led his men forward, climbing slowly to a ridge of high ground where he hoped to find a vantage point overlooking Liddington fort and its southern approaches; then, less than a mile beyond a small farmstead at Upham, he reached the crest of a ridge some eight hundred feet high that gave him a clear view of the hill-fort. Crossing an ancient track-way to take advantage of the wooded area of the escarpment, he found a commanding position overlooking the Roman road that ran from Mildenhall to Wanborough. It was the ideal look-out post: his men were hidden, and Cymen could watch for any sign of Icel's war-band approaching the fortress whilst awaiting Cerdic's arrival along the Roman road.

The sudden thunder of a troop of cavalry bearing down the Ridgeway towards them startled Cymen into realising that they were deep in enemy territory without support. As a detachment of Cei's cavalry thundered past a few yards from his hiding place, Cymen could see that the plateau of Liddington fort was now thronging with British troops: a line of cavalry stood proudly along the western ramparts, on guard, and ready for battle. Then, turning to the south, he saw Cerdic's war-band approaching in a cloud of dust as they marched up the highway, shouting and clashing their weapons, oblivious to the danger ahead.

But Cymen could not believe his eyes when he saw another squadron of British cavalry coming from the direction of Barbury Castle and heading eastward along the Ridgeway: Prince Cadwy and his warriors from Dumnonia had arrived just in time to give Cerdic a sharp reception at Liddington. Cei's squadron and Cadwy's warriors were now galloping down the Ridgeway, heading towards each other from different directions, but timing their charge to meet at the point where the ancient track crossed the Roman road. When the two waves of cavalry sliced into their front ranks, Cerdic's warriors recoiled in shock; then, as swiftly as they had attacked, the mounted warriors returned, trampling the Saxons who stood in their path.

Mindful of Arthur's instruction to avoid contact with the enemy, Cei and Cadwy pulled back from the skirmish to form a double rank of battle-horses that barred Cerdic's way forward; to Cymen in his hillside hide-out, it appeared to be a confrontation prior to a full-scale battle. But Cerdic realised that the odds for success were stacked against him; it was late afternoon, the sun would soon be down, and without the visible support of his allies Ochta and Icel, his small war-band would almost certainly be run-down and wiped out by the enemy cavalry. *"Where are my allies?"* he shouted in exasperation. Then, without a further thought he ordered his remaining men to withdraw: *"Yield to the woods!"* he cried, as he took flight from the phalanx of cavalry confronting him.

As soon as the last of the British troopers returning to Liddington had passed the wooded hide-out, Cymen and his scouts crossed back over the Ridgeway and re-traced their steps towards Aldbourne. Ochta's look of chagrin on hearing of Cerdic's retreat, turned to anger when he realised that his master-plan had been thwarted by Arthur: he could hardly believe his misfortune when Cymen reported the absence of his allies, and the hard fact that Arthur's army had taken command of Liddington ahead of him.

Now, just as the sun was setting, he would have to act quickly to find a defensive position before nightfall; he remembered an escarpment that rose steeply to the east of Aldbourne, and moved his troops a mile or so back down the valley where he turned onto a rough track-way that led him to the top of Marridge Hill. At over five hundred feet, it was almost the highest point in the area, and it gave Ochta a good vantage point; but looking to the north-east across the gently rising landscape he saw, about a mile away in the dim light of dusk, what appeared to be a hill-fort crowning the ridge.

Ochta had, by chance, stumbled across the old Roman fort of Badon, now disused by the military, but housing a few local villeins whose huts nestled close to the inner ramparts. When Ochta's warriors battered their way through the south gateway, the inhabitants fled to the north in fear of their lives. Ochta thanked Woden for his good fortune: it seemed as if the great God of War had heard his prayer and granted the favour of a fortress for his protection.

Arthur and Catwallaun's cavalry squadrons reached Liddington as dusk turned to night, their arrival lit by the flames of camp fires fuelled by spit roast deer and pigs that had been hunted down or bartered to feed the troops. Prince Cadwy, Cei and Theodoric welcomed Arthur to his new military base, leading a rousing cheer for their great battle leader.

Although tired and hungry after the long march, Arthur ensured that all his men had food and drink before he sat down to eat; then, without delay, he called his commanders together to plan the battle. Cei briefed Arthur on his earlier clash with Cerdic's war-band, confirming that there had been no sign of Ochta's army, nor the sighting of Angles approaching from the east. Just before midnight, one of Cei's keen-sighted young scouts reported to the command tent: he explained with excitement how he had seen a patrol of Saxons crossing the Ridgeway track before sunset, and had followed them down into the valley at Aldbourne. Whilst keeping a safe distance he had trailed the Saxon army a far as Badon Fort, where they had camped for the night.

"*Well done boy!*" exclaimed Arthur, "*your position report is just what we need to plan for the morrow.*"

"*Now we have those galley-slaves trapped,*" shouted Arthur, "*we can either starve them to death, or go in for the kill when we choose.*" He looked triumphantly towards his commanders: "*Order your men to battle-readiness at first light: we'll surround Badon Fort by its four quarters, and we'll lay full siege to Ochta's army before noon tomorrow.*"

At daybreak Arthur rallied all his troops together in Liddington fort's central compound to give the orders for the day:

"*My countrymen,*" he began, "*by now, most of you will know why we are here: Ochta and his band of marauders have stolen a march on us. By their secret, underhand enterprise they have broken our peace treaty: in a traitorous action they have stormed Calleva, slaughtering our garrison commander and his valiant men, and setting fire to the city without remorse. Ochta's fanatical desire for the conquest of our homeland gives us great cause for alarm. His new army, linked with his prospective allies, will form a most serious threat to our freedom; but, my fellow Britons, you have no reason to be afraid, for together we have proved to be the masters in the game of battle. Today, if we act quickly, we can declare "Check-Mate!" on the field of Badon. Our scouts report the enemy host to* number about twelve hundred men, so we are outnumbered by more than two to one against them. This means that each one of you is tasked with despatching two or more of Ochta's men, if we are to win."

"But time and good fortune are on our side. To weaken our opponents we plan to lay siege to Badon Fort for three days and three nights: and while we have provisions and plenty to drink, they will starve and their throats will become dry and parched. Then, on the fourth day, with our enemy weak and weary, you will muster all your strength, courage, and fighting skills to launch our attack. Be brave, and fight well my good warriors, for on this hill of Badon we fight the Battle for Britain!"

Following Arthur's rousing speech, Bishop Baldwin of the City of the Legion, who had accompanied Arthur to Liddington, addressed the company:

"Good Christian soldiers and brothers in Christ, you stand here today ready to fight for the land of your fathers and to show your loyalty by saving your fellow countrymen from slaughter. Remember that your enemies are the sons of Hengist's Saxons who traitorously murdered the Elders of Britain in Vortigern's time, and from that day to this, their ambition has not changed, for they wish to conquer our land by fair means or foul; but do not be afraid, for the Lord is with you in your fight against the pagans; and God, who is the Great Arbiter of battles, will give you the strength to overcome the oppressors."

"I beseech you, therefore, put on the whole armour of God: let the Lord be your rock and your salvation; put your trust in Him and He will deliver you from all evil; and should any one of you suffer death in this battle for the sake of his fellow countrymen, then be assured that he offers himself as a living sacrifice to God by following Christ himself, who laid down his life for our salvation." Bishop Baldwin paused for a moment; he could see that his military congregation was becoming restless:

"I see that you are impatient for the battle, but wait one moment longer, for I have a gift for you all: it is the cross of Christ, so that in the coming battle you may be ever mindful of the Lord, who is your gift from God Himself."

Arthur thanked Bishop Baldwin for his gift, placing the white silk surplice over his shoulders; as it fell to cover his chain-mail tunic, the bright red cross emblazoned on the front and back became clear for all to see. "God be with you all!" shouted the bishop at the top of his voice, as Arthur led his army forward towards Mount Badon.

Cei and Theodoric led their squadrons onto the Ermine Way, setting a brisk pace to cover the seven miles to their target position before sunrise; Arthur and Cadwy, proudly led by the scout who had spotted the Saxon host, took the track into the Aldbourne Valley, and climbed the steep escarpment of Marridge Hill to bring them to a holding position south of Badon Fort.

As the sun broke through the early morning mist, the British commanders moved stealthily into position, Cei taking the north, Theodoric the east, Prince Cadwy to the west, with Arthur holding the southern quarter. Detailing his second troop of cavalry to cover sections of the south-east and south-west, with detachments from Cadwy's and Theodoric's squadrons covering the north-west and north-east, Arthur had effectively surrounded Badon Fortress from every point of the compass. His siege strategy was in place: now the waiting game began.

When the first rays of sunlight stirred the Saxons from their slumber, Ochta had the shock of his life to find that he had been completely surrounded by the British. With a steely look of fear in his eyes, he called an emergency meeting with his commanders, calling on Cymen and Wlencing to advise on a plan for the oncoming battle. There appeared to be just two options open to them: either to make a quick break-out to the south of the fort, or to hold their ground and defend the fort against enemy attack.

On the first count, it looked as if the Saxons outnumbered the Britons by about three to one, news that was reassuring to Ochta, who now realised that his initial fear of an inevitable bloodbath had been unfounded. For a while, Ochta's renewed optimism restored the confidence of his men; but there was to be no vote on the matter for Ochta had now made up his mind:

"*We'll hold firm and defend the fort,*" he declared. "*They will attack from the level ground to the north... just where our ramparts are strongest. We must concentrate our forces in the northern quarter of the fort if we are to oppose and repel the enemy.*"

"*See to it that we have a constant watch along the north and east palisades, but leave a light look-out to the south and west, for only a fool would undertake an uphill attack on this fortress!*" shouted Ochta, as he grasped his weapons.

Arthur's men pitched their tents about five hundred yards from the ramparts of Badon Fort, just far enough to give them time to scramble into a defensive line should the enemy make a break-out. Each squadron was divided into two watches, the first on duty from sunrise to mid-day, then from sunset until midnight; the second watch would be on guard from mid-day to sunset, and from midnight to sunrise. During the day, the duty watch would patrol the boundaries of their sector of the ramparts, and at night would light fires to distract the enemy and keep them awake.

Soon after mid-day Cei returned to the encampment at Badon having secured provisions from the neighbouring farmsteads, and arranged for water to be brought up from the freshwater spring at Lambourn. Just as Cei and his bodyguard approached the fort, they came across Marcellus and his infantry who had marched thirty miles from Cirencester. Cei welcomed them to the camp and gave them food and fresh water, before ordering the soldiers to take up their siege stations on each wing of his own cavalry troop.

At nightfall Arthur called his commanders together once more to finalise the battle-plan. During the next three nights, detachments from each squadron on watch would be given the task of undermining the gates at the north and south entrances to the fortress. This would be carried out secretly and silently, so that, on the signal to attack, the defences could be quickly overwhelmed, giving the cavalry access to the inner compound of the fort. Cei and Theodoric, together with Marcellus' infantry troops would start the first attack on the north and north-east ramparts, with Catwallaun's squadron in reserve, while Prince Cadwy would re-position alongside Arthur's squadron and join the attack from the south.

Arthur had been well versed in Roman battle-tactics by Ambrosius, his great mentor, and he remembered the story of the siege of Alesia in the year 52 BC, when Caesar had out-witted Vercingetorix, the leader of a powerful Gallic army. Following an unsuccessful attack on Caesar's army, Vercingetorix and his allies had retreated to the fortified hill-town of Alesia. Caesar laid siege to the town: he ringed the city with siege-works that surrounded Vercingetorix and prevented relief forces from coming to his rescue. In a great battle for freedom, the besieged Gauls launched a desperate attack on the Roman fortifications, filling in their defensive ditches with clay and hurdles, and launching missiles from siege-engines to strike the defenders in their turrets. As they began to tear down the timber ramparts with hooks, Caesar sent in reinforcements, and heading the counter-attack, he ordered part of the cavalry to follow him to confront the Gauls, and the remaining cavalry to ride around the fortification and attack the enemy in the rear: it was this action that changed the course of the battle. As Vercingetorix' troops began to break through the ramparts, the Romans abandoned their javelins to engage in hand to hand fighting. When the cavalry appeared suddenly behind the attacking Gauls, they turned away from the ramparts and took flight. Caesar's cavalry struck with devastating effect, and slaughtered their enemies. Caesar declared a victory and Vercingetorix was later paraded through Rome; but his captors showed no mercy, and he was put to death.

Arthur had neither the time nor resources to build siege ramparts as Caesar had done at Alesia; he could only hope and pray that Ochta would consider his best chance of survival lay in defending the fortress. If Arthur could mount a siege for three days and nights, he would not only succeed in weakening the enemy by depriving him of food, but it would give him the much needed time to rest his own men and build his force to full strength. With the arrival of Marcellus' infantry from Gloucester that afternoon, and the reserve force of fifty cavalry from the Longthorpe garrison due to reach Badon on the second day of the siege, Arthur's battle group would reach the full complement of six hundred and fifty men.

As the sun rose on the morning of the fourth day of the siege, Cei's sturdy, experienced warriors launched the opening move of the Battle of Badon: with hooks and grappling irons they moved up to the palisade of the outer wall, close to the northern gateway of the fortress. Simultaneously, Theodoric's cavalry charged towards the eastern ramparts in a co-ordinated attack, while Catwallaun's troop prepared to reinforce Cei's break-in.

A shout rang out, echoing along the ramparts: *"To arms! To arms!"* called the Saxon look-outs, and men scrambled in a panic to climb to the top of the ramparts and repel the Britons. The two attacking squadrons drew the enemy's fire in different directions, diverting attention from Marcellus and his infantry who ran into the deep ditch between the main ramparts with wooden ladders prepared for the assault.

Jostling shoulder to shoulder on the parapet thirty feet above, the Saxons unleashed a hail of spears that flew high over the stockade and rained down on the warriors below, splintering shields, splitting helmets, pinning men to the ground with penetrating force. Marcellus gave the order for his men to advance in the Roman 'testudo' formation, holding their shields above them as they crouched closely together to form a protective tortoise-shell. They manoeuvred into position close to the inner ramparts, and seized an opportune moment to manhandle their ladders against the timber palisade, in a brave attempt to scale the fortress wall.

It was a feint attack: to climb the ladders and breach the parapet thirty feet above them would have been suicidal for Marcellus and his men, but their bluff was successful: the action teased the enemy host into a swarm along the northern rampart, where they amassed in a disorderly throng, discharging their spears skyward in the hope of hitting a random target.

Suddenly the shrill, sharp staccato of Arthur's horn pierced the din of battle: the south gate was breached, and Arthur spurred his charger ahead of an echelon of cavalry reinforced by Prince Cadwy's squadron who formed the second wave of the attack. Arthur appeared resplendent in his bright scarlet cloak, brandishing Rongwinion his four-bladed, steel-tipped spear; and sheathed by his side, his trusty sword Excaliburn, its golden snakes-head hilt glinting in the sun.

Ochta turned to face his enemy, for a moment mesmerized by the awesome sight that met his eyes as three hundred mounted warriors thundered uphill towards him. In an instant he was transfixed by the bright red cross centred on the white silk cotta that Arthur wore over his shoulders, draped over his chain-mail tunic and furling in the breeze as he galloped forward, fearless against a fearsome foe. And in that moment, transfixed in time, Ochta knew that he was trapped: outwitted by Arthur's superior tactical command of the battle, outmanoeuvred but not outnumbered. Ochta's heart sank in despair: he knew that he was finished, but in true Saxon spirit he rallied his men: *"Fight to the death….to the death!"* he cried.

The battle squadrons began to pick up speed as they reached the northern end of the enclosure, wheeling to the right before spurring their mounts for the final charge into the enemy's rearmost ranks. Arthur gripped his spear, and aimed for the first Saxon in his path; as he made the first strike, he saw the fear in the pallid face of his young opponent who reeled backwards with the shock of the impact. The battle-hardened war-horses flew over the heads of terror-stricken youths who had been drafted into the front line to oppose them; weak with hunger, and petrified by the thundering onslaught, most of them stood frozen to the spot, praying to Woden for deliverance as their swords and shields were sent spinning through the air.

Flying through the ragged shield line, Arthur and his vanguard ploughed into the melée of the Saxon host, charging towards the inner ramparts to do battle with Ochta and the older warriors who had survived the slaughter on the Blackwater front many years before.

"*We put our trust in the Lord!*" shouted Arthur, "*and the Lord our God shall deliver us!*" he cried as he slashed his way through a ring of flailing bodyguards to challenge Ochta himself.

"*More spears!*" demanded Ochta: but there were no more, for all the spears had been launched in volleys over the palisade in the frenzy of the first attack. Ochta gasped in disbelief when he saw another squadron of cavalry sweeping into the fort from the north gate. Cei's men had awaited Arthur's signal before battering down the main gateway and charging into the compound: Cei forced his way into the battle, swiftly followed by the two squadrons led by Theodoric and Catwallaun. The Britons cut their way into the Saxons' right wing just as Cadwy's warriors wheeled eastward to penetrate their left flank.

Cei cut a swathe into the thick of the battle: the strongest of men, most renowned battle chieftain, Cei harvested Saxons as if they were sheaves of wheat under a scythe. When his mount reared-up at the fray, young soldiers ran in fear from the reach of his sword; while others ran forward to attack him until their swords, arms, heads, were swiftly parted from their bodies. Cei, the deadly reaper, killed Saxons by the hundred.

At the climax of the battle, with the enemy host surrounded by British cavalry and hemmed-in against the northern ramparts of the fortress, the ground of Badon Hill became a killing field: the young warriors of the Saxon shield-wall, motionless in life, now flayed, had become a motionless shield-wall of brothers in death. Among them lay Prince Catwallaun, Arthur's own brother, felled by a Saxon's axe.

Defeat was an unspoken word in the Saxon language for it was ignominious, a shameful experience for any battle leader: it was better for a Saxon to perish by the sword than to show cowardice, or to admit defeat in battle. But for many of Ochta's young soldiers the stark fear of death overwhelmed their pledge of honour to the Saxon cause: stricken with panic as the second wave of battle-chargers tore into their ranks, the hindmost ran for their lives.

Prince Cadwy, ever the kind-hearted commander, saw the pitiful plight of these young German whelps, some of them not much more than fifteen years of age, their faces pale with fear, and their bodies trembling for want of food and water. Momentarily, he turned away from the dishevelled blood-stained remnants of Ochta's corps of young warriors as they crawled and staggered towards the battered south gateway to make their escape.

But this token of mercy was not bestowed to all: Cadwy did not spare the lives of the experienced, able-bodied Saxons who would otherwise have lived to fight another day. The sons of warriors survived to tell the tale of Badon, but their fathers perished that day on the field of battle. Indeed, for the young men of both armies, this was a shocking initiation to the bloody carnage of hand-to-hand warfare; but their commanders had become hardened to the remorseless killing and the harvest of death.

For both Arthur and Ochta, Badon was their fifth challenge as opponents in battle; the two great chieftains were men whose youthful appearance in the days of the Blackwater campaign had mellowed into middle-age, but whose strength had not diminished. Arthur came to Badon Hill with eleven victories to his credit: tall, strong and powerful, no man had more experience in battle. Wielding his bright, keen-edged sword Excaliburn, Arthur was indefatigable.

The final stage of the battle of Badon was set to be a clash of champions: Ochta had gone to war with hatred in his heart, a man governed by an overwhelming greed that coveted the very land of Arthur's Britain: conquest was his cause, and in its wake came destruction by fire and death by the sword.

Arthur's cause was the love of his country and his fellow Britons. He knew that his future and the future of Britain depended on the outcome of this battle: the Battle of Badon was to be the Battle for Britain.

Arthur's first strike found its target, lancing Ochta's right shoulder with a deep, painful wound that drew blood and crippled his sword-arm. Then, as Ochta grasped his long, unwieldy sword with his left hand, Arthur drew his light, perfectly balanced cavalry-sword to parry his enemy's lunging thrust. A moment later, as his white stallion reared up at the clash of battle, Arthur caught a glimpse of a young Saxon swinging a blood-stained axe in a vicious attack from behind. In peril, Arthur turned away from Ochta to fend-off the attacker as the axe arched towards him. Suddenly, in a split second, a spear pierced the Saxon's breast, lanced clean through from behind by a keen-eyed young Briton who had seen the instant threat to Arthur's life.

*"God save you this day!"* cried the battle-commander in thanks to his young warrior, as he turned again to face Ochta's lunging sword with a clash of steel and an angry shout. *"I'll give you measure for measure Ochta. I'll have your blood for the blood of my men slain at Calleva, you Saxon traitor!"*

By the time the sun had passed the point of noon, bodies of warriors, Briton alongside Saxon, lay heavy upon the blood-soaked field of battle. Gradually, Arthur's men, who at the first assault were heavily outnumbered by Ochta's army of infantry, but were now reinforced by Cei's battle-chargers, together with Cadwy and Theodoric's squadrons on each wing, began to gain the upper-hand over the enemy host. Their commander's mastery of tactical warfare, demonstrated by the three-day siege, the opening feint assault on the palisade, immediately followed by a surprise cavalry charge that came uphill and out of the sun, swept the enemy off their feet, giving the Britons the opportunity to corner the remnant throng and go in for the kill.

Inspired by the sight of Arthur charging into the thickest ranks of the enemy to challenge Ochta, his battle-worn warriors rallied to his support, and when they saw Arthur's spear pierce Ochta's shoulder, they redoubled their efforts, dealing out death on all sides. Sensing the climactic moment of the battle, Arthur's standard bearer advanced towards the duelling commanders. Ochta looked skywards, distracted by the pennant's Red Dragon snaking menacingly in the breeze. It was the moment that Arthur had been waiting for: in a second he swung his sword back over his left shoulder; then, like the release of a coiled spring, Excaliburn's blade flashed through the air in a wide arc that encompassed Ochta's gaze. The Red Dragon of the Britons was the very last image he saw: with empirical force the scything steel severed Ochta's head from his shoulders. Suddenly, the decapitated body of the king of the Saxons fell at Arthur's feet as his bearded head rolled down into a pool of dead men's blood.

The three-day siege of Badon Fortress culminated in a battle that lasted less than three-quarters of a day: it was a massacre, a bloodbath on a scale that exceeded every one of Arthur's previous battles. The Battle of Badon was unmatched for the shock of its beginning, the ferocity of the fighting, and the unexpected suddenness of its ending, when the Saxon king fell to Arthur's sword.

With a shrill blast of his horn, Arthur, certain that he had won the day, called off the slaughter. Grey faced men and youths, sick with hunger and shaking from the shock of battle, knelt before him pleading for mercy, while the British marshals crossed the field to count the dead, friend and foe alike.

Remembering the honourable gesture made by Ambrosius to Hengist, his lifelong enemy, Arthur allowed the Saxons to make a rough timber bier for their king; forlornly they carried his body from the field, moving slowly down into the valley, where, one mile to the south of Badon Hill, Ochta reached his final resting place.

The marshals returned to announce that Aelle's sons Cymen and Wlencing had been slain and numbered with nine-hundred and sixty enemy dead; altogether, with an estimated two hundred and fifty or more British casualties, over twelve hundred lives were lost that gruesome day. Shocked to hear that his brother had fallen in the fight, Arthur staggered over the dying and the dead to find Catwallaun's body, and he wept quietly as he knelt to pray for his brother's soul.

It was a momentous victory for Arthur and his courageous British warriors; exhausted but elated, the blood-stained soldiers staggered from the battlefield, pausing only to cleanse the blood from their armour in Badon's small pool of spring-water close by the northern gateway of the fort. Arthur, mindful of the great courage and valour shown by his men, called his chieftains and their troops to assemble on the plateau that formed the highest ridge of Badon Hill. Distinctions and rewards were granted to those soldiers in each squadron who were commended by their commanders for brave action in the battle. Finally, Arthur called forward the young warrior who had saved his life; as he bowed before his supreme commander, Arthur placed a solid gold circlet upon the crown of his head: *"Accept this gift as a small measure of my sincere thanks to you for your action this day in our battle for Britain,"* and after a moment's pause, *"I thank you for saving my life!"* said Arthur softly, with a warm smile.

In unison there rose a mighty cheer from every proud Briton on the field.

❧❧❦❦

The small band of Saxons who survived the Battle of Badon dragged themselves and their wounded comrades-in-arms as far away from the battlefield as their legs would carry them. Eleven miles to the east they came across a small elevated mount that offered the prospect of a defensive position where they might shelter for a while, at least until their wounded had recovered. This would be their Mount Badon, named in memory of their compatriots who had lost their lives in the battle. In time, the survivors built a rampart to secure their small settlement around the hill-top, and in a vale one mile to the south they laid their dead warriors to rest: they had reached their world's end. The Saxon settlement is now called 'Beedon' and the burial ground is known as 'World's End.'

In Kent, the young Eormenric inherited his father's kingdom; but Saxon women grieved for the sons and husbands who had been massacred in the Battle of Badon.

235

They did not thank Ochta for taking their loved ones on a perilous mission of conquest, for it was a campaign that brought them nothing but endless sorrow.

᷇᷇᷇᷇

At the entrance to Membury Airfield there is a permanent memorial to the men and women of the United States Airborne Forces who gave their lives in the Invasion of Europe during the Second World War.

Close to the airfield that served as their military base, nature has claimed the killing field of Badon Fortress as its own memorial garden to the warriors who lost their lives in the greatest battle of the sixth century. Today, mature beech trees tower above hazel and hawthorn saplings that surround the shield-line of the ancient fort and, in the spring, a carpet of bluebells covers the ramparts and washes the woodland in a haze of blue.

# CHAPTER 15

# The Strife of Camlan and the Isle of Avalon

*"Gueith camlann inquo arthur & medraut corruerunt et mortalitas in britannia et in hibernia fuit."*
*"The strife of Camlan in which Arthur & Medraut fell, and there was plague in Britain and Ireland."*
The *Annales Cambriae*

Together with Nennius' list of Arthur's twelve battles, the record of events penned by the Dyfed cleric who compiled an updated copy of the *Annals Cambriae* in the early ninth century, have given us the earliest and most significant evidence of Arthur's last battles. By crediting Arthur as the battle-leader and victor at Badon Hill, fighting with the cross of Christ as his emblem against pagan invaders, the entry in the annals for the year 518 redeems the glaring omission of Arthur's name by Gildas, when he mentioned the battle of Badon in his book, *De Excidio et Conquestu Britanniae*.

Following the entry for the death of Saint Brigid in 523, the Battle of Camlan is recorded in the year 539: *"The strife of Camlan in which Arthur and Medraut fell, and there was plague in Britain and Ireland."*

This record not only confirms the year of Arthur's death, but it marks the twenty-one years of peace between Badon and Camlan as Arthur's lifetime achievement: it was this period of peace that in future years would be looked upon as a golden age.

But it was Geoffrey of Monmouth who first suggested that, following the battle of Camlan, Arthur had been carried off to the Isle of Avalon where his wounds might be healed. In his *History of the Kings of Britain* completed in 1136, Geoffrey set Arthur's last battle by the river *Camblam* in Cornwall where Arthur's nephew and arch-enemy Mordred had mustered an army of eighty thousand men. For good measure, Geoffrey brought together all Arthur's known enemies, the Scots, Picts and

Irish in an alliance led by Mordred to oppose Arthur: *"the lines of battle suddenly met, combat was joined, and they all strove with might and main to deal each other as many blows as possible. It is heart-rending to describe what slaughter was inflicted on both sides, how the dying groaned, and how great the fury of those attacking. Everywhere men were receiving wounds themselves, or inflicting them, dying or dealing out death."*

Finally, leading his troops forward, Arthur and his men hacked their way through the thick of the enemy, slaughtering with their swords: Mordred, the accursed traitor was killed, along with thousands of his men. *"Arthur himself, our renowned King, was mortally wounded and was carried off to the Isle of Avalon, so that his wounds might be attended to."*

Geoffrey of Monmouth later added more detail to the description of Avalon in his final work, the *Vita Merlini*, the *Life of Merlin*, in which he draws the renowned bards Merlin and Taliesin together to recall Arthur's transportation to the island of apples:

*"It is also known as the Fortunate Isle because it produces fertile crops, grapes and apples in abundance. The nine sisters who live on the isle give a genial welcome to the people of our land; Morgen, their leader, is the most experienced in the art of healing and is an excellent doctor, for she knows the healing power of every herb and uses her knowledge to heal the sick."*

*"To that place after the battle of Camblam we brought Arthur, hurt by wounds, with the aid of our captain Barinthus who knew the sea and who navigated by the stars at night. With him at the helm of our ship, we brought our leader to Avalon; and on our arrival, sister Morgen received us with honour, placing the King on a golden couch in her chamber. With her own honourable hand she uncovered his wound and looked at it for a long time. At last she said that the King could be restored to health only if he stayed with her for a long time and accepted her healing treatment. We rejoiced at this favourable news and committed the King to Morgen's care. We then set sail and returned to our own country with a favourable following wind."*

Just over half a century after Geoffrey of Monmouth's revelation of Avalon, the monks of Glastonbury Abbey made the fortuitous discovery of Arthur's grave, claiming that Glastonbury, then an island site that was surrounded by flooded marshland and linked to the Bristol Channel by the river Brue, was indeed the Isle of Avalon to which Arthur had been transported after the battle of Camlan. With 'Arthur's body' exhumed and translated to a prominent sanctuary within the Abbey, Glastonbury's fame was rekindled, and pilgrims flocked to Arthur's shrine to pay homage to the famous king. The contemporary historian Giraldus Cambrensis confirmed that 'Glastonia' was anciently called 'Insula Avalonia' and that Arthur's body had been found deep inside a hollowed oak coffin in the old cemetery of

Glastonbury Abbey; by recording these findings in his book *De Principis Instructione* he set the seal of authenticity on a clever but devious scheme devised by the monks to replenish the ailing coffers of their monastery.

The evident success of the monkish trickery at Glastonbury brought about a fit of clerical chagrin at Aberconwy Abbey in North Wales, for the abbot adhered to the tradition that Arthur belonged to Gwynnedd, and to Gwynedd he should return: in his opinion, the monks of Glastonbury had no right to claim Arthur for themselves, let alone prosper from his fame. In a surge of ecclesiastical jealousy the Abbot of Aberconwy decided to make a counter-claim for Arthur's last resting place.

Some years after Giraldus had published his treatise on Glastonbury, Aberconwy issued their own revised version of the battle of Camlan, with Arthur being carried off to the Isle of Avalon, now located in Gwynedd. To ensure the story would be believed, the document was entitled *Vera Historia De Morte Arthuri, The True History of the Death of Arthur.*

This 'true story' amended Geoffrey of Monmouth's account of the final stage of the battle of Camlan: Arthur fell to the ground, seriously wounded, but became vulnerable when he ordered his soldiers to remove his armour; whereupon a young warrior holding an elmwood spear, its tip tempered by fire and water, and dipped in adder's venom, seized the opportunity to attack. He launched the spear at Arthur, who quickly withdrew it from his body and threw the spear back at his attacker, piercing his heart. His fate sealed by the venomous spear, Arthur ordered his men to take him to Gwynedd, for he wished to sojourn in the delightful Isle of Avalon because of its great beauty. In a small chapel dedicated to the Virgin Mary, Arthur's funeral took place; but the entrance to the chapel was so small that Arthur's body would not fit through the doorway and had to remain outside. A tempestuous storm arose during the service, a mist descended, and when the mourners came to bury Arthur, the body had vanished and his tomb was found sealed by a single stone.

The introduction of the venomous spear was a clever idea, for it sealed Arthur's fate: there would be no time for a sea voyage to an island somewhere over the western horizon, or even as far as Glastonbury. Gwynedd was much closer, where Arthur would soon be laid to rest in hallowed ground. With the disappearance of his body, and the tomb sealed, the monks of Aberconwy would have no need to exhume an ancient corpse to prove their story, nor to reveal the exact location of Arthur's grave.

But the *Vera Historia,* whether or not true, was believed only by the faithful few of Gwynedd. Having gained the seal approval from King Richard I, Glastonbury's claim became widely accepted. Arthur and the Isle of Avalon now firmly belonged to Somerset.

In a late fifteenth century version of the story, Sir Thomas Malory featured

Arthur's last battle in a climactic ending to his epic *Le Mort d'Arthur, The Death of Arthur*. The tragic battle made a dramatic conclusion to the romantic tales of Arthur's Court gathered together by Malory from the traditional Welsh, Breton and French sources, embroidered over the years by bards and troubadours with a rich variety of ideas that encompassed all the facets of medieval chivalry, courtly love, and bloody warfare, interwoven with the magical element of the quest for the Holy Grail.

Undoubtedly influenced by King Edward III's great interest in King Arthur that culminated in the re-making of a magnificent round table for Winchester Castle, Malory set Arthur's Camelot at Winchester, the capital city of the English kings of Wessex. Camlan is not mentioned, and instead, Malory placed Arthur's final battle somewhere near Salisbury. Keen to retain the key elements of the traditional story of Arthur's demise, the chapel by the sea, and the voyage by barge to Avalon, Malory unwittingly gave himself some major geographical problems, for not only is Salisbury over thirty miles from the sea, but the round trip by sailing barge to Glastonbury's Avalon would have entailed a voyage of four hundred miles.

With the prospect of a proposed peace treaty to hand, the assembled armies of Arthur and Mordred drew back from the brink of battle, on the understanding that the first to raise a sword would signal the start of hostilities; but when an adder bit one of the assembled knights, he drew his sword to strike the snake. Seeing the glint of a drawn sword, both armies charged into battle. A long day's slaughter ensued until only four men remained standing: exhausted, Mordred leant on his sword among his dead soldiers, while Arthur was supported by Sir Lucan and his brother Sir Bedivere.

*"Now give me my spear"* said Arthur unto Sir Lucan, *"for yonder I have espied the traitor that all this woe hath wrought."* Arthur gripped his spear with both hands and, summoning all his might, pierced Mordred under his shield and ran the spear right through his body. Now locked in mortal combat, Mordred delivered a vicious blow to Arthur's head, splitting his helmet and drawing blood with the last stroke of his sword.

With Mordred lying dead, and Arthur mortally wounded, Sir Lucan died from his wounds while struggling to lift Arthur, leaving Bedivere to take the king to the water's edge. Arthur then commanded Bedivere to throw his good sword Excalibur into the water, but Bedivere, seeing the bejewelled pommel and haft, could not bring himself to discard this special weapon of such great value, and hid the sword under a tree. On his return, Arthur enquired: *"What saw thou there?"* *"Sir"* replied Bedivere, *"I saw nothing but waves and winds."* Knowing his answer to be untrue, Arthur asked Bedivere once more to dispose of his sword, but again he faltered by the waterside, failing his task for a second time. *"Ah, traitor untrue!"* exclaimed the king, *"Now thou hast betrayed me twice."* However, on the third request, under pain of death, Bedivere complied with Arthur's last wish: *"then, binding the girdle about the hilts he threw the sword as far as he might into the water. Then, an arm and a hand rose out of the water to catch Excalibur, brandished the sword thrice, and vanished into the waves."*

Bedivere carried Arthur on his back down to the water's edge where a small barge was waiting. In the barge were three queens, Queen Morgan le Fay, the Queen of Northgalis, (North Wales) and the Queen of the Wastelands, together with Nimue, the chief Lady of the Lake. As the boat rowed away from the land, Arthur called to Bedivere: *"Comfort thyself and do as well as thou mayst, for in me is no trust to trust in; for I will into the vale of Avilion to heal me of my grievous wound; and if thou hear never more of me, pray for my soul."*

Malory concludes his story with an honest summary, *"More of the death of King Arthur could I never find, but that ladies brought him to his burials. Yet some men say in many parts of England that King Arthur is not dead, but had by the will of our Lord Jesu gone into another place; and men say that he shall come again, and he shall win the holy cross. I will not say it shall be so, but rather I will say here in this world he changed his life. But many men say that there is written upon his tomb this verse: Hic jacet Arthurus, Rex quondam, Rexque futurus."* Here lies Arthur, the once and future King.

&#x0222B;&#x0222B;&#x0222B;&#x0222B;

The distinct differences between Geoffrey of Monmouth's and Malory's account of Arthur's last battle suggest that Malory drew his information from a source other than *The History of the Kings of Britain*. Although the names of the central characters are the same, Arthur and Mordred fight their last battle in different locations, Geoffrey's at Camblam in Cornwall, and Malory's battle near Salisbury. Arthur's arch enemy is named Mordred by both authors, but Geoffrey calls him Arthur's nephew while Malory casts him first as Gawain's older brother, and later as Arthur's father.

In the *Vita Merlini* Geoffrey's almost matter of fact description of Arthur's voyage across the sea to the Isle of Avalon is transformed by Malory into a mystical, otherworldly experience following the magical appearance of the arm that draws Excalibur down into the waters, fulfilling the ancient Celtic tradition of warriors offering their weapons to the gods of the underworld, that is readily exemplified by the recent finds of ancient weapons once surrendered to the depths of Llyn Cerrig Bach in Anglesey. But contrary to popular conception, Arthur's sword may not have been thrown into a lake: Bedivere throws Excalibur into the water from the same waterside or embankment where the barge is berthed to take Arthur on a sea voyage to 'Avilion,' so the most likely location would be a quayside within an estuary not too far from the battlefield. Malory's barge rows away from the land; Geoffrey's barge sets sail for Avalon: both are plausible, for in Arthur's day, a barge would have resembled the design of a Roman barge powered by a combination of oars and sails.

By chance, Geoffrey reveals a major clue to the location of Avalon when he describes a feature of the voyage back to Britain, *"We set sail and returned to our own country with a following wind."* Aware that the prevailing winds in the English Channel and the Irish Sea are south-westerly, this would indicate that captain Barinthus took a south-westerly course to Avalon from the estuary or quayside near Camlan. On the outward voyage, the barge would not have been able to sail directly into wind, forcing the helmsman to steer a zig-zag course, tacking the ship through the eye of the wind. Returning from Avalon, the following wind filled the sails and Barinthus was able to run a straight course to the north-east with the wind backing his sails all the way home. But before we can find the Isle of Avalon by navigation, we need to know the true location of Camlan; we can then search for the most plausible point of embarkation for a voyage to the south-west.

Malory gives us a glimpse of his 'Avilion' in a much earlier chapter of *Le Mort d'Arthur:* Dame Lionesse and her brother Sir Gringamore live in the Castle Perilous beside the Isle of Avilion, and they arrange a jousting tournament between the Knights of the Castle and King Arthur's Knights, to take place on the festival of Our Lady's Assumption. The lost land of Lyonesse is a well-known and respected feature of Cornish legend, a tradition that claims a great town called the *City of Lions* exists under the sea, close to the Seven Stones Lightship anchored twenty miles due west of Land's End. The very name '*Castle Perilous*' evokes the suggestion of a perilous sea journey, and the mention of the celebration of the Assumption of St. Mary indicates that there is a strong religious association with the Isle of Avilion. But if Castle Perilous and Avilion suffered the same inundation of the sea as the *City of Lions*, then they may yet be found in the depths of the Atlantic Ocean somewhere between Land's End and the Isles of Scilly.

An early Saxon map of the known world in the fifth century depicts the Isles of Scilly as a single island that was known in Roman times as '*Sylina Insula,*' an island that was associated with the Hesperides of Greek mythology. Often called the '*Islands of the Blessed,*' the '*Elysian Fields,*' or simply '*The Fortunate Isles,*' it was a place where the islanders enjoyed beautiful meadows full of flowers and long days of sunshine. From ancient times Sylina was known as the resting place of kings and princes who had made their last voyage to this beautiful island close to the western horizon, where the sun went down into the sea. Amongst the islets of the Eastern Isles that lie a mile or so to the north of St. Mary's, now the largest island, is a small rocky island named

*Great Arthur.* Could this be the site of Avalon, Arthur's last resting place, in keeping with the traditional rites of Celtic kings of Ancient Britain?

Another strong contender for Geoffrey of Monmouth's Avalon is the *Ile de Sein*, a small island off the western coast of Brittany first described by the Roman geographer Pomponius Mela in 43 AD in his *De Situ Orbis, A Description of the World*. He mentions the island's renowned Gallic Oracle whose nine sacred priestesses, known as *Galliceniae*, were reputedly able to raise storms, change themselves into animals, as well as to cure wounds and diseases, and to be able to predict the future: but they gave their healing remedies only to those wayfarers who came by sea to ask for their help.

Geoffrey clearly drew upon Pomponius Mela's description of the Ile de Sein but took the opportunity to update his version by making up the names of the priestesses, whom he referred to as 'sisters.' Unusual names such as *Gliton* and *Glitonea* are clearly derived from *Galliceniae* whereas *Moronoe* and *Tyronoe* are distinctly Irish, as is the name of their leader *Morgen*. The Druid priestesses of the first century now appear to have changed into a sixth century community of Christian women who are 'sisters in Christ,' Catholic nuns under the supervision of *sister Morgen*. Indeed, this explanation may very well account for the idea developed by early medieval storytellers that Morgen was Arthur's sister who possessed magical powers, and who evolved over the years into Morgan le Fay (Morgan the Fairy) of Arthurian legend.

But the Ile de Sein was not the only island in the Celtic world where Druid priestesses practised their powers of healing. Another famous pagan shrine stood at Carnsore Point on the south-eastern tip of the Wexford Coast of Ireland. On this site it is believed that a natural stone monolith was used by Druids as a temple dedicated to the sun.

Just two miles to the north of this ancient site, a sacred island is surrounded by the waters of an inland lake that is protected from the sea by a wide sand-bar. The Irish name for this island is *Cluain na mBan, the Meadow of the Women,* and according to local belief it was, in pre-Christian times, inhabited by female Druids. Perhaps in the same way that St Brigid established her first simple oratory on a pagan site at Cill-Dara, inheriting the eternal flame of the Druids and using it to symbolize the eternal power of the Holy Spirit, so the sacred island of the Druid priestesses evolved into a place of Christian worship and healing, inspired by St Brigid's enthusiasm and example.

Local tradition asserts that the island's earliest Christian community was centred on a small chapel dedicated to St Mary, that was founded in the sixth century by St Abban of Moyarney, nephew of St Ibar, and its reputation as a place of pilgrimage and devotion to the Virgin Mary was well established by the year 600 AD.

But since that time the island has had a chequered history. Following the Norman invasions of the late twelfth century the island fell into the hands of Milo De Lamporte, who built a feudal stronghold there in 1195. Forty years later his son Rudolph added a defensive tower with ramparts; but before leaving to fight in the Crusades, Rudolph gave his land to the Church and asked the Canons of St Augustine to take charge of the island, and to pray for his soul. In his absence, the monks built a small stone church on the site of St Abban's original chapel, dedicated again to St Mary; but sadly Rudolph did not return to see their good works, for he was killed in battle in the Holy Land. Thus Rudolph's gift of the island of Cluain na mBan unexpectedly became a magnanimous bequest of great benefit to the Augustinian monks.

Then, in 1649 the island was caught in the political strife between King Charles II's Royalist Alliance and Oliver Cromwell's army, sent by Parliament to eliminate the threat posed by Charles' plan to use Ireland as a springboard from which to invade England. After storming Drogheda, Cromwell marched south to Wexford, where he offered the Royalist commander terms for a peaceful surrender; however, negotiations broke down, and Cromwell attacked the town, killing over two thousand soldiers. Determined to eliminate the practice of Catholicism, Cromwell sent his men to destroy places of worship. The Augustinian monks of Cluain na mBan refused to bear arms against their own country and were murdered by Cromwell's soldiers; their church was desecrated and the roof destroyed, and the Norman castle was burned to the ground.

Eventually, when Cromwell had gone, the faithful country-folk returned, and just twenty years after the massacre, pilgrims were flocking to the island once more. Later in the seventeenth century, when merchants arrived from France, they changed the name of the island from *Cluain na mBan* the *Meadow of the Women*, to *Olean Mhuire* the *Island of Mary*; this was their way of confirming the sanctity of the island with its dedication to St Mary that had lasted unbroken through eleven hundred years of tempestuous history.

Today, people come to Our Lady's Island from far and wide to celebrate the Feast of the Assumption of the Blessed Virgin Mary. The annual pilgrimage begins on August 15th with mass celebrated at the out-door altar, followed by a procession of the Blessed Sacrament around the island: pilgrims recite the rosary as they progress round the island and end their visit with a final prayer of penance in the church. The season concludes with a torch-light procession and mass on the evening of the Feast of the Birth of Our Lady.

☙❧☙❧

But where was Camlan? Malory's relocation of Arthur's last battle from Cornwall to Salisbury was resented by west countrymen who firmly believed Geoffrey of Monmouth's account of the battle, for it was now widely accepted that Camlan had been fought in a meadow beside the river Camel at Slaughter Bridge near Camelford. The discovery of a sixth century memorial stone lying on the embankment of the river Camel was claimed to mark the site of Arthur's grave, and evidence of dead men's bones and horse-harnesses unearthed from the meadow, strengthened the local tradition that this was indeed the site of Camlan.

But when the field at Slaughter Bridge was excavated, the gruesome finds were attributed to a battle between Cornishmen and Saxons early in the ninth century when the Saxons had advanced to the west in their final conquest of Cornwall. No evidence of an earlier battle was revealed, and the memorial stone wishfully attributed to Arthur was found inscribed to *Latinus son of Magarus.*

When Malory embellished the legend with his story of the disposal of Arthur's sword, Dozmary Pool, a large windswept lake in the middle of Bodmin Moor, became renowned for the magical scene where Arthur's sword Excalibur had been drawn into the depths by the Lady of the Lake. To Cornishmen who knew the story of Arthur's birth at Tintagel, and of his demise in a battle just four miles to the south near Camelford, it seemed as if Arthur's life had come full circle; Dozmary Pool fitted more or less with Malory's story, Arthur had returned to his own people, and the legend had been fulfilled.

Not to be out-done by the Arthurian claims of their Cornish neighbours, the people of Somerset soon found their own ideal site for Camlan beside the Cam, a river that coursed through meadows within sight of Cadbury Castle, the British hill-fort long renowned as Arthur's Camelot. Local tradition held that, after the battle, Bedivere had carried the wounded king across the ancient causeway that linked Cadbury Castle to Glastonbury, casting Excalibur from Pomparles Bridge into the river Brue, before bidding farewell to Arthur as he departed for Avalon and his last resting place at the Abbey, less than a mile upstream!

But these west-country locations for the Battle of Camlan, made popular by a sincere belief in local tradition, have been challenged by the recent claim by some historians that the battle took place in the north, by the association of Camlan with the Roman fort of Camboglanna, which overlooks the river Cambeck at Castlesteads on Hadrian's Wall. Situated ten miles to the north-east of Carlisle, Camboglanna would have been in the firing line of Pictish and Saxon war-bands raiding from the north. However, the western reaches of Hadrian's Wall were strongly defended by the king of Rheged who was a faithful ally of Arthur, and whose forces would have been powerful enough to repel an enemy challenge against Arthur in the north.

Both the memory of the victory at Badon, and the aftershock of the battle of Camlan emanate from the earliest Welsh sources. One enigmatic but anonymous story called *The Dream of Rhonabwy* is included in the *Red Book of Hergest,* together with a collection of Welsh tales known as the *Mabinogion* dating from the middle of the twelfth century, possibly earlier. Significant from a historical point of view, *The Dream of Rhonabwy* is the only early medieval story that links Arthur to both Badon and Camlan, and although the author reflects an awareness of Geoffrey of Monmouth's locations, he introduces personal names and places that are unique to this story:

Rhonabwy and his companions Kynwrig Red Freckles and Cadwgwn the Stout were soldiers of King Madawg son of Maredudd, the ruler of Powys. Whilst on a mission to find Ioworth, the Kings brother, the three soldiers sought shelter at the house of Hneilyn the Red, grandson of King Iddon of Gwent; they received a cool welcome in a smoke-filled hall, where an old hag gave them a meagre supper of barley-bread, cheese and watery milk. A storm blew-up as they retired to bed, but Rhonabwy could not get to sleep on the flea-ridden straw covered only by a threadbare blanket. At the other end of the hall he found a yellow ox-skin much more comfortable to lie on, and as he fell asleep, Rhonabwy dreamed that he and his companions were transported back over six hundred years to the time of King Arthur.

Approaching the Severn Valley they came to Rhyd y Groes, the Ford of the Cross, where they met Iddawg son of Myno, who explained that he was better known by his nick-name *Iddawg the Churn of Britain,* because he had caused the battle of Camlan. When the Emperor Arthur sent him to remind Medrawd that Arthur was his uncle and foster-father and to plead for peace, Iddawg spoke so rudely to Medrawd that he provoked him into battle.

As Arthur's army assembled tents and pavilions on both sides of the road a mile away from the fort, Iddawg took Rhonabwy to greet Arthur as he sat between bishop Bidwini and Gwarthegydd, son of Caw, on a flat islet below the ford. When he saw the little men, Arthur's grim smile betrayed the sadness that he felt *"at this island being in the care of such puny men, after the sort that had held it before."*

By the time all the cavalry troops had arrived from different parts of the country, Caradawg Strong Arm advised Arthur to prepare for the Battle of Baddon, to fight against Osla Big-Knife, and Arthur led the assembled host across the ford in the direction of Kevyn Digoll, followed by Iddawg and Rhonabwy. When they reached the fortress of Baddon, Cadur Earl of Cornwall, the armourer, presented Arthur with his sword; all could see the design of two serpents on the hilt, but when it was unsheathed, flames of fire appeared to glint from the serpents' mouths and it became too bright for anyone's eyes.

A surreal scene followed as Arthur and Owein, the Prince of Rheged, played *'gwyddbwyll'* a game similar to chess, with gold game-pieces on a silver board. As the battle raged, Arthur refused three times to stop the killing by calling-off his men from their attack on Owein's ravens. Arthur said nothing other than *"Play on."* As one game finished they started another, but this time Arthur's men were being beaten by Owein's ravens: *"Owein, call off your ravens,"* demanded Arthur, but Owein replied *"Your move, lord."*

The battle continued with great uproar and screams of men being pulled apart by the ravens, until a messenger arrived to greet the Emperor with the news that his pages and squires had been killed, together with all the sons of the nobles, so that henceforth it would be difficult to defend the island of Britain. *"Owein, call off your ravens,"* demanded Arthur. *"Your move, lord,"* said Owein.

But the ravens intensified the battle against Arthur's men, ripping them apart and dropping armour and pieces of men and horses to the ground. Straight from the battle, a rider carrying a gleaming gold-hilted sword and brandishing a blood-stained spear, angrily informed Arthur that the ravens had killed his retinue and the sons of the nobles of the island of Britain, and begged him to get Owein to call off his ravens.

As he made the last request, Arthur crushed the gold game-pieces on the board to dust, whereupon Owein ordered Gures, son of Rheged, to lower his standard: this signalled the end of the battle and the two sides accepted peace. Finally Arthur's councillors, who included Cadwr Earl of Cornwall, Avaon son of Talyessin, and Gildas son of Caw, met to negotiate a truce with Osla Big Knife; Cei then rose to invite all Arthur's followers back to Cornwall.

As an allegorical tale that features some of the most controversial moments of Arthur's life, the *Dream of Rhonawby,* with its introduction of surreal imagery and time travel to an earlier age, is possibly one of the most thought provoking early medieval texts. The idea of Arthur's messenger Iddawg being blamed for starting the battle of Camlan clearly echoes the fact that, when the *Dream of Rhonabwy* was written, the real reason for the battle remained hidden. However, reading between the lines of Iddawg's story, it becomes clear that Arthur's nephew was not the *Medraut* of legend, but Maelgwyn, Prince of Gwynedd; and it was the fact that Arthur had made a plea for peace that did not fit Maelgwyn's determined plan to destroy Arthur that caused his anger, not Iddawg's brusque delivery of the message.

Iddawg is sent to remind Maelgwyn that Arthur is his uncle and foster-father; just as Arthur had been fostered as a youth by Cei's family in the accepted tradition, so Arthur's brother Catwallaun Longhand lodged his son Maelgwyn with Arthur's household where he would learn, first-hand, the art of warfare, and grow up with his cousin Cuneglass under the care and instruction of Arthur, Britain's great battle-leader.

But Maelgwyn proved to be a traitor: he was the enemy within Arthur's own hall, and this is confirmed in the fourteenth century romance *The Awntyrs of Arthure* by the ghost of the mother of Queen Gaynoure (Guinevere) who prophesies, with the benefit of hind-sight, Arthur's last battle and the destruction of the noble fellowship of the Round Table:

> *"And all the honourable members of the Round Table*
> *They shall die on a day, all the valiant warriors together…*
> *In King Arthur's hall*
> *the child, he plays with the ball*
> *who shall one day destroy you all*
> *most powerfully…"*

No names are mentioned, because the few who knew that Arthur's nephew caused his downfall were sworn to secrecy: following the battle of Camlan it would have been tantamount to treason to name Maelgwyn in connection with Arthur's death. Surprisingly, there was one person in the country brave enough to address the murderer for his evil actions: it was Gildas, known by his contemporaries as the wisest, and now clearly the bravest man in Britain:

*"What of you, dragon of the island, you who have removed many of these tyrants from their country and even their life? You are the last in my list, but first in evil, mightier than many both in power and malice, more profuse in giving, more extravagant in sin, strong in arms, but stronger still in what destroys a soul, Maglocunus."* (Maelgwyn)

*"Did you not, in the first years of your youth, use sword and spear and fire in the cruel despatch of **the king your uncle** and nearly all his brave young warriors, whose faces in battle looked just like lions' whelps. You did not heed the words of the prophet, 'Woe to you who plunder, will not you yourself be plundered? And to you who kill, will you not also be killed? And when you have ceased to plunder, then you will fall.' "*

Gildas' condemnation of Maelgwyn is complete; furthermore, his opinion is endorsed by Taliesin, the pre-eminent poet who was a contemporary of the king and the monk. In his poem *The Defence of the Chair*, he wrote:

> *"I have been to Deganwy to contend*
> *with Maelgwyn, the greatest of criminals."*

The author of the *Dream of Rhonabwy* mentions real place names that give his story an air of authenticity; this suggests that he was a man of Powys who was familiar with the local folklore that linked Arthur with *Rhyd y Groes* and *Kevyn Digol*. Arthur's army is encamped one mile to the east of *Rhyd y Groes:* by referring to the Ordnance Survey Map of Roman Britain, we find this to be the exact location of Forden Gaer, the Roman Vexillation fort of Levrobrinta, which was a defensive out-post of the legionary base at Wroxeter. *Kevyn Digol* is derived from *Cefn Digoll,* now known as Long Mountain, just four miles to the north-east of Forden Gaer.

It appears that the original story of Arthur's army rallying at Forden Gaer, then crossing the river Severn at *Rhyd y Groes* and marching westward into battle, may have been confused with the story of another great sixth century battle between Cadwallon, king of Gwynedd, and Edwin, king of the Northumbrians, that took place at *Cefn Digoll* over ninety years after the battle of Camlan.

With the real location of the battle of Badon long forgotten, local tradition settled on the nearby hill-fort of Breidden as the site of Arthur's great victory: Breidden is only four miles north of *Cefn Digoll* overlooking Offa's Dyke to the west, and it is quite plausible to suggest that the author had this fortress in mind for the battle of Baddon featured in Rhonabwy's dream. From Forden Gaer an army would have only to march north along the Roman road that ran below *Cefn Digoll,* to reach Breidden.

This seemingly insignificant geographical anomaly that depicts Arthur leading his army from Forden Gaer westward to cross the river Severn should not be overlooked, because it may offer a sign-post to the site of the battle of Camlan. Arthur's rallying position at Forden was already twenty-five miles to the south-west of his military headquarters at Wroxeter: it would have been the best defensive position and the logical rallying point to await reinforcements, before marching to encounter an enemy threat, not at Baddon, but on the western borders of Powys. Just as Cadwallon had marshalled his forces at Forden having returned from refuge in Guernsey, so Arthur may have reached Forden on his return from an expedition to Cornwall or Brittany; responding to emerging news of an invasion in the west and without time to return to Wroxeter to re-arm, he may well have paused his force at Forden Gaer in order to prepare for battle. But it was Cadwallon who marched north to *Cefn Digoll* and Arthur who marched west … to Camlan.

The surreal events witnessed by Rhonabwy reach a climax when Arthur plays 'gwyddbwyll' with his opponent Owein, prince of Rheged, while the real battle rages. The silver gaming-board and the solid gold players represent the precious metals that were the foundation of Arthur's military power; the game reflects the fact that Arthur planned his battle campaigns like a game of chess, moving his men and their cavalry squadrons around the country in a tactical game-plan designed to defeat his enemies. Once the battle has begun and his forces are engaged, he resolutely refuses to call off his men. Whether at Badon or Camlan, Arthur fights to the bitter end; he achieves victory at Badon, but suffers total defeat at Camlan. If the *'gwyddbwyll'* game had an ending similar to chess, then the *Check-Mate* was against Arthur: as his warriors were annihilated on the battle-field, he crushed the gaming-pieces to dust. Arthur's war game was over.

ஒஒஒஒ

No two words in the English language have generated more speculation than *'Medraut'* and *'Avalon.'* Over the years 'Medraut' became synonymous with Arthur's mortal enemy at the battle of Camlan, changing in time to the English form 'Mordred' and later, by association with Arthur's brother-in-law, to 'Medrod.' Medrod ap Cawrdaf was held in high esteem at court as a paragon of courage and kindness; he was appointed Provost of Cornwall by Arthur, but after Arthur's demise Medrod's name became linked with Mordred, Arthur's traitorous enemy at Camlan, and he was unfairly damned to eternity.

Curiously, however, there is no known genealogy for any sixth century Briton by the name of 'Medraut.' In short, apart from the single entry in the *Welsh Annals*, there is no evidence that Medraut ever existed; it begs the question: *"Is it possible that Medraut was never actually a living person?"* Perhaps the word *'medraut'* was not a personal name at all, but an adverb or an adjective with a meaning that was most pertinent to Arthur's condition at the time of receiving a severe battle wound? It would not be too difficult to imagine that the cleric who compiled the original report of the battle had either mis-heard his informant or had made a simple scribal error when transcribing the text from an earlier source.

The Latin word *'corruer'* means *'to fall'* or more explicitly *'to fall to the ground,'* a description that would allow for Arthur to fall wounded from his horse and take time to recover from his injury. In the original text, personal names are not distinguished by a capital letter, so that a word like *'medraut'* that had no significant meaning, could have been easily mistaken for a personal name. Conversely, it is possible that *'medraut'* could be an adverb that described the cause of Arthur's fall to the ground: as Arthur was mounted for battle, this could have occurred when he received a blow or an injury that caused him to fall from his horse.

But *'medraut,'* although it appears to be a Latin word, has no equivalent in the Latin dictionary. However, the Brythonic word *'meduaut,'* current in Arthur's day, could easily have been misconstrued either from the original report of Arthur's

*250*

demise, or from the earliest written account of the battle of Camlan. '*Meduaut*' means '*intoxicated by mead*' so if the original text had been written: "*Arthur ou meduaut corruerunt*" this would give a completely different interpretation of the situation at the end of the battle:

> "*Arthur was drunk, and fell from his horse!*"

Although most unlikely, this scenario would not be beyond the bounds of possibility, especially if Arthur had been celebrating his return from abroad with festivities where mead was flowing until the early hours. If a messenger had arrived with news of invasion in the west, Arthur would have been caught off-guard: having quaffed a few too many goblets of mead in the merriment of the occasion, he was suddenly faced with an emergency and forced to prepare for battle.

But to give Arthur the benefit of the doubt raised by this suggested version of events, there are two other Latin words that could possibly replace '*medraut*' in our controversial text: first, '*mortidare*,' meaning 'to slay' or 'to kill,' is closer to '*mordred*' than '*medraut*;' but '*morderunt*' which means 'to hurt, sting, or cause pain' is more relevant to the text as well as being similar in pronunciation. Sounding like the English word '*murdered*,' and similar to the French '*modre*' and Spanish '*mordedura*,' both meaning 'bite' as in dog or snake-bite, the word '*morderunt*' might easily have been shouted-out by a warrior: "*Arthur est morderunt!*" meaning "*Arthur is hurt!*"

The vernacular Latin, spoken with a Brythonic or early Welsh pronunciation, could have been written thus:

> "*arthur ut morderunt corruerunt.*"
> "*Arthur, as he was hurt, fell to the ground.*"

A further simple error, where a copying scribe later mistook the Latin '*ut*' (meaning 'as') for '*et*' (meaning 'and') and neatly penned the ampersand (the symbol for '*and*') as it appears in the earliest text of the *Annales Cambriae*, thus linking arthur to '*medraut*,' a word derived from '*morderunt*' that was mistaken for a personal name because it had lost its original meaning.

Thus the suggested original entry above, was later copied in error and written:

> "*arthur & medraut corruerunt.*"

Furthermore, the idea of the snake-bite story, first mentioned by Geoffrey of Monmouth as the cause of the battle of Camlan, and later by the monks of

Aberconwy Abbey, whose *True Story of the Death of Arthur* introduced a warrior who attacked Arthur with a spear dipped in adders venom, appears to attest to the early presence of a word like '*morderunt*' that meant 'hurt' but could also be taken to mean 'sting' or 'snake-bite,' and in the general confusion evolved into '*medraut*' and even later into '*mordred.*'

Thus from a simple 'cri de coeur' from the field of battle, a mass of fictitious fable has been attributed to the infamous 'Mordred,' a man who never existed. This leads to the suggestion that the text which most clearly relates the sorrowful conclusion of the civil strife at Camlan should read thus:

*"Gueith camlann, inquo arthur ut morderunt, corruerunt."*
*The strife of Camlan, in which Arthur was hurt, and fell to the ground.*

❧❧❦❦

First mentioned by Geoffrey of Monmouth as the place where Arthur's sword 'Caliburn' was forged, the 'Isle of Avalon' simply means the 'Island of the Apples.' Avalon comes from the Welsh word '*aval*' meaning 'apple' and can be traced back to the Brythonic language of Arthur's day; a good example of this is found in the late sixth century poem by Myrddin (Merlin) called *Afallanau, The Apple Tree*.

But there must have been more to Avalon than just an island of orchards, as the name suggests. Arthur, after all, was not going to a picnic: seriously wounded at Camlan, his first wish would have been to find a refuge far enough away from his enemies, where his wounds could be tended, and where he could recover in a peaceful environment; and for his own safety that place would have to remain secret, known only to his closest friends and to the nurses appointed to care for him.

More than a decade after Geoffrey of Monmouth had first introduced the idea that the wounded king had been carried away to Avalon, he added a postscript to the story within his epic poem, the *Vita Merlini*, bringing Merlin and Taliesin together in a conversation that revealed more details about the story of Arthur's last journey.

When stripped of the embellishment that Geoffrey appears to have taken straight from Pomponius Mela's description of the Ile de Sein, we are left with a core of information that he must have gleaned either from extant copies of the bards' sixth century texts, or from the '*very ancient book written in the British language*' given to him by his friend Walter, Archdeacon of Oxford. Walter the Archdeacon just happened to be the Provost of the Augustinian college of St George's in Oxford, whose canons included the eminent Robert de Chesney, Bishop of Lincoln. Geoffrey of Monmouth was one of the prime signatories to legal charters connected with Augustinian religious foundations in and around Oxford; acting in such a privileged position, Geoffrey may himself have been an elected canon of the college of St George, giving him legitimate access not only to ancient books and texts held in the college collection, but also to the closely guarded secrets of the inner sanctum of the Augustinian order that were passed only to the select few by word of mouth.

One of the Augustinians' most closely guarded secrets was the true story of Arthur's sojourn, death and burial on the Isle of Avalon; a secret that they had kept for exactly six hundred years at the time Archdeacon Walter passed this knowledge to his trusted friend, Geoffrey of Monmouth. Honour bound to keep the secret of Arthur's last resting place but in need of every scrap of historical detail to include in his forthcoming book *The History of the Kings of Britain*, Geoffrey coined the name 'Avalon' from his ancient sources, adding a description of the Ile de Sein to conceal the identity of the real Avalon, but allowing the discourse between Merlin and Taliesin to relate for posterity the authentic account of Arthur's sea voyage to the island; it appears to be nothing more than a logical sequence to the battle of Camlan, a plausible report on Arthur's escape from his enemies, and from his beloved island of Britain:

*"After the battle of Camblam we brought Arthur to Avalon, the island of apples, sailing across the sea with our captain Barinthus to guide us, for he knew the channels and could navigate by the stars. When we reached our destination, we took Arthur to Morgen who tended his wound; she was the senior healer of the nine sisters who were skilled in the art of herbal remedies. We left the king in their good care, for sister Morgen had advised us that Arthur would need a long time to recover. We returned to our ship and sailed back to our own country with a following wind."*

Arthur led his army from Forden Gaer across the river Severn at Rhyd y Groes: he marched to the west, out of Rhonabwy's dream and into the reality of the steep and craggy passes of the Cambrian Mountains, where, on the field of Camlan beside the meandering Afon Dyfi, Arthur would face his enemies for the last battle. Beyond Machynlleth, just nineteen miles south of Camlan, Arthur's sailing barge *Pridwen* lay moored by the quayside at Aberdyfi, with captain and crew awaiting his command.

For captain Barinthus, a safe voyage to an island refuge with a wounded king would be governed by the most expedient logistics; for example, the Island of Sylina (Scilly) was 225 miles to the south-west of Barmouth and it would take a good forty hours to get there. Ile de Sein, off the north-west coast of Brittany was 125 miles further south, with a journey time of sixty hours or more depending upon the wind and weather conditions; but Cluain na mBan, Our Lady's Island, just to the south of Rosslare, was only 100 miles from Barmouth, a voyage that would take only seventeen to twenty hours at the most, and in the event of a rough passage, Barinthus knew that he could find shelter in the safe haven of Wexford Harbour. His outbound course would be west-by-south, reaching into the south-westerly wind; but on the return voyage, his reciprocal heading would be east-by-north, and he could run homeward helped by the prevailing south-westerly, the *"assisting wind"* mentioned by Geoffrey in his *Vita Merlini*.

Avalon was known as the Isle of Apples, but the Welsh name for Ireland was *Iwerddon,* pronounced *Iverthon,* a name from which Avalon could also have been derived, particularly if Cluain na mBan had been referred to as *the Isle of Iverthon* as a way of obscuring its true identity; but true to its earlier name *the Meadow of the Women,* the island had hosted a Christian sanctuary of nuns from the early years of the sixth century. The Celtic name for a sanctuary of nuns was *addoldai llein,* pronounced *atholdalion.* There is no 'v' sound in Welsh, so that any variation in the sound of *atholdalion* would have arisen from the English pronunciation of the original Welsh word, possibly changing it to *avoldalion,* a word that comes curiously close to Malory's *Avilion.*

Geoffrey of Monmouth's revelation of Avalon did not give away the secret of Arthur's isle of rest, but it was a name that would leave everyone looking for an idyllic island somewhere between reality and the mythical otherworld. If there was a clue in the name, it certainly did not deter the monks of Glastonbury claiming Avalon for themselves thirty five years after Geoffrey had died, and could say no more on the matter.

Malory completed *Le Mort d'Arthur* in 1470, over three hundred years after Geoffrey's death and over nine hundred years since Arthur's demise; yet, from an unknown source, he gleaned some information about *Avilion* that added to Geoffrey's scant clues. First, he described *Castle Perilous* as being *"beside the Isle of Avilion;"* secondly, he associated Arthur with a jousting tournament held at Castle Perilous by the invitation of Dame Lionesse, who declared that the knights shall *"come by land and by water;"* and finally, that the tournament would be held to celebrate the *"Feast of the Assumption of Our Lady."* Malory's story appears to echo an earlier tale that brought Arthur to Avalon, not as medieval king armed in full array for the joust, but as a Dark Age warrior who had been invited to the Isle of Avalon to celebrate the festival of St Mary. Malory's extraordinary revelation that Castle Perilous was close by Avilion suggests that Arthur had made the journey to Avalon in happier times, perhaps many years before he was forced to seek refuge there after the battle of Camlan.

If Geoffrey of Monmouth intended to give a clue to the location of the Isle of

Avalon in the name, then it was cleverly concealed; Myrddin's poem introduced the idea of apples with the Brythonic *Affalan,* a word that sounds very similar to *'Iverthon'* meaning Ireland: evidently, *Avalon* could have been derived from both words. But Malory's *'Avilion'* appears to have been derived from a different source; if this source was indeed the Welsh word *'avoldalion'* then all the word clues can be combined to give a clearer meaning: *an island sanctuary of nuns in Ireland.*

If this suggestion is correct, then, together with the navigational evidence from a sixth-century text, there is only one conclusion: that the legendary Isle of Avalon is in fact Cluain na mBan, the Meadow of the Women, with its island sanctuary of nuns and their small chapel dedicated to St Mary, that is now known as Our Lady's Island, in County Wexford, Ireland.

The leaning ruins of Rudolph de Lamporte's Norman Castle still stand guard over the causeway that links Our Lady's Island to the mainland, for it is none other than Malory's 'Castle Perilous' that lies close by the Isle of Avalon.

Our Lady's Island, Wexford, Ireland: the legendary 'Isle of Avalon.'
Photo, © Oliver Doyle

# CHAPTER 16

# ARTHUR'S LAST BATTLE

*"The host is sure to be bowed, fading away*
*as in the great contention*
*of the Battle of Camlann."*
Cynddelw (1155 – 1195)

As Arthur and his battle-weary warriors entered the south gate of the city of Wroxeter, the citizens flocked into the streets to give him a hero's welcome, and as the news of his overwhelming victory at Badon spread through the towns and villages, the people of Britain rejoiced and celebrated the prospect of peace.

Reaching the marshalsea, the warriors dismounted from their blood-soaked destriers, leaving the stable lads to lead the powerful war-horses away to be washed down and fed from a manger of fresh hay and the finest oats, a fair reward for these great stalwarts who had been so fearless in battle.

But Arthur was not yet ready to celebrate his victory, for after the cut and thrust of battle, the gushing blood and the stench of death, he wanted nothing more than to ride into the forest to hunt deer. Before sunrise the next day, Arthur called his marshal to saddle-up his finest coursers and prepare for the hunt.

A small privileged band of young warriors who had been recognised for their bravery and courageous action at Badon Hill, were invited to join Arthur and his trusted commanders Cei and Bedivere for the hunt. After breakfasting in the great hall at twilight, Arthur led his huntsmen south to follow the river Severn, crossing over the bridge by the hamlet of Cressage. Then, as the sun rose above Much Wenlock, Arthur rode to the south-west, leading the chase along Wenlock Edge towards Clun Forest, his favourite hunting ground.

The hunting party reached the forest well before noon, making their assembly at the fort of Bury Ditches, which provided a secure encampment within an oval shaped compound protected by four defensive ramparts and ditches. Crowning the summit of Sunnyhill the fort afforded a commanding view over the surrounding forest, and from this central position Arthur could range the hunt to follow Hopton

Heath in the east across to Black Mountain, some fourteen miles to the west; in this fertile and secluded vale, herds of deer and roebuck ranged free, protected from poachers by the king's foresters.

Arthur's master of the hunt returned from an advanced foray with his lymers, bloodhounds trained to locate the quarry in silence that were sent out before the hunt to find the lay of the game; on this occasion they had sniffed out a herd of red deer whose adult males were vying for the supremacy of the herd. This was good news for the assembly, and as Arthur rallied the hunt on his shrill horn, the huntsmen rode forward towards the hamlet of Cefn-Einion to position greyhounds in relays along the predicted path of the chase. Arthur hunted '*by force of dogs*' using relays of greyhounds to chase the quarry to exhaustion: the hunters would then move in for the kill.

Barely three miles into the forest, Arthur and his young noblemen found the herd grazing in a clearing beside a stream. Moving stealthily, their hearts pounding as if they were going into battle, the hunters closed-in on their quarry. At this moment it was Arthur's right to choose the animal most worthy of chasing to the kill, but he graciously deferred his privilege to Cei as a reward for his unflinching bravery on the field of Badon.

Cei marked out his quarry, a magnificent stag, crowned with mature antlers of more than ten tines, well worthy of the hunt. Arthur lowered his spear and spurred Cabal, his impetuous greyhound, into the chase. The roe-deer scattered in fright at the sudden appearance of the hunters, but the dogs were onto the stag, now running for his life. The hunt chased at the gallop along the stream's embankment for almost a mile; then the great stag faltered as he reached the rising ground of Edenhope Hill. With the hounds at his heels, exhausted from the chase, the stag turned defiantly to face his hunters.

Cei's elm-shafted battle spear flew through the air like a flash of lightning, finding its mark, bringing the stag crashing to the ground. Arthur and his huntsmen encircled Cei as he despatched the animal with his sword, its life-blood flowing into the earth. All gathered around at the kill, shouting in triumph and trumpeting on their horns in a great din as they waited to witness the 'unmaking of the deer.' Then the master of the hunt hacked into the carcass, apportioning the joints and the delicacies in the traditional order; even the dogs were not forgotten and the best hounds were thrown the choicest bits of offal. Finally, the gristle at the end of the breast-bone was thrown to the carrions, for this was the 'raven's fee.'

Mindful that taking stags in the spring was not the best way of engendering the herd for the summer, Arthur restricted the kill to one each for Cei and Bedivere with one marked stag for himself; and during the three day hunt, each young warrior was given free rein to track and kill the barren roe-deer, without adhering to the formal rules of the traditional hunt. Even so, by sunset on the third day of the hunt, enough game had been slaughtered to feast an army on venison for a week or more.

With the trauma of battle now far from their minds, the proud hunters broke camp and found the Roman road that led north from the forest of Clun to Viroconium; as darkness fell, Arthur brought his weary band into Caer Caradoc for a night's rest. By noon the next day, the hunting party had reached Wroxeter: Arthur, Cei and Bedivere cantered into the fortress, line abreast, looking very pleased with their tally.

Arthur, now in jubilant mood, declared a holiday to celebrate his great victory over the Saxons: there would be festivities for fifteen days for the citizens of Viroconium and the people of Powys. Confident that the tally of deer would provide enough venison for a feast, Arthur rode down to the south gate to oversee the arrival of horse-drawn cart-loads of deer, but he was surprised to find the first three carts full of wounded men, bloody and dishevelled, who had been brought back from the battlefield of Badon. Arthur escorted them to the courtyard of his military headquarters where Guinevere and her nurses provided fresh straw mattresses for the men and dressed their wounds.

Several cart loads of disembowelled deer followed the wounded soldiers into the city; the butchers would have to hang the carcasses for three or four days before preparing them for the kitchens. With short whetted knives they cut through the shoulder-bones, sliding them carefully out of the carcass, leaving the sides intact. Deftly cleaving the chest in two, they ripped out the shoulder and rib fillets and cleaved the spine down to the haunch. After hacking the haunch from the chine and cleaving the thigh-forks, they severed the deer's head, sliced up the flanks and cut off the forelegs. Haunches were hung by the hocks ready for roasting, the neck-meat diced for stewing and the shins of roe deer set aside for the commanders' wives; served with shallots, this was Guinevere's favourite dish.

But Guinevere's thoughts were far from the delicacies of the dining table while she dedicated her days to the care of wounded warriors returned from battle. For the seriously wounded men whose limbs had been sliced and shattered by swords and axes, with wounds unhealed and becoming gangrenous, their only hope of survival was the surgeon's saw. Four stalwart orderlies lifted a young soldier onto the flat oak operating table in the hospital quarters, while the nurse administered a herbal anaesthetic of ground opium poppy mixed with henbane leaves.

While the orderlies held the man down, the surgeon made a deft incision with his scalpel, cutting through the flesh down to the bone just above the knee joint. The surgeon flinched as the soldier recoiled from the sudden pain with a bloodcurdling scream; then, ramming a pine dowel between his teeth, he cut deeper round the bone with the scalpel, pulling back the flesh to reveal the bare bone. Then, grasping a small fine-toothed saw, he cut through the bone close to the flesh. Writhing with intolerable pain but pinned down by the weight of four powerful men, the young warrior became unconscious, allowing the surgeon to complete his onerous task by filing smooth the end of the bone, drawing the loose skin back over the bone to seal the wound, and finally sterilizing the suture with vinegar.

This patient was one of the fortunate survivors whose wounds healed after the painful amputation; many of his comrades with more seriously infected limbs were condemned to their deathbeds, tortured with pain. Not least of the Commander in Chief's moribund duties was to bid a sorrowful farewell to his dying warriors, praying for their souls and giving them a Christian burial; but for Arthur the most difficult task was to bear the heart-rending news of their death to the warrior's beloved mother and father, with words of comfort to the bereaved and a commendation for their son's bravery in the Battle for Britain.

Eight mounted warriors escorted Prince Catwaullan back to Wroxeter, where at sunset his body was laid in a hollowed oak coffin, and placed at rest in the small chapel. Soon after dawn the following day, Arthur led his brother's cortege to the burial ground of the kings of Powys. Situated between Castell Dinas Bran and the Wrekin hilltop fortress, the Berth was a sacred site, where six years earlier king Uther Pendragon had been laid to rest with great ceremony. The circular rampart of an ancient fort enclosed the burial ground; lying amid meadows and overlooking a circular lake to the south, it was an idyllic rural resting place.

The procession paused by the north bank of the lake; Arthur dismounted, drew Catwaullan's sword from its scabbard resting on the bier, and flung the sword into the dark waters of the sacred lake. This ceremonial despatch of his brother's sword fulfilled the Celtic tradition of presenting the weapon as a gift to Nimue the water goddess, the legendary 'Lady of the Lake' who withdrew the sword to the underworld where it would ensure protection and good fortune for its owner in the afterlife.

As the oak coffin was lowered into a small chamber lined with stone slabs, Bishop Baldwin committed Prince Catwaullan to his grave with a Christian blessing. Distraught with grief, his widow pleaded with Arthur to take her seven year old son into his care. *"I would like to become a great warrior like my father!"* exclaimed the young Maelgwyn. *"Come with me,"* said Arthur, *"and I will teach you and your cousin Cuneglass to become great warriors together."*

There was a time for sorrow and a time for celebration, events that were circumscribed by the hunting and hanging of the deer, for within five or six days the hung venison would gain flavour; but after a week without salting, the meat would start to rot. Thus the day of Arthur's great feast was set to take place five days after the kill. A team of young men prepared the spacious hall of Viroconium's ageing basilica, setting boarded table-tops on trestles and setting out benches for the many guests. At the head of the hall, the top table was set on a raised platform backed by a Turkestan tapestry wall-hanging that had been draped over suspended wooden poles to form a simple canopy; kindling and logs were gathered at the other end of the hall and a great fire was laid in the hearth.

At sunset Arthur's guests arrived and took their places in order of rank: then, as flaming cressets were lodged in their brackets along the walls of the hall, Arthur and Guinevere and their companions, escorted by warriors armed with spears and shields, moved forward to their places on the dais. Prince Cadwy took the place of honour next to Arthur; seneschal Cei was seated next to Bishop Baldwin and Bedivere next to Guinevere. Gawain and Theodoric, with their wives, took their places in turn.

Arthur welcomed all his guests, thanking the Bishop, his military commanders and their wives, and his warriors and their families for their loyalty and support through the long arduous years of strife and endless warfare. Their steadfastness and courage had brought its own reward: victory over the pagan invaders, and with God's help, victory in the battle for Britain. Turning to Guinevere, he thanked his wife and her nurses profoundly for their vital role in caring for the wounded, and for saving the lives of many of his young warriors.

After raising a toast *"To Victory,"* Arthur called for his venison, and with the Bishop's blessing, the festival began. First, the stewards served a meaty broth with beans and lentils; later, when the venison was brought to the guests, with the choicest cuts of steak, ribs and hams, each feaster helped themselves to a seemly portion of the fare laid before them on the tables. The torches and bright flames of the log fire gave a warm glow of ambience to the hall; with mead and Celtic beer flowing freely, all joined in the merriment and joy of the occasion. Gwyneira, a fair young maiden with golden tresses that fell to her shoulders, played the harp, accompanied by a minstrel who sang the praises of Arthur and his victorious warriors.

To follow the venison, serving maids brought plums and pears preserved in Gallic red wine, complemented with mature farm cheese, goats cheese, and rough oatcakes to complete the feast. Then, to a drumroll and a staccato burst of hunting horns, three tumblers made a surprise entrance at the far end of the hall, each juggling firebrands high in the air to the amazement and pleasure of the guests, as they progressed towards the top table. Before Arthur and Guinevere they formed a triangle, flicking their flaming torches back and forth, faster and faster, all the while moving round in a circle to entrance their audience. Suddenly, the jugglers extinguished their torches in a half-barrel of water, bowed and disappeared into the smoky shadows.

When all had enjoyed the extravagant feast, Arthur rose to join his guests and to give an encouraging cheer to the young warriors who were engaged in a wrestling match in the open space in front of the fire. Finding his friends Gwynn and Olwen from the farm at Llandegwn, Arthur welcomed them with a warm embrace. Their invitation to Wroxeter had been a complete surprise, and now they were astonished to find that their new-found friend Owain was none other than Arthur, the great Leader of Battles.

*"We were complete strangers when you welcomed us to your home, yet you graciously shared your hospitality and entertainment with us!"* exclaimed Arthur:

*"Now it is our great pleasure to return your kindness, and this night you shall stay with us as our most welcome guests."*

⤞⤞⤝⤝

News of the British victory at Badon spread like a shockwave through the enemy territories in the east: from Kent in the south, through Anglia and the eastern seaboard of Lincolnshire and Yorkshire, and to the north as far as the small Saxon colony of Bernicia in Northumberland, word that Ochta and his new Saxon army had been annihilated by the Britons spread fear and foreboding amongst the Germanic settlers. Most now believed that Arthur was invincible: many of the more adventurous Saxons who had dared to move west of the river Blackwater to settle in the Thames Valley, now feared Arthur's retribution. Bereft of their husbands and sons, the warriors who had been massacred at Badon, many Saxon families abandoned their new homes in southern Britain and sailed back to their deserted villages in Saxony.

Yet following his landmark victory over the Saxons at Badon, Arthur could not claim that at last the land of Britain was free from the foreign invader, but he had succeeded in delivering a mighty blow that would make them think twice before launching another campaign of conquest in the west. Even so, Arthur did not drop his guard, for despite the prospect of peace, the threat of invasion was ever present in his mind. Unwilling to rest on the laurels of his now fearsome reputation, Arthur knew that his priority was to maintain a strong army by training new recruits at Wroxeter who would replace the warriors lost at Badon, and also allow him to reinforce the front-line garrisons that secured the heartland of Britain, namely York, Lincoln, Colchester and St Albans. Nor would Arthur neglect his second line of defence: the key fortresses of Cadbury, Gloucester, Warwick and Chester were the bulwarks that protected western Britain from invasion.

The strategic defence of Britain on this scale demanded significant financial support, not least from the treasuries of the allied kings, but also, despite clerical resistance, from the coffers of the Church. Yet inevitably, the final burden fell upon the people: ordinary Britons found themselves forcibly subscribing to Arthur's equitable system of taxation by payment, not in cash, but in kind. Farmers contributed grain, cattle, leather and wool, together with fresh fruit, vegetables, cheese and provisions for the soldiers; and in lieu of payment, skilled craftsmen, carpenters, farriers, blacksmiths and armourers, gave their services to the military free of charge in exchange for their daily bread, meat and beer. But it was the mineral wealth extracted from tunnels deep beneath the ground that provided Arthur with a seemingly endless source of wealth, a beneficial godsend that would guarantee the long-term survival of the British army. Tin from Cornwall, iron from Gwent, lead and silver from Powys, and copper from Gwynedd: these were the prized commodities controlled by the kings of Gwynedd. The monopoly over these minerals and metals had enabled them to become the wealthiest and most powerful kings of Britain.

Uther Pendragon, the Head Dragon of Gwynedd, controlled the largest copper mine in Europe. Just to the north of Llandudno, the Great Orme is a prominent headland that juts out into the Irish Sea; below the surface, a maze of tunnels were gouged into the dark red sandstone, penetrating the depths of an enormous copper mine. Such was the importance of the site that it was guarded by twin fortresses: Penrhyn Rhianedd to the east, known as Din Arth, or Arthur's Fort, and two miles to the west Deganwy Fortress was controlled by Catwallaun Lawhir. Thus Arthur and his brother shared the responsibility of defending the mine that was the fount of their family wealth.

When king Uther died, Arthur inherited the kingdom of Powys, and Catwallaun the kingdom of Gwynedd; they strengthened their guardianship of the Great Orme copper mine, and shared the revenue generated between them. But Catwallaun's untimely and unexpected death at Badon forced Arthur to take on his brother's responsibilities, not only to foster his young son Maelgwyn, but also to take control of the kingdom of Gwynedd until his nephew came of age as the new Prince of Gwynedd. Holding power over Gwynedd and Powys enhanced Arthur's prestige, increased his wealth, and strengthened his role as the Duke of Britain, the Commander in Chief of the British army.

Now, after his victory at Badon, and at the peak of his military career, Arthur ranked amongst the most powerful kings, but his wish was the same as it had been at the very beginning of his battle campaign: to win the battle for Britain, and to secure a lasting peace for the British people. To set the seal on his victory, Arthur re-affirmed peace treaties with the Angles and Saxons: Aelle's south Saxons were confined to their settlements along the South Downs from the river Arun to the river Ouse. Ochta's son Eormenric, who had inherited the kingdom of Kent after his father's death at Badon, now submitted to Arthur's demand, accepting that his western border would be defined by the river Blackwater. King Guechan of the East Angles was allowed to hold his existing settlements to the east of Thetford, and king Icel of the Mercian Angles was granted the freedom of coastal lands to the east of Lincoln, with the river Trent defining his western border and the Humber his northern boundary. Finally the small Anglian settlement of Deira to the east of York, as well as the old Saxon colony of Bernicia north of the river Tyne, agreed terms with Arthur that held their leaders to a peaceful occupation of their existing settlements.

To prevent further bloodshed, Arthur had drawn a line from north to south that divided the Britons from their unwelcome neighbours, the Angles and Saxons; he had, in effect, ceded one third of Britain to his enemies in order to secure what he hoped would be a lasting peace. The vivid memory of the bloody slaughter of Badon Hill became Arthur's long term deterrent to the enemy: let woe betide them if they crossed the line!

Arthur now turned his attention to the recalcitrant kings of the south-west: Cunomorus, also known as king Marcus of Dumnonia, and his son Constantine, were powerful overlords who held free reign over their territories, and who enjoyed a luxurious lifestyle sustained by wealth accrued from the mining and export of tin. Proud and independent, these men resented the authority of Arthur, who was nevertheless determined to levy a tax on the export of tin from their west-country ports.

Constantine complied with Arthur's demands, but his father Cunomorus was altogether more evasive. From Villa Banhedos, his fortress at Castle Dore overlooking Fowey, his sons administered the court and guarded his assets, while Cunomorus continued to annex estates in Brittany. From his new headquarters at Carhaix, Cunomorus dreamed of conquering all the territory to the north of the river Loire: for he planned to become king of all Brittany.

Cunomorus' absence from Dumnonia made it easier for Arthur to assert his authority over the south-west by force; without delay Arthur appointed Theodoric, his naval commander, to act as guardian of the western ports. Partly as a reward for his loyalty and dedication to the British cause, and partly in recompense for his new peacetime role in the west, Arthur bestowed Theodoric with land and estates close to St Ives, Falmouth and Padstow. With his ships riding at anchor in each port, Theodoric was able to patrol the north coast from St Ives to Tintagel, and along the south coast from Penzance to Plymouth.

With Theodoric's naval force on guard, Arthur's next priority was to find a loyal, intelligent officer who would safeguard his interests and ensure his suzerainty over the constituent kingdoms of Dumnonia, a country that reached from Glastonbury to Land's End. Close to home in Powys, Arthur found such a man in Modred ap Cawrdaf, his own brother-in-law, the husband of Guinevere's sister Gwenhwyfach. A kind-hearted and good natured commander, Modred was respected for his courage in battle and his courteous manner at court. As Provost of Cornwall, Modred, ever the diplomat, would handle the wayward kings with a velvet glove, persuading them to pay their taxes for the greater good and for the defence of the whole country of Britain; and should they fail to comply, the iron fist of Theodoric would come crashing down upon them.

Arthur's Battle for Britain had been fought through thirty years of bloody and gruelling conflict: a victory hard won, through sacrifice and dedication to duty, with the loss of many young lives. No fewer than eight battles had been fought against invading Angles and Saxons; three battles against the Picts; one against the marauding Irish, and another against the Irish colonists of Brecon and Dyfed. Far from a parochial theatre of war confined to the borders of Gwynedd and Powys, Arthur's battle campaigns had ranged from Caledonia in the north to Blackwater in the south-east, and from the east to the west coasts of Britain; furthermore, his final victory had been won in the very heart of southern Britain at Badon Hill, just a few miles to the west of the Lambourn Downs.

The years that followed Badon gave Arthur and his commanders an uneasy peace, for they had no way of knowing whether or not the peace would last; nevertheless, young men were recruited to train as warriors and the garrison commanders maintained a state of alert. Just as in wartime, they were prepared and ready for the call to battle.

But as the years went by, the new English kings honoured their treaties with Arthur, allowing Britons to return to peacetime occupations. In the towns and cities that had survived the destruction and privations of half a century of war, magistrates and officials held their positions and citizens carried out their work with renewed enthusiasm.

Arthur had championed the Christian cause, riding into battle, first with the image of the Holy Virgin, and finally with the cross of Christ as his emblem; to most Britons, this was affirmation that God had granted the greatest victory to their battle leader. Now, with their faith strengthened, Christians flocked to church and chapel to pray for peace and to give thanks to God for deliverance from their pagan enemies; but not one of them dared to cross the eastern border to spread the word of God to the Saxons.

Arthur was proud that his military policy had been successful for it brought the prospect of long term peace. With forceful leadership combined with his ability to cajole and coerce the independent kings, Arthur had gained support for his ideal of a united Britain under a central government, backed by a strong military force that upheld the law and defended the realm against foreign invasion.

A decade or more without war gave Arthur the opportunity to enjoy peacetime leisure pursuits and time to coach Cuneglas and Maelgwyn, the young princes who would one day inherit the kingdoms of Powys and Gwynedd. Hunting with dogs in the forests of Powys gave them the chance to perfect their riding skills and to become accurate spearmen; and sailing with Arthur in *Pridwen* to Ireland they gained some experience in navigation, beating the wind and tide, and taking the helm of the great sailing barge through a storm at sea. Fishing for salmon and trout in the clear rivers and streams of Wexford was a fair reward for their rough voyage across the Irish Sea.

In their fifteenth year, the young men were enrolled at Wroxeter to begin their military training, joining the other recruits without rank or privileges. Issued with a wooden sword and light round shield, their first lesson in the martial arts involved hours of practice sword-play against a large wooden post driven vertically into the ground. Once familiar with their weapons, recruits would be pitted against each other, thrusting and parrying in a mock battle and scoring points for successful body hits. Elm-shafted battle spears were issued for javelin throwing practice at lime-washed targets packed with straw; then, as the targets were moved progressively further away, points were awarded to the aspiring soldiers for the distance and accuracy of their throw. Only the fittest of men with the highest scores in weapon training were selected to join the cavalry, where they would have the good fortune to be trained in the fine art of mounted warfare by the highly experienced warriors who had fought in the Battle of Badon. Five years of intensive training saw these privileged young men develop from raw recruits to fearsome fighters, and their efforts were rewarded by a token from Arthur when they paraded before him as fully fledged warriors.

While garrisoned at Camulodunum during his training, Cuneglas had become an expert charioteer and had revived the ancient sport of chariot-racing at the Roman circus, the racing arena that had fallen out of use when the Romans abandoned Britain. On his return to Wroxeter, Cuneglas became Arthur's charioteer, employing his skill to drive his father across the country to meetings with the garrison commanders; on one occasion he drove Arthur all the way to Cornwall to visit Medrod, the new Provost of Cornwall, and Theodoric, his naval commander.

When rumours of a battle in the south-west reached Arthur, he decided to ride south to find out for himself, and as soon as they met, Medrod confirmed that Theodoric had routed Fingar's fleet when the Irish pirate sailed into St Ives Bay with a force of more than seven hundred men. Fingar had planned to join forces with

Guiner, his Breton ally, who sailed into Marazion on the south-coast with a smaller force; but sharp-eyed coastal scouts had raised the alarm an hour or more before the ships made landfall, giving Theodoric the chance to ambush Fingar and his pirates as they came ashore at Hayle in the fading light.

Guiner's fleet, heading from Brittany against a northerly wind, arrived late, and received a steely reception from Medrod's cavalry as they ran ashore; but on the north coast Fingar had fallen to Theodoric's sword; half his crew were killed on the beach at low tide, and his ships were torched. Guiner turned tail at the sight of British warriors, swiftly turning his prow downwind and slipping into the darkness: sparks from the glowing embers of burning ships followed him south.

Arthur congratulated Medrod and Theodoric for their rapid response and their successful action against the marauders; nevertheless, he was concerned that Guiner had escaped to Quimper where he could shelter under the wing of his uncle Maxentius. *So we have an enemy amongst our friends in Brittany,* declared Arthur, *we must keep a watchful eye on this rebellious adventurer!*

During the festivities that evening, Medrod updated Arthur on the news from Cunomorus at Carhaix, where he had found himself in the midst of a cockpit of feuding kings who would stop at nothing less than murder to achieve their own advancement and the acquisition of neighbouring territory. Arthur was shocked to hear that king Riwal of Dumnonie, who ruled northern Brittany from St Brieuc, had killed Meliau, the son of Arthur's good friend and ally, king Budic.

Budic and his brother Maxentius ruled western Brittany from Quimper, but just as Riwal attacked westward to take the towns of Leon and Achm, Maxentius ousted Budic from their shared kingdom, forcing him into exile. Fearing for his life, Budic embarked with his family and sailed for Demetia, hoping to find a safe refuge in South Wales.

Arthur was so enraged when he heard of king Budic's misfortune, that he resolved to do everything in his power to restore this good friend to his rightful kingdom, even if it meant leading an expedition to Brittany to censure Riwal and Maxentius by force. Theodoric volunteered to put his ships and men at Arthur's disposal; but first they would need to meet Budic to discuss a plan of action.

On the return journey from Cornwall, Arthur took the opportunity to visit South Cadbury to show Cuneglas the formidable fortress that he and Prince Cadwy had rebuilt many years before, making it the strongest fort in the west. Prince Cadwy was pleased to see them and welcomed his unexpected guests with jugs of mead and a supper of venison. At Cadbury Castle Cadwy maintained his cavalry troop at battle-readiness and patrolled from Glastonbury to Dunster on the north coast. As the protector of the eastern border of Dumnonia, Prince Cado played a vital role in

Arthur's strategic plan for the defence of Britain; a lifetime ally and a faithful friend, he shared Arthur's dream of a united and peaceful Britain.

Arthur was very excited about the prospect of mounting a military expedition to Brittany with the aim of restoring Budic to his rightful realm. Arthur had not drawn his sword in anger for over twenty years and a campaign in western Gaul would be a challenge, both for himself and for his commanders; but it would also serve to give his young warriors valuable battle experience.

Budic had sailed into Carmarthen Bay, navigating his ship into a safe anchorage in the sheltered estuary by Kidwelly. Agricola, Arthur's newly appointed Protector of Demetia, welcomed Budic to his castle in Carmarthen and dispatched a messenger to inform Arthur of the arrival of his royal guests. By return, Arthur invited king Budic, Agricola and Theodoric to attend a war council meeting at the Roman fort of Isca at Caerleon, for it was conveniently situated equidistant from Wroxeter and Carmarthen and only a few miles upstream from Casnewydd, Newport, on the Usk estuary, where Theodoric could berth his sailing barge.

Arthur welcomed Budic into the great hall of Caerleon Castle, offering his condolences to the king on the sad loss of Meliau his son, and vowing to seek vengeance upon his murderer, king Riwal. Budic told Arthur that Meliau's marriage to Riwal's daughter had set a seal on a new alliance of kings who ruled the northern provinces of Brittany; but Riwal's criminal act was all the more heinous, for he killed his son-in-law before stealing his lands.

All agreed that the prime target would be Quimper, the capital of Budic's province now usurped by Maxentius, his evil brother. Arthur proposed to launch the invasion within three months, long enough to muster ships, men, horses and supplies, allowing a maximum of eight weeks for the duration of the campaign. God willing, this would enable them to return before the September gales swept in from the Atlantic Ocean.

Agricola volunteered to muster a force of two hundred foot-soldiers from Demetia while Arthur pledged two troops of cavalry with the possibility of drafting reinforcements from Warwick or Gloucester; Theodoric would provide six ships from Cornwall for the invasion fleet, together with Budic's ship that would be laden with spare horses and supplies. Looking at his map, it appeared to Arthur that Caerleon would be the best place to rally the troops prior to embarkation at the port of Casnewydd, but Theodoric tactfully pointed out that if they could sail from Abertawe, Swansea, it would cut fifty miles off the voyage to Brittany and save half a day's sailing time. With a reluctant smile, Arthur agreed; he knew that a three hundred mile voyage would be quite long enough for the ship's crews, his soldiers and their horses.

Torches shed a flickering light on the grey stone walls of the refectory, and a huge log fire cast a warm glow over the war councillors as they sat down to supper. Arthur toasted his guest with a goblet of mead: *"To king Budic, and to our success in Brittany!"* All those present echoed the toast aloud. Then Arthur had a sudden flash of inspiration: *"By God!"* he exclaimed, *"We've completely forgotten about Cunomorus. There he is sitting in his fortress right in the middle of Brittany. Carhaix cannot be much more than forty miles from the coast; that's a day's march at the most!"* he exclaimed.

*"Excellent idea,"* agreed Theodoric, *"we must enlist him as our ally in this venture."*

*"But he only has a light bodyguard,"* added Budic. *"Then we'll have to reinforce his bodyguard,"* shouted Arthur, and turning towards Theodoric, *"On your return to Cornwall, send a messenger to Brittany to find out if Cunomorus is willing to join us, and if he is, we'll reward him with a shipload of good warriors in advance of our landing."*

A spirit of eager anticipation spread through Arthur's military headquarters at Wroxeter when he announced his plan to lead an expedition to Brittany: sparks flew from the smithies' furnaces as new swords and spearheads were forged and brightly honed; new shields were lime-washed to bring them to peak whiteness; and new recruits, keen for action, were trained to battle-readiness.

Now it was time for Arthur to reveal his campaign plan to Cuneglas and Maelgwyn and to delegate to them a measure of responsibility while he was away in Gaul. Since they had both declined to accompany him on the expedition, Arthur appointed them jointly to guard their most precious asset, the copper mine within the Great Orme.

*"Cuneglas, you will take over my fortress of Din Arth, and Maelgwyn, you will make Deganwy Castle your headquarters: both of you will share the responsibility of defending the Great Orme between the twin bastions of Din Arth and Deganwy,"* instructed Arthur.

*"But we cannot defend the mine without troops and weapons!"* exclaimed Maelgwyn. *"Then I will agree to post one hundred trained soldiers to reinforce each fortress against enemy attack,"* volunteered Arthur, *"but the revenue from our great copper mine must pay for its own protection and long term security."*

*"In your absence, I shall rule Gwynedd, for the kingdom is my birth-right,"* declared Maelgwyn.

*"Then I shall rule Powys!"* countered Cuneglas.

*"I think not,"* bellowed Arthur, with an angry scowl, *"not while I am alive as your king and commander,"* he declared, *"I shall appoint our cousin Modred ap Cawdraf to govern while I am in Brittany: he will move to Wroxeter, and both of you will obey his command."*

*"And Guinevere?"* asked Cuneglas. *"Guinevere will stay at Castell Dinas Bran under Bedivere's close protection, for he is my most trusted friend,"* replied Arthur.

Seven British ships broke through the early morning mist on the third day of their voyage from Abertawe. Arthur's invasion fleet looked resplendent with their square flaxen sails billowing in a fresh westerly breeze that powered the heavily laden sailing barges on their course due south. *"Ushant a mile off the port bow!"* shouted the lookout as he peered ahead through the thinning mist: *"Keep her steady to the south,"* Theodoric called to the helmsman, *"when Ile d'Ouessant is on our northern horizon we'll ease off to the south-east and run with the wind into the port of Douarnenez."*

*"And when will we arrive?"* enquired Arthur. *"Soon after mid-day, if this kind westerly holds,"* replied Theodoric, and he smiled reassuringly.

Cunomorus and his recently reinforced band of warriors stood guard on the quayside as the ships turned into wind, one by one coming in to berth alongside the old Roman wharf at Douarnenez. *"Welcome to Little Britain,"* he called to Arthur and Theodoric as they disembarked. *"We are very pleased to have your support,"* cried Arthur. *"Thank you for securing the port for our arrival. We'll make our base-camp here tonight and march at sunrise."*

By the time Budic's sailing barge had docked and discharged its cargo of horses and supplies, bright flames from the camp fires were licking around soot blackened cauldrons as the soldiers cooked their first hot meal of dried meat and vegetables. Arthur welcomed Budic to the command tent where Cunomorus and Theodoric had already laid a piece of flaxen sailcloth over a trestle table-top as a makeshift map.

*"Introduce us to your city,"* said Arthur, beckoning Budic towards the map-table and handing him a stick of charcoal. Budic drew a vertical line on the canvas to represent the river Steir; he then drew another line from north-east to south-west to show the river Odet: where the rivers met, he drew a square. *"Here is the ancient Roman 'Civitas Aquilonia' once famed for its sanctuary of Aphrodite, the Greek Goddess of Love,"* he explained, *"but now, we call our city by the Breton name "Kemper" meaning 'confluence,' for the city was built where the rivers Steir and Odet meet. As you can see, our supply of fresh water is guaranteed; and from here, the Odet estuary reaches fifteen miles to the sea with plentiful fishing."* King Budic completed his map by sketching in the coastline from Benodet to Douarnenez:

*"From our present position, we will only have to march fifteen miles to reach Quimper,"* he said reassuringly, *"but our obstacle is the bridge over the river Steir: we*

*will need to cross to the east bank of the river before we can attack the main gateway into the city."*

*"It'll be no good trying to get the whole army over that bridge two by two,"* declared Arthur, *"we'll need to advance on both sides of the river at the same time."*

*"We crossed the river here,"* Cunomorus volunteered, pointing to a position on the map a few miles east of Douarnenez. *"This ford is further upstream, where the river is much narrower, and we can get the horses across with ease."*

*"Excellent!"* exclaimed Arthur, *"then Cunomorus and Theodoric will lead the attack on Quimper from the east bank of the river Steir; I will accompany Budic and we will take the bridge from the west. We'll join forces at the north gate for the main assault on the city."*

At first light the staccato horn-blast of reveille pierced the ears of the slumbering soldiers. Then, as dawn broke over the distant Monts d'Arrée, Arthur rallied his cavalry and foot-soldiers, giving Cunomorus a head-start to cross the river Steir before leading his troop south towards Quimper. At mid-day Arthur and Budic advanced towards the bridge with some concern, for there was no sign of Cunomorus. Suddenly, a detachment of cavalry led by Maxentius charged from the north gate of the Roman fortress. Ordered to attack across the bridge, the Breton soldiers ran head-first into Arthur's front line of cavalry who felled their opponents, spearing them in pairs as they crossed the bridge. Then, with half the enemy troop fallen, Arthur and Budic led their cavalry over the bridge, swords slashing, cutting and thrusting, they unhorsed their opponents and tipped the enemy soldiers over the parapets into the river below.

Just as Arthur had reached the east bank, Cunomorus and Theodoric appeared from the north, launching into the remnants of the enemy troop, and allowing Arthur's cavalry to cross the river unhindered. Maxentius, realising that he was out-numbered, beat a hasty retreat towards the north gate, followed by a few of his cavalry who were closely harried by British soldiers: such was the force of their headlong charge that the Breton defenders who attempted to close the city gates were either speared or trampled to death by the onslaught of horses and armed warriors.

Maxentius took refuge in the Roman Principia, the headquarters building that he was now using as a palatial villa. Women and children screamed and ran for their lives when Theodoric's men rushed forward with drawn swords to attack the palace guards; then Arthur charged forward, pressing through the melée to challenge Maxentius to a duel. Steel clashed against steel, until, with a forceful swing, Arthur flicked Maxentius' sword from his hand, and as the sword went spinning to the ground, Arthur pinned Maxentius to the wall, his sword pressing into Maxentius' throat.

"*Spare him!*" cried Budic, who had followed Arthur into the Principia, "*I cannot murder my own brother! We must negotiate a truce.*"

Maxentius eyes pierced Arthur like the steely stare of a trapped tiger as he writhed under the scales of his black chain-mail; but his captor was in no mood to negotiate: "*Half your kingdom or your life,*" growled Arthur, as he pressed the keen edge of Excalibur into Maxentius' thick neck. "*Spare me!*" he pleaded with Arthur, "*I give you my word that I will surrender half my kingdom to Budicus.*"

By the time Maxentius and his retinue had departed towards the northern region of Leon, the citizens of Quimper had flocked to the streets to cheer the return of their rightful king. Budic, in thanks to Arthur and Theodoric, celebrated his restoration with a feast, extending an open invitation to his honoured guests to stay in Quimper for as long as they wished; and Cunomorus sealed his dynastic allegiance to the king by asking Budic for his daughter's hand in marriage.

In a gesture of goodwill, Cunomorus seconded his British squadron to reinforce Budic's depleted bodyguard while Arthur rounded up a corps of healthy recruits to train as soldiers, making it clear that they would ultimately be responsible for the defence and security of their own country.

Six weeks after deposing Maxentius, Arthur and Theodoric bade farewell to Budic and returned with their forces to Douarnenez. Keen to barter for supplies while he was in Gaul, and with time in hand, Arthur took the opportunity to sail south to Nantes where shipmasters from the Mediterranean traded wine, olive oil, and spices from the east, luxuries that were highly prized in Britain. Theodoric loaded four ships with soldiers and horses for the return voyage to Abertawe, leaving two sailing barges with a master and crew under Arthur's command for the excursion to Nantes.

Two days sailing brought Arthur's ships to the wide estuary of the river Loire; from there it would take the best part of a day to reach Nantes, thirty miles upstream. As the sun went down, Arthur steered his ships to the south of Ile de Nantes, turning about the eastern tip of the island to head up the northern channel towards the long quay of Porte Saint-Pierre, on the north bank of the river.

For three days Arthur bargained with wine merchants and haggled with merchant traders from the Mediterranean, bartering his cargo of copper, tin and lead, for wine from the Loire and Burgundy, olive oil from Spain, and frankincense from the Dhofor region of Southern Arabia. This most expensive commodity Arthur bought as a gift to the chapel at Castell Dinas Bran, to provide the sweet incense for festival services.

With his trading done and the precious goods stowed securely in the ships' holds, Arthur was pleased to receive an invitation from Caradoc the Duke of Brittany, to join him for a celebration of Holy Mass at the Romanesque Cathedral of St Peter. Founded in the fourth century, the cathedral church was an inspiring edifice to the work of Martin, Bishop of Tours, who had first converted the Nantais to Christianity. Kneeling at the altar, the Duke of Britain and the Duke of Brittany humbled themselves before God, and received the consecrated bread and wine as token of the Body and Blood of Christ, in remembrance of their Saviour's sacrifice for all mankind.

Inspired by this simple act of faith, when kings knelt together with carpenters, shepherds and fishermen, Arthur knew in his heart that all men were equal in the sight of God.

Escorted by the Duke's household guards, Arthur and Caradoc rode the short distance from the cathedral to the imposing Roman fortress. Built on the command of Julius Caesar during his conquest of Gaul, and later strengthened when the Emperor Probius re-organised the vulnerable defences of the Empire's north-western front in the third century, the walls of this mighty fortress stood intact, with its garrison safeguarding ships in the Porte Saint-Pierre to the south, and defending the city of Nantes to the north.

Caradoc's castle reminded Arthur of Portus Ardaoni, Porchester Castle, for its walls and bastions were almost identical in design; but within the great square enclosure Caradoc had built a large timber feasting hall, flanked by the garrison huts, grain stores and workshops that were needed to maintain his militia.

That evening the garrison guards lit open fires and turned spit roasts of pork that were served to Arthur's men with a generous supply of beer and rustic bread, while Arthur and his commanders joined Caradoc and Ysenne, his beautiful wife, for supper in the refectory of the great hall.

"*How fortunate you are to have won two decades of peace!*" Caradoc exclaimed, beckoning Arthur to take the seat of honour on his right hand side, "*A fair reward for all your battling, and for all the bloodshed,*" he added with a wry smile.

"*Our peace is a fragile blessing,*" affirmed Arthur, "*We have enemies in every quarter and we have to be vigilant: we are constantly on guard.*"

"*For us there can be no peace!*" exclaimed Caradoc, "*the Franks threaten us from the east and our Breton cousins in the north forever squabble amongst themselves.*"

"*It is so sad when the kings of our provinces are in disagreement,*" explained Ysenne, "*when wars spring up brothers fall, spoils are seized and houses are burned; and the land is made desolate to slaughter and solitude.*"

"*And what of Clovis, the mighty conqueror of Gaul?*" enquired Arthur.

"*Clovis the Frank is dead, and his kingdom quartered, divided by the rightful law that governs the inheritance of kings and princes,*" declared Caradoc, "*Now Theodoric* rules Rheims, Chlodomer holds Orleans, Clothar occupies Soissons, and Childebert commands Paris: so now we have four Merovingian kings on our doorstep, instead of one."

"But we bring you some good cheer," cried Arthur, with an encouraging smile, "We have restored Budic to his headquarters in Quimper and sealed his alliance with Cunomorus; and we have deprived the venomous Maxentius of half his kingdom and booted him off to the north."

"Then you must add Maxentius and his young beagle Guiner to your list of enemies," declared Caradoc.

"I have indeed done so," assured Arthur. Then he thanked Caradoc and Ysenne for their hospitality and kindness and bade them farewell, returning to his ship before midnight.

At sunrise, just as Arthur's crews hoisted their great square sails in readiness for the long voyage home, a colourful caique from Alexandria sailed up to the quayside with a cargo of silks and spices from the far-east. This was an opportunity not to be missed, and Arthur went aboard to buy a roll of pure silk, as a special gift for Guinevere on his return to Castell Dinas Bran.

With a light southerly breeze abeam to port, the heavily laden ships slipped their mooring lines and sailed slowly downstream from Nantes towards the Atlantic. The young skipper, who had been well trained in seamanship and navigation under Theodoric's strict command, went over his planned course with Arthur. "By midnight we'll have Belle Ile abeam to starboard," he explained, "then we'll steer north-west until tomorrow night, when hopefully we should find Ile de Sein twenty miles or so to the east."

"Then we head north," suggested Arthur. "Yes, until we reach Land's End," replied the skipper, "and tonight, if we have a clear sky, we'll be able to steer a true course by the North Star. Then, for the last leg of the course, we'll steer north-east for Dyfed; if the wind holds we'll be there by mid-day on the fourth day of our voyage."

"That's good," said Arthur, "for it will be exactly eight weeks since we departed; we've certainly done well in that time."

Three armed scouts reined in their horses at the cliff-top as they watched Arthur's two ships sail slowly into Abertawe harbour. The Red Dragon of Arthur's pennant unfurled and caught the breeze at the mast-head of the leading barge, confirming his return to Britain. It was the signal that Maelgwyn's scouts had been waiting for. As the ships docked and began to unload their cargo, one scout galloped north to inform Maelgwyn of Arthur's return, while the others kept watch on the quayside from a safe distance.

Before nightfall, Arthur's young soldiers loaded the ship's cargo onto carts;

covered with flaxen canvas and securely lashed down, they were made ready for the one-hundred mile march back to Wroxeter. After four days and nights at sea his men were weary, and they all cheered in unison when Arthur called the march to a halt at the Roman fort of Nidum, Neath, just four miles north of Abertawe. Here in their own tents and on firm ground, they would at last be assured of a good night's rest.

Early the next morning, Arthur led his brigade of cavalry across the river Neath, following the valley that took the route of the Sarn Helen, an ancient trackway that linked Glamorgan with Gwynedd over a distance of one hundred and sixty miles. Winding in a north-easterly direction through the Rheola Forest, the trackway led to the small fort of Coelbren before climbing towards Forest Fawr in the heart of the Brecon Beacons.

With a vanguard of fifty armed cavalry, and a rear-guard of another fifty horsemen, the caravan of precious goods was well protected; but the heavily laden pack-horses dragged the progress of the column to a slow walking pace. Arthur had hoped to travel at least fifty miles each day, his yardstick the average distance covered by the Roman postal service; but as they climbed slowly through the mountain pass between the high peaks of Fan Gihirych and Fan Llia, he realised that he would be lucky to achieve thirty miles a day.

By nightfall, as the weary troop reached Brecon, Arthur decided to make camp in the old Roman fort of Y Gaer, a border fort built in the first century to accommodate a force of five hundred cavalry. The original timber barracks had long since vanished, allowing Arthur's men to pitch their tents in the central grass compound of the fort.

Maelgwyn's scouts, following at a safe distance, reached the south bank of the river Usk at nightfall, to find a group of Arthur's soldiers bathing in the cool moonlit water of the river; but the onlookers remained hidden on the opposite bank, holding their cover until the bathers had refreshed themselves and returned to the camp. Then the spies parted company: one heading for Gwynedd to report to his master, the other remaining within sight of Y Gaer, waiting to track Arthur's progress north.

In the small hours of the morning a lightning bolt jolted Arthur out of his dream: it was the prelude to a late autumn storm that blasted the night with thunder and lightning, bolting jagged flashes of fire into the Brecon peaks. Unable to sleep, Arthur twisted and turned on his straw filled palliasse, forced to listen to the deafening overture that marked a seasonal change in the weather. His pleasant thoughts of returning to Castell Dinas Bran, where he would hold a magnificent feast to celebrate his homecoming and his re-union with Guinevere, were dashed by the sudden shock of the storm.

Arthur was not superstitious by nature, for he had faith in God and trusted in the beneficence of the Lord; but with the sudden clash of the storm, Arthur imagined that he was once more locked in battle. He arose before dawn with a deep sense of foreboding, acutely aware that he neither knew his enemy, nor could he tell from which direction they might strike.

Anxious to take up the reins of government, Arthur spurred his men northward, following the Honddu Valley from Brecon to Builth Wells and onward towards the Ithon Valley. By sundown they had marched another thirty miles, and Arthur called a halt at Castle Collen; men and horses had made good progress but they were weary and needed refreshment. Arthur was concerned that at their present rate it would take another two days to reach Wroxeter, sixty miles away. Now low on provisions, his resourceful troopers caught fish to cook over their camp fires; but with their attention devoted to appeasing their hunger with a makeshift supper, no-one noticed the shadowy figure of Maelgwyn's scout riding north along the Roman road to Caersws.

At dawn, Arthur challenged his troops to march onward to Forden Gaer: if they could cover forty miles by nightfall, they would find shelter at this small vexillation fort close to the river Severn, and hope to complete their journey to Wroxeter the following morning.

কপকপ্৵কপ৵

Arthur's absence in Brittany had given Maelgwyn's lust for power and Cuneglas' greed for wealth the opportunity to blossom into a treacherous conspiracy of cousins whose foremost aim was to bring Arthur's reign to an abrupt end. Arthur's demise would enable them to claim their rightful inheritance as the Princes of Gwynedd and Powys, sharing the bountiful wealth of the Great Orme between them to become the most powerful kings in Britain.

Thus the last act in the dramatic story of Arthur's reign was staged by his nephew Maelgwyn, who was in league with Cuneglas, Arthur's own son. Masterminding a clever but devious plan that they determined to expedite with brute force, the cousins conspired to draw Arthur and his army into a tactical trap where he would be outnumbered and overwhelmed; a trap from which there would be no escape. If one or more of Arthur's known enemies were invited to play the role of protagonist, confronting Arthur and challenging him to battle, then his subsequent demise would be put down to enemy action, and they would escape blameless from the scene of the fateful battle.

Arthur's enemies were not difficult to find. Messengers were dispatched by sea to Maxentius in Leon, and to Serach in Dun Laoghaire. Maxentius, still smarting from the chagrin of his eviction from Quimper by Arthur, was only too pleased to sponsor his nephew Guiner on a combined raid that would do some damage to Arthur in return; and Serach welcomed the chance to avenge the death of his father-in-law king Illan, killed by Arthur at Chester.

Maelgwyn and Cuneglas together were able to muster a force of only two-hundred men, namely the warriors given to them by Arthur to guard the Great Orme. If they were to win a battle against Arthur, they would need to conscript at least another hundred men; but they would also have to find a way of turning the loyalty of soldiers who were faithful to Arthur.

The royal cousins declared their intention to depose Arthur and seize power in Gwynedd and Powys. They demanded an immediate oath of allegiance from the guards: those who refused were thrown into the dungeon of Deganwy Castle, strapped to the rack, and pulled apart limb by limb until they either renounced their oath to Arthur, or expired from ruthless torture.

Cuneglas employed his own expedient method of turning a soldier's allegiance by forcing the man to witness the torture and dismembering of a close relative: wives, daughters, mothers; all were threatened, some sacrificed as hapless victims of Cuneglas' callous and remorseless butchery of his own people: it was the beginning of a reign of terror that would sink Britain into a dark and bloody pit of civil strife.

From the moment Arthur stepped ashore at Abertawe, he was a marked man. Maelgwyn's scouts, his eyes and ears, observed Arthur's every move: they tracked his progress and reported back to their commander at Deganwy. The Sarn Helen, the highway made famous by Helen of the Hosts, wife of the Emperor Maximus, who established the route in the fourth century as a military link between the Roman forts of Carnarvon, Caerleon and Carmarthen, gave Maelgwyn's first messenger the fastest road to the north. From Abertawe he followed the Neath Valley to the Roman road at Sennybridge and turned west towards Llandovery; reaching the old fort of Pumsaint, the sentinel post for the Roman gold mine at Dolaucothi, he then turned north. From Llanycrwys, the Sarn Helen tracked due north via Pont Lanio and Bronnant, crossing the Rheidol Valley at Pen-llwyn; then, passing through Machynlleth and Dolgellau, the road skirted Ffestiniog before running along the eastern edge of Snowdonia to the fort of Caer Lugwy near Bryn y Gefeilian, overlooking the Swallow Falls. From there the mountain highway descended, following the Vale of Conwy to Canovium, the Roman fortress at Caerhun that had once controlled the Conwy estuary.

Riding through most of the night and braving the elements of the storm, the scout reached Deganwy late on the second day of his gruelling journey. Gaunt, hungry and aching with exhaustion from riding over one hundred and sixty miles, he announced the news of Arthur's arrival in the south. Maelgwyn shrewdly estimated that Arthur would have already advanced sixty or seventy miles towards Wroxeter; there was no time to lose. Maelgwyn moved swiftly to put his master-plan into action.

At dusk, Cuneglas, leading his warband of one hundred and fifty warriors, galloped throught the gateway of Din Arth, and headed south towards his campaign base at Caersws. Maelgwyn rallied his troops and marched to Caerhun, where he dispatched a signalling party to Pen y Gaer with instructions to light a beacon on the summit of Foel Fras, one of the highest mountain peaks on the northern edge of the Carneddau ridge. Thirty miles to the west, Serach's lookout, perched on the north face of Holyhead Mountain, saw tongues of fire streaking slowly skyward from Foel Fras: it was the signal to attack. Serach ordered his men to oars, and one by one his ships slipped the safe harbour anchorage of Holyhead and sailed south into the darkness.

The signallers returned to Caerhun just before daybreak. A flicker of light from Holyhead confirmed that the Foel Fras beacon had been seen and understood. Now Maelgwyn could advance, knowing that all his forces were moving towards their strategic targets. At dawn he led his war-band out onto the Sarn Helen, tracking through the forest to Swallow Falls and over the pass to the east of Mynedd Cribau. Crossing the Afon Lledr at Pont y pant, Maelgwyn forced his troops forwards at a relentless pace, pushing through the rugged mountainous terrain towards Ffestiniog. By sunset, Maelgwyn had reached his objective: the disused vexillation fort at Brithdir, to the east of Dolgellau, that would provide him with a safe base for the night. Weary after the forty mile march, his men pitched their tents and refreshed themselves in the Afon Wnion, a clear mountain river that ran close by.

❧ ❧ ❧ ❧

A solitary mounted warrior stood guard in the eastern gateway of Caersws, his face in shadow, silhouetted against the mid-day sun. Suddenly the clatter of cavalry approaching from the north spurred Maelgwyn's scout into action, and he rode out to meet Cuneglas.

*"I passed Arthur before midnight at Castell Collen,"* he shouted, *"he'll be here by mid-afternoon if he takes the Roman road towards the Severn Valley, but if he marches up the Ithon valley, then I would expect him to make Forden Gaer by night-fall."*

*"Good work!"* called Cuneglas, *"We'll prepare a welcoming party."*

The strategic value of Caersws was not lost on Cuneglas, who realised that it would give him a central base in a commanding position from which he could first intercept Arthur on his return from Brittany, and later lead a rear-guard action against him. Built by Agricola in 78 AD, Caersws was designed with triple ditch and rampart defences enclosing an area just under six hundred feet square, just large enough to accommodate a cavalry unit of five hundred men. Of great strategic importance in the Romans' conquest of the rebellious Ordovices of mid-Wales, the fort was named *Mediomanum* '*The Central Fist*.' From here, the Romans delivered crushing blows to defeat the unruly tribes of western Britain.

Another great advantage of Mediomanum's position was that it was situated at the centre of the river sources, for within a radius of seven miles, over twenty fresh water springs gave rise to tributaries of the Severn and the river Ithon; but the arm of the military reached out ten miles to the east of the fort, where it took control of the eastern ridge of Mount Plynlimon, the source of the river Severn. Mediomanum later became known as *The Fortress of the Sources* or *Caer Sws*, a name derived from the old French word 'sors,' meaning *"to spring forth."*

But Cuneglas had discovered a spring of a different kind, a spring that oozed a black, evil smelling slurry: less than four miles from Wroxeter, and just to the west of the Roman road that ran south from Wroxeter to Bravonium, Cuneglas had located the Romans' source of pitch that was used extensively in the construction of their military buildings at Wroxeter. However, Cuneglas had another idea in mind for the ivory black crude oil that seeped profusely from the strata of the underlying sandstone; his discovery would enable him to introduce weapons of fire to his arsenal, but the source would remain his closely guarded secret.

The afterglow of sunset had faded from the western horizon when Maelgwyn's third scout rode wearily through the weathered oak gateway of Caersws. He had been in the saddle for three long days, tracking Arthur's march for a hundred miles or more, from Abertawe to Forden Gaer. Dismounting in front of Cuneglas' battle tent, he was clearly relieved to have completed his mission. *"Arthur has reached Forden Gaer and his men are making camp for the night,"* he reported.

*"Then we shall join him!"* shouted Cuneglas, *"For now it is time to eat , drink mead, and be merry,"* he exclaimed, as he mounted his great stallion, calling his bodyguard to follow him to Forden. *"Greet me with your news at dawn,"* he ordered. Maelgwyn's scout raised his right hand in acknowledgement.

Arthur's dishevelled caravan of cavalry and cart-horses pulled off the Roman road into Forden Gaer sometime after dusk. The exhausted men lit camp fires and erected their tents ready for a night in the fort; but their rations were low, with barely enough to feed a dozen men. A wave of discontent spread through the camp, and Arthur wondered how he could appease his hungry men. He paused for a moment's thought; then, with a deft swing of his sword he cut the bonds from one of the wagons, allowing several casks of wine to roll to the ground. *"Help yourselves to a taste of fine Burgundy!"*

he shouted, *"A small reward for all your hard work, and for your faithful company."*

His soldiers cheered and rushed forward to share the wine with the whole company; but at that moment a tall imposing warrior cantered through the fort's gateway, bringing his mount to a sudden halt as he approached Arthur: *"Welcome home father,"* he said in a gruff voice, betraying no emotion. Dismounting, he came forward to embrace Arthur.

*"Cuneglas, my son, it is good to see you!"* exclaimed Arthur, *"but how did you know of our return?"* he asked. *"Word travels,"* replied Cuneglas curtly, *"and a good thing that it does, for now we can welcome you back to Powys."* With that he beckoned a small troop of his own men into the fort, each laden with prime hanks of ham, ribs of pork, freshly baked bread and fruit, beer and mead; enough to make a feast for hungry men.

Very soon, with rib-roasts spitting over open fires and strong wine flowing freely, the air of gloom soon dissipated into an atmosphere of good cheer and hearty merriment. Cuneglas assured Arthur that all was well: while Medrod and Bedivere had supervised military training at Wroxeter, both he and Maelgwyn had strengthened their defences at the Great Orme.

*"But you and your men came in from the south,"* observed Arthur. *"Yes indeed, because we are at Caersws for a few days,"* Cuneglas hesitated for a moment, *"working to clear the springs and watercourses before winter,"* he reassured Arthur, as he filled his father's goblet to the brim with Burgundy.

By midnight the joyful celebrations had turned into more of a serious drinking competition between Arthur's exhausted men and Cuneglas' troopers who were fighting fit and ready for a challenge; but the plentiful supply of strong red wine, reinforced by mead when the wine ran dry, eventually knocked Arthur's men into a drunken stupor. One by one they fell to the ground. Even Arthur was *meddw-rhawd,* 'as drunk as a trooper;' he had been taken off-guard by the strength of the matured Burgundy wine.

*"Take care of the men!"* he called to Cuneglas as he crashed down into his tent. *"I will,"* replied Cuneglas, *"Sleep well!"*

࿐࿐࿐࿐

*"To arms! To arms!"* cried Maelgwyn's scout as he rode through the rows of tents at Forden Gaer where Arthur and his men slumbered beyond day-break.

Cuneglas, still fully armed after the night's vigil, woke Arthur, and his guards turned Arthur's troops out of their tents, throwing buckets of cold water over them to shock them out of their dreams.

*"Report to Arthur,"* ordered Cuneglas, ushering the scout into the commander's tent.

*"Seven warships have pulled ashore on the long beach above Borth, my lord,"* advised the scout. *"Who is our enemy?"* asked Arthur. *"Serach and his Irish seadogs, with five ships; and Guiner's pirates, in two ships that bear the standard of Maxentius,"* revealed the scout.

*"And their position?"* enquired Arthur. *"Moving north towards Machynlleth,"* the scout replied, *"but they are on foot and their progress is slow."*

*"Then we could intercept them at Aberangell, where the Afon Dyfi valley narrows between the hills,"* declared Arthur. *"Ride on to Wroxeter: call Medrod and Bedivere to arms, and tell them to bring every fighting man they have, even the recruits,"* commanded Arthur. *"We'll await their arrival; but we'll do battle this very day."*

*"Cuneglas, send your scout to alarm Maelgwyn at Deganwy, although I fear he is too far north to reach us in time for this action,"* said Arthur.

*"I will return to Caersws and prepare for battle,"* replied Cuneglas.

*"Follow us westward to Mallwyd; we will advance when Modred's reinforcements arrive, and that I trust will be soon after noon, or we'll not engage the enemy before sunset,"* exclaimed Arthur.

Enemy numbers had not been confirmed, but Arthur made a shrewd guess that Serach's combined war-band would number between two hundred and seventy, and three hundred fighting men. Arthur's cavalry, combined with the reserve force from Wroxeter, would at least equal that number. Cuneglas' squadron would tip the balance in Arthur's favour: four mounted Britons to every three enemy footsoldiers: Serach's men would be scythed to the ground like wheat at harvest time.

Arthur and his men were the worse for wear: most were still inebriated from the celebrations of the night before, and in no fit state for battle; but the cold, fresh running water of the Severn offered some reprieve. Every man was ordered to strip-off and take a dip in the river before running half a mile or more back to the fort to re-arm. Arthur himself led the exercise, for he would never ask more of his men than he was prepared to do himself. Ever the soldier's soldier, Arthur cherished, honoured and rewarded his warriors, and they, in turn, pledged their loyalty, love and respect to their leader and their king.

Killing time before a battle, when fear strikes at the young heart like a poisoned arrow, wrenching the guts and weakening the knees, is the young soldier's greatest challenge; and that day many young lads with pale faces and shaking hands went about the business of preparing for battle, whetting their swords, adjusting their mounts' bridles, donning their mail tunics and desperately trying to conquer the fear that welled up inside them.

Arthur had the more sanguine attitude of the experienced battle-hardened commander: he preferred to pass the time with the challenge of a game of chess, a battle game that kept his mind alert and responsive, so that when the time came for action he would be relaxed, clear-minded and fearless. He caught the attention of one of his troop commanders:

*"Young Owain!"* he called, *"Come! We have time for a battle of wits before our reinforcements arrive."* Arthur pulled his chessboard from its worn leather case and placed it upon the folding oak map-table outside his campaign tent. Owain gasped in wonder at its simple beauty: the board was crafted from pure silver, inlaid with black squares of polished Whitby jet that contrasted with the etched cross-hatched squares of silver. The chess-men had been carefully crafted to complement the precious materials of the board, fashioned from solid silver and polished jet.

*"Very well,"* said Arthur, *"let battle commence!"*

An almost religious silence fell upon the players as the game progressed: pawns were lost equally on both sides, and then serious tactics were brought into play. Arthur admired his young opponent for his youthful looks and his quick-minded reactions to his own carefully considered moves, while Owain sensed that Arthur was always planning three moves ahead, anticipating every advance, and keeping a tactical surprise up his sleeve, true to form as an experienced battle commander. But he also saw the sign of weariness in Arthur's eyes; he did not know Arthur's age, but guessed that he must be in his mid-to-late sixties. Tall and strong, he could still wield a sword as powerfully as a warrior half his age; but the furrows in his brow seemed more marked than ever before and his face appeared pale and sallow beneath his distinctive grey beard. For a moment Arthur's attention wandered, and Owain seized the opportunity to move his Queen into the attack, close to Arthur's King. Arthur moved a Knight to protect his King, but Owain took Arthur's Knight with one of his own. Now, between his Castle, Knight, and Queen, Arthur was trapped: *"Check Mate!"* cried Owain triumphantly.

*"You caught me off-guard for a moment,"* protested Arthur, *"What was I thinking?"*

*"Well done Owain!"* declared Arthur with a generous smile, *"You have beaten your commander,"* and after a moment's thought, *"and for that achievement there must be some special reward. Today you will take nine of your troopers and guard the wagons and the precious goods from Nantes."* As he spoke Arthur packed away his chess-men and handed the leather case to Owain, *"And look after this for me until I return, for today you are excused from battle."* Arthur moved towards the wagon nearest to his tent, and pulled out the roll of silk, *"and if by chance I do not return, please give this to my Lady Guinevere at Castell Dinas Bran, with my blessing."*

*"I shall honour your command, my lord,"* replied Owain, *"but I pray, sire, for your safe return."*

At that moment Modred and Bedivere arrived at Forden with a force of two hundred men from Wroxeter. Arthur explained his plan to advance twenty five miles to the west, following the Banwy Valley to Mallwyd, where his scouts would report the enemy's position. When the number of the enemy host was known, Arthur would decide how to deploy Cuneglas' squadron; until then, he was content to hold his son's troop in reserve.

Bedivere suggested that it might be wise to hold off the attack until the morning: after a fifty mile trek from Wroxeter the horses would be tired, and his young recruits unready for a battle just before sunset. But Arthur was impatient and would have none of it.

*"I'll not have Serach and his pirates wandering at will around the borders of Gwynedd and Powys,"* he shouted angrily: *"We will push him back into the sea before nightfall."*

Arthur took up his spear and shield, mounted his white stallion and led his troops to the west, crossing the river Severn by the ford at Rhyd y Groes, followed by Modred and Bedivere with their cavalry squadrons in full battle array. After marching for ten miles, Arthur brought his army to a halt at Llanfair Caereinion, where the Roman road from Caersws crossed the river Banwy, and where he expected to find Cuneglas marching north to meet him; but there was no sign of Cuneglas or his the squadron from Caersws, and following a pause to refresh the horses, Arthur decided to move forward: *"March on!"* he called to his troops, *"For we must engage the enemy before sunset."*

Leading his small army through the narrow neck of the Dugoed Valley, Arthur crossed the river by the oak-timbered bridge below Cwm Cewydd, followed the river bank for a while, and brought his men to rest in a pleasant meadow beside the stream. Looking out across the Dyfi Valley, Arthur stared defiantly at the waning autumnal sun, now sinking slowly towards the western horizon and casting long shadows from the surrounding hills. For a moment he marvelled at the beauty of this tranquil scene: to his right the fast flowing Dugoed streamed through verdant pastures to join the Afon Dyfi as it meandered south towards its wide estuary. Ahead, majestic hills rose steeply to form the western escarpment of the long glen, with the peaks of Mount Camlan and Mount Aran distinctly silhouetted against the early evening sun; and to the north, Mount Moeldyvi appeared to enclose the vale like an amphitheatre; while the highest mount, Esgair Ddu, shaped the long, steep escarpment that defined the eastern reach of the valley.

Arthur's moment of meditation was rudely interrupted by the sudden arrival of two of his scouts who had galloped into Mallwyd from the south, leaving a dust-trail along the highway track. With a sense of urgency they announced that the enemy had reached Aberangell and were now moving north towards Mallwyd. Arthur realised that he had lost the opportunity to trap the enemy at the narrowest neck of the valley just north of Aberangell, where the river winds closer to the mountainside; he called his commanders forward to the cross-roads at the centre of Mallwyd to look for the enemy war-band and to get the lie of the land ahead.

The Afon Dyfi Valley, towards Maes y Camlan, Gwynedd, North Wales.
Photo, © Aaron Jones

As a glow of evening sunlight streamed along the Dyfi Valley, Arthur concluded that this would be the perfect arena for the battle: Maes y Camlan, the field below Mount Camlan was wide enough to muster his force, and long and level enough to allow a five hundred yards cavalry charge at the enemy.

*"Call our warriors to arms!"* shouted Arthur to his commanders, *"We'll advance to battle positions as soon as we see the enemy."* Then, as Arthur scanned the valley to the south, he was surprised to see an elderly priest approaching him from a small chapel that lay just to the east of the highway. *"My name is Tydecho,"* he explained, *"and this is the chapel that I built to serve the people of Powys."*

*"And my name is Arthur, and I too serve the people of Powys,"* exclaimed Arthur,

*"but I am about to engage in battle, and you should return to the safety of your chapel."*

*"I am at your service,"* replied Tydecho humbly. *"Then you may give us all your blessing before we fight,"* said Arthur, *"and I pray that you will give those who die this day a Christian burial."*

A dust cloud sweeping up from the highway to the south gave advance warning of Serach's arrival: they were now just over a mile away from Mallwyd, and Arthur turned his horse around to meet Modred and Bedivere.

*"God be with you, my lord!"* called Tydecho. *"And with you!"* Arthur shouted as he galloped away.

Arthur headed his own troop as they marched forward, crossing the main highway onto the trackway that led towards Pont Mallwyd, a narrow bridge over the Afon Dyfi; half-way down this dusty track Arthur wheeled his cavalry to the left, and marshalled his warriors across the widest reach of Maes y Camlan.

*"Take up your battle formations!"* he shouted, as Modred and Bedivere brought their squadrons into line, ready to charge. Half a mile away Serach and Guiner led their war-band off the highway and down towards a narrow stretch of grassland beside the river; then, as they emerged at the southern end of Maes y Camlan, the pirates spread out into a disorderly shield line, three ranks deep, shouting in unison and clashing their swords on their shields to alarm their opponents.

But it was Serach who was most alarmed when he saw Arthur's force drawn up in front of him in an immaculate wedge formation that comprised three echelons of cavalry with thirty mounted warriors to each wing of an echelon, supported by two single columns of cavalry on each side of the main force that were ready to attack from each wing of the formation. Arthur stood proudly at the centre of the force, his spear deflected; Modred ap Cawdraf commanded the second echelon, with Bedivere to the rear, leading his squadron of recruits. Behind the standard bearer, Arthur had drawn up a line of sixty cavalry in reserve, ordered to hold the rear-guard position until reinforcements were called upon.

Serach was duly concerned: there was no sign of Maelgwyn or Cuneglas, and he began to wonder if he had been lured into a trap, only to be slaughtered by the hand of Arthur. He silenced his men, and pulled back to the edge of the field. Guiner suggested that against Arthur's cavalry they would have no hope of surviving the battle; perhaps they should negotiate a peaceful withdrawal. It was a moot point, which Serach had little time to debate.

Arthur's mounts were champing at the bit, sensing the tension before the battle-charge. Realising that something was amiss in the enemy ranks, Arthur ordered his cavalry to advance one hundred yards into the field so that he could see what course of action his enemies were intending to take. To his surprise he saw Serach hand his spear to Guiner, draw his sword from its sheath, and thrust the blade into the earth; then he paced forward towards Arthur:

*"We need time to reconsider our position,"* he shouted, *"We wish to pursue a peaceful settlement: we are willing to withdraw for the sake of peace."*

*"Stand down your men and sheath your swords,"* shouted Arthur in return, *"I will consult my commanders."* He wheeled around to face Modred and Bedivere, calling them forward for their counsel, but just as they had broken ranks to join Arthur, a squadron of armed warriors appeared at Mallwyd.

Cuneglas and his cavalry quickly formed a battle-line in the north-east corner of Maes y Camlan, just beyond the Mallwyd cross-roads. Simultaneously mounted warriors began crossing the Afon Dyfi at Pont Mallwyd: Maelgwyn led his men forward from the cover of a nearby wood to take his position in the north-west corner of the field.

At first, Arthur was relieved that Cuneglas and Maelgwyn had arrived with reinforcements and he raised his spear to them in acknowledgement. Maelgwyn replied to Arthur's gesture by drawing his sword and raising it high in the air; he paused for a moment, and then charged forward to attack Arthur's rear-guard.

Maelgwyn's drawn sword was the rebels' signal to attack: at the same moment Cuneglas unleashed a barrage of flaming arrows into the cavalry on the left wing, while his mounted warriors jettisoned flaming spears into Arthur's confused rear-guard. Serach, seeing the glint of Maelgwyn's sword, pulled his own sword from the turf and rallied his war-band to attack.

Arthur was stunned with shock: he looked aghast. Surprised by Maelgwyn's unexpected appearance from the woodland cover on the far side of the Dyfi, Arthur was horrified by the sudden attack: Cuneglas and Maelgwyn together. At first Arthur could hardly believe his eyes; then, when the attack hit its mark and the killing began, he suddenly realised the shocking truth: this was nothing but treachery.

*"Traitors! Traitors!"* Arthur bellowed at his attackers, *"Murderers!"*

He glanced around to find Serach's rogues clattering up the field, gathering speed apace and preparing to attack Arthur's front line. Assessing his perilous situation in a flash, Arthur decided to split his force into three. Arthur gave his last command: *"Bedivere!"* he shouted with all his might, *"Your squadron to attack Maelgwyn. Modred! Your troop against Cuneglas. I shall deal with Serach and his ruffians."*

In that shocking moment Arthur realised that he had been cajoled into a trap by his own son Cuneglas and his nephew Maelgwyn. How clever they had been! How cunning! How treacherous!

It was these traitors, men of his own flesh and blood, who had planned Maes y Camlan as their chosen killing field. Now Arthur and his faithful warriors found

285

that they themselves were the target, right at the centre of this killing field, and subject to the most deadly tactical device of warfare: a triple pincer movement, from which they were unlikely to escape.

In that moment the odds of battle had changed instantly from being in Arthur's favour to turning overwhelmingly against him: instinctively, he knew that this would be a fight to the death.

*"Chaaarge!"* Arthur bellowed, and unflinching he led his echelon of sixty mounted warriors into battle. Hooves ripped at the soft turf as the cavalry surged forward; warriors lowered their spears and steeled themselves for the clash. Even before they had reached the full speed of the charge, they were spearing and hacking their way into the triple ranks of Serach's mob, splitting shields, shattering helmets, piercing mail tunics and severing limbs with their keen-edged swords; Arthur's great battle-horses trampled men to the ground on the summer meadow of Maes y Camlan, a green meadow that was fast becoming stained purple from bloodshed.

Spreading the fear of death by fire, Cuneglas employed his new weapon with relentless force, raining sheaves of flaming arrows down upon the tortured, twisting mass of horses and their mounts, spreading chaos and confusion. Medrod's echelon split into two loose columns and wheeled round to counter Cuneglas' attack: there was no time to charge, but spurring their mounts forward into the fray, they took the brunt of the firestorm unleashed upon them. The few survivors pressed onward, cutting into the line of archers first with spears, then with swords, scything the bowmen down and spilling the black liquid bitumen through their ranks, spreading a fire that engulfed them.

The sun had set beyond the western hills and the lengthening shadow of Mount Camlan cast an ominous gloom over the battlefield. As evening turned to dusk, the smell of smouldering fustian and the stench of scorched flesh pervaded the air; burning warriors writhed with excruciating pain, shrieking profanities as they rolled in the blood-soaked earth in a desperate attempt to extinguish the flames, while others threw themselves into the river Dyfi.

Bedivere led his squadron of young recruits into the field like lambs to the slaughter: Maelgwyn's men, their hearts hardened by torture, fell on the young cadets, sparing them no mercy. A group of Arthur's cavalry, who had survived the initial attack, pushed forward to reinforce Bedivere's section, but they were outnumbered two to one against Maelgwyn's warriors.

Bedivere charged towards Pont Mallwyd to clash swords with Maelgwyn, venting his anger upon the traitor with crushing blows of his sword, but his young opponent was tall, strong and agile, and soon gained an advantage over the old commander, dealing him a forceful blow that spun Bedivere from his mount and sent him crashing down into the swirling waters of the Afon Dyfi. Unconcerned for his survival, Maelgwyn left Bedivere to drown; he turned his horse away from the riverbank, for his mission was to destroy Arthur.

Modred forced his way through the tangle of horses and thrashing, bloody soldiers, trampling over the bodies of the Britons who had been felled in the first attack: one by one he struck down Cuneglas' guards, and then he closed in to challenge Cuneglas himself. Wielding powerful sword-strokes, Modred pressed Cuneglas back to the northern edge of the field; but Cuneglas parried the blows, steel clashing on steel, for he was fighting for his life. Cuneglas lunged at Modred with a mighty sword-thrust, splintering his shield and knocking him off balance. For a moment, Modred lost his guard, and Cuneglas struck hard a second time, thrusting his sword in deep below the tilted shield, piercing the mail, drawing blood: his mount reared up and Modred fell to the ground.

Arthur's first charge had put Serach's force into disarray: the sheer force of the echelon of heavy battle-chargers had driven a wedge into the centre of his host. Then Arthur split his squadron, each troop wheeling round and charging in to attack the enemy war-band from each wing. Derfel Gadarn, who had fought with Arthur as a young commander at Badon, singled out Guiner and speared him to death. Arthur's small force fought valiantly, but they were outnumbered four to one; gradually the cavalry warriors were hemmed in by the larger force of foot-soldiers, and as dusk fell, Arthur and his surviving soldiers had been pushed back into the centre of the battlefield, where they were joined by the few who had survived the vicious onslaughts of Maelgwyn and Cuneglas.

As the enemy forces closed in from three sides to deliver the final blow of the triple pincer attack, these faithful few formed a defensive ring round their commander in the centre of Maes y Camlan. In the last moments of the battle, no-one doubted that Arthur and his valiant young warriors would stand and fight to the death.

Arthur's brave band of Britons stood firm, their courage overcoming fear. *"I thank you with all my heart!"* cried Arthur to his men, *"God be with you all this night!"* and before he could say more, a flight of firebrands arched through the darkness, thudding into the warriors close to Arthur.

Arthur's great white stallion reared up in fright, and Arthur, still half intoxicated with mead from the celebrations with Cuneglas, lost his balance and fell backwards from his horse. Maelgwyn saw Arthur fall, spurred his mount, and charged in towards his target. At full gallop he threw his elm spear with full force at Arthur's prostrate body: the steel-tipped spear split Arthur's helmet, gouging a deep wound into his temple and embedding itself into the soft ground beside him. Glancing back at his quarry, it appeared to Maelgwyn that his spear had pierced Arthur's skull. His mission was accomplished, and not wishing to be identified as Arthur's murderer, he galloped away from the battlefield and into the night.

Arthur lay motionless, the central figure within a ring of dead and wounded warriors. The sudden, violent catastrophe of Camlan was complete: darkness, cold mists, and the stench of death fell upon the meadow, now silent from the sounds of strife, save for the groans of dying men.

# CHAPTER 17

# THE VOYAGE TO AVALON

*"For I will into the vale of Avilion to heal me of my grievous wound:*
*and if thou hear never more of me, pray for my soul."*
Sir Thomas Malory: *Le Mort d'Arthur*

Le Mort d'Arthur. This imaginary painting by the Victorian artist James Archer depicts the
mortally wounded Arthur, tended by three Queens as they await the barge that will take him
to the Isle of Avalon.                                            © Manchester City Art Gallery

Downstream from Pont Mallwyd the Afon Dyfi runs through a narrow channel,
flowing fast over a rocky slate ridge and tumbling over a shallow waterfall into a pool
below. A fine mist fell over Bedivere's bloodstained body while he lay spread-eagled

at the edge of the river; gradually the cool spray from the waterfall revived him, and in the darkness he cupped his hands into the stream and washed the congealed blood from his wound.

In the heat of battle, Derfel Padarn had been forced into the river when Maelgwyn's troops surged forward to attack his cavalry on the right wing of the field, and he had been swept downstream, away from the battle. It was a fortuitous event that saved his life, for by the time he had struggled across to the opposite bank and pulled his horse from the river near Aberangell, the enemy host had withdrawn and faded into the darkness.

But Derfel was concerned for Bedivere: he had witnessed his duel with Maelgwyn and had seen Bedivere flung from his horse, tumbling headlong down the embankment. Taking the riverside track north towards Pont Mallwyd, Derfel watched as a band of Serach's men waved flaming torches in the air and clattered their way back to their boats at long Borth. Derfel crossed the bridge, tethered his horse, and slipped quietly down the riverbank to look for Bedivere.

*"Our battle is lost!"* whispered Derfel as he pulled Bedivere to his feet and helped him up the embankment. "Now we must find Arthur," declared Bedivere. *"He was over here, in the thick of it, when I saw him last,"* Derfel replied. Stumbling through the gruesome mass of deformed and twisted bodies of horses and men, Bedivere and Derfel staggered blindly towards the centre of Maes y Camlan where the flame of a small oil lamp flickered over the macabre scene.

While tending the wounded, Cynwyl, a young cleric from the chapel, had found Arthur lying unconscious in the field. He extracted the spear, carefully removed Arthur's damaged helmet, and gave him some water to drink. Bedivere couched Arthur's bloodsoaked head in his arm, *"Arthur! Thank God you're alive!"* he cried.

*"Save yourselves!"* whispered Arthur softly, *"I am finished!"*

*"We need to find you a safe place, away from your enemies,"* said Bedivere.

\* *"Cui Bono?"* asked Arthur, hoping for some confirmation of a reality that he could not grasp, and did not really wish to believe. *(who benefits?)

*"Maelgwyn and Cuneglas,"* Bedivere confirmed the worst: *"for now they will rule Gwynedd and Powys between them!"* *"Then I shall die with a heart full of sorrow and sadness"* replied Arthur, *"for these untimely usurpers of my kingdom are my own kith and kin."*

*"It is a sad day for you and for Britain,"* concluded Bedivere as he mopped the blood from Arthur's brow.

*"To the victors the spoils of battle,"* said Arthur bitterly. *"And Serach has taken Mallwyd and the Dyfi Valley as his prize,"* added Cynwyl. *"I heard him boast that we are to be called 'Illan's Town' in memory of King Illan of Leinster."*

Seeing two figures approaching in the shadows, Bedivere called for help, *"Arthur is hurt and has fallen from his horse; we need your help."*

The two survivors emerged from the darkness: one Sanddev Bryd Angel was a handsome, fair haired young warrior; the other, Morfran ap Tegid was a short hoary old soldier whose leathery face was as wrinkled as his battle-worn riding boots: *"We can help,"* he called, *"we've found a haycart for the wounded."*

*"We have a king for your haycart,"* replied Bedivere, *"Arthur is wounded, and we need to find him a safe haven before dawn."*

*"Take me to Iverthon, where I'll be safe from my enemies,"* said Arthur softly, *"on the Isle of Atholdalion you will find the sisters of Saint Mary who are skilled in the practice of healing, and there I will rest until my wound is healed."*

Together, they carried Arthur to the haycart that had been pulled half-way along the track on the north side of the battlefield. Then Bedivere explained his escape plan to the others: Cynwyl would take Arthur's horse Hengroen and gallop as swift as the wind, south to Aberdyfi, where Arthur's sailing barge was moored; there he would call upon captain Barinthus to muster his crew and sail to Barmouth. On the flood tide he would be able to sail into the Mawddach estuary as far as the old quay at Fegla Fach, where Arthur would rest under cover until *Pridwen* arrived.

*"Couldn't we take Arthur straight to Aberdyfi?"* asked Cynwyl. *"No,"* replied Bedivere, *"there's too great a risk of us running into Serach's men. Now that Maelgwyn has withdrawn, it will be safer for us to escape to the west, skirt around Dolgellau and follow the farm tracks below Cadair Idris, along the eastern side of the Mawddach estuary. If we can cover the seventeen mile trek to Fegla Fach by morning, then we'll be safe."*

*"God be with you!"* called Cynwyl, as he rode off towards Aberangell. *"Godspeed!"* replied Bedivere.

In the thicket on the far side of the river, Derfel rounded up the horses that had survived the battle to give Arthur a mounted escort through the dangerous Cerist Valley, as they made their way down to Dolgellau. Derfel rode well ahead to scout for the enemy, leaving Sanddev Brydd Angel to care for Arthur in the haycart, while Morfran took the reins and Bedivere led the motley procession of forlorn warriors into the twilight.

By the time the sun had pierced the morning mists over the rugged peaks of Cadair Idris, the 'Chair of Arthur,' Bedivere had guided the king's rescuers along the mountain track to the woodland cover of Arthog. Derfel found a sheltered grove by a freshwater stream that tumbled down the hillside to a waterfall; here they could safely rest for a while and refresh themselves in the clear streamwater. Arthur was in severe pain from the head-wound inflicted at Camlan, and had suffered the jolting ride in the haycart stoically, passing in and out of consciousness with sheer exhaustion and loss of blood.

Sanddev Bryd Angel kept guard by the waterfall while the others slept, but Derfel was restless and decided to ride the last mile across the brackish heathland to Fegla Fach, where he could keep a lookout for *Prydwen*. Climbing to the top of the 'little hill' he had a magnificent view across the Mawddach estuary and the entrance to Abermaw harbour. The tide was on the turn and the mudflats revealed the deep-water channel that curved in close to Fegla Fach before winding its way to the harbour mouth and the sea; Derfel reckoned that it would be mid-afternoon before the spring tide had flooded, giving Barinthus enough water to sail into the estuary. Now, in this peaceful spot, he could rest awhile.

The rushing sound of the waterfalls at Arthog lulled the king's guardians into a deep sleep; but Arthur was distressed and in constant pain. His mind could not escape from the traumatic experience of the battle, his betrayal, and the loss of almost all his men. For Arthur, the great war-leader, the soldier, the Bear of Britain, this was the most harrowing time: he was desolate. Thus Arthur's hiding place by the waterfall became known as 'Arthog,' a Brythonic name that means 'bear harrow' or in a broader sense, 'the harrowing of the bear.'

When Derfel awoke he saw *Pridwen* turning into the channel a mile or so off

The Mawddach Estuary near Fegla Fach, Gwynedd. During World War II, the Royal Marines established a naval base here at Fegla Fach to train men for landing craft operations, in preparation for the invasion of Europe.                     Photo, © Liz Dawson

the harbour entrance. Spurring his horse, he galloped back to Arthog to alert Bedivere. *"Prydwen is here,"* he called, *"approaching the harbour."* *"Thank God!"* exclaimed Bedivere, *"then take us to Arthur's ship before the tide turns."* Derfel led the way down the rough trackway that led to Fegla Fach.

Arthur's four faithful warriors lifted him bodily from the haycart and carried him to a grassy embankment in the shade of five ancient oaks, their branches weathered and bowed by the wind. Arthur smiled grimly, still in pain but pleased to see Barinthus turning *Pridwen* into wind, as he steered the great sailing barge gently towards the lichen covered rocks that formed a natural quay at Fegla Fach. Derfel and Sanddev secured the mooring lines fore and aft, pulling *Prydwen* into the berth.

Arthur and Bedivere, two great warriors together, and companions through half a century of war and peace, knew in their hearts that this would be their last farewell. *"Look after Guinevere for me,"* pleaded Arthur, *"King Budic's grandson Melor is a man of God who has himself taken refuge from Maxentius at Amesbury: he will help you."*

*"God knows what will become of us without you, Arthur,"* said Bedivere, *"for now we are at the mercy of our enemies."*

*"Have faith,"* replied Arthur, *"now put all your trust in God, and all will be well."* Arthur unbuckled his sword and presented it to Bedivere. *"Bedivere, I ask you to return*

Fegla Fach, looking west towards Barmouth, Gwynedd. Photo, © Liz Dawson

*Excaliburn to Katrine, my Lady of the Lake, who made my fine battle-sword in her forge by the river Caliburn at Balquidder."*

*"It will be a long and difficult journey for me to ride as far north as Caledonia,"* said Bedivere with some reluctance. *"Promise me Bedivere. This is my last request, in the tradition of our Celtic warriors, to surrender my sword to Loch Voil beside Calair Burn."*

*"Very well, my lord, I give you my word,"* agreed Bedivere.

*"Farewell Bedivere!"* cried Arthur, *"Now I leave for Iverthon to heal me of this grievous wound: if you hear no more of me, pray for my soul."*

*Pridwen* slipped away from Fegla Fach, moving slowly into the main channel on the ebb tide, pulled by the oarsmen until the wind caught her sails. By mid-afternoon, Barinthus made a broad turn to the north to clear the bar at Abermaw, and then brought *Pridwen* round into the sun, heading west by south for Ireland.

The Mawddach Estuary, 'Nature's Symmetry'. Photo, © Claire Carter

Arthur looked back longingly towards the Mawddach estuary and the beautiful mountain range beyond, his gaze transfixed until at last the Peaks of Cadair Idris fell below the horizon. With a fair breeze on her port quarter, *Pridwen* ploughed into the oncoming breakers, sending sea-spray chasing over the foredeck; and as night fell, Barinthus, with Polaris as his guide, held a steady course for Rosslare Point.

The dawn mist obscured the coastline, but by mid-morning Wexford had appeared off the starboard bow, and Barinthus trimmed the sails to bring *Prydwen* safely into Rosslare harbour. The ship's crew helped Arthur into a horse-drawn carriage, and Barinthus, with a bodyguard of four warriors, escorted Arthur to the Isle of Atholdalion, just a few miles to the south.

The noon-day sun shimmered across the lake as Arthur's carriage reached the sanctuary. Weary from the long voyage and suffering the deep pain of his wound, Arthur was relieved to have safely completed his journey. Surveying the peaceful scene, the island meadow set in a silver lake and protected from the ocean by a long sandbar tipped with marram grass, Arthur saw that little had changed since his first visit with sister Brigid over thirty years earlier. The small chapel dedicated to St Mary had been washed with lime to a pristine white, and thatchers were working on the roof to dress in the new reeds before the winter storms arrived.

Sister Morgen was shocked by the unexpected appearance of captain Barinthus and his wounded king; and as she ushered them quietly into her small house, she was doubly shocked to see how haggard Arthur looked, with his pale complexion, and his bloodstained clothing.

*"Since we met those many years ago, sister Morgen, I have fought many battles,"* said Arthur softly, *"I have saved Britons from the Saxons and our enemies; but at Maes y Camlan, the thirteenth great battle, traitorous Britons turned against me, and as you can see, I am sorely wounded and seek your help and healing."*

Barinthus and his guards carried Arthur to a couch and sister Morgen uncovered his wound and examined it for a long time. At last she spoke to Arthur, *"I think we can restore you to health, but only if you are prepared to stay with us for a long time, and of course, if you are willing to undergo our treatment."*

*"I am in your capable and healing hands,"* Arthur replied.

This was hopeful news, and Barinthus and his men rejoiced and committed the king to Morgen and the healing sisters of Atholdalion; it was agreed that Arthur would stay in their care for as long as it would take to heal his wound. Then, with a sad farewell, they returned to the quay, unfurled their sails and allowed the south-westerly breeze to set *Pridwen's* course for home.

The nuns of St Mary prayed day and night for Arthur's recovery and sister Morgen dressed his wound with honey and herbs; in an attempt to relieve Arthur's pain, she mixed ground opium poppies with henbane leaves for a salve, gave him milk and honey to drink and prepared fresh fish and home-made bread for his well-being.

After a while, Arthur responded to the loving care of his nurses and the healing herbs administered by sister Morgen. He seemed to be getting stronger; but as the days passed, Arthur's deep wound refused to heal, and his pain became unbearable. Slipping in and out of consciousness, he knew that his life-force was ebbing away.

As the evening sun faded in the western sky, Arthur summoned all his strength to speak. *"Sister Morgen,"* he called faintly, *"please bury me on Fion Magh, on your bright plain; it is such a beautiful and tranquil place, I will be at peace there,"* Arthur paused for a moment, *"and be sure to keep my passing a secret, for my enemies must not hear of my death."*

*"I respect your wishes, my lord,"* replied sister Morgen, with tears in her eyes, *"You have my word."*

*"I thank you with all my heart,"* said Arthur.

*"Sleep now,"* said sister Morgen, as she gently made the sign of the cross upon Arthur's forehead, and softly blew out the flickering candle flame.

That night, Arthur passed into the long sleep of death.

☙ ☙ ❧ ❧

When abbot Abban of Moyarnez heard of Arthur's death, he expressed the wish to give him a Christian burial service in the island's small chapel dedicated to St Mary. With deep respect for the king, Abban's monks placed Arthur in a coffin of hollowed oak, and transported his body to the chapel. As the short funeral service began, a tempestuous storm blew in from the Atlantic Ocean; flashes of lightning startled the sisters and the loud thunder momentarily drowned sister Munroe's skilled cittern accompaniment to the psalms.

Grey sea mists blew across the sacred Island of Atholdalion as the mourners progressed from the chapel; sister Morgen led the cortege to the meadow that overlooked the silver lake where the island pointed towards the ocean's horizon. Here, on the bright plain, the monks laid Arthur to rest, and abbot Abban commended Arthur's soul to God. Morgen and her sisters wept in sorrow, their tears washed away by the torrential rain of the storm; but the squall quickly passed, and a ray of sunshine burst through the fleeting clouds across the bright plain of Avalon.

Well before winter, the abbot's stonemason secretly carved a single piece of stone that remained uninscribed but was chamfered towards the top and shouldered at the base to resemble the outline of the capital letter A, and the monks of Moyarnez helped to erect the heavy headstone on Arthur's grave at Fion Magh, the Bright Plain that is now known as *Buncarrick*.

To the few who knew the secret of Arthur's passing, this was the memorial to the soldiers' dearly loved soldier.

Eardownes Great Standing Stone, also known as the Buncarrick Stone, County Wexford, Ireland.

Photo, © 1998 Pip Powell

# 'Arthur Emeradaur'

*"I saw Arthur, the emperor, strife's commander"*
'*Geraint ab Erbin*:' a ninth century poem from the *Black Book of Carmarthen.*

*"We have taken Arthur to the Isle of Iverthon for the healing of his wounds,"* explained Barinthus when he returned to Powys: *"and we hope that one day Arthur will return!"*

But as Arthur's bright star waned, Maelgwyn's rising star ascended as he assumed power in Gwynedd and extended his control to rule over all Wales. The mention of Arthur's name was forbidden, lest the secret of his disappearance became known to the Saxons, and to silence Britons who had begun to question the circumstances of his last battle; but despite his newfound power, Maelgwyn feared that Arthur might return to take his life in revenge for Camlan. Although he had totally destroyed Arthur's army, Maelgwyn now took the precaution of destroying his powerbase at Wroxeter by dismantling all the military facilities and removing them piece by piece to Pengwern in North Wales, leaving Cuneglas to torture Arthur's loyal citizens until they submitted to his callous rule of terror.

But Arthur did not return. After his death, a pall of sorrow descended over the land of Britain like a dark grey cloud obscuring the sun. Even the weather mourned for Arthur, shedding tears for months on end: and like an ill wind, with a dearth of good fortune, a deathly plague was delivered to Britain and Ireland.

Arthur's life was cut short at Camlan in the year 539; but that catastrophic defeat did not diminish his heroic record as the great British commander who had defended the land of Britain for half a century, a warrior king with twelve major victories to his credit and who had, since his landmark victory over the Saxons at the siege of Badon Hill, presented his fellow Britons with twenty one years of peace.

Arthur's success at Badon, when he charged into battle like a Crusader, emblazoned with the Cross of Christ, determined to show his pagan enemies the power of God, was as much a victory for Christianity as it was for the Britons; but the overwhelming effect of the battle as a monumental deterrent to his enemies was unprecedented in his lifetime, and for many years after his passing. Badon effectively stalled the Saxon advance into southern Britain. It would be another fifty-nine years before Cealwin, the Saxon king of Wessex, struck inland, killing three British kings at the battle of Dyrham in 577 AD, conquering Gloucester, Cirencester and Bath; and almost a century passed before Aethelfrith, the Saxon king of Northumbria, attacked the British stronghold of Chester in 616 AD.

In adversity, and threatened by enemies on all fronts, the people of Britain looked to Arthur as their saviour. Following his first victory against the invaders, Arthur had, in the eyes of his people, earned the laudatory title of *emeradaur*, a title that equated to the Roman rank of *Dux Britanniarum,* the Duke of Britain and military Commander-in-Chief.

Thus, behind the legend of King Arthur and his Knights of the Round Table, we can clearly see Arthur *emeradaur,* the leader of the Council of the Kings of Britain, allies who had been drawn together by Arthur to fight in the Battle for Britain.

Arthur's quest to re-unite Britain under a supreme commander, an imperial concept that had welded the independent tribes and provinces of Britain together under Roman rule, was dashed by treachery at Camlan. Inevitably, under the rule of greedy and selfish tyrants, the strength and security of Arthur's Britain eventually disintegrated into civil strife and chaos. The advantage passed to the gradual but relentless onslaught of the English, whose kings, admiring Arthur's 'Golden Age,' challenged each other and fought for the coveted prize of *Bretwalda,* kingship over all the kings of Britain.

It would take another thousand years for the disparate factions to be hammered and crushed in the crucible of Britain's political and military arena before Arthur's ideal of one United Kingdom was finally achieved.

# BIBLIOGRAPHY

## Source Material

A CELTIC MISCELLANY, edited by Kenneth Jackson, Penguin Books, 1971

ARTHUR'S BRITAIN, Leslie Alcock, Penguin Press, 1971

ARTHURIAN PERIOD SOURCES VOL 7, Gildas: *The Ruin of Britain*, edited and translated by Michael Winterbottom. Phillimore, 2002

ARTHURIAN PERIOD SOURCES VOL 8, Nennius: *British History & the Welsh Annals*, edited and translated by John Morris. Phillimore, 1980

CELTIC BRITAIN, Charles Thomas, Thames & Hudson, 1986

DARK AGE NAVAL POWER, John Haywood, Anglo-Saxon Books, 1999

HADRIAN'S WALL IN THE DAYS OF THE ROMANS, Frank Graham, 1984

HISTORY OF THE KINGS OF BRITAIN, Geoffrey of Monmouth, translated by Lewis Thorpe, Penguin Books, London, 1966

KING ARTHUR, DARK AGE WARRIOR AND MYTHIC HERO, John Matthews, Carlton Books, London, 2004

KING ARTHUR: MYTH MAKING & HISTORY, N.J.Higham, Routlege, London, 2002

LAYAMON: *The Brut in Arthurian Chronicles*, translated by E. Mason, Everyman Library, 1962

LE MORT DARTHUR: Sir Thomas Malory, edited by A.W.Pollard, Macmillan, London, 1900

MEDIEVAL ENGLISH POETRY, John Spiers, Faber and Faber, London, 1957

MEMBURY AT WAR, Roger Day, 2012: roger@ramsburyatwar.com

ROMAN BATTLE TACTICS, 108 BC – AD 313, Ross Cowan, Osprey Publishing Ltd, 2007

SIR GAWAIN AND THE GREEN KNIGHT, translated by Brian Stone, Penguin Books, 1959

*TALIESIN: THE LAST CELTIC SHAMAN by John Matthews with Caitlin Matthews, published by Inner Traditions, a division of Inner Traditions International, Vermont, 1991. All rights reserved. http//Innertraditions.com Selected texts reprinted with the kind permission of the author and publisher.

THE AGE OF ARTHUR, John Morris, Orion Books, 1995

THE ANGLO-SAXON CHRONICLE, translated by Anne Savage, Coombe Books, Godalming 1995

THE ARTHUR OF THE WELSH, edited by Rachel Bromwich, A.O.H.Jarman, Brynley Roberts, 1991

THE BLACK BOOK OF CARMARTHEN, translated by Meirion Pennar, Llanarch Enterprises, Felinfach, 1989

THE EARLIEST WELSH POETRY, Joseph Clancy, Macmillan, London, 1970

THE GODODDIN OF ANEIRIN, edited and translated by John Koch, University of Wales Press, Cardiff, 1997

THE GRAIL FROM CELTIC MYTH TO CHRISTIAN SYMBOL, R.S.Loomis, University of Wales Press, Cardiff, 1963

THE MABINOGION, translated by Jeffrey Gantz, Penguin Books, London, 1976

THE OXFORD GUIDE TO ARTHURIAN LITERATURE & LEGEND, Alan Lupack, Oxford University Press, Oxford, 2005

THE QUEST FOR ARTHUR'S BRITAIN, Geoffrey Ashe, Pall Mall Press, 1968

TWO LIVES OF GILDAS, by a monk of Ruys and Caradoc of Llancarfan, translated by Hugh Williams, Llanarch Enterprises, Felinfach, 1990

WROXETER, LIFE & DEATH OF A ROMAN CITY, Roger White & Philip Barker, Tempus Publishing Ltd, 1998

## *Internet Resources*

ancienthistory.about.com

archaeology.co.uk

bbc.co.uk/history

britarch.ac.uk

earlybritishkingdoms.com

en.wickipedia.org

geography.org.uk

glastonburyshrine.co.uk

historyfiles.co.uk

megalithic.co.uk

ourladysisland.ie

roman-britain.org

roman-empire.net

stbrigid.org

take27.co.uk

ucc.ie

woodland-trust.org.uk

yourlocalhistory.info

# ACKNOWLEDGEMENTS

I wish to express my thanks to Colin Wilson for his help with the translation of Latin texts; to Judy Williamson for locating a wide range of reference books for my research; and to Frank Hopton for proof-reading my manuscript and for making many helpful suggestions for improvement.

I would also like to thank those who have freely given permission to include their personal illustrations and photographs, contributions that have helped to reveal the real locations and battle-sites mentioned in the story: Julian Baum, Walter Baxter, Claire Carter, Liz Dawson, Jim Eastaugh, Roger Day, Oliver Doyle, Gareth Houghton, Kate Jewell, Arron Jones, Richard Lee, Stuart Low, Mike Page, Tom Parnell, Philip Powell, Gordon Scammell, Don Summers, David Swarbrick, Helen White, and Andrew Wynne; also to English Heritage and Bracknell Forest Council Library for supplying photographs and illustrations without charge; and to my son Jonathan who designed the book-cover, and my nephew Chris Walmsley who designed and printed the maps of Arthur's Britain.

I must also include a note of special thanks both to Professor Joseph Clancy for his kind permission to quote freely from his book *The Earliest Welsh Poetry* (Macmillan, London, 1970), and to John Matthews for his permission to quote selected passages from *Taliesin, The Last Celtic Shaman* (Inner Traditions, Vermont, 2002).

Quotations from *Arthurian Period Sources* Volume 7, *Gildas,* (ed. & trans. by Michael Winterbottom), and from Volume 8, *Nennius,* (ed. and trans. by John Morris) by kind permission of Phillimore & Co Ltd, London and Chichester.